GERMANY UNDER THE OLD REGIME

Longman History of Germany

Germany in the early middle ages c. 800–1056
Timothy Reuter

Germany under the Old Regime, 1600–1790
John G. Gagliardo

Germany under the Old Regime, 1600–1790

John G. Gagliardo

Longman
London and New York

Longman Group UK Limited

Longman House, Burnt Mill, Harlow,
Essex CM20 2JE, England
and Associated Companies throughout the world.

*Published in the United States of America
by Longman Inc., New York*

© Longman Group UK Limited 1991

First published 1991

British Library Cataloguing in Publication Data
Gagliardo, John G.
  Germany under the old regime, 1600–1790. —
  (A history of Germany).
  1. Germany, 1600–1790
  I. Title II. Series
  943.04

  ISBN 0–582–49106–1 PPR
  ISBN 0–582–49105–3 CSD

Library of Congress Cataloging in Publication Data
Gagliardo, John G.
  Germany under the old regime. 1600–1790/John G. Gagliardo.
    p. cm. — (The History of Germany)
  Includes bibliographical references.
  Includes index.
  ISBN 0–582–49105–3 : £25.00. — ISBN 0–582–49106–1 (pbk.) : £12.00
  1. Germany — History — 17th century.
  2. Germany — History — 1789–1900.
  I. Title. II. Series.
DD175.G34 1991   90–46361943 — dc20 CIP

Produced by Longman Singapore Publishers (Pte) Ltd.
Printed in Singapore

Contents

List of maps

Preface

It is at least arguable that no lengthy period in the history of Germany since the time of Charlemagne has proved more difficult for historians to present clearly to the wider reading public than the almost two hundred years covered by this volume – the seventeenth and eighteenth centuries, comprising the largest part of what might be termed 'early modern Germany' or, as in the title of this book, the Germany of the old regime. The difficulty arises chiefly from the fact that the Germany of this period offers so few of the characteristics of the coalescing 'nations' that were emerging more and more clearly in much of the rest of Europe at the same time. Many of the most important factors and tendencies making for stronger national unity in such large countries as England, France and even Spain and in various smaller ones as well, were either absent in Germany or, if they existed at all at the beginning of the period, were often actually weakened by events which occurred during the period in question. Thus, while for historians the various integrating forces contributing to the increasingly coherent nationhood of other countries can and usually do form an organizing principle for the presentation of their history – in which the factors of disunity can be treated (however extensively) merely as qualifications on the main movement – the absence of such integrating forces in Germany in the early modern period makes the employment of any such organizing principle dubious or actually impossible for its history; indeed, the centripetal impulses which can give meaning to the history of other European countries in this time are replaced in Germany by predominantly centrifugal ones.

This fact in itself does not necessarily make German history of the seventeenth and eighteenth centuries intrinsically less understandable than that of any other country of Europe in the same period. But it does pose an unusually serious problem for the historian who has the task of making it understandable to others. For example: while there were many things about the Germany of this time that marked it as a single *society*, there was almost nothing to mark it as a single *state*; and while a major theme of much modern European history deals with the increasing identification of national state with national community, that theme would be particularly inappropriate for Germany. In particular, the single national monarchy which provided the central and increasingly pivotal reference point for 'national' development in the early modern period elsewhere in Europe was notably lacking in Germany. The Holy Roman Empire of the German Nation which was its only pretense to a national political structure was in fact a polyglot congeries of literally hundreds of virtually sovereign states and territories ranging in size from considerable to minuscule, whose various rulers defined their common imperial bond far more as an entitlement to a self-seeking independence from each other and their titular overlord, the emperor, than as a mandate to cooperation and the preservation of a common German polity.

This political fragmentation of the Empire was the single most salient characteristic of German history throughout the period; it underlay and conditioned developments in all areas of public life and must therefore be regarded in itself as a major historical theme. The imperial political structure, to be sure, provides no good thematic device for a general history; but its very weakness allowed a number of political and other problems and tendencies to become sufficiently important as national issues as to provide threads of continuity and even consistency to both the internal and external history of the various states and territories of the Empire – and these will appear prominently in this history as variations on the general theme of *diversity*, consecrated by permanent territorial fragmentation, which will largely guide the composition of this volume. On the other hand, underneath the almost kaleidoscopic complexities of its political landscape it is also possible to find something resembling a single German society, if not yet a German nation. That possibility, indeed, derives from the eternalization of the weak imperial political structure itself, since the individual territories, spared by the political modesty imposed by their own small size as well as by the absence of coercive external authority from much pressure for internal change, remained largely stuck in the complacently traditional patterns of a parochial and conservative political, social and economic mentality which varied only in relatively insignificant detail from one area to another. The common features arising from this mentality and its slow evolution, thus form another theme of this book, scarcely secondary to the first.

It may be noted that the periodization of this volume departs from the rather more standard practice of beginning the history of Germany in the old regime with the Peace of Westphalia of 1648. By starting at 1600 and including the background and history of the Thirty Years War which led to that peace, I give expression to my conviction that the history of the war itself is essential to a thorough understanding of the interests represented in the terms of the peace and of how those interests were repeatedly refined throughout the long years of armed struggle. The war itself, furthermore, tells us much about the reasons for the immobility or inertia of the imperial structure for the remainder of the period and also goes far to explain the prevalence and persistence of socio-political attitudes in which the reconstitution and protection of the 'good order' so terribly disrupted by the war came to be seen as the chief responsibility of peoples and governments alike and in so doing reinforced the socially static and defensive mindset which so largely defined the old regime.

Another innovation of this volume – and one that I hope will invite general imitation in future English-language books on German history – is my use of the original German spellings of proper nouns and especially personal names. Most previous works have shown an annoying inconsistency in this, Anglicizing some such nouns but not others and with no apparent rule to determine the choice. I have remained with the German in all cases except those in which the inveteracy of English usage is indisputable; thus, for example, the cities of Köln and Wien will become Cologne and Vienna, but Nuremberg will change to Nürnberg and I will breach my rule on personal names only in the single case of Frederick II of Prussia, who does not come across well in English as *Friedrich* the Great.

Finally, it is my pleasure to acknowledge the assistance I have received from Boston University in the preparation of this work: a sabbatical leave granted to me in the spring of 1988, as well as the cheerful and expert work of the interlibrary loan staff of the Mugar Library were indispensable to the timely completion of the book. My very special thanks go also to James T. Dutton, the Departmental Administrator of my own History Department, who introduced me to the mysteries of electronic word-processing and coached me through its often frustrating intricacies with almost apostolic patience and good humour; his help and friendship in this and many other things are of inestimable value to me.

John G. Gagliardo
Boston, Massachusetts

IN DER MORGENDÄMMERUNG
DER WIEDERVEREINIGUNG DES DEUTSCHEN VOLKES:
DEN GROSSEN HERRSCHERN
DER DEUTSCHEN KAISER– UND KÖNIGSHÄUSER
HABSBURG UND HOHENZOLLERN
IN TIEFER EHRFURCHT GEWIDMET
VON DEM VERFASSER

CHAPTER ONE
Germany in 1600: The Land and the People

The difficulty of dealing with the history of Germany in the early modern period begins with even the coarsest facts. The boundaries of Germany are a case in point. Because most modern maps of Europe in this period conveniently outline the borders of the Holy Roman Empire with a heavy line and because the Empire embraced most territories which were unarguably German, it is always tempting to equate the borders of Germany with those of the Empire. In fact, however, even contemporaries did not do that. While most educated Germans in 1600 still cherished images of the vaster medieval Empire and its 'universal mission' which were powerful enough to engender a sense of pride in this sprawling political corpus and in its German leadership, they were aware that it was a body which, though German in its core, was multinational at almost every point on its periphery. Partly under the influence of ethnic and linguistic criteria popularized by Italian humanism, Germans (and other Europeans, too) had by well before 1600 learned to speak of a Germany distinct from the Empire.

Even this Germany was defined differently by different people, however. Thus, while linguistic criteria probably provided the steadiest guideline, it was necessary to recognize that largely German-speaking places such as Holstein, (East) Prussia, Livonia and Switzerland were either ruled by non-German regimes or for other reasons could not be spoken of as political constituents of Germany. Linguistically mixed areas such as Schleswig, Alsace and Lorraine, Luxemburg and Bohemia created problems of classification; and when ethnic standards were mixed with linguistic ones, it became possible to include parts of northern Italy and the Netherlands as part of a German Europe. While such borderlands were the marginal and

1

disputed cases, general agreement existed on certain rough frontiers beyond which no Germany could meaningfully be spoken of: the Baltic Sea and Atlantic Ocean to the north, France to the west, Italy to the south and Poland and Hungary to the east. This agreement leaves us with a geographical definition of Germany which, while inexact in detail, is accurate enough to serve us as well as it did those who employed it with comfortable imprecision four centuries ago.

While the boundaries of the Holy Roman Empire are not terribly helpful in defining Germany geographically, they are more useful for describing the formal structure of politics within which the Germans lived. The Empire was an elective monarchy, headed by an emperor to whom, in theory, almost 2500 inferior authorities who exercised actual governmental powers over the German people were directly responsible. Some 2000 of these authorities were Imperial Knights whose tiny, scattered enclaves comprised not much more than 250 square miles of land. The remainder – almost 400 – were divided among some 136 ecclesiastical and 173 secular lords, as well as 85 Free or Imperial Cities.[1] The Imperial Knights were not entitled to representation in the imperial diet, the legislative body of the Empire, but all the others, known as 'estates' of the Empire, were entitled; and were placed for voting purposes there in one of three councils. The first, the Council of Electors, was composed of the seven princes who elected the emperor by majority vote: the archbishops of Mainz, Trier and Cologne, the king of Bohemia, the duke of Saxony, the margrave of Brandenburg and the Count Palatine of the Rhine. The second, the Council of Princes, consisted of all the other ecclesiastical and secular lords. The third embraced the Imperial Cities. The three councils deliberated and voted separately on legislation, then resolved their differences, if any, informally; if two of the three agreed, the legislation was presented to the emperor for his approval, after receiving which it became law, binding all members of the Empire to its observance. The Council of Electors was the most prestigious of the three curias and contained the most powerful imperial princes, though the Council of Princes represented more of the total territory and population of the Empire. In any case, the more powerful lords essentially controlled the diet

---

1. These figures are drawn from the Imperial *Matrikel*, or list of assessments, of 1521 and could change over time. In 1648, totals both overall and in the separate categories were different, mostly lower.

by virtue of the separateness of the Council of Electors and by means of a complex arrangement which denied lesser lords voting rights equal to those of the greater in the Council of Princes. The Council of Cities played an increasingly negligible role in the diet after the mid-sixteenth century. The diet could only be convoked by the emperor and met in various Imperial Cities until the 1660s, when Regensburg became its permanent seat.

The emperor ranked first in dignity in the hierarchy of European royalty; and though the office was elective, the Habsburg House of Austria, as the most powerful single German dynasty, controlled it continuously from 1438 until the end of the Empire in 1806, with but one brief lapse in the mid-eighteenth century. By well before 1600, the powers of the emperor over the individual territories of the Empire (except his own) had been severely restricted, not only by promises extracted by the electors and other princes as a condition of election (the so-called Electoral Capitulation), but also by the persistent refusal of the diet to grant the emperors the money or other means by which the apparatus of an effective central imperial government could be created. Provision for taxes and other contributions existed, but these were voted irregularly and never in anything approaching the quantity required to establish a civil service or an army under the direct and undivided command of the emperor. An Imperial Army (*Reichsarmee*) did indeed exist – on occasion – but it was only a motley collection of territorial units raised and paid for by the individual princes, theoretically on the basis of a quota system voted by the diet, but in reality, usually, only at the whim of individual rulers. Created only in time of general peril, its existence was always short; the only standing armies were in the territories. And with the exception of the Imperial Cameral Tribunal – a high court established by the princes in 1495 (partly as the result of hostility towards the emperor) and subsequently sustained by them in an often rather insouciant and niggardly fashion – almost no other agencies of a true imperial government existed.

It was of course always possible for the emperor, who was in one sense merely the greatest of the territorial princes, to call upon the resources of the Habsburgs' own patrimony to support his policies both inside and outside Germany; and so in addition to the so-called Aulic Council – a sort of second imperial supreme court, having a roughly concurrent jurisdiction with the Cameral Tribunal, but staffed by judges more responsive to the emperor than to the princes – the Austrian government included several agencies which handled imperial business either exclusively or in addition to family and territorial affairs. There was also a dynastic army, which contemporary usage carefully distinguished from the Imperial Army referred to above, usually referring to the former as the *kaiserliche Armee* – the emperor's own territorial army. The resources of Austria, however, were never adequate by themselves to overawe the rest of the Empire and unless she could make common cause with a significant group of German princes to achieve aims common to both, the goal of resurrecting a true German monarchy would remain forever elusive. Thus, for example, the strong Catholic loyalties of the Habsburgs tempted them to solve the various problems that had arisen with the Reformation by main force with the aid of other Catholic princes in the Empire. But since these princes were no more eager to see their own territorial independence submerged under an imperial despotism than were the Protestants, the kind and amount of such aid would always have limits. Emperor Karl V, to his chagrin, discovered this after his great victory over German Protestantism in 1547 disintegrated into the compromise Peace of Augsburg in 1555, due in large part to the growing reservations and suspicions of his German Catholic allies. This balance of power between emperor and princes was to remain a cardinal fact of German history throughout the early modern period.

As far as population is concerned (and excluding the more dubious borderlands), the Germany of 1600 is estimated to have had some sixteen to seventeen million inhabitants and a population density of 75–80 people per square mile. These numbers represent an upward trend that was to continue until about 1620 and a net increase of perhaps as much as 40 per cent from a century earlier.[2] Of this population, more than 85 per cent lived in rural areas and the remainder in somewhat over 3000 towns and cities, of which only a very few had as many as 50,000 permanent residents; not many more were even half that size and over nine-tenths had fewer than 1000 inhabitants. Rural Germany was absolutely dominated by a nobility of varying ranks, including territorial princes at the top, which not only exercised lordship over rural inhabitants, but also, together with the church (itself largely a preserve of the nobility), owned

2. K. G. A. Jeserich, H. Pohl and G.-C. von Unruh eds., *Deutsche Verwaltungsgeschichte*. Vol. I: Vom Spätmittelalter bis zum Ende des Reichs (Stuttgart, 1983), p. 218. Population density varied considerably from region to region; it was greatest in the Rhine Valley and southern Germany, thinner from the northwest through central-eastern Germany and relatively sparse east of the Elbe. Hajo Holborn, *A History of Modern Germany*, 3 vols. (N.Y., 1959–69), I, p. 37.

virtually all the agricultural land of the country, excepting only the relatively insignificant amounts held by the small number of free peasant proprietors and by various cities, particularly the Imperial Cities. This land also contained the various iron, copper and silver mines, forges and foundries which were important to the German (and European) economy well into the seventeenth century and which provided a significant part of the income of a number of territorial princes, who along with capital-rich merchants from the cities entered the mining and metallurgical fields as entrepreneurs. The vast majority of rural dwellers were peasants whose legal status and rights of land tenure in different parts of the country were so varied as to defy general description. Pending further discussion below (Chapter Twelve), however, it can be remarked that one or another form of serfdom, denying both personal legal freedom and choice of land tenure, was the rule for the great majority of German peasants. Furthermore, the sixteenth century not only witnessed a general increase in peasant obligations to their landlords and to the civil authorities, but also, in much of eastern Germany, greatly intensified a movement begun in the fifteenth century towards the establishment of great noble latifundia, with attendant abolition of individual peasant farms and a marked worsening of the peasant's status, legally and in every other respect. There seems little doubt that in 1600 the average peasant family in Germany had less to be thankful for than its counterpart of 1500, or even 1550 – though, as suggested above, it is not easy to speak meaningfully of an 'average' peasant family.

It is just as difficult to speak of 'average' cities in the Germany of 1600, given their great diversity in size and character. Two basic types of cities immediately strike the eye, however: the Imperial City and what for lack of a better term might be called the territorial city. The former, like the territorial princes, whether secular or ecclesiastical, and the Imperial Knights possessed what was known as 'immediacy', which meant that they were subject only to the authority of the emperor himself. In fact, however, they were virtually autonomous and self-governing entities, of greatly varying size and prosperity. The territorial cities, by contrast, were subject to the authority of some territorial lord; and while many of them enjoyed some degree of self-administration, this was a precarious privilege which might be curtailed or abolished according to the will and power of the prince. Belonging to neither of these types was a group of semi-autonomous cities whose size and economic strength was sufficient to sustain a substantial and virtually permanent independence from surrounding territorial authorities, even though no formal right to independence existed. Cities in both latter categories normally had representation in territorial diets, but not, like the Imperial Cities, in the imperial diet. Regardless of their differing relationship to higher or outside authorities, most cities of any size had developed constitutions which, however different, usually drew an important distinction between full citizens (*Bürger*) and residents (*Beisassen*), only the first of whom were theoretically entitled to participate in governing the city through eligibility to membership in the city council. In fact, however, by well before 1600 most city councils had fallen more or less permanently into the hands of a small group of wealthy patrician families of varied economic origins and had increasingly taken on the character of authoritarian governing bodies.

Both rural and urban Germany had by 1600 undergone some notable changes as the result of important economic developments in the sixteenth century. Since the chief income-producing activity of Germany as a whole was agriculture and its associated industries, the entire country was affected by a steep rise in agricultural prices from the late fifteenth century onward, caused by a rapidly growing population and the inflationary influence of vast increases in the supply of gold and silver bullion. Such increases came partly from improved silver production in Germany itself, but even more from huge imports from the New World through Portugal and Spain. The price of grain – the most basic and therefore also the most income-inelastic foodstuff – rose throughout central Europe by some 260 per cent between 1470 and 1618. Animal products in the same period rose by around 180 per cent, lesser availability (the result of transferring land from stock-raising to grain cultivation) being somewhat offset by lessened demand due to the higher cost of grain. Prices of manufactured goods also climbed, but substantially less. Wage increases, meanwhile, remained significantly behind the above levels.[3] Amidst an almost frantic rush to get all available arable land under cultivation and to open up new lands, especially in the second half of the sixteenth century, different groups of people were affected quite variously by the inflation. Agricultural producers (in this case meaning landlords) did generally very well in this market; but with some exceptions – and these only in areas where he had free disposition of his produce – the peasant failed in almost every respect to benefit. The establishment and expansion of latifundia with their

3. Jeserich *et al.*, *Deutsche Verwaltungsgeschichte*, I, p. 222.

oppressed peasant populations in the eastern areas of Germany was greatly stimulated by these favourable market conditions; and elsewhere, even where landlords' income from peasant tenants was fixed by statute or custom, devices were quickly found to deny peasants of all or most of the increased income of their labour.

The towns and cities were affected in both positive and negative ways by the inflation. On the one hand, it appears that the creation of more disposable income in some segments of the rural population led to some increase in demand for manufactured goods from the cities, as did the fact of a growing population by itself; and the rapid spread of the domestic system of production (*Verlagswesen*), introduced by the great wholesale merchants, led to a notable decrease in unit costs of some kinds of production, especially in mining and the metal trades, thus helping to hold down the inflation rate and to moderate decrease in demand. Nevertheless, since the price of foodstuffs rose so substantially faster than that of hard goods, economizing became necessary for much of the urban population except the very wealthy and considerably quickened the pace of social stratification by wealth within cities, which had been proceeding for a long time already. The few rich – especially those who knew how to take advantage of an inflationary cycle – in fact got richer, but the large majority became poorer, some of them much poorer. Other causes contributed to sap the vigour of the urban economy. Greater reliance on seaborne trade from the eastern Mediterranean to western and northwestern Europe caused a fundamental shift in the geography of European commerce which was very hurtful to a number of Rhenish and south German cities, in particular; and while a few other cities such as Frankfurt, Leipzig, Hamburg and Danzig actually rose in economic importance after 1550, their good fortune could not right the overall balance of decline. The dissipation of accumulated capital through loans made to periodically bankrupt governments in Austria, Spain and France by such large commercial and financial houses as the Fuggers and Welsers in Augsburg and by others in Nürnberg and elsewhere, was accelerated by a couple of generations of conspicuous consumption. While their distant posterity can still admire the magnificent public and private edifices which are the most obvious surviving evidence of this consumption, contemporaries might have done better to curb their self-indulgence in the name of prudence.

There is no doubt that the 'golden age' of the German renaissance city was drawing slowly to a close by the beginning of the seventeenth century. But while the Germany of 1600 presents an overall economic picture more dominated by prosperity than by poverty and one with a particularly vigorous agrarian sector, it appears obvious not only that the general standard of living of most Germans had slipped, relative to the first half of the sixteenth century, but also that the distance between upper and lower economic strata was growing. This process of social differentiation and urban decline was accompanied, furthermore, by a gradual but quickening reinvigoration of the nobility as a class. Beset by economic and political problems of their own (which to some extent were related to the simultaneous rise of the cities), the lower and middling ranks of German nobility, beginning in the fifteenth century, had experienced a decline of fortunes which approached crisis proportions by the later sixteenth century. Then, however, assisted partly by a newly thriving agriculture, but even more by the increasing opportunities offered them by the rapidly expanding civil and military administrations of the one segment of the nobility – the territorial princes – whose fortunes had prospered throughout the period, the rest of the nobility underwent a revitalization which was to become perhaps the most important single factor in the development of German society for the remainder of the early modern period.

The decline of the cities and of standards of living in general between 1500 and 1600 had a counterpart in the realm of culture as well – though it is hardly possible to ascribe this to economic recession alone. Furthermore, progress in some areas offset regression in others, so that here as in other aspects of German life in 1600 we have no really uniform picture. On the negative side, it is doubtful that any informed German in 1600 could compare favourably the quality of effort of his contemporaries in the area of humane letters with that of the heroic age of early German humanism as represented by such figures as Conrad Celtis, Crotus Rubeanus, Aventinus, Heinrich Bebel, Ulrich von Hutten or Johannes Reuchlin. The same was true of the graphic arts, in which no equally gifted successors to a Matthias Grünewald, an Albrecht Dürer or a Hans Holbein the Younger were to be found. Furthermore, the originally very powerful stimulus to a broad social dissemination of humanistic thought and letters that these and other individuals had given weakened after the mid-century. Partly this was the result of the deepening religious controversy, which increasingly dissolved both the ties of communication and the moral and intellectual consensus that had bound the community of early humanists together and diminished the enthusiasm for the establishment of new and better secular schools and curricula at middle and lower levels which had been vigorously pursued in the first half of the century. It is worth noting, in this connection, that the numbers of readers of books, as well as the literacy rate of the population as a whole – relatively very high in the few decades after 1500 – also began a long decline after the mid-century.

There was a positive side too, of course. The number and quality of printed works, for example, rose steadily throughout the century and a notable increase in the number and size of libraries and art collections occurred, especially at the thriving princely courts. And if painting and sculpture showed less in the way of brilliance than they once had, at least there was enough talent still available to adorn the castles and other public buildings which were either newly built or renovated in quantity in the years around 1600 – strong testimony also to the vitality of late renaissance-style architecture. Further, while the fierce religious disputations of the Reformation era had clearly left their mark on the universities, the humanistic tradition still remained powerful in the faculties of several new universities founded between 1575 and 1625, especially in Protestant territories; and in the work of the pansophist disciples of Paracelsus von Hohenheim (died 1544) there were even strong hints of important changes in thinking about the natural world and the physical sciences which in some ways adumbrated the 'scientific revolution' of the seventeenth century. But there were dubious aspects even to some of these evidences of progress. For example, a considerable proportion of the increase of printed literature in the sixteenth century was religious in nature – much of it homiletic or polemical – which did little to advance the frontiers of knowledge and only exacerbated the confessional conflict. Even several categories of secular literature – historiography and works on imperial and canon law, for example – were affected, sometimes negatively, by hardening religious differences. And while the addition of new universities resulted in the production of a more numerous educated leadership elite, the universities themselves, hostage to the opposing religious purposes which had led to their creation in the first place, lost much of the fecundity which might have helped to link them into a single national community of higher learning. Nor, finally, did such levels of learning attained by the leadership elite prevent it from presiding over literally thousands of witch trials, whose numbers peaked in the years just before and after 1600 and about which more will be said below. Whatever their origin, these judicial processes do not point to any notable increase of enlightenment among the upper classes generally, even by the standards of the time.

The life style of both upper and lower classes of society, as one index of cultural standards, again demonstrates the difficulty of forming a simple impression of the Germany of 1600. For example, there were some definite and encouraging signs that a civilizing and socializing process was occurring within the nobility, symbolized by an already established trend towards abandonment of their hilltop fortresses and armouries, echoing with the noises of domestic and farm animals and stinking of gunpowder, mould and animal ordure, in favour of mostly rather modest lowland dwellings which were closer to the sources of their income and not much more vulnerable to the new artillery than their old domiciles.[4] This physical rapprochement with the rest of society was accompanied not only by an increased literacy rate, but also by a more frequent (though still not really typical) pursuit of higher education in learned schools and universities, especially as preparation for service in the expanding administrations of the territorial princes. By the later sixteenth century there had even emerged from within the nobility the beginnings of a new agrarian literature of real quality, which not only extolled the virtues of rural life, but also aimed at agricultural reform and improved estate management.

But now the qualifications arise. This same agrarian literature, to begin with, was to some degree an indirect response to one of the favourite diversions of scores of humanist writers since the fifteenth century and which may colloquially be referred to as 'court- and noble-bashing'. Around 1600, this already fashionable critique of the often raw, coarse and vulgar life style of nobles high and low reached new heights of frequency and severity. The drunkenness, gluttony, conspicuous and unproductive consumption and dissolute sexual behaviour of the upper classes was a leading theme of humanist social critics. At the same time, there was so enormous a criticism of the life style of the middle and lower classes among those who knew them best – the Catholic and Protestant clergy – as to suggest almost a denunciatory conspiracy between the faiths. If the intensity of all this criticism does indicate an actual and substantial decline in public morality, its origins, as one historian has recently suggested, may lie less in the psychological stresses associated with sinking standards of

4. Heinrich Lutz, *Das Ringen um deutsche Einheit und kirchliche Erneuerung: von Maximilian I. bis zum Westfälischen Frieden, 1490 bis 1648* [Propyläen Geschichte Deutschlands, vol. IV] (Berlin, 1983), pp. 52, 54–5.

living than in an anomie which was the result of the destruction of old social norms and values by the religious quarrel and by the attempt of territorial authorities to impose by ordinance new standards of social behaviour which for a long time were more successful in eliminating old practices than in supplanting them with new ones.[5] The courts and persons of the princes also did not escape critical attention for their dissipation, venality, malfeasance and other abuses; indeed, the literature on this subject constituted a permanent genre throughout the entire early modern period. But for better or worse, it was these princes, their administrations and their public policies which were increasingly to dominate and give direction to German culture and society during the seventeenth and eighteenth centuries. As will become apparent below, the peculiarities of the German scene gave them a power to do good which was considerable, but which was also limited by many of the same factors which curbed their power to do evil.

If one nation could be distinguished from others by a 'national character' discernible from the forms and habits of the daily life and social intercourse of its people, as the humanists were wont to think, then the above comments might lead to the supposition that an active coarseness and crudity of life would occupy an important place in literary attempts to define Germany. And so it was. Many French and Italian humanists, in particular, basing their views on both contemporary observation and ancient sources – Tacitus, above all – routinely ascribed to the Germans a physical and spiritual life on the wild side which was usually dubbed the *furor teutonicus* – the 'Germanic madness'. This madness not only involved an uncouthness which set Germany off from the more civilized nations (especially of Latin Europe), according to these sources, but was also held responsible by some of them for the occurrence, as well as the conflicts and indispositions, of the Reformation. Many German humanists, interestingly enough, accepted much of this, but with significant alterations in perspective and emphasis. For them, for example, Tacitus had described and praised a Germany peopled by a race of manly warriors of vigorous and independent disposition, not a loutish collection of drunken layabouts. In Tacitus's time, as now, averred these Germans, German 'madness' was in fact only the ferment of ceaseless physical and mental activity, German 'barbarism' only a refusal to accept current fashions of a degenerate and debilitating overrefinement; and German morality, profundity and

5. Ibid., 376–7.

vigour were contrasted sharply to the corruption, indolence and superficiality of the Latin peoples. For evangelical Germans, furthermore, Martin Luther's successful revolt against Rome was a shining moment in European civilization, representing the triumph of characteristic German spirituality and honesty over equally typical Latin materialism, treachery and deceit.

Beyond this, if Germans of the sixteenth century had been asked to provide examples of their nation's contribution to European civilization, certainly most would have pointed first to the invention and continuing perfection of printing. Germans were well aware of the enormous and still growing influence of what for a long time they proudly referred to as 'the German art'. A renewed emphasis on scripture – 'the Word' – in the German Reformation served to heighten appreciation of the new art. Printing also became the chief means whereby the Germany of 1600 had achieved a much more nearly uniform national language, at least for the literate, than it had in 1500: in the publishing world, High German had established permanent dominance over Low German (which was almost a different tongue); and while Latin for a long time remained the primary scholarly language (and kept its importance even as a literary language in Catholic Germany), High German, slowly but steadily refined over the years, penetrated more and more deeply into both learned and popular discourse.[6]

In any event, according to the cultural standards employed by those contemporaries who concerned themselves with such matters – the humanist scholars, primarily – Germany was indisputably a 'nation' in 1600. By other standards, unhappily, this was much less true. Thus, for example, if uniformity of religious belief was integral to nationhood – and for many people it was – then Germany was no nation at all. Even in a Europe where religious division was by now present in virtually every country, creating confessional minorities which challenged the majority (and normally 'official') religion, such division was of the very essence of German public life. By 1600, it was even difficult to speak of religious minorities in Germany as a whole, since the Protestant faiths had become so solidly anchored and embraced so significant a percentage of the entire population. Since mutual toleration as policy had been rejected in principle by the militant Catholicism of the Counter-Reformation (and was not a popular position in many Protestant quarters either, especially

6. Ibid., 79, 385–6.

among Calvinists) and since nothing had so far demonstrated the absolute impossibility of imposing (or reimposing) a uniformity of belief, the relative parity in numbers between the contending faiths was itself dangerous. While the balance of forces may have worked for peace, because it discouraged the idea that any quick, decisive military action against a small minority might solve the problem for either side, it also meant that if a major clash of arms, absent since the 1550s, ever were to occur, it was almost certain to be long and bloody. As earlier suggested, the religious quarrel in Germany ran very deep and coloured almost all aspects of public life. It dominated politics and influenced literature and the arts; and because the churches remained a primary source of influence on public opinion in all classes, but especially among the middling and lower sorts, their concerns and perspectives quickly became the stuff of intense daily discourse and debate.

The fractionalization of religious nationhood in Germany was made worse by the uneven geographical distribution of the reformed faiths and by the fact that by 1600 Calvinism had established itself as a Protestant alternative to Lutheranism – a fact as unwelcome to Lutherans as to Catholics. Both these circumstances, however, derived from a common political source which must be regarded as one of the most important characteristics of Germany in the early modern period: the federative nature of the Holy Roman Empire. Of all the other great nations of Europe, none had evolved a constitutional structure which assured as much power and independence to the individual territories which composed it as had the Empire. Indeed, during the very period from the late middle ages onward in which dynastic monarchs in England, France, Spain and elsewhere were slowly asserting a more dominant role over the noble grandees of their realms, the high ecclesiastical and secular nobility in Germany was steadily increasing its independence from all central imperial agencies, including the emperor. This independence was represented by the term *Landeshoheit*, perhaps best translated as 'territorial lordship', an authority recognized neither formally nor informally as conferring true sovereignty on the territorial rulers of the Empire, but which approached that position more and more closely from the sixteenth century onward. At whatever their level of power, the princes were extremely jealous and protective of their *Landeshoheit* against outside interference from the emperor, the diet, the imperial law courts, or their individual fellow princes. Even the famous *Reichsregiment* of 1500 – an attempt of the imperial states to form a permanent governing council to supplement (or even supplant) the authority of the emperor – failed in two years, a victim of an uncooperativeness ultimately traceable to *Landeshoheit*. Nor was any similar scheme even approaching the seriousness of the *Reichsregiment* ever again to appear in the Empire.

When the first period of military confrontations over religious issues ended at the Peace of Augsburg in 1555, it was entirely consistent with the steady strengthening of the autonomic content of the concept of *Landeshoheit* that each ruling prince was accorded the right to determine the official religion of his own territory, with correspondingly sweeping rights over ecclesiastical organization, discipline and doctrine, not to mention the lives and consciences of his subjects. Since conversions and reconversions continued to occur after 1555, Germany's confessional map resembled a periodically changing checkerboard into the time of the Thirty Years War; and because no one was sufficiently strong or willing to prevent it, Calvinist territories soon took their place alongside Lutheran and Catholic ones, even though only the latter two had been recognized in imperial law as 'official' alternatives in the Peace of Augsburg. The triumph of territorial particularism in the Empire, then, though not fully celebrated until the Peace of Westphalia in 1648, had proceeded far enough by 1555 to guarantee that the religious conflict would work together with political fragmentation to deny the Empire the unanimity it required to be a full nation, much less a true state.

But while Germany was in these respects less than the nation many of its neighbours were, or were becoming, and would suffer for it, it was in another regard also more than a nation – and would suffer no less for that. The fact is that Germany was hostage to supranational – imperial – interests which were of no real concern or value to almost any of its princely houses, but which had much potential to drag them into conflicts not of their own making. That was because the one German house whose geopolitical situation and dynastic ties were most internationally complex was the Habsburg House of Austria, whose grip on the emperorship, moreover, had become permanent by 1600. It was a fateful circumstance for Germany that the lands ruled by the Austrian Habsburgs, comprising far more territory than those of any other single German house, were located on the southeastern periphery of the Empire, where borders with Italy, Poland and Hungary (with all their domestic and international problems) not only conferred on Austria interests in non-German areas as compelling as those in Germany itself, but also – and more to the point – encouraged the emperor to look at

Germany as an auxiliary to be called upon in the service of Austrian needs as required. Strong loyalties to the Catholic cause in all parts of Europe, as well as to the Habsburg rulers of Spain, widened the range of interests the Austrians accepted as their own and complicated their German connections considerably. Though it was no real fault of their own, the cunning of their history and geography had made it virtually impossible for the Austrian Habsburgs to view Germany in the same way the more centrally rooted 'national' dynasties of other European states looked at their countries: as a challenge, however vaguely grasped at this point, to forge the bonds of a strong national community – the precursor of the nation-state. No single political fact about early modern Germany is more important than its lack of a *national* dynasty at its head.[7] The unfortunate consequences of this fact had appeared in Germany before 1600 on several occasions and had led to a widening of the gulf between the interests of the emperor and the Empire; but no previous consequences could compare with those which were soon to come as the result of what Germans for many years after it were to call 'the Great War' – the Thirty Years War – whose origins must now be explored.

CHAPTER TWO

Drifts and Eddies Towards War

It is common and appropriate, for accounts of the origins of the Thirty Years War to begin with the religious Peace of Augsburg of 1555 – not because that treaty settled forever the political-religious issues that had created so much turmoil in Germany for some years previously, but because it did not, thereby demonstrating that the time had not yet arrived when the raging waters of the religious conflict could be dammed up by good (or not so good) intentions and mere signatures on any one or several pieces of paper.

What the Peace of Augsburg did do was to recognize certain developments as at least temporarily irreversible without further and unacceptable sacrifice on the part of both Catholic and Protestant contenders. The terms of the peace itself were hammered out at the Diet of Augsburg on the basis of an understanding reached at Passau in 1552 between King Ferdinand – acting for his brother, Emperor Karl V – and the German princes. They can be summarized in three categories according to the descending levels of genuine agreement they represented between the parties. From this perspective the strongest points were those which recognized two 'official' religions in the Empire – Catholics and 'members of the Augsburg Confession' (Lutherans) – and which gave to all estates (territorial rulers) of the Empire the right to determine the religion of their subjects; those of the latter who could not accept the now 'official' territorial religion were to go elsewhere, subject to certain conditions respecting person and property that were intended to be reasonably generous. Less strong was the provision that in those Imperial Cities which were at the time not already entirely Catholic or entirely Lutheran – and there were only eight – both faiths were to coexist in parity. The weakness here was that no recognition was given to the possibility that the admixture of confessions in one or more cities might someday become so lopsided in favour of one or the other that toleration of the minority was no longer realistic; or to the eventuality that a city wholly of one faith now might become strongly mixed later. Consequently, no provision was made for any mechanism whereby parity might later be abolished or created. Least strong of all were those terms which did not receive the formal approval of the imperial diet at all, indicating strong reservations in one or another quarter. Unfortunately, these included some potentially very troublesome issues. One was the so-called 'ecclesiastical reservation', inserted into the peace only by imperial insistence and which was designed to prevent any further Catholic losses of ecclesiastical principalities. Unlike the hereditary rulers of secular territories, the ecclesiastical princes came to their thrones through election by a 'chapter' – a mixed body of clerics and laymen (mostly nobles); this provision forbade continued rulership of such territories by any prelate who might convert to Protestantism by requiring the chapter to elect another Catholic in his place. Finally, there was the so-called 'Declaration of Ferdinand', which was not a part of the treaty at all and therefore not binding in imperial law; this was a secret assurance made to Protestant princes by King (later Emperor) Ferdinand I that nobles and towns within the ecclesiastical territories which were already practising Lutheranism would not be hindered in the continued exercise of their religion. This promise, not generally known for some twenty years, was accepted by the ecclesiastical princes as reluctantly as was the 'ecclesiastical reservation' by the Protestant princes.

Most important, however, is the fact that neither of the religious parties looked upon this peace as a permanent one; and since each anticipated not only that further disagreements over its terms would arise, but also that such disagreements would work to its own unique advantage, neither had a compelling interest in eliminating the vaguenesses which glossed over what both knew were some serious problem areas. It is indicative of the durability of this dangerous attitude that no general conference to iron out the burgeoning problems arising from this treaty was seriously proposed in the several decades thereafter.

At the very least, however, the Peace of Augsburg had recognized the permanence of a Protestant faith in Germany and had assured it a relative security. The impulses which carried it to this point continued to favour the expansion of Protestantism for another quarter of a century thereafter, assisted by the nonconfrontational policies adopted by Emperors Ferdinand I (1555–64) and Maximilian II (1564–76). Ferdinand made a determined effort to pacify the Empire by giving equal hearing to the advice of the more important princes of both faiths and by encouraging theological compromise between the two – an undertaking which never succeeded. Maximilian, for his part, though never formally deserting Catholicism, was in some respects almost a crypto-Lutheran and followed a political path of careful neutrality towards both religions. Paradoxically, this policy may actually have helped to save Catholicism in the Empire by encouraging Protestants to believe that all of Germany might be converted by the sheer spiritual power of their faith, unassisted by political or military measures. Their gains between 1555 and 1580 certainly did not discourage such a view, since by the latter date Protestantism was triumphant in virtually all of Germany east of the Weser River and territories either totally or predominantly Protestant were not only almost wholly contiguous geographically, but also occupied perhaps three-quarters of the map of Germany. Still more ominous for Catholicism was the cir-cumstance that even in territories which officially continued to adhere to the old faith, large percentages of the nobility and towns had turned Protestant and had forced some sort of recognition of religious freedom on their rulers. Dire predictions of the imminent and total eclipse of Catholicism in Germany could be heard in many quarters in these years and such forecasts were reinforced by the collapsing morale of the Catholic clergy itself, which more than ever before presented a picture of ignorance, moral dissolution and spiritual apathy.

Great success, however, can breed overconfidence, and while in both moral and material terms Protestantism in the late 1570s seemed overwhelmingly superior to its Catholic opposition, its political representatives – the princes – allowed an excellent chance to convert the whole Empire by means of a coordinated political offensive to slip away forever. Coordination, of course, had never been a notable strength among the Protestants in any case. Doctrinal dispute, especially between the 'original' Lutheran faithful, who believed they held the key to the correct interpretation of the master's words and the followers of Philip Melanchthon (frequently called 'Philipists'), who championed various modifications and different emphases in Luther's teachings, was commonplace even before Luther's death in 1546 and became more frequent and acrimonious thereafter. The territoriality of the Lutheran churches did nothing to dampen this quarrelling, since individual rulers sometimes felt obliged to support

their theologians against those of other princes. It was therefore a
hopeful event when the three Protestant electors (Saxony, Brandenburg and the Palatinate) in 1580 signed the so-called Formula of
Concord, whereby many disputes within Lutheranism were laid to
rest. Less reassuring was the fact that a number of Protestant princes
refused to accept the Formula and, worse yet, that the agreement
caused the defection of many frustrated Philipists to the growing
persuasion of Calvinism.

Calvinism had not been a force on the German scene before 1555,
which of course accounts for its exclusion as an 'official' religious
alternative in the Peace of Augsburg. But it is certain – if one can
judge from the nasty relations obtaining between Lutherans and
Calvinists a quarter of a century later – that most Lutheran princes
would have opposed its inclusion as vigorously as the Catholics.
John Calvin's theology, even in its normally modified German form,
was as repugnant to most Lutherans as were the high-energy political
acuity and activism that tended to distinguish the regimes that
adopted it. Those characteristics flowed from the more strongly
international appeal of the movement, with its accompanying
awareness of threats to its existence in Switzerland, France, the
Netherlands and now Germany from various powerful sources,
including the French and Spanish courts and, of course, the papacy.
On the whole, Calvinist regimes tended to look at their Lutheran
counterparts in Germany as allies against the common Roman
enemy, but this hopefully friendly attitude was not reciprocated by
most Lutherans. Thus, since a number of German princes – foremost
among them the Elector Palatine Friedrich III – adopted Calvinism
before 1580, the idea of a united Protestant front for a final conquest
of Catholicism in Germany had been rendered dubious even before
the Formula of Concord – and, more importantly, before the
appearance of the first real challenges of the Catholic Counter-
Reformation in Germany.

The revival of the sagging fortunes of the Church of Rome in the
second half of the sixteenth century is one of the most remarkable
stories of early modern European history. Beginning with the several
sessions of the Council of Trent (1545–63), the Catholic Church
undertook a sweeping series of reforms designed to eliminate the
inner weaknesses of the church as the first and necessary condition of
successful resistance to further inroads of Protestantism and the
reconquest of lost lands. Through identification, clarification and
reaffirmation of the central teachings of the church, by definitive
rejection of compromise with Protestantism and by construction of a

programme for thoroughgoing reform of the training and morals of the clergy, the foundations were laid for a vigorous long-term counter-attack against the 'heresies' which had penetrated so close to the very vitals of the church. Indispensable to this effort, as it unfolded, was the Society of Jesus – the Jesuits – founded by the Spaniard Ignatius Loyola and accepted as an order of the church in 1540. Tough-minded and pragmatic, but also thoroughly educated and ideologically driven, the Jesuits – 'soldiers of the pope', as they were styled – had from the beginning an organisation and dedication matched among Protestants only by the best of the Calvinists; both contrasted strongly with the more relaxed and comfortably inactive generality of Lutherans. Like the Calvinists, too, the Jesuits from the outset appreciated the impact of a properly conceived education (or indoctrination), begun early, on the shaping of inflexible adult attitudes. Arriving in Germany in increasing numbers from Spain and Italy, along with trained clergy from other orders, the Jesuits founded scores of schools at various levels which began to educate a new elite of loyal, disciplined laymen who were not only impervious to the blandishments of Protestantism, but fiercely eager to assist in destroying it. The fact that a certain number of these students rose to positions of rulership, military command or other influential posts in civil and ecclesiastical government – not to mention the Society of Jesus itself – was a benefit well understood and intended from the outset. More than a few Jesuits themselves became personal confessors, confidants and advisers to various German Catholic princes.

The upswing of Catholic fortunes in Germany after the 1570s was fully as dramatic as had been their virtual collapse over the preceding decades. Apart from the early successes in reestablishing religious uniformity registered by such resolute Catholics as Albrecht V of Bavaria, one episode of the 1580s occupies such an important place in the revival of hope and confidence among Catholics as to justify calling it a turning point in the heretofore headlong retreat of Catholicism before the Protestant onslaught. In late 1582 the elector and archbishop of Cologne announced that he had converted to Protestantism and shortly thereafter granted freedom of worship to Protestants. Most members of the chapter refused to accept this and the pope declared him deposed, thus clearing the way for the election of Ernst of Bavaria, a brother of its duke, who was already possessed of several other bishoprics. A minor war resulted, in which the deposed elector received support from the Dutch Netherlands and the Palatinate – though not from either Saxony or Brandenburg –

and the new archbishop was helped by Spanish and Bavarian troops. This episode was a fundamental test of the 'ecclesiastical reservation' and was of special importance because it involved an electorate, where a change of religion would for the first time have given a majority in the Council of Electors to Protestants, thus making possible the elevation of a Protestant to the imperial office at the next election; worse yet, it might have encouraged the other two archbishop-electors – Mainz and Trier – to consider similar conversions. Earlier, to be sure, Protestants had gained possession of some ecclesiastical territories by successfully insisting that the 'ecclesiastical reservation' covered only conversions of existing ecclesiastical princes, not the election of new (Protestant) ones; but their clear failure in Cologne almost immediately dissipated the force of those earlier successes, most of which – notably in several important Westphalian bishoprics – were reversed in the twenty years or so following the acceptance of Ernst by the other electors in 1585.

The Catholic revival, as it gathered steam, consisted thus partly in the recovery of whole territories, but also and just as important, in the total re-Catholicization of territories previously accepted as mixed by their Catholic rulers. This was especially the case in a number of ecclesiastical territories, where the protection of the 'Declaration of Ferdinand' was now systematically ignored. However, even in secular territories to which the Declaration had never applied, but in which the number and social importance of Protestant converts was so great as to have forced concessions on Catholic rulers, strenuous efforts were now undertaken to reverse the Protestant tide. As previously mentioned, in this endeavour the dukes of Bavaria, beginning with Albrecht V (1550–79), provided models of success to other Catholic princes, including Emperor Rudolf II (1576–1612) who, while generally respecting the terms of the Peace of Augsburg in his policies towards the Empire, began in his family lands to restrict or abolish religious freedoms and privileges extracted from his immediate predecessor, Maximilian II. For more than a quarter century of Rudolf's rule, slow but steady progress in the closing of Protestant schools and churches throughout the Habsburg inheritance was apparent. It was not the nobility, but rather townspeople and peasants, in particular, who bore the brunt of this policy, partly because no formal promises of toleration had ever been made to them and partly because by the 1570s such a vast proportion of the nobles in some parts of the realm – probably 90 per cent in Upper and Lower Austria, for example – had converted to Lutheranism that as a practical matter it was impossible to coerce them.[1]

In the Habsburg territories, however, as elsewhere, the trend of re-Catholicization was not an altogether uninterrupted one. Emperor Rudolf's progressive incapacity after 1600 – the result of illnesses and mental degeneration – not only caused a family coup in 1609, whereby his brother Matthias removed the territories of Austria, Moravia and Hungary from his hapless older brother's rule to his own (leaving only the imperial and Bohemian crowns to Rudolf), but also permitted a strong reassertion of demands for religious concessions from the Protestant estates – concessions which had to be granted in almost all Habsburg lands and of which some were more extensive than ever before. On other fronts, however, Catholics generally fared better than did Protestants. In 1592, for example, the bishopric of Strassburg was barely prevented from falling into Protestant hands by a compromise which, by dividing the bishopric temporarily, made possible its full recovery by Catholicism in 1604. In 1598 Emperor Rudolf, with the assistance of Spanish troops, threw out a new Protestant municipal government in Aachen and restored the city to Catholicism, thus permanently settling in the latter's favour the legal question of whether Imperial Cities not originally designated as Protestant in 1555 could alter their religion.

Protestants unhappy about the outcome of this important issue soon received even worse news. The south German city of Donauwörth, with a mixed population in 1555, had been designated a 'parity' city in the Peace of Augsburg. But the subsequent growth of a strong Lutheran majority had delivered the city council over to the Protestants, while the Catholic presence had for all practical purposes shrunk to a single monastery and two chapels. Conflict between Protestant burghers and monks and other Catholics – sometimes degenerating into street brawls – became commonplace and the city council appeared powerless to do anything about it. In 1606, on complaint of the bishop of Augsburg, the imperial Aulic Council – the emperor's own 'supreme court' – threatened to place the city under the imperial ban. Further disturbances resulted in the actual imposition of that ban in late 1607 and Rudolf II empowered Duke Maximilian of Bavaria to execute it in defence of the religious rights of the minority. Maximilian not only took over the city and

---

1. A number of these nobles, in fact, preserved the privilege of private – not public – worship through the entire Thirty Years War.

dismissed the Lutheran administration, but later, with Rudolf's permission, reimbursed himself by annexing the city. Donauwörth, henceforth only a Bavarian territorial city, was quickly re-Catholicized with the eager and efficient assistance of the Jesuits.

With these latest ill tidings barely digested, the Protestant princes approached the imperial diet convoked at Regensburg in early 1608 in a mood of anger and frustration. While the actions against Donauwörth seemed to them plainly illegal, it was even more important that a militant Catholicism had pushed forward onto entirely new ground. They therefore demanded an imperial reconfirmation of the terms of the Peace of Augsburg as the first order of business. With the religious issue so conveniently raised by their opponents, the Catholics took this opportunity to demand the restoration of ecclesiastical lands seized by Protestants after 1552 in defiance of the understandings reached at Passau. After much bickering, the Palatine delegation, joined by Brandenburg and most of the other Protestant estates, simply walked out and the diet dispersed without passing any legislation at all. It was not a good sign for the future that the diet − a national forum for possible compromise between the religious parties − had collapsed, thus joining in futility the Imperial Cameral Tribunal, whose already weak authority had been totally destroyed by the adamant refusal of the Protestant estates to take part in its appeals process.

It is clear evidence of the loss of faith in imperial remedies that a militarily (if also defensively) oriented alliance of Protestant princes was formed only nine days after the formal dismissal of the Regensburg diet. On 12 May 1608, a 'Protestant (or Evangelical) Union' (hereafter called simply 'the Union') composed of the rulers of the Palatinate, Württemberg, Neuburg, Baden, Ansbach, Anhalt and three Imperial Cities was created and was later expanded (for a time) by the addition of Brandenburg, Hesse-Kassel and a few more south German cities. Though the most considerable prince of the Union was the Elector Palatine Friedrich IV, the major force behind its creation was the forever-scheming Christian I of Anhalt, the small size of whose own north German principality did not prevent him from plotting against Catholicism and its purveyors on a pan-European scale. Friedrich IV, whom Christian served in several different posts, was named head of the Union, while the Anhalt prince became its lieutenant-general. Because its membership remained small − partly due to persistent hostility between Lutheran and Calvinist princes and partly because the city membership (from which it drew a significant portion of its very considerable budget) was extremely chary of any purposes which might be construed as offensive, or which might reach beyond the borders of Germany – the Union neither began as, nor ever became, the giant-killer Anhalt had hoped it might be.

The novelty of the Union's existence, however, as well as the simple fact that it represented some degree of military and political cooperation among Protestants, was almost bound to produce some tighter bond among the Catholic princes, especially if a new religious crisis should arise within the Empire. When that crisis came in March 1609 in the form of a disputed succession to the duchies of Jülich and Cleves, and the Union made some vague noises about military support for its candidates to the succession, the formation of a new Catholic League in the summer of the same year could have surprised no one. Consisting of Bavaria, the three ecclesiastical electorates and various prince-bishoprics of Bavaria, Swabia and Franconia, the League expressed its general purposes as the defence of Catholicism and opposition to the secularizations illegally carried out by Protestants since 1552. Maximilian of Bavaria was chosen as leader. Divisions similar to some of those which plagued the Union soon appeared, however, especially between the ecclesiastical electors and the south German members, including Bavaria. Not as confrontational or bellicose as the latter, the electors (led by the imperial archchancellor Mainz) within five years not only forced a decentralization of the League into three regional directorates, but also, after inviting Austrian membership, located one of the directorates in Vienna. Generally disgusted by the weakness he saw arising from the decentralization scheme, but also very suspicious that the Habsburgs would not hesitate to subvert the purposes of the League in their own interest, Maximilian resigned from it in 1616. But when Emperor Matthias dissolved the League in April 1617, as part of a general programme to reduce tensions in the Empire, Maximilian immediately recreated a smaller but tighter and more purposeful alliance; and it was this new League, firmly under Maximilian's control, which was to carry the banner of militant Catholicism into the maelstrom which lay ahead.

The first opportunity for a direct clash between League and Union had been provided even before this. In March 1609, the Catholic duke of Jülich and Cleves and their dependencies, died without direct heirs. His fairly considerable inheritance occupied a strategic position on the lower Rhine which was of great importance to Spain as a military bridge in and out of the Netherlands. For this reason, as well as because the two best legal claims to the territories were raised by Lutherans, the succession was also important to Emperor Rudolf II, who wanted to delay a decision on the inheritance in the hope that a Catholic could be found to raise a reasonable claim to the succession. In the following months and years, his forces and representatives, together with those of the two Protestant claimants – Duke Wolfgang Wilhelm of Neuburg and Elector Johann Sigismund of Brandenburg – occupied various parts of Jülich-Cleves at different times. The Union supported the claims of the Lutheran princes, both of whom belonged to the alliance and for the first time made some hard contacts with foreign governments, resulting in minor interventions of French, English and Dutch forces. Maximilian's Catholic League also mobilized an army under the command of the able Count Johann Tilly and Spain considered intervention even at the cost of breaching the twelve-year truce with the Dutch that had been in force only since 1609. All parties, however, recognized the explosive nature of the issues involved here and that a general European war was not only possible but likely unless real restraint was exercised. While none of the greater powers believed in either the possibility or the utility of perpetual peace, they were disinclined to want war except over issues and at a time of their own choosing; so they welcomed the new quarrelling which erupted between Wolfgang Wilhelm and Johann Sigismund over the latter's attempt to enlist Saxon support for his claims, as well as his conversion to Calvinism in 1613. This widening rift led the aggrieved Wolfgang Wilhelm to seek the advice and assistance of Maximilian of Bavaria and his League – an initiative which, surprisingly, led not only to his conversion to Catholicism, but to marriage with Maximilian's sister as well. This unforeseen conversion of one of the claimants to Jülich-Cleves opened the way to a compromise settlement, embodied in the Treaty of Xanten of 1614, by which the original inheritance was divided: Wolfgang Wilhelm received Jülich and Berg, while Johann Sigismund took possession of Cleves and the territories of Mark and Ravensberg.

In 1612, in the midst of the Jülich-Cleves conflict, Emperor Rudolf II died. In precipitously declining physical and mental health for years, he had already been shorn of most of his governing powers by other members of the Habsburg family. A considerable anxiety existed among Habsburg supporters that the anger and disarray within the Empire arising from the as yet unsettled dispute over Jülich-Cleves might lead to an attempt to deny the imperial office to Rudolf's younger brother and presumed successor, Matthias. In the event, however, Matthias was elected emperor unanimously and with surprising ease, owing this good fortune to the same desire for stability that had prevented major armed clashes during the whole succession crisis. Once in office, however, the new emperor delivered the conduct of his government almost entirely into the hands of his close confidant, Cardinal Melchior Khlesl, who had been bishop of Vienna since 1598 and whom Matthias now appointed as his chancellor. Khlesl's policies were determined by his conviction that the resurgence of Protestantism among the nobility and towns of the Habsburgs' own territories since 1600 or so was a most serious problem, requiring an urgent and undivided attention such as could be managed only if the Empire beyond were kept quiet and orderly. To this end, Khlesl adopted a rhetoric of compromise and conciliation towards the German Protestants and hinted at various concessions the imperial government might be prepared to make to clear away old fears and new grievances of the Protestant princes and to restore life and meaning to those imperial institutions such as the diet and the Cameral Tribunal which had collapsed into uselessness partly because of hostility between head and members of the Empire.

Unfortunately for the chancellor, as well as for his programme and his master Matthias, Khlesl's overtures to the Protestants, while producing no very tangible benefits, created a great deal of suspicion and opposition on the part of many Catholics, including Maximilian of Bavaria and some members of the Habsburg family in both Austria and Spain. This attitude, over time, increased the credit of Matthias's much younger cousin, Archduke Ferdinand, who was governor of Inner Austria and the man chosen to succeed Matthias on his various thrones. With the approval of (and some pressure from) King Philip III of Spain, whose favour was courted by Ferdinand, the archduke was put forward as candidate for the thrones of Bohemia and Hungary; he was crowned in the former in June 1617 and in the latter in July 1618. By the latter date, however, Bohemia was already in full revolt against its new king and the growing legions of Cardinal Khlesl's Catholic opponents, taking the rebellion as conclusive evidence of the bankruptcy of his policies, moved to exclude his influence from government. Matthias's brother Maximilian, long in favour of Ferdinand's advancement to full rulership of all the Habsburg territories, arrested and imprisoned Khlesl in a palace coup that effectively ended Matthias's reign in July, 1618 – an event he survived by only eight months. While it is reasonable to suppose that Matthias, left to himself, would not have chosen such an inglorious end to his life, he would have been more reconciled to it had he known that the great troubles he had seen were as nothing compared to those soon to arise in profusion for his cousin and successor, Ferdinand.

CHAPTER THREE

The Nightmare Begins: The Bohemian War

While almost the entire Austrian inheritance of which Archduke Ferdinand had now become master was riddled with religious dissension, nowhere were his Protestant subjects more vigorous or vocal in the defence of their religious rights and privileges than in the troublesome kingdom of Bohemia[1], where no less than five non-Catholic denominations – Hussites, Utraquists and Bohemian Brethren, in addition to Calvinists and the much more numerous Lutherans – coexisted in more or less friendly fashion. Since well before 1600, the largely Slavic Bohemians had proved to be extremely defensive about traditional rights of various kinds, including that of choosing their own religion; and the facts that the Bohemian crown was elective and that the citizenry was not shy of rebellion as a means of chastising overmighty rulers had helped them to maintain an unusually large measure of political autonomy from their kings. The most recent evidence of their power was the so-called Letter of Majesty which they had forced out of Rudolf II in 1609 – a royal promise which guaranteed them free choice of religion and permitted them to establish a permanent committee to monitor observance of the promise. No Habsburg had ever liked these and other similar guarantees, which were regarded as pure extortion and Rudolf's successor Matthias had already begun an active effort to strengthen Catholicism wherever it seemed possible to do so – chiefly on crown and ecclesiastical lands not covered by the Letter of Majesty. After his accession to the Bohemian crown in 1617, Ferdinand not only stepped up this activity, but also directed his

---

1. The authority of the Bohemian crown extended to the provinces of Silesia, Moravia and Lusatia as well as to Bohemia proper.

Council of Regents in Prague (whose membership Matthias had already altered to favour Catholics) to disregard the protests of the monitoring committee.

It is of course peculiar, in retrospect, that the Bohemian estates should ever have accepted Ferdinand as their ruler, given their knowledge of his background. An able and eager product of Jesuit indoctrination, Ferdinand, in spite of some pleasant personal qualities, was a religious fanatic of the first water and as governor of Inner Austria had demonstrated both a harsh and inflexible attitude toward heresy and a fine aptitude for destroying it. But whether from an inertia born of carelessness, inability to agree on another candidate or fear of electing someone else, the Bohemians, after receiving a promise, which none of them believed, to respect the Letter of Majesty elected Ferdinand anyway. Less than a year of experience with him convinced them that they had made a serious mistake. Reacting to his regents' studied indifference to their mounting religious concerns, an angry group of nobles stormed into the royal palace in Prague on 23 May, 1618 and ended a turbulent meeting by throwing two of the regents – Martinitz and Slavata – out of a second-storey window.

This so-called Defenestration of Prague did no lasting damage to the unfortunate regents; but the same cannot be said about the relations between the Bohemian estates and their new king. A majority of the estates, backing the lesser nobility and gentry who were primarily responsible for the revolt[2], approved the establishment of a provisional government – a directorate of some thirty individuals who were to generate measures for the defence of the country. Declaring themselves opposed not to Ferdinand himself, but only to his wicked agents (specifically the Jesuits), the Bohemians called upon the other provinces to join their revolt. While only the estates of Silesia signed on more or less immediately, both Moravia and Lusatia had come into the fold by the summer of 1619, making possible the drafting of a constitution for a confederation of the four provinces of the Bohemian crown in July of that year. The following month, the confederation made an agreement with the estates of Upper and Lower Austria providing for mutual support in the struggle to extend and defend political and religious liberties. This already enlarged alliance achieved a final

2. Most of the very wealthy landowning nobles had converted to Catholicism after 1600 or so and remained strong supporters of the Habsburgs. Their refusal to support the rebellion was a serious flaw in the façade of rebel unity.

success when the Calvinist ruler of Transylvania, Bethlen Gabor, having already decided that the time was ripe to seize the Habsburg crown of Hungary for himself, concluded an offensive and defensive alliance with the Bohemian confederation, also in August 1619.

With rebellions of the estates either overt or just below the surface in all of their major territories, it might appear that the Habsburg inheritance in central Europe was about to collapse entirely; indeed, intelligence to that effect was widely noised about by gleeful agents of Protestant persuasion. But while the situation was indeed serious, it was kept from being fatal by a number of factors, first among which was the inability of the Bohemians to attract enough assistance from outside to strike a mortal blow either at the decisive early moment or, as it turned out, at any time thereafter. The rebels' own resources were much more scanty and their political organization and cooperation much less effective, over the long term, than the ease with which they achieved their initial successes might suggest. While various leaders of the rebellion since long before 1618 had developed an almost incredibly complex network of correspondence with Protestant rulers and statesmen all over Europe[3], in which bellicose statements against Catholicism and the Habsburgs vied with easy promises of mutual support and assistance against both, very little concrete help was offered when it was needed. The only early military aid came from the duke of Savoy – a prince of the Empire – who saw in the Bohemian revolt a chance to further his own schemes to embarrass the Habsburgs in Italy and who offered the Protestant Union a small army of 2000 which it had earlier permitted him to recruit on its territories. The Union, whose first and belated response to the Bohemian uprising had come in the form of a condemnation of Ferdinand's violations of the Letter of Majesty, together with a plea to its members not to permit on their territories recruitment of troops for use against the Bohemians, now accepted the Savoyard offer and placed the army (commanded by the neither able nor estimable mercenary general Ernst von Mansfeld) at the disposal of the directorate in Prague.

---

3. Particularly in view of the great difficulties of transportation and communication then obtaining, the volume of letters, reports and dispatches which circulated to the most remote places in Europe and between even the smallest courts or cities and their political agents, is astounding. Unquestionably, the excitability and paranoia of this age of religious conflict increased this volume substantially. Unfortunately, rumour – some of it deliberate, some just the result of imperfect information or blind fear – spread as widely and perhaps even more rapidly and did nothing to calm the atmosphere of an already badly overheated political and religious climate.

What Mansfeld's army and that of the Bohemians themselves (commanded by Count Matthias Thurn), were able to accomplish in the year or so after the rebellion broke out – the conquest of the Catholic stronghold of Pilsen, for example and the successful occupation of Moravia – was not altogether insignificant; but more indicative of the course of future events were the failure of Thurn's attempt to take Vienna in June 1619 and the reversal Mansfeld suffered in Bohemia a bit earlier. In response to Ferdinand's desperate pleas to his Spanish cousins, veterans from the Army of Flanders had begun arriving in Vienna in some numbers as early as the late spring of 1619, as did large money subsidies from the Madrid government; and while this help could not yet turn the tide decisively in Ferdinand's favour, it did stave off what might otherwise have been irretrievable disaster.

More significantly, it was becoming steadily more apparent that the foreign assistance on which the Bohemians had always counted, in view of their own lack of resources, would simply not be forthcoming. The majority Lutherans among the rebels, for example, had hoped that Elector Johann Georg of Saxony, the foremost Protestant prince of the Empire, would volunteer his help and were even prepared to offer him the Bohemian crown once Ferdinand had been declared deposed. But the Saxon refused their entreaties – partly from timidity, partly from a genuine conviction that the rebellion was an illegal act against a legitimate ruler and partly from a profound distaste for Calvinists, kept active by the fulminations of his stiff-necked, pompous and fanatical court preacher Hoë von Hoënegg, who was convinced that the revolt was a Calvinist plot. The Protestant Union, for its part, was badly split between those who were delighted that the cosmic showdown between the Word of God and the Roman antichrist had now arrived and those who devoutly hoped that it had not. Christian of Anhalt, chancellor to the Elector Palatine Friedrich V, of course belonged to the former group. He had, in fact, been preparing for this Armageddon for years through ceaseless negotiation with the enemies of the Habsburgs, whether Catholic (as in the case of Venice and Savoy) or Protestant. His success in arranging an English alliance in 1612, sealed the following year by the marriage of Friedrich V to Elizabeth, the daughter of King James I of England, was the crowning achievement of his spider web of formal and informal alliances and one that he hoped would bear instant fruit in case of just such a crisis as had now arisen in Bohemia.

Alas, it was not to be so. James I, angling for a reconciliation with the Spanish court, proved quite unresponsive to the needs of the Bohemians; and even after his son-in-law Friedrich accepted the Bohemian crown, deeply conflicting feelings about the illegitimacy of the rebellion, on the one hand and his own daughter's new royal dignity, on the other, prevented him from asking even minimal support from his Parliament until it was too late to do any good. Greatly more disposed to give help, from the outset, was the Dutch stadholder Maurice of Nassau, who was also eager to resume the war with Spain that had been in truce since 1609; but deep turmoil over domestic religious and political issues neutralized this source of aid as well. A third country from which help might conceivably have been forthcoming, in view of its long history of enmity to the Habsburgs, was France; but the French monarchy found itself in that strange interlude between the assassination of the forceful Henry IV in 1610 and the rise to power of Cardinal Richelieu in 1624, during which the combination of the inexperience of the young Louis XIII and the revival of a fanatical Catholic fervour in and around the court created conditions under which a coherent foreign policy of any kind could scarcely be formulated, but especially not one favourable to a foreign Protestant interest.

Finally, of course, there was the German Protestant Union. After its early verbal support of the Bohemians' 'defence' of their traditional rights and liberties and the subsequent acceptance of Savoy's small military offering for the rebels, the Union's first major decision respecting the crisis was its agreement in June 1619, to raise an army of 11,000 – a force, however, which was to be employed only for its own defence. From this time on and especially in the face of the studied neutrality of the rest of Protestant Germany, the solidarity of the alliance began to crack; and in November, at its first plenary meeting after Friedrich V had accepted the Bohemian crown at the hands of the rebels, only two of its members expressed support for Friedrich's decision. The Union's position was therefore becoming clear even before a final decision for neutrality was made in mid-1620 as a result of events discussed below.

Since much of the above intelligence was available to Friedrich, his decision to take up the Bohemian crown offered to him in August 1619, seems exceptionally foolhardy – as indeed it was. But Friedrich – young, tentative and susceptible to the advice of others older and more experienced (if not necessarily wiser) than he – listened more attentively to his old retainer Christian of Anhalt than to others who were more dubious about the enterprise, including his father-in-law James I and elected to take what he knew was a great risk for a great prize. Still, one must remember not only that elements of genuine religious conviction and obligation were involved in this fateful choice (along with the handsome prince's childish but disarming desire to please his young and beautiful wife), but also that at the time of his acceptance (late September 1619) Bethlen Gabor had just been chosen 'Protector of Hungary' by the Hungarian diet – an achievement which at the time seemed more impressive than it really was – and that the various agreements by which his nemesis Ferdinand finally acquired the means to save himself were either unknown to Friedrich and his advisors, or had not yet been made. Furthermore, as late as November 1619 troops commanded by Count Thurn and Bethlen Gabor were able to advance against little resistance to lay siege to Vienna a second time; and while this attempt was no more successful than the first, it helped to give the Bohemians a false sense of their own military security. From these perspectives, even the smallest amount of optimistic self-deception could make the chances of success or failure seem more even to the participants than to the historian many centuries after the fact.

Ferdinand's relative inaction for the first year of the rebellion, though partly the result of unreliable and conflicting intelligence concerning the magnitude of the crisis in Bohemia, was due chiefly to a need for caution imposed by the obstreperousness of the estates of Upper and Lower Austria, which extracted concessions from him as the price of their recognition of his rulership, as well as by the usual political and diplomatic delicacies attending candidacy for the now vacant imperial throne. While Ferdinand had begun some negotiations with both Spain and German Catholic princes early in the summer of 1619, the real push for support against the Bohemians did not begin until after his unanimous election as emperor in late August – an election even the Palatine representatives chose not to contest. While these much intensified negotiations were in mid-course, Friedrich V's acceptance of the Bohemian crown became known and it was that fact which determined the nature and terms of the alliances by which Ferdinand acquired the help he so desperately needed.

In the first place, the Spanish ambassador to Vienna, Count Oñate, looking ahead to the expiration of the truce between Spain and the Dutch in 1621, promised significant new military aid from the Army of Flanders under its veteran general Spinola, primarily with the aim of seizing and holding the strategically important Rhenish Palatinate.

Oñate also persuaded Ferdinand to grant to Maximilian of Bavaria generous terms by which the Catholic League would raise an army to serve the Habsburg cause. This bargain of October 1619 was predicated on the imperial ban to be pronounced at a later date on Friedrich V by the emperor and by which the former's territories and electoral title would be declared forfeit for himself and his posterity. The League was to raise an army of 25,000 men, paid for from Maximilian's own bulging treasury; but he was authorized to recoup his expenses (and more) not only by holding in lieu of payment those of Ferdinand's lands he disciplined (Upper Austria), but also by annexing to Bavaria such territories of Friedrich V (the Upper Palatinate) as he might conquer while executing the promised ban against him. As a final inducement, Ferdinand promised to transfer the forfeited electoral title to Maximilian as soon as politically feasible. This already formidable coalition was soon strengthened not only by the permission granted by King Sigismund III of Poland to allow Catholic forces to recruit on his territory, but also by the promise of financial support from Pope Paul V, who temporarily reversed the curia's traditionally hostile attitude towards the Habsburgs in the name of Catholic solidarity.

Unfortunately for the Bohemians, such solidarity was not to be found on the Protestant side. The most shocking evidence of this was the decision of the Lutheran Johann Georg to help Ferdinand subjugate Bohemia. The Saxon elector had watched the amassing of Catholic forces with a concern rooted in his growing conviction that all of neighbouring Bohemia would soon be re-Catholicized, with the double danger of extinguishing Lutheranism there and, worse, of exposing his own territory to the possibility of Catholic recovery of various Saxon bishoprics secularized since 1552. With these reasons to court Ferdinand's favour, in March 1620 Johann Georg promised both the emperor and the Catholic League that he would restore obedience in Silesia and Lusatia and was in turn assured not only that he could hold Lusatia for the duration to defray his costs, but also that consideration would be given to his other concerns. Other Protestants behaved perhaps less reprehensibly towards their Bohemian coreligionists than Johann Georg, but not much more courageously. The Protestant Union, for example, which became more weak-kneed and divided in measure as its information on Catholic actions and intentions increased, finally neutralized itself entirely on the basis of an agreement with Maximilian in July, 1620, by which League and Union promised not to attack each other's territories; furthermore, since Bohemia was not a member of the

Union (which also agreed to respect the ban against Friedrich V), this meant that the Protestant alliance would not interfere with actions against either Bohemia or the Palatinate.

The actions of the various auxiliary parties in the Bohemian crisis to this point serve to call attention to the complexity of motives of all major parties in this evolving struggle. The young Friedrich V, wrestling with divided advice and his own conflicting feelings, did not undertake his Bohemian adventure lightly. Nor did the astute Maximilian accept Ferdinand's bargain, advantageous though it was to him, without a certain dread of the consequences of the military actions now in prospect. As a sincere Catholic, however and one who furthermore believed that the Bohemian rebellion and the acceptance of the Bohemian crown by Friedrich represented a usurpation of legitimate authority and a serious breach of the imperial constitution, it was perhaps easier for him to reconcile his motives than it was for Johann Georg, who to be sure had many of the same constitutional objections to Friedrich's actions, but whose attitude on this point was traceable more to fear for himself than to principle. Otherwise, only the unpraiseworthy motives of avarice and a blind hatred of Calvinism explain the actions of this less than admirable prince. The members of the Protestant Union, on the other hand, who abandoned their leader to his fate in Bohemia, did so without joy or satisfaction and with no positive gain for themselves; and they could at least argue that as a group they had never encouraged or supported Friedrich's gamble, which most saw as endangering the permanent interests of Protestantism. For these participants, then, as for others later, selfishness and selflessness were thrown together in a variable and changing mixture which defies simple explanation. In fact, even the attempt to isolate distinct motives from their inseparable comingling in individuals' minds and hearts can be historically misleading. Thus, for example, to term 'ideological' a ruler's apparently spiritual desire to protect and advance his religion in his own territory by excluding other faiths ignores the fact that this was a part of his *political* interest – a duty to his own people which was as fully expected of him by them in this time as protection of the principle of religious toleration was to be in a later period of European history. Contemporaries, in short, would not even have understood a question which, in asking them to distinguish their motives along the above lines, would distort reality by failing to appreciate the power resulting from their inseparable comingling.

But while in such cases motives could reinforce one another, in others they could be mutually combative. Thus, Friedrich V's desire to nurture and protect Protestantism in Bohemia and his wish to be king there proved to be destructive to both. Just as important, the Bohemians' strong will to preserve their religious freedom ultimately clashed with their equally strong attachment to political autonomy and helped to bring both to an end. In the beginning, to be sure, resistance to the forceful imposition of an unwanted religion went hand in hand with opposition to the Habsburg attempt to construct a more powerful and centralized regime which would severely reduce or eliminate the cherished autonomy of each city, diet, province and faith. But the excessively independent and particularistic attitudes which served to unite the Bohemians against what they did not want also in the end prevented the kind of cooperative effort that might have stayed the disasters which befell them. One example: after their arrival in Prague in October 1619 Friedrich V and his Palatine advisers (whose own frivolous and extravagant living was hardly designed to win the enduring affection of their new Bohemian subjects) discovered to their chagrin that the leaders of the rebellion were in no mood to install a strong monarchy in the place of the one they had just thrown out. Thus, while the Palatine elector's personal popularity began to sag and his Calvinist entourage began to attract increasing criticism from Bohemian Lutherans, he found himself denied the funds, the army and the governing apparatus necessary to protect Bohemia against the growing legion of its enemies.

Since no other kind of regime emerged to fill this gap and to assume the all-important tasks of systematic collection of revenues, organization of defence and so on, the Bohemian cause appears in retrospect never to have had a real chance against its foes, whose military campaigns began in earnest in late July 1620. In that month, a League army of some 30,000 men under the command of Count Tilly invaded and rapidly subjugated Upper Austria, while Count Buquoy led a smaller imperial force – Ferdinand's 'own' army, so to speak – into Lower Austria. Even in this earliest of campaigns, some of the ferocity and bestiality of armies towards civilian populations, which later became a horrible but standard feature of the war, could be seen in the behaviour of Buquoy's troops, which were less well disciplined than those of the League because their pay was less regular and certain than that guaranteed to the League army by Maximilian's fat treasury – one built up with unusually assiduous care for many years. With Upper Austria now under Maximilian's governance (and his tax collectors), the combined Catholic armies moved into Bohemia, while in the north Lusatia was occupied by

Johann Georg's Saxons. The main Bohemian army, under the joint command of Count Thurn and Christian of Anhalt, fell back upon a position at White Mountain, very close to Prague and there, on 8 November 1620, engaged the enemy force in a battle which lasted only an hour. At its conclusion, the Catholics had won a victory which was not only as decisive as any that was fought over the next quarter century, but which also had the enormous political result of instantly terminating the Bohemian rebellion.

It is, in fact, remarkable how rapidly and utterly resistance in most of Bohemia collapsed following the battle at White Mountain. Friedrich V and his wife, with a small band of followers, fled the scene immediately and even after the full extent of the terrible retribution to be exacted by the victors had become clear, there were no stirrings of popular protest. The passivity with which ordinary Bohemians accepted the harsh punishments meted out to their erstwhile leaders and to themselves, shows how faint their identification with the rebellion had always been. The lesser nobility, gentry and urban patricians who were the real force behind the revolt had made no sacrifices to gain the active support of the common folk, who simply had no stake in the sorts of privileges and immunities defended by their aristocratic leaders against the Habsburgs. With no opposition to cause delay, the victorious party rushed to implement its vengeance: twenty-six rebel leaders were publicly executed in Prague in June 1621, while corporal punishments and imprisonments were ordered for many others. Even before this, a sweeping programme of property confiscations had begun, whereby an estimated half of all landed estates in Bohemia changed hands within a few years. While some of these lands were taken up by newcomers – court favourites, military officers of Austrian or foreign origin and so on – most of the confiscated properties fell to already existing Bohemian noble families which had remained loyal to Ferdinand; and most of these estates were not given away, but sold to pay off Habsburg debts. Similarly, while new titles of nobility appeared, these were awarded mostly as 'upgrades' to existing notables; no large class of really 'new' nobles was created.

These massive confiscations and transfers of landed property were inevitably accompanied by a considerable amount of financial speculation, which redounded to the particularly great benefit of a few individuals. One such was Prince Karl von Liechtenstein, the new royal governor of Bohemia, who in 1621 also supervised a deliberate debasement of the coinage by 25 per cent – a figure which had risen to 90 per cent by the end of the following year![4] It was this factor which, by driving already badly depressed land prices into the ground and totally destroying confidence in the currency, nearly wiped out the once-thriving commerce of the country – a development accelerated by the vigorous persecution of Protestant burghers now set in motion. The resulting economic ruin brought not just immiseration but genuine destitution to most Bohemians and the economic shock waves, especially from the currency manipulations, reached well beyond Bohemia itself.

This rapid impoverishment of both town and countryside in no way impeded Ferdinand's new military government from the efficient pursuit of its religious and political goals and may even have facilitated it. Protestant ministers of whatever persuasion suspected of having been active in the rebellion were expelled within less than a year after White Mountain and all the rest not long thereafter. Protestant schools and churches were closed everywhere and previously lost souls were returned to the old faith by various forceful means. By the late 1620s Protestantism as a public confession had disappeared almost everywhere except in Silesia, where a significant minority managed to hang on and in Lusatia, which as matters turned out was to remain permanently under Saxon rule. Not coincidentally, a document of 1627 which amounted to a new constitution for Bohemia not only declared the Catholic church to be the sole church in Bohemia and its clergy the 'first estate' of the kingdom, but also formalized the political programme which had accompanied the religious reconversion. By its terms, the persistently troublesome elective crown of Bohemia was declared henceforth hereditary in the Habsburg family, while its powers in legislation, military command, appointment of officials and other areas of government were greatly augmented; and a new advisory and administrative body to manage Bohemian affairs was established in Vienna. Bohemia would henceforth be governed not by the estates in Prague, but by Austrian laws and the agents of the crown in Vienna.

---

4. Geoffrey Parker, *The Thirty Years' War* (London, 1984), p. 89. It is worth noting that this level of debasement was caused by a consortium of fifteen individuals to whom the imperial treasury, for immediate gain, had leased control of the coinage in all the mints of Bohemia, Moravia and Lower Austria for one year, beginning in January 1622. Some of these individuals also sat on the so-called Court of Confiscations which judged the degree of guilt or innocence of supporters of the rebellion and it was common, even in cases of only partial confiscation of the estates of guilty parties for *all* their lands to be taken, with the 'innocent' portions paid for with this debased money. Ibid.

The battle of White Mountain, because it was the real watershed in the struggle for Bohemia, was also an enormously important event in the entire history of the Habsburg central European inheritance. The triumph there not only returned an immensely significant bloc of territories to obedience, but also put the seal on the still precarious victories achieved earlier over the Protestant estates in the several provinces of Austria itself. It has always been recognized that the real beginnings of the age of absolutism in these Habsburg lands lay in the period surrounding the onset of the Thirty Years War. But the enormously important thing at stake in this case was not the elevation of the position of the monarch relative to other traditional sources of public authority: it was the survival of the dynasty itself. The merest glance at the political map of Germany in this period shows clearly what could, and in fact very nearly did, happen to the various provinces which comprised the Habsburg patrimony: a breakout to a political autonomy not much if at all less complete than that which characterized the *Landeshoheit* enjoyed by the other territories of the Empire. Thus, while the long shadow of White Mountain darkened the sad path of the many thousands of Protestant emigrants, nobles and commoners, who fled Bohemia, Upper and Lower Austria, Styria and Carinthia in and after 1620, Ferdinand II and his Catholic allies had emerged in the sunlight on the other side of disaster.

CHAPTER FOUR
Habsburg Triumphs, Protestant Defeats

While there are many ways to explain why the war apparently so convincingly ended at the battle of White Mountain did not end and instead grew wider and more intrusive into the politics of Germany and of Europe, one may begin with the simple fact that the parties to the Bohemian war themselves would not let it end. After a period of enforced travel, the young Friedrich V – now already in some quarters styled 'the Winter King' because of the brevity of his majesty in Bohemia – was received into a comfortable exile in The Hague by his Dutch friends in April 1621. Encouraged by them and others, he disregarded the advice he had received earlier in that year from his father-in-law, James I, to renounce the Bohemian crown as a possible means of restoration to the Palatine lands and titles declared forfeit in the imperial ban pronounced on him by Ferdinand II in January. Emboldened by the knowledge that some of his military forces had escaped the disaster in Bohemia, as well as by the belated acquisition of some new allies and the expectation of still more, Friedrich clung stubbornly to his royal pretensions.

Since Friedrich's decision played directly into the hands of his adversaries, it has usually been condemned as a foolish one. But apart from the fact that the sheer enormity of his defeat left him with little to lose by insisting on his vanished dignities, it is also likely that abandonment of the Bohemian crown would have made no difference to the future conduct of his enemies, all of whom had the strongest reasons to expropriate his Palatine inheritance regardless. Maximilian of Bavaria, to begin with, would under no circumstances renounce the Upper Palatinate and the electoral title promised him as the price of his assistance by the emperor. Ferdinand, for his part, was by now so deeply in debt to Maximilian – whose troops still occupied Upper Austria as surety for the repayment of that debt – that he had little choice but to keep his end of the bargain. And aside from these business considerations, of course, Ferdinand was determined on moral, religious and constitutional grounds that Friedrich should suffer mightily for his transgressions. Philip III of Spain agreed with his Austrian cousin for all these reasons and also because he wanted his troops to remain in the strategically important Rhenish Palatinate, which they had seized in September 1620 – a circumstance which became even more urgently important under his successor, Philip IV, who resumed Spain's war with the Dutch immediately after the expiration of the twelve-year truce, in March 1621.

With such compelling reasons to continue the war on the part of such potent foes, Friedrich's cause, in retrospect, appears to have been lost from the beginning. To contemporaries, however, that outcome became perceptible only gradually; indeed, there were some initial reasons to suppose that a successful resistance to the Catholic forces could be mounted. No one, perhaps, put much stock in the military efficacy of such small Protestant units as had escaped Bohemia to the east to join up with the ever-unreliable Bethlen Gabor, whose annoying presence to the Habsburgs in Hungary was in any case temporarily neutralized at the peace table in January 1622. But more considerable forces under Ernst von Mansfeld, who in the meantime had formally signed himself into Friedrich V's service, had also successfully withdrawn into the Upper Palatinate; and although they were pursued and dislodged from there in the fall of 1621 by Maximilian and his general Tilly, who then occupied the territory, Mansfeld was able to blunder his way into the Rhenish Palatinate and to cross the Rhine into Alsace. By early 1622, living off the enforced courtesy of the plundered Alsatians, he was able to build up an army of some 43,000 men. The Dutch contributed significant monies for this army and James I of England, in spite of serious and continuing reservations about the whole affair, dispatched both money and a couple of English regiments for service in the Palatinate.

There were, to be sure, some less favourable developments in the course of 1621. For example: in spite of their deep unhappiness over constitutionally dubious aspects of the ban pronounced on Friedrich by the emperor – and especially the extension of the ban to Friedrich's posterity, which caused much genuine outrage in the Empire – the members of the Protestant Union had come to look at their association as not merely useless (which had long since been proved beyond doubt), but also as downright dangerous to themselves and therefore dissolved it in May 1621. But whatever psychological setback this event may have caused – and it was not much – appeared more than compensated by the new activism of two German princes who declared support for Frederick and who began to assemble military forces to assist him: Margrave Georg Friedrich of Baden-Durlach and Christian, the Protestant administrator of the bishopric of Halberstadt and younger brother of the duke of Brunswick. Georg Friedrich, a devout Calvinist who was worried about the future of his own territory because of its proximity to the Palatinate, put together an army of some 11,000 men in the winter of 1621–2, while Christian – called the 'mad Halberstadter' because of his bawdy language and his adventuresome and warlike character – assembled a force of about equal size which he financed by pillaging and looting the neighbouring bishoprics of Münster and Paderborn.

By early spring 1622, there were therefore three separate Protestant armies prepared to offer resistance to Tilly and to Spanish forces in or near the Rhenish Palatinate. But inability to combine these forces led to the defeat and dissolution of Georg Friedrich's army, while the other two, finally achieving juncture at Mannheim, were inadequate to defend the Palatinate against the now cooperating armies of the League and Spain and their commanders ordered a strategic retreat into Alsace – accompanied, as usual, by plundering. This was really the decisive moment of the war for the Palatinate; for while it was not until March 1623 that Frankenthal, the last stronghold defended by a Protestant garrison, was surrendered to the Spaniards – Heidelberg and Mannheim having fallen to Tilly the previous autumn – the conditions for a Catholic victory were put fully in place through the final abandonment of the Palatinate by Mansfeld and Christian of Halberstadt in early summer 1622. The forlorn Friedrich V, who had already been warned by James I early in the year that a much longer continuation of the fighting would entrain a forfeiture of English support, dismissed both Mansfeld and Christian in mid-July 1622 and declared himself at last prepared to negotiate to recover his electoral inheritance. But the moment for that – if such had ever existed since the débâcle of White Mountain – was long past; Friedrich had nothing left to negotiate with but his dreams, which were increasingly his alone and which held no interest whatsoever for his Catholic foes against the reality of their conquests. While the 'Winter King's' erstwhile military lieutenants Mansfeld and Halberstadt sold themselves and their badly needed troops into Dutch service and moved north, Tilly permitted his men to entertain themselves at the expense of the physical and material well-being of the citizens of Heidelberg, who also soon found their spiritual solace removed through the dissolution and proscription of their Calvinist church. For a long time, the only smiles to be seen in Heidelberg were on the happy faces of the scores of Jesuits who now flooded into the area to begin their work of reconversion.

A superficial review of events in the two years between the end of the Bohemian war and the final conquest of the Palatinate in late 1622 might fairly lead to the conclusion that the Habsburg emperor, together with his Catholic allies Spain and the League, had achieved a position of such invincibility that a reconquest of all of Germany for the Roman church was now not only possible but almost inevitable. But this was not so and Ferdinand II himself knew it was not. In the first place, while the Habsburgs had indeed dramatically reversed the alarming dissipation of their monarchical authority in the Bohemian crown lands, as well as in Austria itself and while in Friedrich V an annoying and momentarily dangerous Protestant prince had been neutralized, there was still a powerful and resourceful Protestant Germany to reckon with. Its so-far debilitating disunity and its failure to call upon or receive much foreign assistance could not be counted on to last forever. Secondly, the impending and then actual renewal of hostilities between Spain and the Dutch, though a major reason for Spanish assistance in the campaigns so far, could – always depending on the course of that conflict – become such a major absorbent of Spanish energies as to deny to the House of Austria in the future the sort of aid which had been so indispensable to this point. Finally, Ferdinand II could not deceive himself that the programmatic cooperation that had so far existed between the imperial court and the members of the Catholic League would extend to any and all plans he might make – especially if those plans included any diminution of the cherished *Landeshoheit* of the territorial lords, Catholic or otherwise, in the name of a stronger and more effective German monarchy.

The first and last of these points became unmistakably clear to Ferdinand in the course of 1622 and in a rather unusual manner. In March of that year had appeared a book entitled *Cancelleria Hispanica*, edited and with extensive commentary by Ludwig Camerarius, one of Friedrich V's most experienced and astute advisors. This volume, which has recently been termed 'one of the publishing coups of the century'[1], consisted partly of correspondence between Ferdinand and

---

1. Parker, *The Thirty Years' War*, p. 67.

Maximilian concerning their bargain relative to Friedrich V's electoral title. The publication of their correspondence (obtained through the capture of a courier by some of Mansfeld's troops) created an instant sensation and howls of outrage in an Empire previously ignorant of the deal and much of the rest of Europe was also taken aback by this news of trafficking in an important imperial dignity. Ferdinand not only delayed conferral of the title because of this stir, but also felt obliged to enlist the assistance of the papacy in a major propaganda effort, lasting for the remainder of 1622, designed to demonstrate to his coreligionists all over Europe the moral and legal correctness – not to mention the political advantage – of the transfer. Furthermore, when Maximilian's own impatience for his reward had waxed to the point where it was impolitic to delay any longer, Ferdinand did not commit the blunder of convoking a plenary diet for the announcement – a meeting with unforeseeable and potentially dangerous results and one which could easily have turned into a full-scale riot of the estates of the Empire – but instead called together a *Deputationstag*, a much smaller assembly of the more important princes. In the event, this meeting of January 1623, turned out to be even smaller than anticipated; it was in effect boycotted by many Protestants (even the always deferential Johann Georg sent only deputies) and the Catholic attendees were themselves grumpy and uncertain about the unusual agenda: only Maximilian's brother, the elector of Cologne, gave really unreserved support to the transfer of the electoral title. In the face of this massively qualified support from the Empire and after a month and a half of vigorous debate, Ferdinand felt compelled to modify his original intention by stipulating that the transfer be made to Maximilian for the latter's lifetime only, thus holding open at least the legal possibility that Friedrich V's heirs might someday recover the title. On these terms, on 25 February 1623, the duke of Bavaria was permitted to add a new and higher title to those he already bore.

For all of the reservations and outright opposition apparent in this *Deputationstag*, it did settle, for the moment, the strictly German issues that had arisen from the Bohemian crisis. The future of the Rhenish Palatinate, to be sure, was uncertain, but also moot for the foreseeable future, since it was under Bavarian administration; and the Upper Palatinate and the electoral title were now firmly and legally in Bavarian hands. Thus, had it not been for the renewal of what is sometimes referred to as the 'Eighty Years War' between Spain and the Dutch Netherlands in 1621, the Empire might have remained at peace for a long time. But Spain and the Dutch both had an absolutely vital interest in the territories of northwestern Germany, in particular, stemming from Spain's need not only to protect her overland communications with the southern Netherlands – that network of highways and byways referred to as the 'Spanish road' – but also, further north, to attempt to block from the east channels whereby the Dutch might provide or receive assistance to or from elsewhere. The Dutch were as aware of the importance of keeping their doors to the east open as the Spaniards were of closing them – as the actions of both in the Jülich-Cleves dispute had shown. It was this concern, specifically, which caused Maurice of Nassau to hire the armies of Ernst von Mansfeld and Christian of Halberstadt into Dutch service after their evacuation of the Palatinate and, after receiving some timely assistance from them against a serious threat from Spinola's forces, to encourage the two German adventurers to recruit more troops in neighbouring German states. Christian, with some appearance of legitimacy stemming from his administratorship of Halberstadt and his familial ties with the ruler of Brunswick, roamed widely throughout the Lower Saxon Circle, recruiting as he went, while Mansfeld, with no legitimacy at all, blundered around East Frisia, adding troops and provisions by his usual ungentle methods.

Of the two, Christian's actions were regarded with particular alarm by Ferdinand II and Maximilian, who suspected that the Halberstadter might be mad enough to attempt a junction of his growing army with that of the forever hopeful Bethlen Gabor, who was once again on the warpath in the east. To obviate this possibility, but also simply as a timely defensive measure, Tilly and the League army were sent northward into Hesse and thence into the southern Lower Saxon Circle. Halberstadt now took the occasion to style himself 'protector' of the Circle, overawing the witless and fearful estates within it which had proclaimed a policy of weakly armed neutrality; but feeling that his forces were not up to a direct challenge to Tilly, Christian instead proposed joining his army with that of Maurice of Nassau to inflict a crushing defeat on Spinola in the Netherlands. The scheme might have worked, had Christian not dawdled so long in Westphalia on his way west, hoping that Mansfeld's army might link up with him. But a determined Tilly caught up with him at Stadtlohn, near the Dutch border and in early August 1623, destroyed all but 6000 of a 21,000-man army. This most decisive of victories left the door open for Tilly to advance into the Netherlands, with possibly fatal results for the Dutch; but his master Maximilian, afraid of an unpredictable storm of foreign reaction (and with an already good and still growing sense of which battles were his and which were not), chose to leave the League army in Germany.

Although Tilly's army was now the only powerful military force in northwestern Germany – a fact which stimulated a good deal of discussion in Catholic quarters about the possibility of reconverting several important bishoprics of the area which had come under Protestant administration since 1555 – the battle at Stadtlohn was the last military action in Germany for some time.[2] Abroad, however, worried reaction to the recent successes of the Habsburg alliance was growing. For a time, England was the most important centre of diplomatic discussions aimed against the Habsburgs – as indeed it had been since Friedrich V's Bohemian fling. James I had always liked to think of himself as the foremost defender of the Protestant faith in Europe – a position called into question by a foreign policy whose only notable consistency for a long time was the king's dogged pursuit of friendship with Spain, the leader of anti-Protestant forces in Europe. This policy had caused James much trouble with his anti-Spanish Parliament, which received his requests to help his daughter and son-in-law in Germany at the same time he was arranging a Spanish marriage for his son Charles with understandable puzzlement. When the Spanish marriage scheme fell apart for good, in the spring of 1624 and under circumstances which were humiliating for both James and Charles, the king and his Parliament agreed on an anti-Spanish policy which became the cornerstone of a gradually forming northern European coalition against the Habsburgs. At the same moment, in France, Cardinal Richelieu was accelerating the reversal of a pro-Spanish interlude in French policy which had already begun to change before his appointment to and subsequent domination of the royal council in 1624. In rapid-fire order a marriage was arranged between Prince Charles and the sister of Louis XIII of France and an alliance was signed between France and the Dutch in June 1624, to which England acceded in the same month. Sweden and Denmark – for somewhat different reasons which will be discussed below – also became involved in serious discussions of a military alliance centred around England.

It is essential to understand that while the general nature of these negotiations, in which even Venice and Savoy took part, was known

---

2. The sheer threat posed by Tilly's presence reconverted one previously Protestant bishopric – Osnabrück – where the chapter elected a Catholic who, for even greater insurance, was a brother of one of Maximilian's chief advisers.

to the Habsburgs through their extensive intelligence network, many of the details were not. But what the courts in Madrid and Vienna did understand very well was that their interlinked dynastic empire had enemies everywhere who were plotting ceaselessly against it; yet since they could not know how ramshackle, tentative and subject to sudden and radical shifts of policy the structure of their enemies' engagements really was, it is not hard to imagine that the simultaneous French occupation of the Valtelline and the Savoyard blockade of Genoa – the southern terminus of the 'Spanish road' – from the north in late 1624 might have seemed to them merely the first strategic moves of a mighty coalition, promising much worse to come. This is clearly what Maximilian and his allies in the Catholic League feared and, knowing that their own army, large and well trained though it was, also had its limitations, urged Ferdinand II to engage substantial new forces.

At the time this advice was given, it was not clear against whom such auxiliary forces would have to be employed, or when, since danger seemed to be everywhere and imminent; but it came as no great surprise when the enemy appeared in northern Germany in the summer of 1625 and in the person of King Christian IV of Denmark. Originally only one of several possible partners in the anti-Habsburg coalition England was trying to assemble, Christian's importance grew as that of other potential allies diminished. France, normally more concerned about events in Italy than in Germany, all but lost interest in northern European schemes after its successful occupation of the Valtelline and distanced itself still further from the coalition after a serious Huguenot revolt broke out in January 1625. Sweden's King Gustavus Adolphus also defected. He had made a serious proposal to James for a large-scale invasion of Germany, but one which required very large contributions of men, money and ships from his allies, including especially James himself; when the latter refused the proposal, Gustavus backed away (taking with him the support of his brother-in-law, the elector of Brandenburg, who would not cooperate except as a partner of Sweden) and soon renewed his temporarily suspended war with Poland. Under these circumstances, Christian of Denmark became the man of the hour. First approached by James in the summer of 1624, he had proved very cautious and sensibly suspicious of England's ability to make good on promises of men and money for a German campaign; but because his traditional foe, Sweden, had made a proposal to lead a campaign involving large forces that could prove dangerous to Danish interests in the western Baltic, he felt obliged to come up with his own plan.[3] Less complicated than that of Gustavus and less expensive to England, his scheme called for an army of some 30,000 men, with provision of subsidies and a certain number of troops by England. With Gustavus' plan no longer on the table, James accepted that of Christian in late February 1625.

Few have entirely dismissed as motives for his invasion of Germany Christian's stated intentions to rescue the endangered cause of Protestantism (he was a strong Lutheran) and to defend the imperial constitution against illegalities such as those perpetrated against Friedrich V (Christian, as duke of Holstein, was a prince of the Empire)[4]; but it is also true that he had some very compelling political motives as well. The most immediate of these, as suggested above, was to forestall Swedish intervention in northern Germany by a Danish one, since Gustavus' future intentions continued to worry him. Scarcely less important, however, was the fact that in 1623 his son had been elected bishop of Verden and that Christian saw a real chance to extend his control over several other north German sees, including Paderborn, Osnabrück, Halberstadt and especially Bremen, whose territory contained the estuaries of the Elbe and Weser rivers. And finally, though more enablement than motive, Christian had a personal fortune of more than one and a half million talers – a sum large enough to start (though not, as it turned out, to finish successfully) a major military enterprise even without the support of his own frugal and cautious estates.[5]

Things started off well enough for Christian. He was elected 'captain' of the Lower Saxon Circle by its estates, which had been in a state of permanent panic since Tilly's great victory at Stadtlohn had put their territories at the whim of Catholic intentions. Furthermore, with the help of Mansfeld, Duke Ernst of Saxe-Weimar and Christian of Brunswick[6], he put together a force of some 34,000 men. And in December 1625 a formal treaty of alliance between England (under the rule of Charles I since April), Denmark and the Dutch Netherlands was signed. But Christian, though not a temperamentally incautious person, had failed to heed his own persistent doubts

---

3. Denmark and Sweden had fought a major war as recently as 1611–13.
4. Since Christian had not only allowed some of his officers to serve with Ernst von Mansfeld, but had loaned money to Friedrich V and his allies in 1620, his credentials in both intentions were better than those of the generality of German Protestant princes who had sat on their hands during the Bohemian crisis.
5. Parker, *The Thirty Years' War*, p. 72.
6. This is the 'mad Halberstadter', who in the meantime had given up his bishopric and taken over the government of the duchy of Brunswick ceded to him by his brother.

about the reliability of English promises and it appears that he had counted rather firmly on support from other quarters that simply never materialized. These included France, Brandenburg, perhaps Saxony and certainly the princes and territories of the Lower Saxon Circle (some of whom, in fact, were continuing to negotiate with Ferdinand II for neutrality even as they voted for their new Danish 'captain'). These errors in judgment, however, glaring as they were, pale considerably against Christian's single greatest mistake: his assumption that the war he was preparing would be fought against only such enemy military forces as were already in being and whose numbers were known. This assumption was a colossal and tragic blunder – colossal because it defeated him, tragic because he had no way of knowing about it before casting his lot irrevocably.

In the spring of 1625, at about the same time Charles I's accession to the English throne was accelerating the Anglo-Danish alliance, a Bohemian nobleman named Albrecht von Wallenstein (born Waldstein) approached Ferdinand II with an offer to raise and finance an army of 50,000 men for the imperial service. Wallenstein – a most fascinating individual even in an age replete with remarkably powerful and colourful personalities – was not unknown to the emperor. Scion of a Bohemian noble family, with a mixed Protestant and Catholic upbringing which seems to have left him with a studied indifference towards all formal religion, Wallenstein had served as a loyal imperial officer during the Bohemian rebellion and had been rewarded with grants of landed estates which he added to others he already owned; with these as security, he borrowed to buy still more properties – some of them confiscated from rebel sympathizers – and then went into the lending business himself. Ferdinand was not the least of his debtors, but showed his appreciation to Wallenstein by the conferral of offices and titles, including governor of the kingdom of Bohemia and prince (later duke) of Friedland, the name given to the some 2000 square miles of mostly contiguous territories the astute soldier-businessman had amassed in northeast Bohemia.[7] Wallenstein was to cast a huge shadow over events in Germany from 1625 until his death in early 1634. He was a firm believer in astrology, yet left as little to chance as possible, always planning for the long term. But there has been much disagreement about his ultimate goals – if indeed he had any consistent ones at all – and his

---

7. E. A. Beller, 'The Thirty Years War', in *The New Cambridge Modern History*, vol. IV (Cambridge, 1970), pp. 322–3.

words and actions, as well as the opinions held of him by contemporaries, were often contradictory.

Ferdinand II, in dire need of new military resources, but without the means to pay for them, accepted Wallenstein's offer, while reducing to 20,000 the number of troops to be raised. Since the emperor's current state of financial embarrassment was not expected to end anytime soon, he gave formal authorization for 'contributions' to be levied on the populations of the territories Wallenstein's forces would conquer in his service. While even Ferdinand could hardly have known the indescribable misery and destitution this dispensation was to bring to wide areas of Germany, it was unusual only in that as a formal decree it was quite illegal in imperial law; other armies had operated on a similar basis from the outset and would continue to do so, with fine disregard of all legalities. It is clear that Wallenstein himself had predicated his initial offer on the supposition that his army – backed for short periods, if necessary, by the resources of his own huge estates – would pay for itself, yet less through random looting and plundering by individual companies than by systematic high-level coercion and extortion from princes and other territorial authorities. And while the nature of the personal gains he expected for himself was rather murky at this point, it is equally clear that he had not undertaken this vast enterprise for entirely altruistic reasons. But such matters, like everything else, now seemed to depend on the course of military events.

Initially, those events unfolded rather slowly. In late July 1625 Tilly marched his army into the Lower Saxon Circle from the south, signalling a readiness to cross swords with Christian IV of Denmark; but the only war conducted at this point was against the towns and peasantry of Brunswick, whose hostility to the invading army was met with the ferocious retribution of arson, plunder and murder. Even the arrival of Wallenstein's new army in Lower Saxony in October did not signal immediate occasion for battle, since its commander's first concern was to secure the bishoprics of Halberstadt and Magdeburg for Ferdinand II's young son, intended as the future bishop of both. This accomplished, Wallenstein's troops went into winter quarters there, as did Tilly's in Hildesheim. Not until the spring of 1626 did the hounds of battle break loose. In late April, Mansfeld's small force of 12,000 men attacked Wallenstein's army at the Weser crossing of Dessau and was repulsed with heavy losses; but the old mercenary reorganized his force after a strategic retreat into Brandenburg and in July was on the move through Silesia, with the intention of joining forces with Bethlen Gabor who, unsurprisingly, was once again pondering an attack in the east. Wallenstein, with an army constantly augmented by new recruits, was forced to chase Mansfeld, but left several regiments in Lower Saxony to help Tilly against Christian IV and his allies – reduced by one in June by the untimely death of the 'mad Halberstadter', Christian of Brunswick, at the age of twenty-eight. The Danish king was caught by Tilly at the village of Lutter, south of Brunswick, in late August and was soundly defeated. Supported now only by the dukes of Mecklenburg and by his fast diminishing hope for English support, Christian withdrew northward to the lower Elbe, while his former allies among the Lower Saxon princes sued for peace.

Wallenstein now reappeared on the scene. His dash to Hungary had cost him perhaps half his army of 30,000 men, mostly from disease and desertion; but he had not only achieved the final neutralization of Bethlen Gabor, but also, through the Transylvanian's promise to cease forever cooperation with Mansfeld, wrote the last chapter in that perennial mercenary's career.[8] Returning to the Elbe through Silesia, where he cleaned out the remnants of Mansfeld's forces, Wallenstein joined with Tilly in September 1627 and in the same month their combined armies overwhelmed a vastly inferior body commanded by Georg Friedrich of Baden-Durlach. This battle was the last of any importance in the Danish campaign. The chastened Christian IV fled to Holstein and thence to the relative security of the Danish islands, while his enemies occupied the whole of the Danish peninsula.

Albrecht von Wallenstein was now well on his way to becoming the military arbiter of northern Germany. Until quite recently, he had not really been as significant a sustainer of the imperial cause as had Tilly and at one point had even offered to resign his command; but Ferdinand, with new and more ambitious plans in mind, still needed him and not only kept him but raised the level of 'contributions' he was authorized to extort. With Tilly out of action for a time because of wounds suffered in the last stages of the Danish campaign, furthermore, Wallenstein now had sole command of forces numbering around 125,000 men. With Ferdinand's blessing, he expanded his military operations eastward along the Baltic coast, occupying all of Mecklenburg and eventually pushing deep into Pomerania. While Ferdinand's as yet incompletely formulated goal of a re-Catholicization of much or all of northern Germany was partly

---

8. Mansfeld died in November 1626 and Gabor, having signed his final peace with the emperor in December of that year, himself died in 1629.

responsible for this, so was a grand plan – originally suggested by Spain – to 'imperialize' the Baltic coast and put afloat a Habsburg navy, with the objective of gaining a share of the lucrative Baltic trade while denying as much as possible of it to the Dutch. Wallenstein, now appointed 'General of the Oceanic and Baltic Sea', did his best either to overawe or to coax the Hanseatic cities of the northern coast into cooperation with the plan; but when most of them refused, he found it necessary to attempt to occupy the entire Pomeranian coastline. He was generally successful, but was stopped short at the important port city of Stralsund, where a determined citizenry, with some help from the otherwise hapless Christian IV and even more from a worried Sweden, outlasted a siege by Wallenstein's forces from April to August 1628. Christian IV, encouraged by Stralsund's successful resistance, made one last fling at retrieving his fortunes by landing a small army in Pomerania; but when this feeble force was overwhelmed by Wallenstein in early September, Christian gave up his futile struggle and sued for peace.

The fairly generous terms he received in May 1629 were conditioned by Ferdinand II's concern over Sweden's recent activism, which made it politic not to throw Christian into the arms of Gustavus Adolphus by embarrassing or embittering the Danish king too much. In return for full restoration of his hereditary lands, Christian agreed to resign his captaincy of the Lower Saxon Circle and to renounce his claims to the north German bishoprics, therewith bringing the Danish phase of intervention to an end. It now remained to be seen how the victorious imperial forces would use their triumph; in their decision lay a future of war or one of peace for Germany.

CHAPTER FIVE

From One Insecure Peace to Another: 1629–1635

By early 1629 the interests of the House of Austria seemed more secure than at any time in recent years. Within the Habsburgs' own territories, serious threats of various kinds had now long since been dissipated: Bohemia was quiet, if sullenly so, under its imposed constitution of 1627–8; closer to home, Upper and Lower Austria had been fully pacified, especially after the fairly easy suppression of a violent peasant uprising in 1626; and in Hungary the unpredictable Bethlen Gabor had been brought to heel once and for all. In Germany, of course, the end of the Danish campaigns had brought imperial domination of virtually all of northern Germany and with it a militarily unchallenged hegemony over the rest of the country as well. Further abroad, Spain's failure to subdue the Dutch was increasingly troubling and some potentially dangerous issues had arisen from the Mantuan succession crisis soon to be discussed; but the overall outlook for Vienna was a solidly positive one.

In the fertile soil of this optimistic climate the seedlings of old plans now grew rapidly to maturity. Neither Ferdinand nor the leaders of the Catholic League had ever forgotten their responsibilities to their faith and all had planned that victory in northern Germany would be followed by a major revision in the religious balance that had evolved over the previous three-quarters of a century. In the event, it was the emperor himself, encouraged by the unbending determination of his Jesuit confessor Wilhelm Lamormainie, who set the specific shape of that revision. In early March 1629 Ferdinand issued the famous Edict of Restitution, a document designed essentially to turn the clock back to the Peace of Augsburg, disregarding all informal agreements or understandings (such as the Declaration of Ferdinand) which were not strictly part of that treaty.

By the provisions of the new edict, all ecclesiastical properties of any kind seized by Protestants after 1552 and all imperial bishoprics and conventual foundations taken by them after 1555, were to be returned to the Catholic church. Rulers of ecclesiastical principalities were henceforth under no obligation to tolerate Protestants in their territories; and, as at Augsburg, Calvinism was not recognized as an 'official' religious alternative. Imperial commissioners with the right to invoke military assistance were established to determine transfers of properties and territories.

The Edict of Restitution was a staggering blow to German Protestantism, before which all earlier setbacks paled in comparison. The loss of two archbishoprics, several bishoprics and almost a hundred convents and other properties instantly beggared a number of Protestant princes and faced tens of thousands of their Protestant subjects with the terrible choice of expulsion or conversion. The provisions of the edict were not and in fact could not be applied and enforced everywhere and at once; and some issues, such as the future of the religiously mixed Imperial Cities, were not addressed at all in the document. But while some princes such as Johann Georg of Saxony were not importuned immediately, others were; and when a city such as Augsburg, with a 90 per cent Protestant population, was placed under a Catholic bishop and city council, with attendant prohibition of Protestantism, no Protestant could reasonably assume anything but the worst for the future.

That future might have been grim indeed had the degree of cooperation that had characterized Catholic efforts to this point continued. But it did not. Hard feelings soon became apparent over the division of the spoils within the Catholic camp and especially over the repartition of the reconverted north German bishoprics between members of Ferdinand's family and those of Maximilian of Bavaria and other League members. Even after that was settled, serious misgivings remained on the part of Maximilian and his allies about Ferdinand's military chieftain, Albrecht von Wallenstein. Almost all princes in the Empire had been outraged when an indebted Ferdinand had elevated the parvenu Bohemian warlord to be duke of Mecklenburg, in place of its deposed rulers, in March, 1628; and many of them also had complaints about the vast 'contributions' Wallenstein's huge army continued to consume even in peacetime. Catholics were also angry about the generalissimo's indifference to their faith as evinced in his widely known belief that the Edict of Restitution was extreme, unnecessary and pregnant with dangers for the future – though of course he also enforced it on cue.

More serious than any of these verbalized complaints, however, was the simple fact that Wallenstein's forces were now significantly stronger than those of the League. Its members were deeply worried about the security of their own positions in a Germany so clearly dominated by a military force devoted only to the purposes of Ferdinand II, since his intentions with respect to increasing his imperial power over all the princes of Germany were always suspect on principle.

In the summer of 1630, a cheerful Ferdinand called together a meeting of the electors at Regensburg; Saxony and Brandenburg did not attend, but those who did were in a decidedly objectionable mood. They listened impatiently to the emperor's request for the election of his son as German King (with the right to succeed automatically to the imperial throne), for assistance to Spain in its increasingly less successful war against the Dutch and for support of the Habsburg candidate for the disputed throne of the duchy of Mantua. Eventually denying their approval to all these requests, the electors also pre-empted Ferdinand's agenda by demanding the immediate dismissal of Wallenstein and a drastic reduction in the size of the imperial army. After some resistance, Ferdinand acquiesced and on 13 August 1630, Wallenstein was sent home to Bohemia. The army, reduced by three-quarters, was combined with that of the League and placed under Count Tilly's command. These measures seemed for the moment to restore at least part of the cooperative relationship between the emperor and his Catholic allies and thus to stabilize the new religious and political order in Germany they had achieved together.

But while no one appreciated it at the time, a problem of wholly foreign origin, which seemed to be nothing but an irrelevant sideshow to the German princes, had already become enormously important to the future of the Empire. In December 1627 the Gonzaga duke of Mantua and Montferrat – territories which flanked Spanish-ruled Milan to the east and west, respectively – died without direct heirs. The most likely successor was a French prince, who was supported by France and Venice; but Spain's extreme sensitivity about these approaches to Milan led her, in alliance with Savoy, to support a different claimant. What resulted was a limited and undeclared war in northwestern Italy between France and Spain (with Savoy). Allowing loyalty to his Spanish cousins to override his political good sense, Ferdinand, at Spain's request, sent a corps of Wallenstein's troops to assist in securing these territories. More important, in the end, than the final resolution of the succession (which was decided in the French candidate's favour in 1631), was the simple but vastly significant realization which now anchored itself in the mind of Cardinal Richelieu of France that the long struggle against Spain was in fact a struggle against *both* Habsburg houses and now had to involve a consistent and determinedly active policy against Austria throughout Germany. The fruits of this realization soon revealed themselves not only in a new alliance with the Dutch and the establishment of a much-expanded network of diplomatic relations with various German princes (including those who attended the Regensburg meeting in 1630), but also, most importantly, in serious negotiations with King Gustavus Adolphus concerning Swedish intervention in Germany.

For reasons of both politics and religion, Gustavus had long been concerned about the rapidly changing German scene. As early as 1620 his able and perceptive chancellor Axel Oxenstierna, with an eye on events in Bohemia and Poland, had felt that a Swedish presence in Germany might someday be necessary and nothing that had happened since had changed either his mind or that of his king. Since Sweden had long aimed at a domination of the entire Baltic Sea and its lucrative trade and at various points had been led into wars with Denmark and Poland in defence of this aim, events affecting its relationship with these states, or which touched the German Baltic coastline that lay between them, were of immediate and urgent concern. Nor should the sincerity of Gustavus's Lutheran faith or his concerns about the declining fortunes of his Protestant co-religionists throughout the 1620s be forgotten – though here, as elsewhere, the connection between politics and religion was inseparable, since for Sweden the political fragmentation of Protestant northern Germany was preferable to the domination brought to the area by a hegemonic imperial Catholicism. The defeat of Christian IV of Denmark was therefore a mixed blessing for Gustavus: it had momentarily eliminated an old Baltic rival (if also a Protestant one), but had done so by an imperial victory of such proportions as to permit Wallenstein to dispatch 12,000 troops to assist Ferdinand's Catholic brother-in-law Sigismund III of Poland, who had been at war with Sweden (again) since 1625.

While the general interests of Sweden made developments in northern Germany a permanent concern of its leadership, there is no doubt that imperial assistance to Poland in 1628–9 was especially worrisome to Gustavus, who suffered some serious reverses there in the summer of 1629. Now convinced that direct intervention in Germany was urgently necessary, the Swedish king was fortunate that Cardinal Richelieu had reached the same conclusion. In September 1629 the latter's envoy Charnacé, having exhausted other alternatives for harassing the Habsburgs in Germany[1], mediated a six-year truce between Sweden and Poland designed specifically to free Gustavus to invade Germany. With strong support from his own people, a small but loyal and extremely well disciplined army consisting mostly of devout Lutheran peasants and sources of income sufficient to fund at least the beginnings of a large-scale military enterprise, the king landed on the shores of Pomerania, at Peenemünde, in July of 1630.

That there were elements of a real gamble in this invasion is clear. While it is true that the armies then available to his putative German foes – Ferdinand II and Maximilian's Catholic League – were soon to be weaker, more dispersed and less battle-ready than at the height of the Danish campaigns, they were still numerically superior to Gustavus's original force; and, much more serious, Sweden began its German adventure with but a single ally: the city of Stralsund, saved from Wallenstein in 1628 largely by Swedish help. Gustavus had made strenuous efforts to engage German support before his invasion, especially from Saxony and Brandenburg; but Johann Georg had flatly refused (and had even threatened to join the emperor), while Gustavus's own brother-in-law Georg Wilhelm of Brandenburg would only talk of neutrality and a possible role as mediator. Even by the end of 1630, the king had acquired only a handful of allies, most of them of dubious value: the deposed dukes of Mecklenburg and of Saxe-Weimar, the margrave of Hesse-Kassel and the secularized bishopric of Magdeburg. But his coastal base was secure and by early 1631, after expelling the last imperial troops from Pomerania, he had moved into Brandenburg, where he established his headquarters at Bärwalde. It was here, in late January 1631, that Richelieu's emissaries finally signed the subsidy treaty Gustavus had counted on as a chief enablement of further campaigning.

The Treaty of Bärwalde was late in coming because of various problems on the French side; but its timing was very opportune for Gustavus, whose growing worries about the costs of maintaining a large and still increasing host of troops at various points around the Baltic were well founded. By the terms of the treaty, France would pay an annual subsidy of one million *livres* for five years in support

---

1. These included attempts to turn Maximilian of Bavaria against Ferdinand (by now almost a fixation of Richelieu) and to convince Christian IV not to give up his already disastrous war.

of a Swedish army of 36,000 men and a war to liberate the North
and Baltic Seas and to restore the 'oppressed' estates of the Empire –
somewhat open-ended goals whose vagueness was desired by both
parties. For both political and religious reasons the French insisted
that Gustavus throughout his campaigning respect rights of Catholic
worship wherever it already existed and that he regard the territories
of the Catholic League as neutral unless they themselves acted
otherwise. This last stipulation was clearly very important to
Richelieu, above all because he still hoped to drive a wedge between
Maximilian's League and the emperor. He had begun attempts to
woo Maximilian into some sort of alliance with France as early as the
mid-1620s and had generally found him interested but noncommit-
tal. But as the Bavarian's suspicions about Wallenstein and the
overall drift of the emperor's policies grew and after the Swedish
invasion and the conclusion of the Treaty of Bärwalde, he became
more receptive to French overtures, making possible conclusion of
the Treaty of Fontainebleau of May 1631. France and Bavaria
promised not to attack each other or to help each other's enemies and
France agreed to recognize Maximilian's electoral title as hereditary.
While this treaty was soon to prove almost meaningless to both
parties, it is of interest because it shows the importance Maximilian
attached to the creation of a Catholic third force between the
emperor and his foreign foes, which might not only prevent new
wars but also safeguard the constitutional liberties of the German
princes and their recent gains.

Not coincidentally, the Protestant princes had issued a document –
the Leipzig Manifesto – embodying very much the same purpose
only a month before the Franco-Bavarian treaty was signed. Saxony
and Brandenburg had been discussing various possibilities for a
Protestant defensive alliance since April 1630; and though Johann
Georg had initially (and typically) proved reluctant to enter into joint
arrangements of any kind, the summer of 1630 changed his mind.
Both the Swedish invasion and the refusal of the electors at
Regensburg to modify the harsh terms of the Edict of Restitution
aroused new fears and old resentments which persuaded him to
convoke a heavily attended meeting of Protestant princes in Leipzig
from February to April of 1631. After much fulmination against the
Edict of Restitution and expressions of anxiety about the Swedish
presence, the princes agreed to set up an armed force of 40,000 men,
dispersed in their various territories, which could only be called into
action by the Saxon elector, who emerged as the leader of the group.
Here again, then, the concept of a third force appeared – this time a

Protestant one, designed to achieve modification or abolition of the Edict of Restitution, but thereafter (as Johann Georg envisioned it) to cooperate with the emperor to expel foreigners from the Empire.

For the king of Sweden, the Leipzig Manifesto was a sharp disappointment, strongly hinting that the enlistment of support from German Protestants would have to be accomplished by action, not by verbal appeals. The city of Magdeburg, an early ally and an important Protestant stronghold at a strategic location on the Elbe, suggested itself as an early objective, especially since it was currently under siege by imperial forces whose assaults it had successfully repulsed for years, thus becoming a widely praised symbol of Protestant resistance. Unfortunately, Gustavus and his relief force arrived too late. Magdeburg was successfully stormed on 20 May 1631 and was handed over to an enraged soldiery for a sacking which was sadly distinguished from the norm by the virtual annihilation of both structures and inhabitants by fire and massacre. The shock waves of this tragedy through all of Protestant Europe, especially, were unusually strong and lent a nasty ideological coloration to some subsequent campaigns. One more or less immediate effect of Magdeburg's horrible fate, however, was to strengthen the Swedish party by the addition of its first major German Protestant ally, Georg Wilhelm of Brandenburg, who in June decided to join Gustavus.

After Magdeburg, the imperial army under Tilly's command moved northeast to confront the Swedes, who in the meantime had greatly strengthened their control of the northern coastline by the conquest of Mecklenburg and its restoration to its original dukes. Thus blocked to the north and with his army in need of food, Tilly proposed to march into the rich and as yet undespoiled territories of Johann Georg of Saxony and asked the latter's permission to do so. In what was perhaps the only genuinely courageous decision of his life, Johann Georg refused. When Tilly crossed the Saxon border anyway, in early September, the elector immediately joined his inexperienced 18,000-man force with the 24,000 troops of the Swedes and formally cast his lot with Gustavus by treaty on 12 September. Only five days later, at Breitenfeld north of Leipzig, the opposing armies met in a fierce battle which lasted just over two hours. With a considerable superiority in numbers, an even greater advantage in artillery and in the tactical brilliance of Gustavus himself (and in spite of the appalling performance of the untried Saxon contingents), the Swedes administered a crushing defeat to Tilly resulting in the loss of well over half his army, all of his cannon and the mobile 'war chest' of the League.

The sheer magnitude of this first great Protestant victory of the war seems to have caught those who had achieved it somewhat by surprise and without any real plans for the future. But with no organized enemy force anywhere in view, it was decided that Johann Georg would lead a Saxon-Swedish force south and east into Silesia and hold there, while Gustavus and his army would saunter to the southwest through the well-stocked Catholic bishoprics along the Main and Rhine, ending up in winter quarters at Mainz – which then became the centre of Swedish administration of the conquered territories. Even now, however, while ordinary Protestants all over Germany and Europe were gushing with gratitude and admiration for their Swedish saviour, the politically minded German princes were not rushing to his banner. Eschewing religious enthusiasm and possible gain in favour of a cautious neutralism which might at least guarantee no loss and mindful of the fact that with only a few exceptions the Swedish king had written treaties with his German 'allies' in terms reminiscent of the relationship of a feudal overlord to his vassals, Gustavus's partners generally had to be threatened into cooperation. But with their help, however grudging and fearful and that of his own Swedish administrators – Oxenstierna at the top – Gustavus instituted a systematic exploitation of the areas under his control. This system was doubtlessly unpleasant, but for the most part not a vicious one and it was made more bearable by the remarkable tolerance the king showed towards Catholics – a policy stemming less from promises made at Bärwalde than from the personal convictions of this quite extraordinary man.

By the spring of 1632 some troubling clouds appeared on Gustavus's otherwise bright horizon. For one thing, the shock of Breitenfeld and of the staggering territorial losses which followed it had begun to produce some determined Catholic countermeasures. Tilly had removed the shattered remnants of his army to the relative safety of Bavaria in November 1631 and thereafter recruited reinforcements steadily, while a small undefeated force under Count Pappenheim in the northwest continued to harass a surprisingly large number of Swedish troops. Furthermore, Gustavus's ally Johann Georg had complicated the strategic map by pushing on into Bohemia, accompanied by a small host of Bohemian exiles, instead of holding in Silesia. But most worrisome of all, perhaps, was the fact that Ferdinand II, urged on by Maximilian, had initiated the recruitment of an altogether new army, by none other than – Albrecht von Wallenstein. After his dismissal from imperial service in August 1630 Wallenstein had returned in sullen resentment to his

Bohemian estates, where he nurtured his grievances against the emperor, Maximilian, Tilly and others who had caused his fall from grace. Obviously enjoying the discomfiture of the imperial court after Breitenfeld, Wallenstein toyed with Ferdinand before finally agreeing to resume his military entrepreneurship in December 1631. Consenting to a long-term arrangement only in April 1632, after he was given complete and undivided military authority *and* the right to negotiate with the enemy, Wallenstein had no difficulty in finding recruits, who remembered well the regular pay and the booty of the good old days of rapine and plunder.

Gustavus was aware of these developments and recognized their seriousness as part of a mixture of negative factors which threatened the grand strategy he had gradually evolved over the winter of 1631–2. That plan, based on the unexpectedly strong position of the Swedes in western Germany, now called for the conquest of Bavaria and then of Austria itself – objectives never so much as dreamed of in the king's original German design. But quick action was necessary to preserve the integrity of the new strategy; and when Tilly did him the favour of forcing a Swedish unit out of the city of Bamberg, thus releasing him from the obligation contracted at Bärwalde to respect the neutrality of the Catholic League, Gustavus marched an army of just under 40,000 men from Mainz to the southeast, through Nürnberg and on to the river Lech – the western boundary of Bavaria. There, at Rain, he forced a crossing in the face of Tilly's considerably smaller army; in the ensuing battle, on 15 April 1632, the Catholics lost not only most of their army but also its commander: the old but ever faithful Tilly, mortally wounded, died two weeks later. Maximilian, making the intelligent but painful decision not to defend his own electorate, but instead to position his forces in northern Bavaria where they might link up with Wallenstein's new army, left Bavaria open to his enemies. The result was predictable: a deliberate pillaging and destruction of major proportions, systematically executed everywhere except in such various towns and cities as were able to buy exemption.

Wallenstein, meanwhile, leaving to subordinates the task of successfully driving Johann Georg and his Saxons out of Bohemia and Silesia, had moved most of his army into the so-called Alte Veste, a massive fortress complex near Nürnberg, where they were joined by Maximilian and his forces. Gustavus besieged him there in a fruitless effort which lasted over two months and cost him a not inconsiderable number of troops. Forced to raise the siege in October, he retreated to the northwest in search of new recruits and supplies, while Wallenstein seized the opportunity to strike northeast into Saxony, where Johann Georg's dispirited troops offered little resistance. After taking Leipzig on 1 November, Wallenstein readied himself for the Swedish attack he was sure would occur momentarily. When it did not, after two weeks, he ordered his army to disperse into winter quarters, only to recall the already-scattering units the very next day because of information that the Swedes were fast approaching his headquarters at Lützen, southwest of Leipzig. On the day battle was joined – 17 November – Wallenstein's army had only reached a size equal to that of the depleted Swedish force; and while neither side, after heavy losses, won a clear-cut victory on the battlefield, Wallenstein's quick troop count in the night following the combat suggested the wisdom of retreat. Abandoning his cannon and supplies to the enemy, he withdrew from Saxony into Bohemia. It then remained for the Swedes to count their losses; and of these, beyond any doubt, the greatest was the life of their brilliant king who, thrice shot, expired on the battlefield of Lützen.

The death of the great Gustavus – attended by outright disbelief which gradually gave way to genuine grieving all over Protestant Europe – left forever unanswered the question of what he might have achieved had he lived a normal life-span, or even just a few years longer. Nor can one really be sure of what dreams of a future Germany may have entertained his imagination, especially after the victory at Rain seemed to open up even the possibility of a Swedish emperor someday reigning over a more or less completely Protestantized Germany. But such visions – if he had any at all – were now moot.[2] The direction of Swedish policy in Germany fell to the astute and tireless chancellor Axel Oxenstierna, to whom almost plenary powers had been granted by the regency government which now ran Sweden in the name of Gustavus's daughter, the child-queen Christina. Oxenstierna, a man who trafficked more effectively in realities than in dreams, immediately set a simple, concrete and – as he saw it – attainable agenda for Sweden in Germany: the retention of substantial Baltic coastal territories under permanent Swedish rule and the recovery of as much (or more) of the costs of Sweden's German involvement as possible.

Circumstances seemed auspicious for the achievement of these objectives: the retreat of Wallenstein to Bohemia left no enemy

---

2. There is at least some reason to suppose that, surprised by his own successes, Gustavus may have improvised his future as he went along and that there was no true 'grand plan' in being at the time of his death.

between the Swedes and their Baltic bases and indeed the overall balance of forces after Lützen was not unfavourable to Sweden. But a way had to be found to keep the leadership of the anti-imperial forces in Germany in Swedish hands rather than those of others interested in seizing it. Johann Georg, for example, coveted the role, but would almost certainly have used it to press for a general peace that would have ignored or opposed Sweden's interests. France's Cardinal Richelieu, on the other hand, who had become downright alarmed by Sweden's unexpected successes (and especially by its strong presence in the Rhineland, for which he had his own plans) and who was annoyed by Gustavus's obvious indifference to the Cardinal's continuing efforts to sow division between Maximilian of Bavaria and the emperor, would have liked to make separate alliances with Saxony and Sweden, in order to dominate both. Oxenstierna's clever solution to this problem came in the form of the Heilbronn Confederation, an association of Sweden with German princes from the four imperial circles of southwestern Germany, of which Oxenstierna was promptly named the sole leader. In the same month, a disgruntled Cardinal Richelieu saw no choice but to renew the Treaty of Bärwalde.

The Heilbronn Confederation was an excellent temporary device, but it became apparent in the course of 1633 that the alliance simply could not cover the costs of men and supplies it had agreed to assume. Even after dumping French and Dutch subsidies into the common war chest, immediate expenses required adoption of various expedients, including, of course, the horrid system of military requisition. One solution to the problem was to expand the Confederation's membership, especially by the addition of large Protestant territories such as Brandenburg and Saxony. Oxenstierna's approaches to the former nearly foundered on the rocks of Sweden's grim determination to keep the duchy of Pomerania at all costs, without regard to a family compact which guaranteed Brandenburg's succession to it upon the death of its heirless duke. In the end, however, Elector Georg Wilhelm threw his lot in with Johann Georg of Saxony, who after rejecting as too harsh the peace terms he himself had solicited from the Habsburgs, reluctantly agreed to cooperate with Sweden in another campaign – though under terms which stipulated that the main Protestant thrust would come in Silesia, the area of greatest interest to him and under officers of his choosing.[3]

3. Parker, *The Thirty Years' War*, p. 136.

That this new Protestant alliance system was not a fully harmonious one was well known to Wallenstein, whose many contradictory actions throughout 1633 have provided historians with a rich choice of alternative motives and purposes for the now physically infirm and mentally unstable veteran mercenary. With the certain immediate aim of exploiting differences between the allies and perhaps with other longer-term goals in mind as well, Wallenstein at one time or another bargained separately or together with Sweden, Brandenburg, Saxony and even with the Czech emigrés, led by Count Thurn, who surrounded the Saxon court. The sheer variety of Wallenstein's initiatives have led to sharply differing interpretations, among them: that he was a German patriot, who wanted a true and permanent peace and unity for the Empire such as would allow it to defend itself against all foreign intrusions and perhaps even to undertake a crusade against the Turks; that he was a Czech (Bohemian) patriot, who wanted peace, unity and independence from the Habsburgs for that kingdom, perhaps with himself on the throne; and finally, that he was simply an enormously avaricious and self-interested warlord-businessman, prepared to make deals with anyone on the basis of his own greatest gain in money, titles or territories – and perhaps especially if such deals were detrimental to the emperor and his henchmen who had betrayed him in 1630. Evidence to support all of these interpretations exists – though it is difficult to find any considerable body of contemporary opinion which gave credence to any but the last.

What was in any case becoming apparent to Ferdinand II and his advisers in the increasingly erratic behaviour of his generalissimo, who fought, stopped fighting, negotiated, fought again, then retreated, was that decisive military action in the imperial cause was not an important part of his agenda. Against enormous financial expenditures, he had accomplished remarkably little throughout 1633 and his exaggerated and intemperate words and actions had begun to dim the loyalty even of his own army. Old and new enemies – including Maximilian, Philip IV of Spain and his brother the Cardinal-Infante Ferdinand and the emperor's own son, also a Ferdinand – persuaded the emperor to dismiss Wallenstein in late December 1633 and, when the latter refused to step down, subsequently to order his arrest, with permission to kill him if necessary. When Wallenstein did in fact attempt to escape execution of this order, a group of officers loyal for whatever reasons to Vienna's purposes murdered him on the night of 25 February 1634.

Wallenstein's demise was lamented by almost no one, but it had the very important result of bringing the imperial army – now larger than that of the Catholic League – under the command of the emperor's son, the future Ferdinand III, who pressed the war vigorously and effectively. The Swedish-German army of the Heilbronn Confederation, commanded by Count Horn and Bernhard of Saxe-Weimar, had some successes in the summer of 1634, but then made the mistake of attacking Ferdinand's army, which was besieging the Protestant city of Nördlingen and which had just been strengthened by the addition of 15,000 Spanish troops led by the Cardinal-Infante. In this battle of 6 September 1634 the power of the Heilbronn Confederation was instantly and forever shattered: almost two-thirds of the army were killed or captured, while the remainder, under Duke Bernhard, retreated all the way into Alsace. By the spring of 1635, after the Swedes were forced to recall all garrisons south of the Main, all of Germany east of the Rhine was securely under Habsburg sway, while Sweden's north German supporters were fast deserting it for a less dangerous alternative.

That alternative, unsurprisingly, was provided by the dependably pusillanimous Johann Georg of Saxony, whose constant readiness to talk peace with the emperor finally bore fruit in a preliminary settlement of November 1634, which in a form somewhat more favourable to the imperial interest was eventually ratified as the Peace of Prague of May 1635. By the terms of the latter, which really superseded the Edict of Restitution, a 'normal date' of 12 November 1627 was established to determine restitution of church lands and rights of religious worship. In effect, it protected the secularizations of most of the north German princes while recognizing Catholic reconversions in the south and southwest, as well as in several bishoprics in the north. Johann Georg was allowed to annex Lusatia permanently and to administer Magdeburg, while Maximilian's electoral title was declared hereditary. Most important, perhaps, a single imperial army of Habsburg, Saxon and Bavarian troops was to be formed for use against foreign forces in the Empire. The army would be under oath to the emperor himself and no separate territorial armies were henceforth to exist. Special alliances among the princes (including the Catholic League) were to be dissolved and were forbidden for the future. Both France and Sweden were invited to become signatories, on condition that their forces quit Germany; both, of course, refused.

The German princes, however, hastened to join, chief among them Brandenburg, whose acceptance of the treaty became the signal for a general accession of Lutheran princes. In doing so, they proved characteristically unconcerned about the fate of their former Calvinist allies, to whom no recognition was given in the settlement; the most important of them – Wilhelm V of Hesse-Kassel – was in fact expelled from his territory by the Lutheran ruler of Hesse-Darmstadt. Besides Wilhelm, only a few other princes refused reconciliation with the emperor, among them Bernhard of Saxe-Weimar, who remained camped in armed unrepentance in Alsace.

The Peace of Prague was at least a moderate victory for Ferdinand II and for Catholicism. The emperor's monarchical position was automatically strengthened by the extinction of a formed opposition among the German princes, as well as by the new all-German military force he now commanded; and the Catholic church, salvaging most of its important gains of the previous decade, had restored itself to a clearly dominant position in the Empire. But the Lutherans, while recognizing this fact, saw the peace as one which at least assured the survival of their faith – an almost submissive posture, perhaps, but one which had always been more acceptable to them than to the Calvinists, whose restless militancy the former had with some reason learned to fear. Yet the most remarkable thing about the Peace of Prague was not that the Lutherans could sign it, but that Ferdinand II did. Some of his advisers did not want him to and in view of his previously ironclad hostility to settlements with any hint of softness about them, they had some reason to suppose he would not. But Ferdinand had by now seen great triumphs and hopes succeeded by equally great defeats and disappointments; he appears to have developed a chastened appreciation of how thin the line separating the former from the latter really was and perhaps even a sense of a causal relationship between them. Influenced in part by the majority judgment of his theologians, but also by the pragmatism of his son and successor, who was not as strongly governed by religious considerations as was his father, the emperor chose not to heed the advice of the naysayers, including the omnipresent Lamormainie, who this time did not have his way. Thus, emperor and Empire resolved at Prague to wrest the determination of their common future from the grip of foreigners. Given the intensity of their desire for peace, they can perhaps be forgiven for their failure to realize that it was simply too late – or too early – for that. Sadly, indeed, the worst miseries of Germany were yet to come.

CHAPTER SIX
Eternal War as Lifestyle

As at two earlier points in the long conflict – first after the general pacification that followed the Palatinate wars and then after the imposition of imperial authority which resulted from the defeat of Christian IV of Denmark and his allies – the Peace of Prague of 1635 seemed to present an opportunity for a united German Empire to iron out its problems and to control its own destiny. in the stillness of peace desired by all Germans. The invitation to both France and Sweden to accede to the treaty was a serious one, generally recognized as indispensable to the immediate cessation of all hostilities. Indeed, if just one of the two had accepted, the same result still could have been expected, since no extensive campaigning in Germany was possible for either without the cooperation of the other. Sweden, in fact, considered signing the treaty as a way of escaping military commitments in Germany in the face of a looming war with Denmark and the expiration of its truce with Poland. But Denmark was temporarily bought off by the cession of Bremen and France – grimly determined to continue its harassment of the Habsburgs – helped to mediate a twenty-five-year extension of the Polish truce, thus freeing the Swedes to pursue their double objective of compensation and retention of north German territories.

It was the French even more than the Swedes, however, who really determined that the afflictions of war would visit Germany more horribly than ever for another thirteen years. With his allies reduced in number and the remaining ones no longer in a position to accomplish his purposes without direct French military intervention, Cardinal Richelieu admitted the failure of his hitherto clever and successful policy of using surrogates to fight his wars: in May 1635 France declared war on Spain in a formal statement which, without naming him, was clearly understood to include Ferdinand II as well. Preceded by a new alliance with the Dutch and accompanied by the occupation of Alsace and the enlistment of new armies under the command of the dissidents Bernhard of Weimar and Wilhelm of Hesse-Kassel, the French declaration of war presumed cooperation with Sweden in Germany as well as a persistent diplomatic campaign to separate the emperor from as many of his German allies, new and old, as possible.

For several years after 1635 the military balance between the imperial forces and those of the French and Swedes did not appear substantially unequal. France, indeed, suffered initial reverses on other fronts (Italy, Lorraine and the Netherlands) which limited its commitments to the German war for a time, while in northeastern Germany the Swedes under Johan Baner had some successes in 1636, but were then forced back into their base areas in Mecklenburg and western Pomerania for most of 1637 and 1638. They thrust far to the south in 1639 and again in 1640–41, but in both cases could not consolidate positions secure enough to avoid withdrawing after each campaign. In the other German war theatre, the west and southwest, similarly, the military situation remained fluid until in 1638 and 1639 Bernhard of Weimar and his 'Bernardines', with French help, were able to inflict severe defeats on imperial forces, especially at Breisach, which resulted in French control of virtually the entire upper Rhine and its important crossings. These victories were of great significance to France in its war with Spain, but subsequent French campaigns – conducted now without Bernhard, who died in July 1639 – were unsuccessful for several years. The Bavarian army carried the burden of war for the Empire in the southwest under such able generals as Franz von Mercy and Johann von Werth and inflicted one defeat after another on French forces still lacking in field experience; but with regular supplies of money and reinforcements and increasingly veteran troops, a French army strengthened by Hessian and Swedish units pushed relentlessly towards the Danube in the summer of 1645 and at Allerheim, near Nördlingen, fought and barely won an unusually vicious battle in early August, during which Mercy was killed.

In the southwest, then, the situation of the imperial forces did not look altogether discouraging until after Allerheim. But circumstances had never looked very hopeful in the east, where a superb new Swedish commander, Lennart Torstensson, struck into Saxony and Bohemia in 1642, placing Leipzig under occupation until the end of the war; and after a decisively successful war against Denmark, in

1643, he again renewed an attack through Bohemia which brought him all the way to the Danube in Upper Austria. This army again had to be withdrawn to winter quarters in the north, but in 1646, under its new commander, Wrangel, it was combined with the French general Turenne's forces in a devastating campaign across the Main and the Danube; Augsburg was taken and parts of Bavaria were laid waste in the winter of 1646–7. This time, therefore, the Franco-Swedish host was able to winter in the south and while Maximilian of Bavaria saved his electorate from depredations throughout much of 1647 by a truce concluded with the enemy in March, his return to imperial allegiance in September and the subsequent defeat of the last real imperial-Bavarian field army at Zusmarshausen in May 1648, led to an even more frightful destruction in Bavaria in the summer of 1648. Prague, meanwhile, was spared as bad a fate by the determined resistance of its now Catholicized citizenry to the siege undertaken by a smaller Swedish force under Count Königsmarck; the belated arrival of the news that peace had been concluded at Westphalia finally lifted the siege.

By any reckoning, the war had gone badly for the Habsburgs and their German allies at least since 1640, by which time a deep war-weariness among the princes had also become obvious. Evidence of this was sufficiently clear in Vienna as to suggest that a timely airing of issues was necessary to prevent individual defections which might become a mass movement. Ferdinand III thus convoked an electoral diet in Regensburg early in 1640 and when that meeting failed to produce results, called together the first full diet since 1613 later the same year. While no serious prospect of general peace was forthcoming from this diet, which lasted over a year, it was significant that the emperor showed a willingness to make concessions on several major issues, including what amounted to a revocation of the Edict of Restitution. But this did not have the desired unifying effect. Friedrich Wilhelm of Brandenburg, elector since the death of Georg Wilhelm in 1640, whose lands had been fought over and then largely occupied by his enemies, arranged an armistice with Sweden in mid-1641 which delivered his patrimony from the ravages of war (if not those of continuing Swedish tenancy). Early in the following year, the dukes of Brunswick – allies of Sweden since renunciation of their earlier acceptance of the Peace of Prague – also called it quits, made their peace with Ferdinand and thus brought the blessings of neutrality to another large area of northern Germany. More importantly, a despondent Johann Georg of Saxony concluded a truce with Sweden in September 1645, taking his electorate out of the war. The most significant admission of German defeat so far, however, came from the staunch Maximilian of Bavaria. Torn between his loyalty to emperor and Empire (and the electoral title which went with it, of course) and his desire to halt the progressive ruination of his territories, Maximilian had begun to negotiate with France as early as 1640, first with the objective of detaching France from its Swedish ally and later to work out terms for a separate peace for Bavaria and some other German Catholic states. Desperation finally drove him to an armistice with France in early 1647 and even greater desperation moved him to break it later in the year and to rejoin the peace negotiations in Westphalia as a belligerent. No one, surely, was happier than he when those long and wearisome negotiations were successfully concluded in October, 1648.

Well before it ended, this war had already lasted long enough to have created what one might term a 'life style' in wide areas of Germany. For the most part, it was a very unwelcome one. The extraordinary misery caused by this conflict almost from the outset had no real parallel in earlier European history. Hunger, disease and systematic mayhem – all of them traceable to the repeated campaigning and rampaging of hordes of soldiers and their camp followers – produced an abundance of horrors so hair-raising as to be remarkable even to a generation of observers already inured to the ordinary and extraordinary cruelties of the imaginative maiming, torture and death regularly visited on some human beings by others in the name of religion and criminal justice. Famine, which became familiar to many areas on an annual basis, produced diets which included grass, bean stalks, dogs, cats, rats (and even their cooked skins), not to mention human flesh, which more than a few accounts mention as procured from the gallows, from graveyards, unwary strangers (or neighbours), or even from new-born babies. Disease, fearsome even in ordinary times, marched with the troops and baggage trains of every army and could become locally and even regionally epidemic with every campaign, reducing the available food supply still further and causing abnormally high mortality among an already mal-nourished population.

The sheer vengefulness of a brutalized and cruelly careless soldiery was also a cause of many deaths; the horrible fate of Magdeburg was only the most widely publicized example of a wanton and almost joyous massacre of civilians which occurred in a number of cities, towns and villages throughout the war, not to mention the almost everyday 'spot killings' of peasants who were unlucky enough to be found at home when a band of armed marauders visited them unexpectedly. To make matters worse, the destruction and death arising from these deliberate acts increased as the conflict wore on; indeed, the last ten years or so were worse than anything that had gone before. The behaviour of soldiers themselves, for one thing, appears to have degenerated from levels that were hardly apostolic to begin with. This was the result not only of inadequate discipline traceable to recruitment problems, but also of the tendency of 'good' soldiers eventually to be infected by the criminality of the bad ones. Then again, because by the later stages of the war looting and marauding had stripped so many areas virtually bare of food and plunder, the soldiers became more intent than ever on extracting whatever was left and by whatever increasingly vicious means were necessary. Also, of course, the areas along the march routes subject to requisitions and plundering had to be steadily widened to provide the pay and other necessities of the armies.[1]

Peasants and small-town dwellers were much more exposed to the recurring ravages of war than were the residents of larger cities, where sound fortifications could often withstand lengthy sieges or where urban wealth could buy off the attackers; and, of course, they were proof against the small raiding parties which were the bane of the peasant's existence.[2] On the other hand, of course, some of the more terrible incidents of deprivation and starvation occurred during very long and unrelieved sieges of such cities, not to mention the general impoverishment which came to characterize many cities which lay in the broad, permanent war zones. Battle deaths occurred in the cities, too, since it was common for burghers to fight side-by-side with the mercenaries whom they housed, fed and paid and often also with peasants called in from surrounding rural areas which were under urban authority.

The recurring losses of life and property among the peasantry were staggering. Even if allowances are made for the undoubted hyperbole which characterized many contemporary accounts, evidences of the suffering and devastation of peasant lands contained in literally thousands of chronicles, diaries, travellers' accounts and

1. This fact may account for the marked increase in the proportion of cavalry to infantry in all armies as time went on, though it is also important to note that it was the cavalry, as the only real offensive weapon available, which decided most battles. Lutz, *Das Ringen*, p. 417.
2. Herbert Langer, *Kulturgeschichte des 30 jährigen Krieges* (Stuttgart, 1978), p. 103.

other sources are too convincing to be dismissed. In spite of the proverbial stubborn loyalty of the peasant to his land, the relentlessness of the war in numerous areas finally led to abandonment of farms by families which saw the hopelessness of growing crops which year after year were either destroyed or seized. Then and for the most part only then, might they join the very armies which had ruined them, or migrate to towns and cities or to safer regions of the country. That they were free to do so, where they did, testifies to the collapse of the authority of the landowning nobility, many of whom had already fled their manors for refuge elsewhere.

Some princes, in order to provide protection both for their territories in general and for the peasantry in particular, attempted to set up *Landesdefensionen* – peasant militias, essentially – which required registration, some training in arms and an alarm system (church bells, usually) which would call a varying percentage of these rustic troops to a common assembly point in emergencies. Generally resented by the peasants, who saw them as both time-consuming and expensive, such schemes were seldom successful. War was indeed conducted by peasants against soldiers, but under conditions very different from those envisioned by the *Landesdefensionen*. On innumerable occasions, individuals or small groups of soldiers found isolated from their units were fallen upon by peasants wielding axes, pitchforks, flails and other crude but effective instruments; and when the numbers were unequal in their favour, the peasants exacted as complete and grisly a vengence as any they suffered from the soldiery. A more organized protective arrangement, developed over time in the relatively permanent war zones in small towns and villages, had some success in limiting loss of life and property: by a system of couriers, bonfires and bells, communities alerted each other to the approach of military units, providing time for residents to hide themselves and their valuables in the woods before the arrival of the troops. This did not always spare their houses or barns, however; and if the soldiers had the time or inclination for a search of the area, the unfortunate civilians were often robbed and murdered in their hiding places.

The legendary cunning of the peasantry, on the other hand, gradually taught some of them not only how to live with the war, but even how to profit by it now and then. Money could be made by serving as guides to armies or their detachments or, less honestly, by following raiding parties to pick up what they left behind, or even by looting abandoned camps and blood-soaked battlefields. In time, peasants learned to sell before they were robbed – as in Bavaria in 1645, where they sold horses otherwise sure to be requisitioned to drovers who were assembling them in herds to be sold in Switzerland.[3] More courageous peasants sometimes appropriated and sold the produce of timid neighbours who had abandoned their farms, or benefited in other ways from their fellows' misfortunes – as in Augsburg during the Swedish occupation, when peasants bought up stolen cattle from soldiers at prices which reflected the latters' ignorance of their real worth. Finally, as C. V. Wedgwood has pointed out, 'Soldiers did not stop to bargain and the village boy who exchanged a mug of beer for a silver chalice did well out of the deal.'[4] Such transactions, however, even if multiplied many thousands of times, were surely a miserable enough compensation for the heavy losses occasioned by this interminable conflict.

If there was a life-style of war for civilians, there was also one for soldiers, who because of the sheer length of hostilities grew to sufficient numbers as to comprise almost an identifiable class by themselves.[5] No really reliable figures exist on the number of troops who fought at one or another time in the war, but one estimate that well over a million may have served (with perhaps 250,000 the top figure for a given time and 210,000 at the cessation of hostilities in 1648) cannot be too wide of the mark.[6] They represented virtually every country of Europe and some beyond, from Scotland to Turkey; Germans were not only always the majority, however, but there was even a strong tendency for their numbers to increase, relative to all foreigners, in the later stages of the war. That resulted partly from the fact that some foreign participants literally used up their available manpower eventually (Sweden being the best example), or employed it elsewhere (as in the case of France); also, however, the impoverishment of an increasing proportion of the population in the battle zones of Germany created unemployment for which enlistment in the ranks seemed the best (and sometimes the only) solution. Religious persuasion was generally unimportant as a criterion for admission to the rank-and-file of any army, especially after the Peace of Prague eliminated most of the confessional aspect of the war. All armies were therefore both nationally and religiously

3. Ibid., 124.
4. C. V. Wedgwood, *The Thirty Years War* (Garden City, N.Y., 1961), p. 495.
5. Marshal Baner of Sweden once referred to his army as a 'widespread state', while Oxenstierna in 1633 commented that he had elevated the army to the rank of a political estate. Ibid., 376. It may be noted that this 'estate' in fact had its own representative, Colonel Erskine, at the final negotiations at Westphalia.
6. Parker, *The Thirty Years' War*, pp. 191, 208. The anti-Habsburg forces outnumbered the imperialists by roughly 2:1 by 1648.

mixed – a circumstance which created occasionally serious problems of discipline and command.

Apart from some numbers of criminals who were either sentenced to military service, or whose prison terms were commuted on that condition, almost all who served were volunteers, whose reasons for joining armies were quite varied. A love of adventure and of what seemed to many a carefree life attracted many young people, as did both immediate wages and the long-term prospects of regular pay and the lure of easy plunder. These real or potential economic rewards became more important to more people as the pauperization created by the war widened; and after a time, war became the only profession they knew. In areas repeatedly ravaged by war, it was often a safer profession than many civilian callings, offering 'the comparative security of being the robber and not the robbed'.[7] Religious conviction impelled some men to fight, at least in the early years; and joining armies under commanders who cared little about the religion of their recruits could also be a way of avoiding forcible conversion – as in the case of the thousands of Upper and Lower Austrian peasants who found refuge under Wallenstein's banner during his second generalship.[8] Some recruits, no doubt, found what they wanted and perhaps even more. A soldier's life could in many respects be a free one and 'free' in a much more than ordinary sense for those many peasants who escaped legal servitude by following the drum; and there did exist some chance of self-betterment for those who worked hard at it. With a standard of living normally no worse than the average of the time and with considerable excitement and variety in his existence, the soldier also enjoyed a position in public life which, while vilified by civilians, was in some respects more elevated than theirs.[9] Carousing, drinking, harassing the citizenry in both innocuous and cruelly vicious ways, the soldier's life had in it something of that joyful and unrestrained primitivity that has never been without some appeal, especially to the young. Only self-interest, based on the need for the continued support of the organization of which they were part, but also reinforced by a savage system of military justice, kept the wanton behaviour of the soldiery within the bounds necessary to preserve military effectiveness.

There was, of course, a very dark side to all this as well. Great battles – and even intense skirmishes – were actually relatively few

7. Wedgwood, *The Thirty Years War*, p. 376.
8. Langer, *Kulturgeschichte*, pp. 89–90.
9. Ibid., 89.

for a war that lasted as long as this one did; that was the result of the strategy of movement eventually adopted by both sides, designed to manoeuvre the enemy into already devastated areas, where recruitment, refitting and resupply would become so difficult as to create both physical hardship and financial exhaustion. Grim indeed was the fate of a number of such armies, whose casualties could run as high as in the bloodiest field engagements. But there were very many battle deaths as well, often resulting from relatively minor wounds which the virtual absence of medical care permitted to become fatal. Within the narrow confines of military encampments, diseases – especially dysentery, typhus and bubonic plague – could easily become epidemic, causing many deaths. The same was true in the huge 'tail' of the camp following of every army, which included servants, wives, children, hostages, pedlars, hucksters, gamblers, prostitutes, suppliers and artisans and which could equal or even exceed the size of the army itself. A soldier also had to reckon with the possibility that the defeat and consequent dissolution of his army, or simply the financial exhaustion of his commander, could terminate his employment for a greater or lesser period of time, casting him into a generally inhospitable civilian environment in the role of a vagabond. The life-style of the soldier, like that of the civilian in war-affected areas, was thus an unpredictable mix of fear, hunger, sickness and death, alternating with hope, coarse pleasures and good times – and not a small amount of sheer boredom. Sadly, the only truly predictable element of life, on good days and bad, was menace; Mars, after all, was a constant companion to all.

An often significant part of the hardship of a soldier's life was the irregularity of his pay – a reflection of the huge problem of war economics faced by all the combatants large and small, and which had a fundamental effect on military strategy and thus on the nature and character of the war itself. No army was immune from serious weaknesses arising from dissatisfaction in the ranks caused by privation; and while mutinies were rare, desertion (sometimes to switch sides) was not and the breaches of discipline and military readiness caused by impromptu foraging expeditions or the drifting of soldiers from one unit to another in search of better provisions was a source of much worry to commanders, who were also aware that their men regularly sold off pieces of their equipment for food and other necessities. By the later years of the war, especially, the danger that an army could lose its coherence through inadequate provisioning was so obvious as to dictate a strategy in which possession of territory for its produce was more important than fighting.[10] Needless to say, this strategy not only lengthened the war considerably, but also guaranteed the progressive impoverishment of town and countryside by steadily increasing requisitioning and by the infamous system of 'contributions'.

It is pointless to ask whether more sophisticated fiscal policies on the part of the major contenders might have prevented the merciless exploitation of civilian resources, with its attendant atrocities, which gave this war its especially horrible character. In fact, fiscal planning for war utterly defeated itself in some cases – as in the monetary crisis of the early 1620s known as the 'Kipper and Wipper' period (so called from the 'clipping' and 'whisking-away' of good coins by money-changers). In the context of a generally increasing confusion and manipulation of coinage within the Empire in the late sixteenth century, which was then worsened by an inflation which made silver more valuable, a number of princes in southern and southwestern Germany, fearing the onset of war, began to mint debased coins as a quick way to augment their financial resources. This ominous trend broadened and escalated suddenly and sharply with the beginning of hostilities in Bohemia and Austria after 1618 and reached crisis proportions in 1622–3. As confidence in the currency collapsed, the tempo of business activity slowed for a time disastrously, thus eroding the fiscal footing on which many princes had hoped to meet the now real military emergency.[11] But no amount of planning prior to 1618 could really have helped to fight the kind of war this one became, whose staggering costs eventually simply outran the ability of every government to pay for it out of anything resembling ordinary revenues. Ferdinand II's resources were inadequate from the outset and neither papal nor Spanish money provided more than temporary relief; neither did the unexpectedly small sums he realized from his Bohemian confiscations. The large treasury of the prudent Maximilian and the carefully hoarded monies of the penurious Johann Georg were eventually exhausted. Even those gifted with more than ordinary foresight into the probable costs of the conflict knew that the war would have to pay for itself. Wallenstein, for example, whose vast estates in Friedland were converted into a huge war manufactory producing both food and every other imaginable kind of campaigning necessity, was untypical of the warlords of the time

10. Wedgwood, *The Thirty Years War*, p. 470; Langer, *Kulturgeschichte*, p. 158.
11. Jeserich *et al.*, *Deutsche Verwaltungsgeschichte*, I, 240; Langer, *Kulturgeschichte*, p. 29.

only in that his exploitations of princes and peoples, being more systematic than theirs, were accompanied by less senseless destruction. Much the same was true of Gustavus Adolphus, whose planned and orderly extortions – especially from large cities such as Augsburg and Munich – usually allowed him to indulge his gentler instincts regarding the treatment of human beings and whose destructions, great though they were, were militarily purposeful, not random.

All, however, relied heavily on 'contributions', a term which embraced a wide variety of expedients: tax assessments on communities in the vicinity, paid either in cash or in kind (in the form of food, clothing, munitions, transport and so on); new tolls, such as those levied in Baltic ports by the Swedes, or by Tilly on the Elbe; or, quite commonly, single-payment demands on cities and towns as the price of avoiding unfriendly occupation. With the sums thus acquired, it was possible not only to pay the troops but even in some cases to let out contracts to distant suppliers for arms, munitions, clothing, horses, cattle and other items in bulk. Production and commerce in armaments, in particular, became enormous, but Germany's earlier position of European leadership in mining, smelting and metal manufactures guaranteed adequate coverage of the basic requirements of the warring princes and cities. Older production centres and entrepôts such as Nürnberg and Essen were now joined by Dresden, Munich, Vienna, Graz and others.

With steadily rising prices, a brisk trade in such commodities as lead, iron, sulphur and saltpetre arose, adding new jobs and wealth to the relatively safe port cities of Hamburg, Bremen and Danzig and even to some interior cities such as Frankfurt am Main. More than a few great fortunes were made by those who dealt in these wartime products, as well as by a number who trafficked in troops – the military enterprisers, who advanced cash to recruiting officers against promissory notes from the governments who commissioned them. Wallenstein was certainly the greatest and best known of these, but he was only one of an estimated total of 1500 who operated at one or another time during the war.[12] War being war, however, there were no guarantees of uninterrupted gain even in these vocations. Foundries and arms factories were often destroyed by armies on the march and while their great profitability often led to immediate reconstruction, there were areas in the permanent war zones where the whole industry suffered a disastrous decline. Some military enterprisers, furthermore, never recovered the loans they

12. Parker, *The Thirty Years' War*, pp. 195–6.

made and were ruined; a good example is Wallenstein's chief financier, the Antwerp banker Hans de Witte, who committed suicide as a business decision following the generalissimo's dismissal from imperial service in 1630.

While a social and economic climate as dominated by military necessity as that of Germany between 1618 and 1648 does not normally provide fertile ground for intellectual and artistic activity, it is difficult to argue that the war alone accounts for the at best mediocre level of German cultural achievement in the period. Certainly, as we have seen in Chapter One, no great wave of cultural creativity was in evidence in 1618 to be cut short by the war; and to the extent that political fragmentation was a factor in preventing the emergence of national 'schools' in literature or the arts, it was no worse during the war than before or after it. Wartime conditions were also essentially irrelevant to the greatest contributions (though not to the personal lives) of the handful of memorable individuals of the time – the astronomer Johannes Kepler (1571–1630), for example, or the composer Heinrich Schütz (1585–1672). Still, the ongoing war did affect high culture in some ways worth noting. Almost all activities which required either large or regular infusion of money suffered to some extent. Schütz himself, for example, lamented the virtual collapse of the organized music establishments of princely courts all over Germany, including that of his own Saxony, because of cost-cutting and the exodus of musicians to other countries. Architecture and to some extent its associated decorative arts, were very negatively affected by shortages of funds: virtually no major new structure of any significance appeared in most of Germany during the war and architects were lucky to find work building fortifications. Higher education was crippled by under-funding, the sporadic closure of universities and a sharp decline in the number of students due to lack of money and the lure of military adventure. For a time, Dutch universities and especially Leyden, had a great attraction for German students, including some who upon their return to Germany achieved distinction as literary figures (Martin Opitz, Andreas Gryphius and Paul Fleming, for example) or as 'natural philosophers' (Otto von Guericke).[13] As individual Germans fled the war for education elsewhere, some important parts of their cultural heritage were also leaving the country as the booty of war. The most famous early example was the Palatina, the most impressive German library of the time, shipped to Rome as a gift to

13. Langer, *Kulturgeschichte*, pp. 186, 223–5.

the pope by Maximilian of Bavaria after his conquest of Heidelberg. Gustavus Adolphus also had a discerning eye for book and manuscript collections and shipped quantities of both back to Sweden from Würzburg and Mainz, in particular. Silesia, Bohemia and other areas were similarly stripped of their cultural treasures, sometimes by Germans, sometimes by foreigners.

The works of German poets and writers of the period – an undistinguished lot for the most part, whose work has largely been forgotten – clearly reflected a preoccupation with the war and its effects. Description of the cruelties of war, together with a yearning for peace and an earnest German patriotism characterized much prose and poetry, including that of Martin Opitz, the most celebrated poet of the time and author of an important treatise on German poetics which became the standard in the field for over a century. Resignation in the face of adversity, the vanity and frailty of earthly existence and an inward-turning religiosity were common themes. Among the major authors, most of urban origin, almost none made a living from his art, but from civilian occupations as physicians, teachers, clerics and officials. But there were also soldier-poets such as Caspar Stieler and Georg Greflinger, who wrote of the excitement, dangers, momentary joys and short lives of those who followed fife and drum. The most important work of military theme – and possibly the best semi-fictional work engendered by the war – was of course Hans von Grimmelshausen's *Adventures of Simplicissimus*, a narrative of the war years as experienced by a peasant lad carried off by soldiers; but it was neither written nor published until long after the war (1669).

Very different from this literature, but extremely important and influential in its own right, was the voluminous body of pamphlets and flyers which became the real popular literature of the period. Much of it was polemical and propagandistic and in that sense was hardly new, since the whole Reformation era was pervaded by confessional pamphleteering. The Swedes published a great deal of German-language propaganda to justify their intervention and their German allies soon joined their presses to the cause. While all parties to the war put out justificatory literature, Protestant Germany had an especially strong tradition of popular publicistics; this was evident in the veritable flood of pamphlets which attacked Spain and the Jesuits, in particular – though Lutherans and Calvinists threw much bilious ink at each other as well. A steady coarsening of language, to the point of extreme obscenity and tastelessness, eventually characterized much of this ephemeral literature, reflecting the increasing numbers of 'authors' who got into this very popular business. The demand for their writings was enormous, because in addition to the polemical purposes they served – whether political, moral or religious – they addressed the pressing social and economic issues and grievances of the day and, most important, provided the only easily accessible news about the parties, personalities and events of the war.[14] Pictures and cartoons played a large role in this literature and were all the more effective because of the widespread adoption of copper etching, which permitted much greater detail and shading of light and dark than the woodcut, which it now virtually replaced. Among the many publishers of pamphlets and flyers, a Nürnberg art dealer named Paul Fürst was particularly prolific; after the mid-1630s, he published literally hundreds of them, with illustrations, verses, songs and stories and purveyed them in quantity at the annual Leipzig fair, where he seems to have been an eagerly awaited visitor.[15]

As this chapter has shown, life indeed went on even during this terrible war. But simply to manage some sort of accommodation with the uncertainties of wartime was hardly the same as a good life. A bell-maker could survive by casting cannon, just as could the peasant who reluctantly traded his ploughshare for a pike; a merchant ruined by siege and arson might survive by the charity of his neighbours, just as a forcibly converted Catholic or Protestant kept his hearth and home only by virtue of a deeply soul-wrenching apostasy. What all had in common was a lack of choice. If this sad situation were ever to be ended, it would be so only by a general and permanent peace. And while it seemed to take forever, peace finally, and miraculously, came.

14. Gerhard Benecke, ed., *Germany in the Thirty Years War* (N.Y., 1979), pp. 55–6.
15. Langer, *Kulturgeschichte*, pp. 235–43.

CHAPTER SEVEN
Peace at Last

Given the length of the war, as well as the tangle of issues and interests which had become involved in it, it cannot be surprising that the making of peace was a long and complicated process and that the final treaty signed on 24 October 1648 incorporated assurances, promises and the substance of both formal and informal agreements made by the various parties over several previous years. The Regensburg diet of 1640–41 had already demonstrated a war-weariness among the German participants so great as to move Ferdinand III towards major concessions on German issues which were aimed at creating the imperial unity necessary for negotiation with the foreign belligerents. That such negotiation would indeed occur was virtually guaranteed in December 1641 by the emperor's acceptance of a Franco-Swedish proposal calling for imperial representatives to talk separately with the French at Münster and with the Swedes at Osnabrück, beginning sometime in 1642. The latter date proved over optimistic: the German princes were not yet finished ironing out either their substantive differences over purely German issues or the very important procedural issue of whether the emperor would be permitted to negotiate with the foreign powers in the name of the whole Empire, as he wished, or whether some or all of the imperial estates could represent their own interests. That the latter alternative finally prevailed was due partly to the combined stubbornness of the elector of Brandenburg and of Landgravine Amalia, the widow of the outlawed Wilhelm V of Hesse-Kassel, but even more to the support of Sweden and France, who saw advantage in it through separating the interests of emperor and Empire.

A large assembly of German princes wrangled over these and other issues in Frankfurt from early 1643 until almost autumn of

1645; their meeting would have lasted longer had Ferdinand III himself not resolved the procedural issue in late August 1645 by conceding a separate right of negotiation to all estates of the Empire, thus in effect constituting the proceedings in the two Westphalian cities as a diet whose determinations would have the force of imperial laws. The Frankfurt conference then closed and the Catholic princes sent their representatives to join those of France, Spain and their Catholic allies in Münster, while the Protestant estates moved to join Sweden and its allies in Osnabrück. When, soon after, the emperor not only agreed not to seek special advantage for Catholics resident in Protestant territories of the empire, but also amnestied even his outlawed vassals to permit them to join the negotiations legally, the talks could begin in earnest and did so with the arrival of the imperial plenipotentiary Count von Trautmansdorff in late November 1645.

The emperor had made these important concessions, of course, only because serious military reverses in Germany made it seem more urgently necessary than ever to conclude a peace. The repeated catastrophes suffered by Spain over the last several years also gave no comfort: a decisive naval defeat in 1639, successful separatist revolts in Portugal, Catalonia and elsewhere beginning in 1640 and the crowning battlefield disaster of Rocroi in 1643 – all set against a backdrop of fiscal problems of unprecedented and increasing proportions. Yet while Ferdinand's overall position was weaker than that of France or Sweden, it was only relatively so; both Cardinal Mazarin of France, left to finish the war started by his mentor Richelieu after the latter's death in 1642 and Sweden's leaders – especially Axel Oxenstierna – were sharply aware of the economic dangers and political risks, domestic and otherwise, of continuing the war forever. It is certainly true, however, that both foreign powers showed a greater willingness to prolong a war not fought on their own soil than did the German belligerents and this was especially true of Mazarin, who almost single-handedly delayed the final treaty from mid-1647 until the autumn of 1648 in the hope of achieving a final victory over Spain; not until a serious revolt against his government convinced him of the need to bring the troops home from Germany did he instruct his diplomats to conclude peace quickly.

One of the factors which delayed negotiations, then, was the more or less conscious decision of the belligerents to continue fighting while talking, all obviously hoping for a new military advantage to buttress their bargaining positions. There were other complications as well. The existence of two chief centres of negotiation – Münster and Osnabrück – though only a short distance apart, necessitated diplomatic relays which were time-consuming, as were also the more lengthy periods required for agents to consult with their principals in the various capitals of Europe. Confused and contradictory instructions, as well as personal animosities between members of one and the same delegation, led to much unnecessary delay. Furthermore, nothing of much importance was accomplished during numerous periods of petty squabbling over rank, precedence and procedure; and ceremonies and entertainments took up far more time than the importance of the diplomats' mission would suggest they should have. The fact that at Westphalia there were no less than 176 plenipotentiaries, acting as agents for 194 rulers and heading delegations which totalled several thousand persons, gives further insight into the problems of the conference.[1] Finally, while issues outstanding between enemies were difficult enough, those between allies often proved to be just as knotty, since peacemaking required a clarification and reconciliation of conflicting interests which warmaking did not.

These delays and problems could have led to an almost perpetual peace conference had a number of issues important to the German participants not been all but settled at a fairly early date, partly because both France and Sweden had agreed that it was in their interest to see the purely German issues resolved first. Some of these pertained to religion and had been addressed by Ferdinand II at the Peace of Prague in 1635 and by Ferdinand III at the Regensburg diet of 1640–41 and later. An already favourable trend for the Protestant interest continued at Westphalia, especially since the extremist Catholic party, resistant to virtually any concessions to Protestantism, did not include either the emperor or Maximilian of Bavaria and failed to exercise a decisive influence on the final terms. Calvinism, first of all, was now recognized as an 'official' denomination. Then, after much haggling, a new 'normal date' of 1 January 1624 was set for secularized territories; all such territories in Protestant hands on that date were to remain so or be restored to them and wherever private worship of minorities had existed at that time it was once again to be tolerated. The 'ecclesiastical reservation' remained, but was also extended to Protestant bishoprics. The principle that each independent territorial ruler had the right to determine the religion of his territory was reaffirmed, but also

---

1. Parker, *The Thirty Years' War*, p. 178.

importantly clarified to include the right to supervise the institutions and public practice of religion, not the private exercise of faith by any subjects, all of whom were free to hold whatever beliefs they had in 1624. Not even the conversion of the ruler was to affect these provisions. And while it was still possible to expel dissidents who had not had rights of worship in 1624, it had to be done within five years; such subjects could also leave voluntarily and in neither case was confiscation of property permitted. Moreover, the treaty explicitly recommended toleration in this situation and indeed the whole tenor of the religious settlement was remarkably more charitable than any which had been hammered out before. Its terms were also largely free of the vagueness and ambiguity which had deliberately been built into the Peace of Augsburg by an earlier and aggressively hopeful generation of Protestant and Catholic rulers who had sought to use equivocation to their own advantage; their descendants had finally learned, at great cost, that lack of clarity could be enormously harmful in many and unpredictable ways. They were determined to avoid it and this time they did.

There were other evidences of a genuine desire not to allow religious disagreements to escalate to the point of armed hostilities. Of these, the most important were designed to restore the ability of several imperial institutions to serve the calmative or intercessory role between the religious parties that had been so tragically lacking in the years before the war. The diet, for example, was protected from one cause of its prewar ineffectiveness by a provision that religious issues which came before it would henceforth be settled not by the usual majority votes (which almost always favoured the Catholic side), but through peaceful accommodation by the entire membership separated into two bodies, one Protestant and the other Catholic – a procedure known as *itio in partes*. The supreme organs of justice in the Empire, the Cameral Tribunal and the Aulic Council, were given greater credibility by the requirement that equal numbers of Protestant and Catholic judges had to be appointed to the former and at least some Protestants even to the latter. The later history of the Empire certainly does not demonstrate that these or any other subsequent reforms restored real vigour and efficacy to any of these institutions; but they were at least removed as sources of grievance between the confessional parties.

The religious provisions of the Peace of Westphalia were to some extent aimed at removing the dangers to public order of territorial conversions and reconversions by eliminating most of the advantages which had accrued to rulers by virtue of such changes, as well as the disadvantages suffered by their subjects. And whether intended or not, changes of religion among the territorial princes after 1648 became fairly rare, while religious uniformity increasingly characterized their lands, resulting in the shrinkage of minorities to numbers so much less than dangerous as actually to encourage the growth of a slow but steady spirit of toleration among both rulers and peoples. Thus, while religion never entirely disappeared as an occasional source of minor public disturbances, or even as a secondary reinforcement to the foreign policies of some territories, the persuasion towards confessional peace for the Empire from which the various religious provisions of Westphalia had emerged was to remain general and permanent. Even the important fact that Ferdinand III refused to bind himself to any general observance of the religious determinations of Westphalia for his own Habsburg territories does not necessarily invalidate this generalization: his refusal to allow the many thousands of Austrian and Bohemian exiles to return, or to consider restoration of estates and other properties confiscated from them and other rebels, while clearly proceeding from self-interest, also embodied the remembrance that the war had started because of the need to preserve the political unity of his patrimony which had been ruptured by these exiles and others like them. Protecting that restored unity by intoleration was a necessity to him and in its own way served the cause of peace as much as did such degree of toleration as now obtained elsewhere in the Empire.

Of the changes in the imperial constitution brought by the Peace of Westphalia, some were more important than others, but none was entirely new in practice. Thus, the recognition of the *Landeshoheit* (*ius territoriale, droit de souveraineté*) of all the estates of the Empire now written into imperial law, conveying the right to keep armed forces and make treaties with foreign states, was already implicit in Ferdinand's decision of 1645 to permit the territories to represent their own interests at Westphalia and, more importantly, was sanctioned by several generations of past practice already. That the Council of Cities was now recognized as having a distinct third vote alongside the Council of Princes and the Council of Electors was simply unimportant; its vote had sometimes been counted, but never as a deciding one and that practice was now in effect continued as the cities declined into political insignificance. Most of the numerous prohibitions and restrictions placed on the powers of the emperor at Westphalia with respect to legislation, taxes, war and peace and so on, were really only restatements of concessions forced out of earlier emperors as conditions of their election and were no more or less binding in practice than those – except that France and Sweden, formally recognized as guarantors of the peace, now had a potential role as protectors of the 'German liberties' which could be threatened by any breach of these restrictions. Finally, the addition of Bavaria to the Council of Electors and the latter's expansion to eight members with the new electoral seat created for Karl Ludwig, the son of the unfortunate 'Winter King', meant that its influence on events in the Empire, constitutional and otherwise, would be even greater than previously. Overall, however, the Peace of Westphalia did not strengthen, or weaken, or even much change the formal constitution of the Empire. What it did do, by its sheer weight in Germany and the rest of Europe, was to lock in place a set of attitudes and conditions – political ones, above all – which virtually eliminated the possibility of a unifying reform movement on the part of either emperor or estates and which eternalized a territorial fragmentation, with all its consequences, which seemed to be the only alternative to an imperial despotism.

The territorial changes arrived at over the several years of negotiations brought some important but not really drastic alterations to the political map of Germany. Ferdinand III found little support from his German allies for resisting the demands of France, which for a relatively small payment carried off most of the district of Alsace, as well as the Rhenish fortresses of Breisach and Philippsburg – bases important both as gates to the Empire and as serious qualifications on any future Austro-Spanish cooperation. The Lorraine bishoprics of Metz, Toul and Verdun, long occupied by France, were now formally abdicated to her. Sweden received the western part of Pomerania, including Stettin and the island of Rügen, the port of Wismar in Mecklenburg and the bishoprics of Bremen and Verden – thus assuring not only a firm coastal base area, but also control of the mouths of all three north German rivers: the Weser, Elbe and Oder. Mecklenburg, deprived of Wismar, was indemnified by permission to annex two small bishoprics. Saxony absorbed all of Lusatia as the result of its old bargain with the Habsburgs. Maximilian of Bavaria, of course, kept the Upper Palatinate and his electoral title, while the Lower Palatinate was restored to the new elector, Karl Ludwig. Most other territories once declared forfeit by imperial decree were restored to their original rulers or their heirs. And, just to clarify old and new ambiguities, both the Swiss Confederation and the Dutch Netherlands were recognized as sovereign entities, independent of the Empire.

Some of the most impressive gains of any German ruler at

Westphalia were those of the elector of Brandenburg and they came only partly as the result of his own persistent and clever diplomacy. The geopolitical position of Brandenburg proved for a change to be an advantage to Friedrich Wilhelm. While in spite of a legal entitlement to the entire duchy he could not avoid losing part of Pomerania to Sweden, he found both the Swedes and the French eager to assist him in finding compensation for the loss. The former, once assured of their other gains, saw advantage in friendly relations with their closest German neighbour, especially in view of continuing hostility between Sweden and Poland; so they favoured compensation for a north German Protestant ruler who might also act as a buffer against a reassertion of imperial power from the south. France, similarly concerned to strengthen a north German counterweight to the Habsburgs in the south, was also worried about Sweden's power and envisioned Brandenburg in the role of a balancer in this respect as well. As a result, in addition to eastern Pomerania, Friedrich Wilhelm was awarded the secularized bishoprics of Kammin, Halberstadt and Minden, as well as the expectancy to the bishopric of Magdeburg, finally annexed in 1680.

While the territorial changes mandated by the treaty were carried out almost immediately and even the religious provisions were implemented beginning in the winter of 1648–9, one final and very serious issue remained: the financial compensation demanded by Sweden for the withdrawal of its troops – perhaps 100,000 of them, mostly German – who were represented by their own negotiator, Colonel Erskine, at Osnabrück. The initially staggering sum demanded was eventually reduced to five million talers, which was supposed to be paid off over a two-year period. But it could not be; and while the Swedish army was the largest single part of the overall problem of demobilization, other armies had to be looked after as well, presenting a general problem of such magnitude as to require the assembly of a general conference at Nürnberg in April 1649. Wrestling with schedules of payment and withdrawal until July 1651, the conferees were witness not only to much restlessness among the various bodies of troops, with desertions and mutinies, but also to formal threats by Swedish commanders in the autumn of 1649 to return to war if an approved plan for withdrawal was not soon forthcoming. Such a plan was finally agreed on in mid-1650, after which the still very real possibility of renewed hostilities diminished rapidly. Even so, the last Swedish troops were not withdrawn to their Baltic bases until May 1654.

The huge payments required for demobilization, initially raised mostly through loans by native and foreign bankers but eventually distributed as assessments on the territories of the Empire, were very painful to both princes and peoples, but were accepted almost gladly as the price not only for the dissolution of the huge armies in their midst but also for reducing the threat of lawlessness and violence at the hands of many thousands of suddenly unemployed soldiers. There were incidents of more or less organized brigandage by some groups of discharged soldiers, or by individuals, some of them requiring suppression by force. But such episodes soon ceased, partly because considerable numbers of soldiers, neither knowing nor wanting any other kind of occupation, quickly found employment elsewhere, thus reducing the quantity which had to be reabsorbed into German civilian life.

The multitudes which participated in the joyful mass celebrations accompanying the conclusion of peace all over Germany in 1648, as well as the numerous lesser ones thereafter which greeted every phase of the demobilization and withdrawal of troops in the localities, can certainly be forgiven, after their long ordeal, for their widespread assumption that this awful war must surely have been the one to end all wars. But had they assiduously followed the long negotiations at Westphalia and read carefully the treaty that emerged from them, they might have seen the evacuations of troops from their fatherland for what it really was: a respite from war, not eternal absolution from it. The treaty reflected no conscious desire to create conditions for perpetual peace, but only every participant's determination to protect his own interests and position to the degree permitted by others under the circumstances of the moment. Thus, to use the best example, France gained new advantage in its most pressing concern – the war with Spain – not only by extracting a promise from Ferdinand III that he would give no more assistance to Spain, but also by territorial concessions making such aid more difficult and by encouraging division between the German princes and their Habsburg emperor. That all or most of the benefits of these concessions to France might someday recoil upon themselves was a consideration lost on the princes, intent as they were on immediate self-protection and assertion of the all-important principle of *Landeshoheit*.

There was much talk at Westphalia about the need for a basic reform of the imperial constitution to transform the Empire into a politically more cohesive body, able to formulate, assert and defend a single German national interest whose absence until now was generally recognized as a major source of the Empire's recent woes.

But that was never to happen, simply because the only common interest the princes were able to act on consistently was the defence of their individual independence. It says much about this issue that the only notable 'reform' to emerge for many years after Westphalia was the establishment of the so-called 'Eternal Diet'. In 1663, Emperor Leopold I convoked a diet at Regensburg to ask for help against the Turks. Deeply suspicious of Leopold's well-known displeasure at all the constitutional restrictions placed on his imperial office, the delegates, after disposing of current business, refused to disband and the diet thereafter remained forever in session at Regensburg. This was a fatal blow to any possibility that the only universal political body in the Empire could ever serve as a focal point for national unity, simply because no one took it very seriously; subsequently, for reasons of time and expense, neither princes nor emperor were often present in person and some estates essentially refused to represent themselves at all.

The princes' suspicion of each other and of the emperor was also much to the liking of foreign powers, especially France, which continually played on the estates' fear of imperial domination for their own purposes. For some years after 1648, fear of renewed war made this easy. As early as 1654, Elector Johann Philipp of Mainz had brought together a group of Rhenish princes in a league (later expanded to include others) designed to protect the Empire from war, above all by dissuading Ferdinand III from assisting Spain in the last years of its desperate struggle with France. Cardinal Mazarin not only encouraged the league, but eventually even joined it as its 'protector' in 1658. He also tried to manipulate the election of a French or Bavarian successor to Ferdinand, who died in 1657; and while he was unable to prevent the succession of Ferdinand's second son Leopold in 1658, his hand (and money) was evident in the promise forced from Leopold by the electors not to give help to Spain. These examples illustrate the real meaning of the Peace of Westphalia for Germany's place in the international power politics of the next hundred years. Each of the major powers involved in the war, unable to establish hegemony over Germany for itself, could at least agree to create a balance of power which denied it to the others. The idea of such a balance was much discussed at Westphalia and influenced not only the specific clauses of the peace but also the way Germany was henceforth to be thought of within the European community, to wit, as a vast and populous area which *as a whole* was not only to be kept essentially non-aligned with respect to its great-power neighbours (including, so far as possible, the Austrian

Habsburgs), but also inert within itself – a mass to be acted upon, perhaps, but not to be an actor itself. The most basic condition of this passive role was the preservation of disunity between emperor and estates, as well as between the estates themselves. Thus, the political fragmentation so consequential for the entire course of German history in the early modern period, already anchored in the self-interest of the territorial princes, was now both consecrated and institutionalized as a mandate of the international system. The Peace of Westphalia, it is well to remember, instantly became not only part of the fundamental law of the Empire, but a very important component of European international law as well.[2] The peace did indeed inaugurate a new international order; but it was a dubious benefit for the Germans that their country was introduced into that order in a role which, while virtually assuring that it would not be dominated by any single foreign state, also guaranteed that it would become a perpetual battlefield for the interests of non-German powers and helped to prevent it from elaborating a common national interest of its own.

The destructiveness of this great war in demographic and economic terms has been the subject of a long and often heated debate among historians. The steady accumulation of local and regional studies over the years has virtually eliminated the grossly exaggerated guesswork of the old 'catastrophist' school (best represented by the nineteenth-century historian Gustav Freytag) whose estimates of population losses ran as high as 75 per cent; but it has also called into question a number of reactive works in which losses were set at 10 per cent or less. Far more such studies will be needed before a confidently close approximation can be given. Furthermore, a permanent qualification on research into this problem is the fact that while contemporary officials, clerics and others were very conscientious record keepers, the primitive state of statistical science, as well as the random destruction of records, during the war or since, simply does not and perhaps never will permit the kind of accuracy on both detailed and broad scales that historians would like.

Recent German historians, on the whole, have tended to set overall losses distinctly higher than their foreign counterparts: the former vary their estimates of rural population decline from 40–50 per cent and of urban losses from 30–33 per cent, with a combined

---

2. Even the absolute rejection of the peace by the papacy, largely on religious grounds, did nothing to change its normative significance for the future.

total of perhaps 35–40 per cent, while the most recent English-language treatment of the whole war sets its averaged total of all losses at 15–20 per cent.[3] The issue is further complicated by two circumstances: first, that a significant number of people – perhaps more than a million – were more or less permanently on the move looking for better conditions; and second, that figures everywhere changed both up and down during the war itself and in particular may not have reflected large temporary gains from refugees, whose numbers might then have to be subtracted from final losses. Historians agree much better on the regional variation of demographic decrement. Much of northwestern Germany was spared destruction, as were the Alpine lands, while eastern, northeastern and central Germany were hard hit; much of southern and southwestern Germany – except for the Palatinate – escaped devastation until fairly late in the war, but then suffered terribly and repeatedly. There were, beyond doubt, individual towns and even territories which lost as much as 90 per cent of their population at some time in the war and others whose population actually increased.

In economic terms, while no historian has argued that the war had anything but a woeful effect on Germany as a whole, a debate has raged over whether the war alone caused an economic downturn, or whether it merely exacerbated a decline already in evidence by 1618 (or perhaps was even partly caused by such a decline). The weight of scholarly opinion now clearly inclines to the latter view which, by placing Germany in a wider European context, emphasizes the early seventeenth century as a period of transition between the long-term economic expansion of the sixteenth century and the more recessionary environment of the seventeenth. Chapter One has already shown that economic signs in Germany around 1600 were at best mixed; and the monetary crisis of the 'Kipper and Wipper' years was hardly helpful. Still, the war was by any standard a genuine economic disaster. It destroyed incalculable amounts of fixed capital – buildings and manufactured means of production – destroyed or displaced a very significant percentage of the labour force and disrupted both domestic and foreign market connections which proved difficult or impossible to recreate or replace. The new local

---

3. Of the German estimates, see in particular Lutz, *Das Ringen*, p. 421; Jeserich *et al.*, *Deutsche Verwaltungsgeschichte*, I, 218; and Rudolf Vierhaus, *Staaten und Stände. Vom Westfälischen Frieden bis zum Hubertusburger Frieden, 1648 bis 1763* [Propyläen Geschichte Deutschlands, vol. V] (Berlin, 1984), p. 60. In English, Parker, *The Thirty Years' War*, p. 211.

prosperity which accrued to a few cities by virtue of their fortunate geographical position in wartime did not represent a net national gain; neither did the booming agriculture of the northwest or the small increases in productivity which occurred here and there as landlords or war profiteers either absorbed or bought up deserted peasant holdings and consolidated them into entrepreneurially-farmed estates. Land, of course, cannot be destroyed; but its return to an arable condition after years of neglect, especially by a decimated farming population, was not a rapid process. Neither was the rebuilding of herds of livestock and collections of other farm animals which had all but disappeared from numerous areas during the war.

Some less direct results of the war on economic life proved to be no less troublesome than its physical destructiveness. A sharp increase in municipal indebtedness – much of it due to 'contributions' – plagued many urban budgets for years and added its influence to that of the overall collapse of business activity in town and countryside as a cause for a drastic reduction in tax revenues which for a long time crippled the fiscal strength of government at all levels. It was a lesser but still bothersome problem for the fiscal system that good coins and precious metals had been removed from Germany throughout the war by the foreigners who fought on its soil, while much of what remained was hoarded. Far harder to evaluate than these problems, which are at least to some degree statistically demonstrable, was the generally depressive effect exercised by the decline of the work ethic and of labour discipline; the repeated destructions of the war created a hopelessness and loss of confidence in the future among many people which resulted in both shiftlessness and a *carpe diem* attitude which discouraged productivity as well as investment.

That the widespread existence of this mentality can be confirmed chiefly only by the impressionistic evidence of contemporary observers again underscores the difficulty of reaching accurate estimates of war damage. Both the highly exaggerated descriptive language so characteristic of the time and the fact that the self-interest of various individuals and groups dictated overstatement of their losses makes absolute reliance on verbal evidence from the period unwise. At the same time, however and regardless of the actual extent of the war's destructiveness, there are few grounds to doubt that contemporary chroniclers and their posterity both immediate and distant *believed* the war to have been a nearly unqualified catastrophe. That is a fact of capital importance: since people after all act not on what is objectively true, but on what they believe to be true, Germans' impressions of the war as a national disaster profoundly affected the way they thought and behaved for a very long time after the conclusion of peace. The Thirty Years War was therefore as important to Germany's future development as a mental construct as it was for any of the physical changes it wrought. This will be greatly evident in the sequel, beginning with the triumph of princely absolutism in the territories of the Empire.

CHAPTER EIGHT
The Development of Territorial Autocracy, I

Probably no piety in the historiography of Germany is more commonly encountered than that which describes the century and a half following the Peace of Westphalia as the period of the development and heyday of princely autocracy in the German territorial states; here as elsewhere in Europe, in other words, it was 'the age of absolutism'. Actually, there is nothing very wrong with this view, which as a generalization is acceptable as long as two important qualifications are kept in mind: first, that 'absolutism' itself is a term of convenience and a somewhat slippery one, whose precise meaning varied greatly in the concrete circumstances of even those territories where it can be applied more or less correctly; and second, that absolutism did not develop in all German territories and that where it did its growth was often uneven and sometimes self-contradictory.

The term 'absolutism' itself derives ultimately from a principle of Roman Law which asserted that the right and power to make and execute law rested solely and absolutely with the prince and that no individual, group or agency external or internal to his jurisdiction had a legal claim to interfere with or call him to account for this supreme legislative and executive entitlement. This principle ran directly counter to the spirit and practice of medieval customary law, which sanctioned the diffusion or dispersal of the power of laws and therefore also of political power, among various personages and corporations in rough accordance with their differing ranks in medieval society. Roman Law refused to admit such actual sharing of power, though it could approve its delegation by the ruler. Recent scholarship argues that this and other doctrines of Roman Law were never 'received' or adopted wholesale as a distinct body of jurisprudence in Germany, designed to take the place of the old law, but crept into piecemeal usage, here and there, over a long period of time beginning in the later middle ages[1]; they exercised their influence both through the procedures and verdicts of the law courts and through the administrative practice of the many individuals who had studied Roman Law at Italian universities and who were later hired as advisers and officials by the territorial princes. Led by the chancellors who supervised the governing machinery of the princes, these civil servants gradually increased the degree of monocratic authoritarianism which characterized both policy initiatives and the daily practice of administration. Still, it cannot be argued that Roman Law, in itself, was much more than a helpful adjunct to the growing authority of territorial princes within their own lands. It was nowhere put fully into place as a coherent code and in fact even its influence was often publicly disavowed by princes and their officials and for two reasons: first, their influential subjects, knowing its tendencies, almost universally despised Roman Law as a loathsome 'innovation'; and second, the princes' own *Landeshoheit*, far from receiving legitimization from Roman Law, was endangered by it, since by any strict interpretation it would confer supreme authority over the entire Empire on the emperor, not on his vassals in the territories.

The evolution of territorial absolutism in Germany, like that of *Landeshoheit* itself, was a long and by no means uninterrupted process; the Peace of Westphalia was only one milestone in a path which started with the breakdown of imperial supremacy in the thirteenth century and, more recently, had led through the shattering ordeals of Reformation and Counter-Reformation. Beyond doubt, the vast increase in supervisory power over territorial ecclesiastical establishments which accrued to both Protestant and Catholic princes as a result of the religious conflict and of the agreements which arose from it tended to strengthen their authority over society as a whole. But this factor should not be exaggerated, since this new empowerment had to be used very carefully: not only was religion a most sensitive matter in all classes of the population, but also the material

1.   Since its establishment in 1495, however, the Imperial Cameral Tribunal had formally recognized Roman Law as part of the common jurisprudence of the Empire and this became a chief cause of its penetration into the territories. Fritz Hartung, *Deutsche Verfassungsgeschichte vom 15. Jahrhundert bis zum Gegenwart*, 7th edition (Stuttgart, 1959), pp. 42, 66.

gains of princely governments (as in the case of the confiscations and alienations of church property by Protestants) were often watched over by the territorial estates as a sort of public trust and were therefore not as subject to free disposition by the princes as has sometimes been supposed. As with Roman Law, therefore, heightened control of territorial churches was but another piece in the complex mosaic of what, in practice, came to be known as absolutism.

A much more important part of the story of the development of territorial autocracy involves the decline of those institutions and agencies which historically had acted as restraints on the power of territorial princes. Of these, the most important external ones were those contained in the imperial constitution insofar as they represented a sovereign authority superior to that of the estates of the Empire themselves. By 1648 that authority had been badly eroded by generations of autonomous practice in the territories, a trend greatly assisted by the ferocious religious quarrelling of the sixteenth century and intensified by the Thirty Years War. The recognition of territorial *Landeshoheit* in the Peace of Westphalia did not, theoretically, absolve the estates from their general obligations to emperor or Empire; but since neither this peace nor any subsequent imperial instrument made any attempt to reaffirm or codify those obligations in specific terms, the estates were left with a broad dispensation to define them for themselves. Naturally enough, they chose to define them in ways which restricted their territorial autonomy as little as possible. The emperor, to be sure, either through the Aulic Council or by himself by virtue of certain prerogative powers, could still confer favours and on occasion prove useful to various princes in the pursuit of their own goals. Consequently, there was a general predisposition throughout the Empire to maintain cordial relations, or at least correct ones, with the imperial court and this was especially true of most of the ecclesiastical and smaller secular princes, as well as the Imperial Knights, Counts and Cities, which for good reason had begun to see in the emperor a protector against the growing ambitions of some of the larger secular estates once the latter, after 1648, had added territorial acquisitions from their lesser neighbours to their list of possible objectives for the future. But while Vienna could and often did request and receive favours in return for its own, this never constituted a generalized subordination of territorial policies to those of the emperor. The large territories, in particular, continued to nurture their long-standing grievances against the Habsburgs and to deal with them as they would with an altogether foreign power. Thus, by virtue of the steadily increasing constitutional restrictions formally placed on his office, as well as of the watchfulness of both the territorial princes and of foreign powers, the emperor after 1648 was largely denied influence on the internal development of the territories.

Having long since decided that the emperor's intervention in their internal affairs was undesirable, the German princes proved no more hospitable to the notion that other imperial institutions such as the diet or the supreme courts should interfere with their virtual sovereignty. There was never any thought of abolishing the diet, of course, because it was useful as a check on the emperor – which was the original reason why it became the 'Eternal Diet' in 1663 – as well as a convenient diplomatic assembly for mutual watchfulness and the exchange of views among the estates. And it could be employed, if very rarely so, to pass legislation which anchored more firmly or actually expanded the powers of territorial lordship and which was therefore acceptable to the majority of princes. A good example arose in the Regensburg diet of 1653–4, which was originally convoked to iron out various problems of imperial obligations left undefined at Westphalia. It did precious little of that, but one article of the so-called 'Latest Recess' which emerged from the meeting confirmed the right of territorial rulers to demand from their subjects funds to maintain existing fortresses and to provide adequate garrisons for them. While most princes currently possessed such funds on the basis of temporary grants from their territorial estates, the new law removed some of the discretionary power of military finance from those estates, making possible the establishment of permanent or standing armies under the direct control of the princes – armies whose size, furthermore, was to be left largely to the judgment of the princes, not their estates.

At the same Regensburg diet, however, whatever final chance there was that the Empire as a whole might establish an even minimal fiscal footing for the achievement of common purposes was scotched by Brandenburg's successful opposition to the emperor's proposal that all estates be held responsible for payment of such imperial taxes as might be voted by a majority of the diet. There were a handful of other matters in the century and a half following Westphalia on which agreement based on common advantage was possible and which resulted in imperial laws: a revision of the structure of imperial military defence in 1681 and ordinances of 1731 and 1772 relating to territorial supervision of the crafts guilds throughout the Empire are the two most commonly cited examples. But they are also almost the only examples; for the rest of it, the diet was not allowed to function as a real legislative body at all and the already exquisite checks and balances built into its organization and procedure in and before 1648 were still more finely tuned thereafter, resulting in an immobility which nicely suited the interests of the larger and more powerful estates.

The supreme courts of the Empire presented a slightly different problem. Even the major princes recognized the utility of an imperial judicial system for adjudicating quarrels between the lesser estates, the Imperial Knights, private subjects of different territorial rulers and so on; they even roused themselves occasionally to reform the organization or procedures of the courts to increase their efficiency. But they wanted no interference from that system in their relationships with other princes or, above all, with their own subjects. They avoided contact with the Aulic Council, in particular, because of its close ties with the emperor, but were nearly as shy of the Cameral Tribunal, before which, in theory, they or their representatives could be dragged on complaint from a number of sources. In the event of an unfavourable judgment with which they refused to comply, they could be coerced by the head ('captain') and other estates of the Circle to which they belonged. In fact, however, this enforcement procedure depended entirely on the discretion of the princes involved, who usually proved unwilling to attempt forceful measures against fellow estates, especially those of any size. But matters often never got this far anyway, since litigation before the Cameral Tribunal took forever and its backlog of cases was so enormous as virtually to guarantee that except in rare instances no defendant was likely to see any case in which he was involved settled in his lifetime, or even that of his immediate heirs – during which time, furthermore, the plaintiff and his heirs might have died or the object of litigation have been forgotten. Finally, some of the potentially undesirable effects of any supraterritorial judicial inter-vention could be avoided altogether by acquiring the privileges of *non appellando* and *non evocando* from the emperor, who dispensed them as favours for services rendered to many of the larger estates after 1648; together, these privileges in effect sealed off the territorial judicial systems from contact with the imperial courts, thus assuring princes of an almost complete control of judicial processes in which their own subjects were involved.

While it is not correct to say that the imperial nexus had no restraining influence whatsoever on the development of autocratic government in the territories – especially in the smaller ones, including the Imperial Cities, the ecclesiastical principalities and the enclaves of the Imperial Knights and Counts – it is clear enough that any notion of genuine subordination to emperor or Empire had an increasingly imperceptible effect on the internal policies of the princes. In fact, even the theory of the political and constitutional nature of the Empire and of the imperial bond was changing to reflect the trend towards the greater autonomy of the territorial lords. The old concept of the Empire as an unalloyed monarchy continued to be preached in some quarters almost until its dissolution in 1806, though with increasingly less conviction as the realities of German political life eroded the relevance of the neat Aristotelian categories on which that concept was based. In his widely read *De Statu Imperii Germanici* of 1667, the philosopher Samuel Pufendorf (1632–94), writing under the pseudonym of Severinus de Monzambano, dismissed the applicability of such categories to the present reality of the Empire and characterized its form of government, which was neither monarchical nor federative, as something of a monstrosity. Thereafter, only a stubborn self-deception (or self-interest) could permit the embrace of any but some sort of theory of mixed government with, if anything, a tendency towards a stronger emphasis on the confederational elements of the constitution, which Pufendorf himself had seen as increasingly important. One variation of the latter construct which was especially important in both Calvinist and some Lutheran circles represented the Empire as a kind of aristocratic republic. It was expressed in its most truculent (though not most sophisticated) form in the 1650s by the Pomeranian Lutheran nobleman Bogislav Philipp Chemnitz, writing pseudonymously as 'Hippolytus a Lapide'. His angry demand for the removal of the Habsburgs from the imperial office as usurpers and betrayers of their trust reveals the fundamental nature of this whole species of argument as one which cast the emperor in the role of a servant of the princes, not their overlord. Theory was therefore slowly brought more closely into conformity with practice in confirming for the princes a steadily increasing freedom from external, imperial constraints.

More serious as an obstacle to the elaboration of autocratic government in the territories than any external interference was the internal problem posed by the existence of the territorial estates (*Landstände*). Such estates existed in almost all lands of the Empire except the smallest, but even by 1600 there was no absolute uniformity in their composition. Traditionally, they were composed of the three 'orders' to which medieval theory and practice had reduced the social structure: the clergy, the nobility and the commons, all of which sent representatives to the territorial diets (*Landtage*) to advise and assist the prince at his request. By 1600, however, the Reformation had all but eliminated the clergy as a separate estate in most Protestant territories, while in many Catholic states the clergy was so closely tied to the civil authority that it could hardly be spoken of as an independent corporation. In a few places – Württemberg is the best example – representation was almost wholly restricted to the towns and cities because the old territorial nobles had succeeded in elevating themselves to imperial knighthood, thus removing themselves and their lands from territorial jurisdiction. In some other territories, the relative weight of towns and nobility in diets was roughly equal, but in a much larger number the influence of the nobility vastly overshadowed that of the urban representatives.[2]

The power exercised by the territorial estates through their plenary diets or committees thereof derived almost entirely from the long tradition that any funds necessary to the prince's government beyond those realized from the revenues of his own domain lands and from a handful of prerogative rights had to be voted by the estates. The prince had no power of general taxation, in other words and when his needs – for war or other emergencies, or to cover debts arising from these or other causes – exceeded his ordinary income, he was forced to ask his estates for grants, or 'contributions', as they were known. By tradition, again, it was generally acknowledged that he had a right to assistance in justifiable cases (usually even when debts from dubious sources such as gambling were involved); but the conditions insisted on by the estates as the price of their grants were often very extensive and could intrude into almost every aspect of the ruler's policy and administration. Almost invariably, the estates called for oral or written reconfirmation of their traditional rights and privileges, including that of voting grants and frequently demanded explanation and defence of whatever policy required the extra funds, how they would be spent and so on. They sometimes insisted on reviewing overall territorial expenditures and frequently recommended reductions in the prince's personal spending. Most important of all, perhaps, they normally set time limits on their grants and, since these were nothing other than taxes on themselves,

2. The peasantry was directly represented in only a few relatively unimportant places, but it was sometimes said to be 'virtually' represented by noble landlords.

they also created and firmly controlled the administrative apparatus necessary to distribute and collect the assessments.

As might be expected, rulers and their estates quarrelled frequently over money; and since money was the basis of power, conflict over the raising and expenditure of tax monies really carried within it the permanent constitutional question of the extent of the sovereign powers of the ruler. Nevertheless, it is not correct to speak of a competition for sovereignty between princes and estates; the latter, to be sure, insisted very stubbornly on certain reserved rights, but they never claimed to share the sovereign powers of state. In the handful of cases where they actually took part in the policy-making process, it was under highly unusual conditions such as unexpected minorities or, as in the case of Mecklenburg, where quarrelling within the ruling house, division of the duchy, the violent actions of the dukes and, finally, the presence of foreign troops led to a rare intervention and execution of imperial agencies which sought the active participation of the estates to restore stability to the government. Oriented almost entirely towards the defence of their traditional privileges and interests, the estates were in no sense politically power-hungry and were in any case incapable of exercising such power on any broad basis since the administrative personnel and institutions they controlled were few, local, uncoordinated and possessed of narrowly circumscribed functions. They recognized that government, as such, was the right and duty of the prince; and apart from the fact that this established a powerful and important presumption in favour of the growth of princely authority as the scope of governmental responsibilities increased, it also resulted in a generally responsive attitude towards requests to fund the legitimate expenses of government. Complaints were frequent, especially during the Thirty Years War with its unheard-of expenditures; but then, as later, a spirit of cooperation between princes and estates was more characteristic than mutual recrimination and the estates' grievances were more often directed against the necessity which forced the prince to request money than against the prince himself.

The princes, for their part, also generally adopted a spirit of conciliation with their estates; it not only lent stability to the internal affairs of their territories but also reduced appeals of aggrieved estates to the imperial law courts and especially to the Aulic Council, which often looked sympathetically on such complaints and rapped the knuckles of the princes with judgments which the latter might often safely ignore, but which resulted in a bad public press that was to be avoided where possible. A further reason for princes to preserve cooperation was that for much of the early modern period they depended heavily on certain services performed by functionaries of the estates in both urban and rural areas: maintaining town and manorial courts of law, performing various police functions, sometimes recruiting troops and, of course, assessing and collecting 'contributions'. This was, in a sense, a bureaucracy parallel to the prince's own, performing duties which his own as yet under-developed administration could not. It was not an efficient system, to be sure; even in a place such as Bavaria, where the estates had been totally neutralized since before 1618 and where no diet met after 1669, their administrative organs continued to function under the supervision of the elector, alongside his own, resulting in an appalling mismanagement of finances far into the eighteenth century. Most rulers recognized the inadequacies of this dual system and many were eventually successful in eliminating it; but all, for a time, had to accept it as a necessary part of a still primitive governmental apparatus.

A final encouragement to a basic harmony between rulers and estates was the similarity of economic interests between the former and the noble landowners who mostly dominated the territorial diets and their committees. For much of this period, the prince was, among other things, the largest owner of landed estates in his territory, who benefited or suffered from the same agrarian factors and conditions which governed the fortunes of the noble families and who could sympathize with their problems in managing the human and other resources of their estates. Thus, while a certain amount of disagreement and confrontation was inevitably present in their relationship, princes and estates approached each other more often as partners in a common enterprise than as natural antagonists; the few widely publicized cases in which their conflict was profound and protracted – as in Mecklenburg and Württemberg (where, in both cases, the estates were victorious) – should not be allowed to obscure the more general pattern of mutual deference.

Still, there can be no doubt that by the middle and late eighteenth century the estates had become less assertive, vigorous and visible in many German territories than in most of the previous century, while in the same period the impulses which animated internal political life emanated more and more exclusively from the princely court and its civil and military administration. The retreat of the estates to a less active role in public life was a gradual process which was continuously nudged along by the determination of the princes to be less dependent for their funds on the changing moods and demands of their estates. It was seldom accompanied by the actual employment of armed force by the princes, though the very availability of such force was a powerful argument against excessively obdurate resistance. That it was available says much about the dilemma faced by the estates in many territories. Some of the most bitter quarrelling between them and their princes came over requests for money to establish standing armies; these, as opposed to mere guards companies, had hardly existed in many places before the Thirty Years War and territorial diets after 1648 were very alert to the self-endangerment which could arise from delivering a permanent military establishment into the hands of the ruler. But in the climate of the post-war Empire they could hardly deny the arguments from military necessity so insistently urged upon them by the princes. Thus, while the latter did not always get an army of the size they wanted – at least not initially – they usually got one of sufficient strength to be perceived as an effective instrument of domestic coercion. That such forces could be maintained and even increased in the face of episodes of resistance from the estates was due not only to an increase in governmental revenues from other sources as the economic crisis of the immediate post-war years was gradually overcome, but often also to subsidies paid directly to princes by foreign powers as inducements to friendship.

One great weakness of the estates in any attempt to preserve a significant advisory and supervisory role in the territories was their failure to maintain a united front in the face of various factors which tended to divide them and which were exploited by the princes. This was most importantly evident in the willingness of the landowning nobility to sacrifice the economic interests and much of whatever remained of the self-governing character of the towns in return for assurances that their own economic interests and their traditional control of local affairs in rural areas would not be compromised. In some areas, to be sure and especially those where towns were numerous and vital, there was enough commonality of interest between urban burghers and landed nobles to resist princely efforts to 'divide and conquer'; but in many others, princes all but liberated themselves from the need to beg for extraordinary grants through the imposition of permanent (usually indirect) taxes which, because they were paid largely by the towns, were approved by diets dominated by the nobility. A certain divergence of interests and loyalties within one and the same estate tended to produce the same overall effect. Towns, for example, were often weakened by social and economic divisions among the burghers which made the relatively disadvantaged less hostile to schemes proposed from the outside which might shield them from the self-serving fiscal powers wielded by their own patrician elders – even if, as often happened, this occurred at the expense of the self-government of the town and resulted in higher overall taxes. The nobility, on the other hand, whose landed estates and other limited sources of income simply could not provide decent livings for families whose size grew with every generation, found a partial solution to this long-term problem by taking employment in the expanding civil service and military establishments of the princes. Over time, this had the double effect of redirecting some noble loyalties towards the prince while at the same time reinforcing the aristocratic character of his government; the former gave him allies against the rock-ribbed traditionalism of the oppositional nobility, while the latter made his administration more acceptable to the majority of the nobility because their kind was so well represented in it.

Thus, what evolved in the century after 1648 was a new relationship between prince and estates (at least the noble estates) representing cooperation on an entirely different basis from the old duality. The earlier estates had not really been 'subdued' or 'conquered'; those terms are simply inappropriate for what actually happened to them: a slow descent into irrelevance, with their own complicity.[3] That irrelevance was based not only on factors already discussed, but also on the growing isolation of the old estates from the rest of society, caused by their inability to escape their character as remnants of an anachronistic political order. Increasingly, their only business was a stubborn defence of a past defined by their own privileges; and because of that, they forfeited such claim as they had once had to represent the interests of society as a whole.[4] That claim was now being asserted with growing success and confidence by the princely regimes, whose steadily more comprehensive administrative intrusion into all areas of public life conferred both the appearance and the reality of a responsibility to the common weal – the good of

3. The growing tendency of princes not to call or consult with plenary diets is one evidence of this. Full diets (which the prince paid for) were not only costly, but were harder to manipulate than the much smaller committees which were empowered to act for the whole diet.
4. Appeals to the general welfare were common as part of the rhetoric of the estates' argumentation, but cannot always be taken very seriously – as too often happens, for example, throughout F. L. Carsten's otherwise very valuable study *Princes and Parliaments in Germany from the Fifteenth to the Eighteenth Century* (Oxford, 1959).

all.[5] The old estates, meanwhile, now all but politically neutralized by the same guarantees which protected their privileges, grumbled periodically as rulers added imaginative new devices to their fiscal arsenals and as old temporary taxes hardened into permanent ones; but they also voted their 'contributions' more or less on cue from their princes.

As this chapter has tried to show, the 'absolutism' which developed in the German territories in the early modern period was partly the result of the weakening of earlier institutional restraints on the power of the territorial princes represented, first, by the rapid decline of the supraterritorial or 'national' imperial government and second, by the eclipse of the political power and influence of the territorial estates. To be sure, neither the former nor the latter faded entirely from view even by the end of the eighteenth century. There were a few very important instances of imperial intervention in the affairs of the member states and a number of much less important ones; but, as noted earlier, these cases were sensational largely because they were so rare. There were also some large territories in which the estates played a quite significant role throughout the eighteenth century – sometimes in conjunction with imperial agencies; this was also true of many smaller ones, including especially the ecclesiastical principalities, where an active and harmonious cooperation between ruler and diet was encouraged by the modesty imposed on princely ambition and pretension by both the elective character of the ruler's office and the meagreness of territorial resources. But the overall picture was one of increasing powerlessness of both imperial institutions and territorial estates, with concomitant lessening of both external and internal restraints on the autocratic power of the princes.

Still, the relative absence of restraints on power does not in itself guarantee either that power will grow, or that it will be exercised effectively, much less in an 'absolute' fashion. For these to happen, the sphere of responsibility successfully claimed by power must expand and an apparatus through which power can flow from the centre throughout the entire body politic must be established. These are two halves of a single self-reinforcing cycle, which together

---

5. It was another part of the dilemma faced by the estates that their obligation to oppose governmental initiatives which were either really or ostensibly intended to promote the common good, but which also clearly violated past practice, often recoiled on them by simply adding to their reputation for selfishness. See Vierhaus, *Staaten und Stände*, p. 113.

eventually strengthened and institutionalized princely authority in what German historians are fond of calling the *Verwaltungsstaat* – the administrative state – whose proceeding realization was of great importance to the definition of absolutism in Germany in the seventeenth and eighteenth centuries.

CHAPTER NINE

The Development of
Territorial Autocracy, II

Even before 1600 a new conception of the political character of the
German territories had begun to solidify in the minds of the princes
and in the practices of their governments. The common medieval
notion that a prince's territory was essentially a personal and private
patrimony, an item of divisible or interchangeable inheritance, was
slowly giving way to a more sophisticated understanding of princely
office and territory as public trusts for whose perpetuation and well-
being the ruler was responsible to God. The heightened religiosity of
the era of Reformation and Counter-Reformation gave new depth
and intensity to this point of view. Vaguely but also strongly
connected to this developing understanding was a concept of
continuity of stewardship and of a responsibility to insure it, which
is evident from the fifteenth century onward in an increasing
acceptance of the principle that territories should be passed undivided
to an heir, whether direct or not – a principle encouraged by a
growing sense of territorial identification on the part of the estates.
As with many other changes in perspective, this one established itself
slowly; it was not absolutely firm even in the larger territories until
after 1600 and in some of the smaller ones not for more than a
century after that. But it gained ground steadily and as a conscious
choice.[1]

There also existed, from the late fifteenth century, an increasingly
strong desire at both imperial and territorial levels to rationalize and

---

1. Hartung, *Deutsche Verfassungsgeschichte*, pp. 63–4. It is interesting, in light of the
   later history of Germany, that the Great Elector Friedrich Wilhelm (1640–88) of
   Brandenburg-Prussia gave some thought to dividing even his realm at his death;
   but considering the dangers of its peculiar geography, that alternative may have
   had much to recommend it at the time.

issue sets of regulations and ordinances which would replace the myriad of existing local and partly unwritten codes which often varied considerably even within fairly small territories. Such codes embodied traditions unknown to the formally educated jurists who in growing numbers were occupying official positions in the princely courts, as well as at the Imperial Cameral Tribunal and whose Roman Law training had instilled a loathing for the disorderliness of medieval customary law in any case. The coincidence of their preferences with what seems to have been a genuine desire in much of society for more uniform bodies of law resulted in the issuance of the many territorial codes which characterized the later fifteenth and sixteenth centuries. Known in German as *Landesordnungen*, these codes, revised and reissued many times – well into the eighteenth century in many of the smaller territories – were not consciously intended to create anything new, but simply to reduce to order what already existed. Inevitably, however, that very process of reduction had two important consequences: first, in the name of uniformity it tended to prune back a number of the special freedoms and privileged practices of a number of social corporations (including the estates) which were seen as complicating variations from a simpler and more practical norm; and second, the assumption of responsibility for codification and promulgation of the new codes lent new visibility and prestige to the prince's government as well as a strengthened precedent for its future claim to unique legislative authority.

Accompanying these attempts at a regularization of legal norms was a deliberate effort to give greater steadiness to the administrative processes by which law was made operative. This was at least partly a response to numerous complaints in the sixteenth century about abuses and deficiencies stemming from the highly personalized, capricious and often self-serving administration of the untrained officials who staffed the late medieval princely household. The notable increase in population of the sixteenth century was no doubt one reason for these complaints, as was the rapidly expanding economy with its accompanying inflation and disturbance of the traditional socio-economic balances, since both contributed to a greater regulatory and intercessory role for government. Thus, a growing desire for greater continuity and dependability in the performance of public services joined with the movement towards codification to produce a transition towards a new kind of state in which normative regulation, emanating more and more exclusively from the princely government, was supplanting the multiple and variable legal standards and sources of authority of the medieval territory.[2]

The Reformation also contributed its share to enlarge the scope of public authority claimed by the princes. This was particularly true of the Protestant territories, where the assumption of supreme episcopal authority by rulers delivered greatly expanded powers and duties in religious affairs into the hands of their governments, including clerical training and discipline, supervision and disposition of church property, ecclesiastical police jurisdiction and even guardianship and control of doctrine and liturgy. And although Catholic princes did not have episcopal powers, many of them exercised supervisory and disciplinary functions which approached (and in the case of some, such as Bavaria, even exceeded) codetermination with the bishops – often with the approval of the popes, who were willing to recognize a greater role for the secular authority as an indispensable condition for victory in the struggles of the Counter-Reformation. In almost all Protestant territories, special administrative bodies (called 'consistories' or simply 'church councils') were established to monitor and govern the activities of the church. In territories of at least medium size, these bodies soon developed subordinate agencies at provincial or local levels and were sometimes joined by a 'synod' charged with examining the reports of church visitations carried out in local areas. Not a few Catholic states adopted a similar system: Bavaria, whose bold intervention in ecclesiastical affairs made an important contribution to the early development of an absolutist regime there, established a 'Spiritual Council' in 1570, which was copied by other territories later.

After 1648, regulation and control of territorial churches by governments, especially Protestant ones, became more complete than ever before and by the mid-eighteenth century in a number of places the old original consistories had been replaced by 'Supreme Consistories' – more politicized agencies designed to coordinate ecclesiastical policy more closely with the overall objectives of the state as determined by the ruler. This new kind of political regimen for the churches was encouraged by conversions of rulers to a faith different from that already established as 'official' in their territories. When the elector of Brandenburg converted to Calvinism in 1613 and agreed to give up his right of reformation for his Lutheran territories, he set a pattern which was followed later in the century in

2. Jeserich *et al.*, *Deutsche Verwaltungsgeschichte*, I, 297.

the Palatinate, Saxony and elsewhere. Retention of episcopal authority over a territorial church which was no longer the prince's own made no sense; but since after 1648 the new understanding of *Landeshoheit* included sovereign powers for the ordering of all areas of social life, confessional uniformity was no longer important and much of the authority inherent in episcopacy was simply transferred to the prince as head of state, who in that capacity supervised the public affairs of all religions.[3] Eventually, therefore, the genuine sense of religious trusteeship with which many princes had originally approached and accepted responsibility for governing the visible church gradually gave way to a more secular and political view of the ecclesiastical establishment as but another, if different, administrative agency in the service of the princely state. In the meantime, of course, the various social disciplinary duties which had been transferred from church to state, including some which touched conscience itself, had added their bit to that relatively unchallenged *Landeshoheit* that was German absolutism.

Even before the Reformation, however, a first major response to the need for greater steadiness and expertise in administration had materialized in the form of the Court Council (*Hofrat*), a body from which nearly all later administrative development proceeded. Created in almost all territories of any size by shortly before or after 1500, this council was staffed by formally educated jurists (many of non-native bourgeois origin); few if any of the old officers of the household had any connection with it and, just as important, it was a permanent body which met regularly according to a set schedule. To the advantages of professional competence and regularity of activity was added that of the council's independence from the territorial nobility – a matter of no small significance, since a major part of its business was judicial in nature and frequently involved nobles as litigants or petitioners. Since the latter had often received preferred treatment from their own kind among the household officials, it is hardly surprising that the estates frequently grumbled about this new institution and its complement of non-native, non-noble personnel – though mostly to no avail. Originally, the competence of the council extended to every aspect of the prince's territorial government, including not only justice and supervision of finances and the internal administration, but also war and foreign affairs. This represented an agenda so full as to preclude regular attendance by the prince

3. Ibid., 361–9.

himself, who, while always reserving the formal presidency to himself, therefore appointed a chairman, or chancellor, to supervise the conduct of business.

In some small territories, the work load of the council was sufficiently modest to permit this arrangement to continue essentially unaltered into the eighteenth century, with only some division of labour among the councillors for specialized aspects of administration; but in the larger territories it soon became apparent that a single council, meeting collegially, could not cope with the steadily increasing burden of duties. One of the first modifications of the simple conciliar model, arrived at in an awareness of the unusually time-consuming nature of the judicial functions of the council, was to separate those functions from its other responsibilities. This was done either by deputing a group of councillors for this purpose alone, or – which had the same result – by creating an entirely new agency, usually known as the Court Tribunal (*Hofgericht*). Only slightly later – from the late sixteenth into the early seventeenth century – this specialization of labour was further institutionalized by the creation of a Privy Council (*Geheimer Rat*). This originated as a group of councillors chosen for their loyalty or special expertise from the membership of the Court Council or the Chamber (which will be discussed below) to confer informally with the prince on matters of special interest or importance to him and which he did not wish to have discussed in the larger forum of the other councils. Both his personal finances and his foreign policy – often related and both concerned with dynastic business – were of this kind and over time the Privy Council (or its equivalent) in many territories came to be more and more exclusively preoccupied with foreign affairs and other concerns of high policy; and while the initially rather personal relationship between prince and Privy Councillors tended to give way to a more objectivized or bureaucratic one, whatever functions the Privy Council may have had as both an advisory and administrative body were gradually narrowed to exclude most of the latter. In some territories, the Privy Council eventually replaced the Court Council altogether and by the early eighteenth century had often grown very large; this sometimes led not only to a redesignation as Cabinet (or Privy) Conference, but also to a separation of the membership into two groups: a larger one whose members kept their titles, but who did little work of any importance and who met mostly on ceremonial occasions only; and a smaller one whose personnel were dubbed Real Privy Councillors to distinguish their working positions from the honorific ones of their colleagues.

It is clear from the table of ranks established by most territorial governments that the Privy Councillors as individuals and as a group had a position superior to that of other officials of the central government. Yet their work was hardly more important than that of the Court Chamber (*Hofkammer*, often called simply Chamber), which because of its economic and fiscal responsibilities was the real nerve centre of all the German territorial governments. Like the Privy Council, the Chamber evolved from the older Court Council as a sort of subcommittee charged with checking the books of the so-called *Rentei*, a combined treasury and accounting office which received the prince's revenues and paid his bills. This responsibility for verifying receipts and expenditures remained a very important one throughout the early modern period; but it was not long before these councillors also began to examine the sources of both revenues and expenditures, as well as the methods and costs of their administration. As the scope of their responsibilities widened, the size of their committee increased to the point where it made sense to separate it from the Court Council and to constitute it as an altogether separate agency: the Chamber. Eventually, the sheer volume and variety of its work became so great that it was necessary to modify the originally fully collegial organization of the Chamber by the delegation of certain tasks to individual specialists or to newly-created subcommittees functioning as departments or 'deputations'. Two tasks were important above all others: first, to preserve existing sources of princely wealth and wherever possible to increase their yield through better management, while cutting unnecessary costs; and second, to provide a reasonably accurate method of balancing revenues and expenditures and of projecting such balances into the future – in other words, to create balanced budgets. The latter task in particular, already difficult because of unreliable statistics and the unpredictability of many kinds of revenue (especially from agriculture), was made still harder by princes who contracted gambling and other debts that could not be foreseen and who in spite of their often good intentions could never quite bring themselves to subject their spending habits to the scrutiny and control of their own functionaries.

Because of the broad and increasing variety and importance of the matters it dealt with, the Chamber eventually became the largest and most significant single agency of the central government in all territories where it existed. Aside from a separate War Council (*Kriegsrat*), or its equivalent, which was common in the larger territories since before 1600, a very large percentage of the administrative bodies which came into being in the century and a half after 1648 were deputed or otherwise derived from the Chamber. In the sizeable states, subordinate agencies were frequently established in the provinces and even in the localities, though in Germany, as elsewhere in early modern Europe, already existing local agencies and officials were employed on a large scale to execute laws and regulations emanating from the centre. Nowhere was there a neat and complete chain of officials appointed directly by the princely government leading from local through provincial to central levels; government in this period was unthinkable without the cooptation of municipal magistracies, the urban guilds, the provincial estates and even the church, together with their associated commissions and instrumentalities.

The Chamber and its derivative organs also came to embody the essential practice of absolute government insofar as that consisted in social manipulation and control through a pervasive and intrusive legislation and administration of police functions and powers. The concept of 'police', as understood in early modern Germany, was vital to the development of absolutism and for two chief reasons. First, from the time of its appearance in the German language in the fifteenth century it carried with it the connotation of a responsibility for the establishment and preservation of civil peace and good order in society – goals which could suggest an almost infinitely expandable agenda of activity. Secondly, while the term was always understood to refer to the administration of justice, it was also a special kind of justice, which permitted the authorities to issue both prescriptive and proscriptive ordinances as binding legal maxims, to keep watch over their observance and to punish offences summarily, without either formal procedure or the possibility of appeal to the territorial courts. Before 1500, such police powers lay in the mostly independent hands of almost as many individuals or institutions as shared in the exercise of public authority in general: the magistracies of largely self-governing territorial cities, the church, the estates and even village communities. The gradual assumption by the prince of an increasingly exclusive responsibility for the issuance and observance of this regulative legislation was extremely significant not just because it increased his actual powers, but also because it legitimized the single most important theoretical component of *Landeshoheit*: the unique authority of the sovereign as lawgiver – which is also the fundamental premise of absolutism.

As the princes absorbed more and more of the obligations for insuring social discipline and order from the Empire[4], from the church and from the estates, they also began to add new ordinances which differed subtly but importantly from the old. Whereas traditional police legislation had aimed primarily at the prevention of change by locking into place relationships between individuals, groups and whole classes which over the years had evolved into a more or less peaceful social balance, the new regulation proceeded not from the premise of preserving the old by timely repairs and additions, but from that of improving the overall well-being of society by prescribing new rules of behaviour designed to serve the common good. For present purposes, the specific directions taken by this new kind of legislation are less important than the fact that it was predicated on a need for change – movement – which added a vastly larger scope of social responsibility and control to what had once been a much more limited wardship of society against dangers to its stability; in doing so, it also attacked the remnants of the minimalist view of the sovereign rights of the prince typical of an earlier and simpler time. At this point, however, from the early eighteenth century onward, the 'police state' of early absolutism began to take on something of a self-contradictory character; still committed to preservation of the essentials of a traditionalist social order within which it had grown up, it had also begun to innovate and reform certain aspects of society and economy in the name of a public good that transcended that traditionalist order in potentially revolutionary ways. Nowhere in Germany prior to the French Revolution did problems arising from this contradiction become serious enough either to alter significantly the social relationships of the old order or to weaken the political claims of absolute government; but attempts at accommodation and adjustment were necessary and form an interesting part of the political history of a number of territories in the later years of the eighteenth century.

As contemporaries became aware of the differences between the spirit of the two types of legislation referred to above, a distinction began to appear within what had previously been a single theoretical and descriptive literature devoted to both, which eventually resulted in a fairly clear division between 'Police Science' (*Polizeiwissenschaft*) and 'Cameral Science' (*Kameralwissenschaft*). The former, true to its origins, was henceforth largely restricted to the principles and

---

4. The imperial diet had passed a comprehensive set of police ordinances as early as 1530, but this legislation was of course drawn up by the princes, who were individually responsible for its implementation in their own territories. It also did not preclude additional territorial legislation.

practices of maintaining law and social order, as well as to prevention and removal of threats of any kind to public health and safety – which could include everything from street lighting to the purity of food and drink and maintenance of sewage systems to supervision of orphanages, workhouses and asylums. The new Cameral Science, on the other hand, while continuing to incorporate aspects of both old and new police theory, added to it both economic theory and a great deal of expertise in administrative practice and resource management, which eventuated in an enormous corpus of suggestions and recommendations designed to increase the overall wealth and prosperity of the princely territory. As such, it gave impulse and direction to the new ameliorative legislation which distinguished governments of the eighteenth century from their predecessors. Its name betrays its original purpose in the seventeenth century as an adjunct to the work of the *Kammer*, the Chamber, as the latter sought to increase the prince's 'own' revenues through discussion and analysis of the needs, expenses, income, accounting practices and administration of the princely household, the domainal possessions and regalian rights. The steady broadening of the Cameralists' purview to include virtually all productive activities instead of just those over which the prince had direct control was the result not only of an increasingly sophisticated understanding of sectoral interdependence within the economy, but also of the gradual enhancement of the prince's right of general taxation, which meant that the entire economy now had to be studied and improved as a means of increasing the overall tax base. And while the influence of the humanitarianism and philanthropism of the enlightenment no doubt injected some genuine concern for a general increase of human happiness into their thinking, the Cameralists never allowed the fiscal needs of the state to migrate very far from the centre of their considerations; almost all of them, after all, were salaried servants of the state, whether as officials and administrators or as professors.

Even the earliest Cameralists – the sometime Austrian and Bavarian official Johann Joachim Becher (1625–82), for example, or Veit Ludwig von Seckendorff (1626–92), who served as councillor to Duke Ernst 'the Pious' of Saxe-Weimar – operated from the premise that the territorial state was an essentially closed political, social and economic unit: a very important practical and theoretical reinforcement of the evolving reality of the *Landeshoheit* formally enunciated in the Peace of Westphalia. Not surprisingly for pioneers, they differed from later Cameralists in having rather modest agendas; and they mixed in a great deal more of the older and narrower police theory and practice with their economic and administrative recommendations than did later ones. They also thought, wrote and acted within an ethical framework strongly shaped by Old Testament precepts, according to which the prince should conduct his government as a firm but loving patriarch to whom power had been entrusted by God for the welfare of his people. This emphasis was quite pronounced in Seckendorff's *The German Princely State*, first published in 1655, whose great popularity resulted in several reprints in his own lifetime and as late as 1754; and the very title of his later work *The Christian State* (1685) reveals the persistent force of this moral view of the final purposes of statecraft. Furthermore, the influence of Christian ethics never disappeared entirely as an undercurrent even in much later Cameralist writings, in which frequent references to the prince as *Landesvater* (father of the country) betray the durability of the patriarchal notion of rulership – a notion long encouraged by a certain familiarity of social and political circumstances engendered by the small size of so many German territories.

Still, as the intensity of religious feelings created by the Reformation and the Thirty Years War diminished; as a few of the German states developed internally enough to play a role as second- or even first-rate powers on the European scene; and, finally, as the influence of the enlightenment began to secularize and politicize ethical thinking even in Germany, Cameralist doctrine lost much of its moral-philosophical content and developed into the 'science' of political economy, finance and police and their administration, that it had everywhere come to be called by not long after the beginning of the eighteenth century. By this time, furthermore, the mercantilist orientation of Cameralism had become quite pronounced. In contrast to an earlier time when regulation of the privately-owned sector of the economy was thought of almost exclusively in terms of its contribution to fairness and economic stability (stasis, even), social balance (frequently implying immobility) and the moral purity of the population, a much more comprehensive and active intervention and encouragement was now recommended and for a new purpose: to increase the economic and financial power of the state in the service of such interests as the prince might establish.

It is thus not incorrect to call Cameralism in its developed form the German brand of mercantilism, which was a European-wide movement of the seventeenth and eighteenth centuries; but it is also necessary to insist on its peculiarly German features, which include not only the unique combination and interdependence of various principles of political economy and finance with administrative theory based on observation and experience, but also the unusually heavy economic emphasis on the extractive industries (agriculture, forestry and mining) because of the commercial and industrial backwardness of the territorial cities and a general shortage of both governmental and private development capital. (There was no lack of interest in the encouragement of trade and manufactures, only a practical awareness that as things then stood a healthy and growing agrarian sector and especially agriculture, was a prerequisite for growth elsewhere in the economy.)

Cameralism was also somewhat different from mercantilism elsewhere because it was less a policy than an increasingly organized and refined body of specialized knowledge – at once 'a learned and practical science', as one of its better-known representatives put it in 1755.[5] As such, it could be and was made into a subject for academic study, first at colleges and academies specifically set up in various places for the training of officials and administrators and later also as a distinct discipline in several universities. In 1727, Friedrich Wilhelm I of Prussia established the first university chairs of Cameral Science at Frankfurt on the Oder and at Halle, where the foundations for such study had already been laid by the famous Christian Thomasius (1655–1728) in a series of earlier lectures on Seckendorff's writings. Thereafter, a number of other universities established their own chairs, which, together with the professorships of the special colleges referred to earlier, provided ample teaching possibilities for all of the more prolific Cameralists: J. B. von Rohr, J. C. Dithmar, G. H. Zincke and perhaps the best known of them all, J. H. G. von Justi (1720–71). Justi's career, which carried him to various formal and informal teaching and administrative positions in Austria, Mansfeld, Saxony, Hanover, Denmark, Hamburg and Prussia – among others – illustrates two important things about the better-known Cameralists: first, that virtually all combined hands-on administrative duties with their teaching and writing; and second, that the demand for their services became almost universal throughout Germany and considerable in northern and eastern Europe as well, resulting in a great deal of movement of individuals from one position to another. Partly by this means, furthermore, Cameralist doctrine and practice was gradually standardized (if also eventually somewhat ossified) and in this normalized form pervaded the entire German scene. Probably

5.   Quoted from Georg Heinrich Zincke's *Anfangsgründe der Cameralwissenschaft* (Leipzig, 1755) in Jeserich *et al.*, *Deutsche Verwaltungsgeschichte*, I, 414.

nowhere else in Europe was *Verwaltung* – administration – invested with the special dignity it possessed both then and now in the German-speaking world and which is traceable to its enshrinement as a scientific discipline by the scholarly and practical achievements of the eighteenth-century Cameralists.

As an increasingly accepted standard of expertise for those who either did or hoped to occupy governmental positions of any importance, furthermore, Cameralism represents a new stage in a long, if somewhat erratic, attempt on the part of the more serious-minded princes to inject more competence and a greater sense of professionalism into the growing ranks of their officials and administrators. At the beginning of the sixteenth century, when much of the business of the primitive princely governments at any level was directly or indirectly juridical in nature, familiarity with local law, customs and conditions, gained from experience and observation, was regarded as an essential qualification for officehold-ing. But as earlier shown, the widespread adoption of learned or formal procedure in the course of that century put a new premium on legal training as a prerequisite for office, leading eventually not only to a general requirement that proof of both formal study and some form of courtroom apprenticeship be presented, but also to the introduction of increasing numbers of non-natives as officials. From this time forward, the double notion that there was a desirable thing known as competence and that it was acquired by some sort of training rather than by birth or the possession of money, made steady though by no means uninterrupted progress.

The character of the prince himself, in a time when personality still meant more than laws or institutions, was a considerable influence on the rapidity and thoroughness with which professional standards penetrated the civil service in the territories. A steady and determined commitment to quality, especially over two or more generations, could have dramatic results, while insouciance and lethargy could prevent, or in some cases reverse, improvement in the levels of bureaucratic competence. A preference for persons of noble birth for positions of real responsibility did not always have to mean low levels of competence, as long as the nobles were chosen for talent – as was generally the case under Frederick II of Prussia, for example. Similarly, venality of office, which in one form or another existed in nearly all places at some time and at all times in some places, was a practice not necessarily productive of uniformly bad results – as long, again, as it was combined with the criterion of merit. But in both cases and even apart from the fact that merit was often disregarded, there lay the real danger of reinforcing the already strong tendency of the officeholder to regard himself as possessed of a private right to his office by virtue of birth, in the one instance, or purchase, in the other. This was a terrible obstacle to the development of the concepts of public law and public service – service to and under a public law – which is one of the earmarks of the modernized state.[6] In most territories where venality of office became institutionalized for any period of time, it was strictly because of the revenue it generated; there was a marked increase in its incidence in a number of places after the beginning of the seventeenth century, where princes' need for money, due to inflation, increased expenses of the court and the establishment of standing armies, had become chronic.[7] Dismissal of venal officeholders was difficult, of course, because to do so without refunding the purchase price of the office would discourage new entrants to the system. Another bane of a thoroughly professionalized civil service was the favouritism of the prince himself, or of his chief ministers – a fault arising partly from the very nature of monarchical government and one never completely overcome anywhere. Charlatans, pretty-boys and fast-talking confidence men cropped up periodically (if also mostly briefly) in important positions in various territorial governments; so also did sons and even the more distant posterity of earlier officeholders, though here it is important to recognise that such appointments often represented an appropriately recognized family tradition of loyal and competent service to the prince. Some other apparently whimsical prejudices of princes turn out, on closer examination, to have had a rational basis; thus, the propensity of Friedrich Wilhelm I of Prussia to hire retired soldiers to fill lower-level positions in his civil service not only solved the problem of how to look after them in retirement, but also took advantage of the invaluable habits of loyalty, discipline and hard work instilled in them by their military careers.

Still, many of the unprofessional practices mentioned above were

6. This obstacle was further reinforced by the custom, established early, of appointing officials without term – which usually meant for life. While in the modern civil service a somewhat similar security of tenure exists and is generally regarded as good, there is also a standard of sufficient performance connected with it which was often missing in this period. Dismissal was regarded by contemporaries as a serious punishment in itself, carrying connotations of disloyalty, dishonesty or gross malfeasance and consequently was seldom employed in cases of mere laziness or periodic inattention to duty. Jeserich *et al.*, *Deutsche Verwaltungsgeschichte*, I, 357–8.

7. Ibid., 355.

increasingly recognized as abuses inconsistent with efficient government and from the early eighteenth century onward various
measures were taken which, over time, noticeably strengthened the
professional capabilities of civil servants. The provision of new
arrangements for formal training, inside and outside of universities,
together with the growth and increasing systematization of the
cameral sciences, produced a steadily increasing pool of qualified
candidates, while examination systems for appointment and promotion were developed to weed out the grossly incompetent. Yet one is
inclined to agree with the recent judgment of a German historian that
even by the end of the eighteenth century these measures had not
produced bureaucracies in the modern sense of the term – even in the
one German state (Prussia) which most closely approximated that
standard. There was still too much that was accidental, fortuitous
and *personal* in the systems – too many individuals hired or advanced
for reasons having little to do with their qualifications for their jobs,
too many dismissed or passed over for promotion in spite of (or
because of) superior qualifications and performance. Most of the
earmarks of genuine bureaucratization did not exist: fixed standards
for employment and promotion and for pay scales; security of place
during good behaviour; a regularized system of old-age and
disability insurance; and so on.[8] There are, to be sure, evidences that
by the later eighteenth century a sense of professional corporatism
was growing in some of the larger and more developed administrative systems, carrying with it a sense of permanence for officials as
public servants of the state, rather than as adventitious personal
servitors of the princes. But while emergent, this sensibility was not
yet dominant and would become so only in the following century.

Regardless of the state of perfection it had attained even by the end
of the eighteenth century, the development of bureaucratic administration was essential to whatever degree of absolutism existed
in the various German states. It underlay the reality of the mature
'police state' which virtually all the territories had become, as well as
the *Machtstaat* – the state successfully cultivating sheer power – that
the largest of them had become. Paradoxically, however, the
developed administrative apparatus also eventually came to set

---

8. Vierhaus, *Staaten und Stände*, p. 125. Some aspects of a kind of 'social security' in the
form of disability and old-age pensions (often simply modest lump sum payments)
as well as provision for the care of widows and orphans did exist in some places; but
it was often irregular and, like so many other things, dependent on the good will of
individual princes. Jeserich *et al.*, *Deutsche Verwaltungsgeschichte*, I, 356–9.

certain limitations on absolutism insofar as the term includes the exercise of arbitrary powers. While the agencies of government at various levels were the instruments through which the will and power of the prince were effectuated, they inevitably subtly altered that will and diluted that power down through the chain of command, while the growing rationalization of administration through more and more complex regulations, codes of procedure and permanent bureaucratic 'job descriptions' actually limited the discretion of the prince by making him to some degree a hostage to his own desire for efficiency. On the other hand, that efficiency should not be exaggerated even in the best territorial administrations of the time; some were certainly greatly more efficient than others, but all rulers were aware of the limitations of their own administrative apparatus. There were many things they could reasonably expect it to accomplish, but there were as many or more that they could not and it could not. Primitive conditions of transportation and communication contributed to this, but so also did the personal foibles and the individual, family and class interests of the numerous officials themselves.

What this intends to suggest is that no German (or European) ruler, with the horrible but also extremely rare exception of some small and often insane princes who committed unspeakably vicious acts only to prove how absolute they were in their tiny territories, had the technical means to push beyond absolutism to real dictatorship, even if he had wanted to. Equally important is the fact that few wanted to. Contemporary usage distinguished sharply between absolutism (meaning the unique authority of the prince to legislate) and despotism (meaning the absence of all 'rights' and the actual ownership of all persons and property by the ruler). Absolutism, however complete, had grown up within a general western tradition which set both divine and natural law above the will of the ruler and in which duty and responsibility for the welfare of his people were inescapable parts of the prince's entitlement to rule. And while working for change, in the sense of the improvement of society, was increasingly accepted as a permissible responsibility of the prince (especially after the enlightenment began to urge it), no German prince was allowed to forget that the ancient and original mandate of his office was *conservation*. Tinkering around with well-intentioned schemes for economic or administrative improvements was one thing; any action resembling an attempt to alter the basic structures and habits of society was quite another and risked forfeiting that passive consent of at least the socially important

121

classes on which even the most absolute governments tacitly rested. All the German territories were *Ständestaaten* – 'societies of orders' – within which the location in the prince's government of a more and more exclusive responsibility for the direction of public affairs developed as a working solution for certain problems arising from the disintegration of an earlier system of political management. People in all walks of life could and did tolerate a great deal of police regulation and even regimentation as long as they could accept it as aimed at preserving justice and fairness, or at improving their prosperity and reinforced rather than threatened their security of place in a traditional social order. Even the actively reforming princes of the eighteenth century, the so-called 'enlightened despots', understood this and with the partial exception of Joseph II of Austria did not step much beyond the lines drawn by the fundamental nature of their own societies.

While the princely absolutism that existed in most of the German states did indeed conform to the basic definition of an unshared power of laws, it is therefore necessary to recognize that that did not imply an unlimited power to shape society to its will. That is a most important qualification on the meaning of absolutism and puts it in proper perspective as a significant vehicle in the process of modern state-building, but not one of social change; it could not be that because, in the end, it was always committed by virtue of its own origins, purposes and character to reaffirm its responsibility to preserve a social structure which was also the condition of its own survival.

CHAPTER TEN

The German Economy, 1650–1800: Population and Agriculture

Any overview of the development of the German economy from the middle of the seventeenth century to the end of the eighteenth century must begin by recognizing two important facts: first, that the regionally severe destructiveness and dislocations of the Thirty Years War created some uniquely acute problems for the German lands; but second, that the economic climate of the whole of Europe was not a very healthy one for most of the seventeenth century and not robust again until around and after the middle of the eighteenth century.[1] These facts mean not only that the badly depressed producer and consumer sectors of Germany helped to deepen the overall European recession, but also that that recession contributed its share to slow the progress of German post-war economic recovery. Over the longer term – until late in the eighteenth century – other factors also limited the progress that could be made beyond the point at which basic recovery was achieved. These included not only several prolonged periods of war from the later seventeenth century onward, but also the growing comparative advantage enjoyed by the maritime states of western Europe – Britain, France and Holland, especially – through their ability to exploit the increasingly important resources and markets of the overseas colonial world, as well as the mercantilist protectionism characteristic of these and other states, which closed their markets to many exports from a Germany more than ordinarily needful of them. Finally, of course, the political and territorial fragmentation of Germany itself, while

---

1. In addition to references cited in footnotes, material for this and the following chapter is taken from Heinrich Bechtel, *Wirtschaftsgeschichte Deutschlands vom 16. bis 18. Jahrhundert* (Munich, 1952), and Vierhaus, *Staaten und Stände*.

nothing new, nevertheless prevented conceptualization and implementation of potentially beneficial economic planning on a national or even regional scale and also imposed significant restraints on economic growth through the almost innumerable transit tolls, customs duties and other protectionist and money-raising measures with which territorial authorities sought both to restore and maintain the traditional socio-economic balance within their societies and to satisfy the fiscal demands of their princely courts and governments. Thus, both internal and external causes combined to limit economic growth in Germany to levels which, while not unimpressive when compared to the conditions of 1648, were only modest when compared with those of its western neighbours.

In general, one may distinguish three broad phases of economic development from the mid-seventeenth to the end of the eighteenth century. The first, from the end of the Thirty Years War until shortly after 1700, was dominated by recovery from the effects of the war and the reestablishment of some sort of balance between the various sectors of the economy which had been affected somewhat differently by the war. The second phase, marked by slow but fairly steady growth from about 1715 into the 1740s, was one of consolidation; population grew much more slowly than in the first period, but the absence of major catastrophes (especially large-scale wars) for most of these years allowed modest progress in living standards. The last phase, from the 1740s onward, was one of accelerated though not spectacular expansion, based on a considerably more rapid growth in population and a long-term increase in agrarian prices; interrupted regionally only by the ravages of the Seven Years War (1756–63), this expansion continued into the period of the wars of the French Revolution. In a rough way, these three phases correspond with early, middle and late stages of the development of Cameralism, or mercantilism – that is, of governmental initiatives to stimulate productivity and its fiscal yield. In the early stage, governmental policy was directed mostly at recovery of resources reduced or destroyed by the war and at nurturing such slow growth as could be obtained by careful supervision and management of current sources of income. Only with the second stage, as a less anaemic economy had begun to emerge, did the dynamic, growth-oriented elements of mercantilism make their full appearance in the form of increasingly coordinated programs of subsidies, monopolies, manipulation of taxes, establishment of government-owned and -operated industries and so on, together with a balanced import-export policy.[2] It was this period which witnessed not only the canonization of Cameralism as an academic and administrative 'science', but also a widespread institutionalization of the policy of growth through the establishment of specialized bodies to study the economy and make specific recommendations for government action. Usually called 'Colleges (or Deputations) of Commerce', these agencies were often short-lived, except in the largest territories, since their parent body, the Chamber, though not well suited to perform their function, was characteristically suspicious of them and tended to reabsorb them. Even where this happened, however, temporary economic commissions composed of both government officials and private businessmen could prove highly successful with sharply defined and limited tasks which did not appear to invade areas reserved to the competence of the Chamber.[3]

The final phase of mercantilism, especially after the Seven Years War, was characterized by contradictory tendencies which presaged its decline as a universally accepted approach to the problem of economic growth. While many of its regulatory practices – protectionism, for example – were more stringent and rigid than ever, the whole system of governmental direction, regulation and control of the economy was coming under increasing attack both in formal theory (by the adherents of the French Physiocratic school and, very late in the period, by the disciples of Adam Smith) and in the everyday experience of ordinary businessmen whose growing confidence in their own competitiveness gave them a correspondingly unfavourable view of state paternalism. Even some governments began to move in directions contrary to 'classical' mercantilism by reducing the number of monopolies granted and in other ways encouraging greater freedom of competition. Yet while these stirrings of economic liberalism pointed towards a future in which the relationship between government and the economy would be quite different, they were not strong enough to alter the basically mercantilist character of the policies pursued by most of the German territories until after the end of the eighteenth century.

Important though the Cameralists and their mercantilist doctrines

---

2. This characterization must be greatly modified for the smaller territories, whose lack of sectoral diversity and dependence on trade with neighbouring territories on all sides made any but a defensive and modestly self-assertive economic policy absurd.
3. Jeserich *et al.*, *Deutsche Verwaltungsgeschichte*, I, 442–5.

may eventually have become to the territorial princes, their insights were hardly necessary to the first phases of the reconstruction of the shattered German economy after 1648. A thousand things cried out so loudly to be done that the only real question was where to begin. The answer given almost everywhere was: repopulation, or as it was commonly referred to at the time, *Peuplierungspolitik*. By their own experience, as well as by the insistence of the early Cameralists, princes knew that people were the ultimate source of productivity and of taxes, not to mention soldiers for their armies; and the noble landowners who made up the politically most important part of the estates in most territories knew that the worth of their own landed properties depended on an augmented peasant population to reinhabit their abandoned farms. One notable feature of repopulation was therefore an attempt to attract new tenants to deserted farms, whether on princely domains or on private estates, by offering incentives for their reoccupation; these could include reduction or remission of taxes, dues and labour services for a period of years, as well as subventions in the form of wood for construction, seed and even farm animals for work and breeding. To the extent this effort was successful, it encouraged more and earlier marriages and childbearing.

The seriousness of the population problem can also be seen in proposals offered up here and there for forced marriages of the healthy and wealthy and punishment for childlessness among married couples; and while no major wave of legislation resulted from such uncharitable ideas, some territories followed their spirit by imposing special taxes on single men. An enhanced concern that foundlings and orphans live to be adults was evident in the establishment of more institutions, with better funding, for both. A very important part of population policy was the encouragement of immigration, often coupled with a discouragement or outright prohibition of emigration. With little concern for nationality, language and frequently even for religious persuasion, German rulers, and especially Protestant ones, eagerly accepted settlers drawn into the vacuum of their underpopulated territories from Italy and Switzerland in the south to the Low Countries, Denmark and Sweden in the north. A not inconsiderable number of immigrants came because of religious persecution: several thousand Bohemians fled from the threat of Jesuit conversions to Saxon Lusatia, while some 30,000 French Huguenots sought refuge in Germany immediately after Louis XIV revoked the Edict of Nantes in 1685 and were followed by several times that number over the next three decades; a further 20,000 Protestants driven from the archbishopric of Salzburg in 1731 were welcomed into German territories further north. A particular beneficiary of these religious immigrations was the sparsely populated electorate of Brandenburg, which took up 20,000 Huguenots immediately (and more later), over half of the Salzburg Protestants and also numbers of Mennonites forced from their homes in Switzerland and southwestern Germany.

While such additions to population from immigration were not unimportant, a much more significant cause of the surge in population after the war came from a great increase in the native birth rate until late in the seventeenth century, predicated partly on the economic opportunity provided by the labour shortage which lasted for many years after the war. This increase brought restoration of pre-war population levels by shortly after 1700 and perhaps 10–12 per cent beyond it by 1750; it would have been even greater except that the death rate remained stubbornly high – the result of several prolonged periods of war affecting various parts of Germany between about 1675 and 1715, as well as of periodic famine and epidemic disease, especially before 1720 or so. In the first decades following the war, the percentage of very young people was predictably high, but that imbalance evened out over time, as also, to a certain extent, did the initially much greater proportional increase of rural over urban population. By 1800, while Germany was hardly urbanized as yet, there had been some startling urban growth since the Thirty Years War: Vienna, with some 207,000 residents, was the largest city in the Empire, followed by Berlin with 150,000 (more than twice its size in 1730 and a twenty-five-fold increase since 1640) and Hamburg with around 100,000. Some sixty cities by that time had over 10,000 inhabitants and about fifteen of those over 30,000. While not all of the latter were territorial capitals – or, better, 'residences' of the ruling prince (or magistracy, as in the case of Imperial Cities) – most of them were and illustrate the powerful and growing demographic attraction of the princely courts and seats of government after 1648 as major consumers of goods and services and therefore also as providers of employment.[4]

4. Rolf Engelsing, *Sozial- und Wirtschaftsgeschichte Deutschlands* (Göttingen, 1973), pp. 92–3. The town of Ludwigsburg in Württemberg is an interesting example: elevated to the status of a residence (alongside Stuttgart) in 1718, its population grew to 5000 by 1733, but quickly sank back to 2800 when the ducal court left it in 1738. Hermann Kellenbenz, *Deutsche Wirtschaftsgeschichte*, vol. I (Munich, 1977), p. 308.

The importance of demographic change and specifically of sheer numbers of population, is nowhere more evident than in the agrarian sector of the German economy, which remained by far the most important sector throughout the entire period, still accounting for as much as 70–75 per cent of the gross national product as late as the mid-eighteenth century.[5] The serious depression that characterized this sector for at least a half century following the war and in some areas much longer, was a result of a relative overproduction of basic foodstuffs, especially grains, which had three causes: the success of rural repopulation efforts, leading eventually to increases in agricultural production which outstripped overall population growth and especially that of the very important urban consumers; the shrinkage of foreign markets because of a European-wide recession; and a notable change in consumer habits towards less expenditure on food and more on other things (such as clothing). Both leases and land prices had collapsed in many areas during the war and they did not recover much for a long time thereafter. Many landlords and peasants had accumulated large debts; and while an attempt was made in both imperial (1654) and territorial legislation to alleviate this situation by capping interest rates and decreeing moratoriums on repayment of loans for as long as three years or more, forced sales of individual farms or pieces of estates were common enough to depress land prices still further, thus hindering the progress of recovery. Taxes, especially excise taxes and transit tolls were either newly imposed or kept at already high levels, thus increasing cost and reducing demand. The development of every aspect of the economy was affected adversely by the troubles of rural Germany, since the fortunes of both commerce and manufacturing were to a considerable degree dependent on disposable income generated in the agrarian sector. Both wages and the price of manufactured goods slowly followed the falling grain prices.

A mild recovery of agricultural prices from the third quarter of the seventeenth century onward mirrored the increasing demand of a growing population, resulting in a stabilization of the balance between production and consumption by shortly after 1700 at a level which, while not promising much in the way of growth, eased the minds of princes whose traditional policy of insuring adequate food supplies at 'fair' prices for both producer and consumer had been

---

5. Hermann Aubin and Wolfgang Zorn (eds.), *Handbuch der deutschen Wirtschafts- und Sozialgeschichte*, vol. I. (Stuttgart, 1971), p. 569.

severely and repeatedly tested in the previous half-century, occasioning a flood of ordinances and regulations concerning prices of basic foodstuffs, movement of grains and so on. By this time, too, many other serious problems arising from the immediate post-war situation had been overcome. Repopulation of peasant farms, achieved either by inducements such as those discussed earlier in this chapter, or by less gentle means, including literally forcing peasants out of cities and towns to which they had fled during the war back into their rural villages, had created an agrarian Germany not too dissimilar in 1715 from that of 1618. One notable exception was the considerable increase in the number and size of estates east of the Elbe farmed as *Gutswirtschaften* – that is, as latifundia not divided into individual peasant tenures but worked for landlord-entrepreneurs as a unit by an unfree peasant labour force bound more tightly to the land than ever before and burdened by extremely onerous personal and family service obligations. In this region, this system even before 1618 had proved to be the easiest long-term solution to the problem of rural labour shortage, a problem the war had worsened considerably in the whole northeast: in Brandenburg, as an example, only about two-thirds of the arable land was back under cultivation even by 1700.[6] A somewhat similar development had occurred in some other regions of Germany following the war and for the same reason, as landlords had found themselves with no alternative but to reabsorb abandoned peasant tenures back into their manorial land and then to increase their service demands on the peasants who remained, simply in order to insure cultivation of the now larger demesne. In these places, however, where desperation played a larger role than avarice in altering a centuries-old tradition of *Grundherrschaft* (as the system of division of estates into individual peasant farms was known), the gradually growing availability of peasant labour usually led more or less naturally to a restoration of the old system.[7]

Where it did not, another part of the agrarian policy adopted by many territorial governments often came into play to assist the process. That was the application of a series of measures, frequently

6. Engelsing, *Sozial- und Wirtschaftsgeschichte*, p. 81.
7. Where landed estates tended to be small or medium-sized, as in most of the south, southwest and west, noble proprietors clearly preferred a profusion of peasant tenancies to entrepreneurial *Gutswirtschaft* in any case, since many of them had lived from ground rents and various outside sources of income for so long as to have lost both knowledge of and interest in agriculture *per se*. Also, of course, the lack of markets provided no inducement to entrepreneurial farming.

decreed as ordinances, designed to protect the viability of the peasantry on the land and which were known collectively as *Bauernschutz*. Proceeding essentially from the same considerations that underlay population policy and with an eye towards preservation of the peasantry as a class rather than towards protection of individual rights as such, regimes in wide areas of northwestern and central Germany, as well as in electoral Saxony and (after 1713) in Brandenburg-Prussia, inserted themselves into the landlord-peasant nexus to prevent physical mistreatment of peasants and their families, to prohibit expansion of the lord's demesne at the expense of peasant tenures, to establish or codify tenure rights of peasants, to limit the labour services required of them and to regulate and supervise the system of manorial justice. How efficacious such policies were depended to a large extent on the political relations that had developed between the prince and the landed nobility; while it was invariably necessary to proceed with circumspection when interfering in any way with the relationship between landlords and their dependants, rulers in the areas named above found that a firm but careful approach could produce more than just modestly successful results. In other territories, however, the domination of the government by the nobility was so complete as to prevent such initiatives altogether; Swedish Pomerania and the duchies of Mecklenburg fit this picture and in the latter, in particular, the peasant's lot was widely known and deplored throughout the eighteenth century as the most miserable in Germany by a considerable margin.

It should be clear, from the foregoing, that the policy of reconstruction from the devastations and disruptions of the war went hand-in-hand with the already venerable tradition of conservation of existing social and economic relationships in the countryside. Recovery was really unthinkable except in terms of a re-establishment of the 'good order' at which all police measures – including the whole policy of reconstruction itself – were always ultimately aimed. This characterization applies equally to a special kind of widely read agrarian literature which appeared during the phases of agricultural recovery and stabilization from 1670 to 1750 or so, known as the 'house-father literature' (*Hausväterliteratur*). Based to a large extent on earlier models, including Johannes Coler's influential *Oeconomia ruralis et domestica* of 1593 (which was reprinted fourteen times into the early eighteenth century), the works of this genre dealt in a very comprehensive if also often rather whimsical and random fashion with the management of landed estates, which for these authors included not just agriculture and its produce, but animals, implements, buildings, servants, the landlord's family relationships, medicines, wine cellars, kitchens and even recipes and food preparation. Neither agriculturally scientific nor even very helpful regarding the business practices of the landlord, this literature pictured the whole estate as a single household and the *Hausvater* as the firm but caring patriarch for whom it set down norms for a just and virtuous stewardship.[8] With an emphasis on equability and preservation of existing resources and hardly at all on change or growth, this literature was entirely companionable to a period of agrarian recovery, followed by one of little or no expansion.

Much of this was to change after 1740 or so. A quickening population growth in Germany and most of the rest of Europe from that time onward exerted a steadily increasing pressure on the food supply. Since new expenditures of capital and labour appear soon to have reached a point of diminishing returns in the existing agrarian system, grain prices rose and were not equalled by wages, because the same principle seems to have operated in the non-agrarian labour market. The result was a mild crisis of subsistence whose primary effect was to create an explosion of new interest in agriculture and its productivity – the booming preconditions for what was to be known as the 'agricultural revolution'. The *Hausväterliteratur*, with its earnest but backward-looking moral message was soon replaced by an almost altogether new literature of agricultural innovation and experimentation – some of it based on English and Dutch example, but most of it home-grown – designed to work changes in methods of cultivation, as well as to increase the amount of land suitable for growing crops. By the 1760s and 1770s this literature had achieved the status of a cottage industry in itself and its exhortations and suggestions were eagerly discussed in many newly-founded agricultural societies patronized by a mixture of princes, nobles, officials, academics, clerics and ordinary burghers. Some of these societies published their own proceedings, but articles on agricultural improvement also appeared regularly in the rapidly growing number of periodicals which made their appearance in Germany after 1770. Prize questions on various problems of agriculture were offered by the Berlin Academy and other similarly prestigious learned bodies

8. Aubin and Zorn (eds.), *Handbuch*, I, 495–6. The works of Wolf Helmhard von Hohberg and especially his *Georgica curiosa oder adeliches Land- und Feldleben* (1682) may be cited as some of the best and most influential of this genre.

and one essay prizewinner, Johann Christian Schubart (1734–87) was elevated to the nobility as 'Schubart of the Clover-Field' by Emperor Joseph II for his suggestions concerning the cultivation of clover as animal fodder on land otherwise temporarily unusable for grain cultivation. While among the sober Germans this 'agrimania' never became quite the festive national fad it was in France (where courtiers pranced about in peasant costumes) or even in England (where George III proudly answered to the name of 'Farmer George'), it did result in important initiatives with an impact on productivity which, if not dramatic, were also not insignificant.

One broad direction of agricultural improvement was towards *intensification* – making existing land produce more usable crops. The single most important innovation here involved a modification of the three-field system which predominated in about two-thirds of the arable land area of Germany. Traditionally, one-third of the fields of any given farm were allowed to lie fallow, by rotation at every planting, to permit the land to regain its fertility. But by planting this fallow with crops which required a different variation of soil nutrients than those immediately preceding, it was possible to produce crops for human or animal consumption: peas, cabbage, lentils or other legumes, or perhaps clover or turnips for fodder. A variation, in areas with especially favourable climate, was to plant all fields in grain one year, followed by pasture crops the next year. A regular rotation of different crops on all three fields was another alternative, again employed chiefly in places with a dependably good climate. To the extent that all three systems could pasture more animals, which then deposited more manure – the only real fertilizer of the day – there was a double or triple gain of more animals, more human food and increased soil fertility. The numbers and quality of cattle and sheep were noticeably improved by the stall-feeding made possible by more fodder (which also facilitated collection of dung), as well as by the luxury of selective breeding permitted by the growth in sheer numbers of animals.

Of the new crops introduced on a large scale, the potato was of enormous nutritional significance and was widely cultivated as a field crop after the famine of 1771–2 which it helped to alleviate. Tobacco also achieved some importance as a field cash crop. Still, grains remained king not only among crops but also against all other food supplies; in Prussia, at the end of the eighteenth century, grains comprised 53 per cent of all food production, with other types of plants and animal products very nearly equal at 23 per cent and 24 per cent, respectively. For Germany as a whole at the same time, grains were similarly dominant, taking up 61 per cent of the total arable land; fallow crops took up some 14 per cent and 25 per cent, in spite of all improvements, still lay fallow at any given planting.[9] This last figure, in particular, says much about the great variation in the intensity of cultivation in different areas of Germany and warns against exaggerating the net gains in productivity from intensified agriculture, which tended to flourish only in those limited areas where the variables of good soil, favourable climate, proximity of markets and availability of relatively cheap transportation coincided. The same caution must be applied to the impact of new inventions and implements; the seed drill, which wasted less seed than the broadcast method in planting, was known, as was the improved iron plough which turned up more fertile subsoil through deeper furrows, but neither was widely employed at any time in this period. Intensification was therefore not the revolution in cultivation that was to be reserved for the truly scientific, rational and eventually mechanized agriculture of the nineteenth century. But it pointed the way in that direction and was at least successful enough to develop and sustain the high levels of interest and expectation necessary to maintain the momentum of improvement.

The second major path towards increased agrarian production was that of *extensification* – expanding the total amount of arable land. State-sponsored efforts in this direction were the most obvious and dramatic, especially in Brandenburg-Prussia, where between 1718 and 1786 several hundred square miles of wetlands were recovered and restored by drainage, dams and other means and then colonized. Frederick II alone brought in as many as 300,000 settlers and by the end of his reign a very substantial proportion of the population of Prussia consisted of colonists or their descendants, going all the way back to the days of the Great Elector. The Bavarian and some other governments also made progress in land reclamation through the clearing of forests and the development of moors and wastelands. Less dramatic than these gains, but possibly more significant in the total amount of land reclaimed, were the literally thousands of private efforts undertaken on individual farms and estates, sometimes with state assistance, to expand cultivation onto small tracts of land

9. Aubin and Zorn, *Handbuch*, I, 523; Kellenbenz, *Deutsche Wirtschaftsgeschichte*, I, 325. A notable decline in meat consumption, relative to earlier times, is reflected in reports from the late eighteenth century that in some places cattle were raised only for the production of manure. Friedrich Lütge, *Deutsche Sozial- und Wirtschaftsgeschichte: ein Überblick*, 3rd ed. (Berlin, 1966), pp. 353–4.

previously regarded as incorrigibly unproductive. There were three other possibilities for increasing the amount of land available for growing crops: first, to reduce or eliminate the extensive village common lands, used mostly as pasturage, by partitioning them for cultivation by individuals; second, to abolish the traditional *Flurzwang*, the community restrictions on land utilization which were originally designed to preserve a distributive fairness among peasant villagers, but which did so by means which frequently limited productivity; and third, to alter inheritance rights so as to stop the fragmentation of peasant holdings into parcels whose increasingly smaller size reduced overall productivity generation by generation. Attempts to achieve these objectives were undertaken by improving landlords as well as by various governments, with decidedly less than gratifying results; alarmingly negative reactions in the peasant communities, combined with the stubborn tendency of the territorial law courts to uphold the 'old law' which sanctioned these customary rights, in most cases forced the abandonment of these initiatives which, in sum, had a generally less than even modest success.

As these last examples suggest, the ability of the traditional agrarian economy to resist change and innovation was, in fact, impressive and was certainly a cause of much frustration to official and private reformers alike. Nor was it only the peasants whose stubborn attachment to centuries-old practices and prejudices set limits to what could be accomplished: landlords, especially in areas where a rapidly increasing demand for foodstuffs was not in evidence, were often loath to make the investments of time and capital initially required by improvement and both the administrators and lessees of state domain lands could find many ways to avoid carrying out reforms ordered from above which they saw as vain, difficult or productive of problems with the peasantry. But there was another side to the coin. Many from the same groups of landlords, officials and lessees were at the forefront of agricultural innovation, taking the time to deal patiently with peasant fears, confusion and complaints and proceeding at a cautious pace consistent with current conditions. The local priest or pastor was often a valuable ally, especially since many clerics were well-read in the literature of improvement. Furthermore, not all peasants fitted the mould of an ignorant and hide-bound traditionalism; and while most of the 'model farms' which sprang up here and there in Germany as instructional showcases for the new agriculture were the creations of princes, improving noble landlords or other 'philanthropic' agriculturists, a few were developed without fanfare, over time, by peasant proprietors who knew the difference between profit and prejudice.[10] Committed local interest and perseverance often accomplished what edicts and decrees from above could not. Still, while German agriculture was healthy and vital as the eighteenth century neared its end, it is doubtful that the steps taken towards either intensification or extensification, no matter how energetic or locally successful, formed more than a small part of that vigour, most of which was simply the result of the conventional response of a traditional agrarian economy to the stimulus of new markets created by a steadily increasing population.

10. Similarly, there were some cases in which partition of common lands and alteration of traditional land utilization was welcomed and even initiated by peasant communities themselves.

CHAPTER ELEVEN

The German Economy, 1650–1800: Industry, Commerce and Finance

Next to agriculture and its closely associated industries, manufacturing was the most important sector of the German economy and one which received a great deal of attention from the territorial princes and their Cameralist advisers and officials. Recovery from the Thirty Years War in this sector occurred more rapidly than in agriculture; the larger cities which housed artisan and other manufacturing activities had generally suffered less direct war damage than smaller towns and rural areas and population losses were less severe, so that the important factors of fixed capital and labour started from levels considerably better than in the agrarian sector. State activity, here as elsewhere in Europe in the age of mercantilism, was directed towards increasing both quantity and quality of manufactures – the former primarily in order to cover domestic demand as fully as possible so as to reduce imports, the latter for both that reason and to increase exports. With problems in both areas from somewhat to greatly more severe than in other countries of Europe until at least the middle of the eighteenth century, the German territories coupled the encouragement of domestic manufactures with a particularly rigorous prohibition of imports of finished goods and of exports of many raw materials, thus not only depriving German consumers of many commodities fairly readily available elsewhere in Europe, but also disadvantaging the commercial sector by reducing it to a handmaiden of the manufacturing economy. The universal recognition of the inferiority of German manufactures, particularly to those of France and especially in high-quality luxury goods, was in fact responsible for some rare legislative activity in the imperial diet: in 1676, 1689 and 1702, imperial laws prohibiting the import of a majority of French goods into the Empire were passed. While in each case passage was eased by the fact that the Empire was at war with France, war was more occasion than cause for these measures, which lay in the desire to protect a still recovering manufacturing industry from foreign competition. The seriousness of the problem is further exposed by the ineffectiveness of the laws, due to non-observance by a number of territories, including especially the Imperial Cities, most of which had opposed their passage in the first place.

While the problem of quality of manufactures was a temporary one, eventually overcome in the course of the eighteenth century by various means discussed at greater length below, it was to some degree related to the more important problem of quantity production. The urban crafts guilds, which for centuries had been the primary producers of manufactured items of common consumption, proved capable of satisfying the demands of the increasing post-war population generally until after about 1700. But since it had always been in the interest of the guilds to produce essentially limited quantities of relatively expensive goods at prices kept up by restricting supply to demand, they could be expected to react strongly against any competition which could produce the same goods for significantly lower prices, even if the quality was somewhat lower as well. In fact, such competition had for some time been growing from several sources, including rural guilds and independent workshops which lay outside the zones in which the urban guilds enjoyed a legal monopoly of production, as well as from some parts of the burgeoning domestic system of production (*Verlagswesen*), in which large numbers of rural inhabitants worked full- or part-time in their homes on materials supplied by a single merchant. The reaction of the guild masters, over time, came in the form of attempts to reduce competition at least within their zones of protection, chiefly by the double means of limiting admission to the lowest rank of apprentice and of sharply curtailing promotion from the second rank of journeyman to the highest rank of master. Since only the masters could actually sell goods at retail, these measures restricted competition at that level, while blockage of the age-old process of promotion for journeymen meant deferment or even elimination of their chance to rise from the status of wage earners to that of small businessmen.

For growth-minded princes and their advisers, the decreased production resulting from the shrinkage in the size of the guilds was bad enough; but it was made worse by rapidly increasing tensions within the guilds between masters and journeymen which led to the formation of local offensive and defensive associations of both. These sometimes expanded to become regional and involved correspondence, polemical pamphleteering and reciprocal blacklisting by journeymen and masters. Bitter quarrelling over family favouritism, wages and working conditions resulted in individual acts of violence which frequently escalated into major street brawls, boycotts of masters and journeymen against each other and long strikes. This represented a severe and growing challenge not just to productivity but also to public order, a matter of serious and immediate concern to territorial authorities. But it proved very difficult to evolve and execute a consistent policy of guild control, not only because of extensive guild privileges and a lack of central agencies capable of assuming the supervisory functions currently reserved to urban magistracies, but also because the cooptation of knowledgeable and experienced elders in the guilds themselves was indispensable to the conduct of industrial policy. Early attempts to abolish the autonomous jurisdiction of guilds over their own membership, or even to eliminate the guilds altogether (as in Prussia in 1718), were largely failures. But when a number of particularly ugly strikes, culminating in an uprising of journeymen clothmakers in one of the provinces of Brandenburg and a months-long strike of journeymen cobblers in Augsburg, drew national attention to the seriousness of the guild problem, Prussia seized the opportunity for a national solution to it. At the urging of its delegates, the imperial diet in 1731 adopted an Imperial Guild Ordinance which not only conferred sweeping powers of guild regulation on territorial governments, but also established for all territories a common floor of basic ordinances designed to discourage the migration of artisans from lands with strict guild controls to those with easier ones. This imperial ordinance, together with another passed in 1772 which both amended and amplified it, brought a degree of tranquillity into the artisan world sufficient to allow not only a continued toleration of the urban guilds but even in many places a renewed commitment to their protection from rural competition.

Nevertheless, while state mercantilist policy could continue to accept the now more orderly guilds, its reliance on other means of industrial production continued to grow and the share of total production accounted for by the urban guilds shrank fairly steadily. Rural guilds continued to multiply and their output was joined by that of the so-called 'Free Masters', individuals permitted by the authorities to set up workshops in both town and country and to hire helpers in often unlimited quantity, but not ones trained as

138

apprentices. By the end of the eighteenth century, there appears to have been a real surplus of guild artisans, especially in much of eastern Germany, where there were actually more masters than journeymen; of the former, in Germany as a whole, as many as half may by that time have worked alone.[1] But the growth represented by all the suppliers mentioned above paled beside that of the domestic system, which became the greatest source of mass production in Europe before its supplantation by the factory system in the nineteenth century. While there was much variation in the details of production, the typical arrangement in the large industry most susceptible to this form of organization – textiles – involved one or more merchant-capitalists who provided raw materials (and sometimes basic tools as well) to rural workers in their own homes, who were paid piecework wages to work the raw material up to a higher stage of completion, after which it was collected and assembled in a central place – a small factory, in effect – for finishing and distribution for sale.

Until the end of the eighteenth century, the domestic system was primarily a rural one, relying on the fact that a majority of peasant households in Germany as a whole probably derived income from farming alone which put them only at or below subsistence level. Thus, while a real exploitation of these families undoubtedly occurred, they desperately needed the added income; a few lucky ones even made enough by it to purchase freedom from their landlords. In areas where dependency on income from the domestic system was both widespread and permanent, a kind of proto-industrial proletariat came into being, whose availability as a labour pool was important to the early stages of the later industrial revolution. The largest segment of textile manufacturing – linen – was also the most rural in organization, while weaving in silk, wool and imported cotton was more urbanized and retail manufacture almost wholly so, especially in the luxury fabrics. Textiles were the most important German industry of the eighteenth century; figures given for Prussia in 1793, for example, indicate that 61 per cent of total manufactures consisted of linens, woollens and silks.[2] German linens were particularly well regarded in European markets, while the cheaper varieties of textiles were one type of commodity in which German producers were able to compete in overseas colonial

1. Aubin and Zorn, eds., *Handbuch*, I, 539.
2. Ibid., 554.

markets reasonably successfully with the maritime states. Overall, the domestic system had come a very long way from its modest roots in the sixteenth century, as demonstrated by one estimate that by 1800 it accounted for some 43 per cent of all German manufacturing production.[3]

Given the strength and advantages of the domestic system, it is not surprising that the state itself in various territories should make some direct use of it, if in unusual ways somewhat reminiscent of the later factory system. Since the early stages of textile manufacturing – spinning and weaving – did not require specialized skills, governments found it possible to organize production in state-run orphanages, workhouses, penal institutions and lunatic asylums; while some of these were government-owned, most were either leased to private entrepreneurs or entirely owned by them, while the state provided labour drawn from the above sources as well as from periodic roundups of beggars.[4] Much more important than these forced-labour workshops was a whole series of industries either founded, funded and managed by the government directly, or encouraged and to one or another degree sustained by grants, subsidies, concessions or privileges. In the former category were many luxury industries which because of special problems relating to high start-up costs, labour acquisition and discipline and market development, among other things, were either originally established as state enterprises or were eventually bought from private ownership. One thinks immediately of the various porcelain manufactories in Meissen (Saxony), Vienna, Berlin and elsewhere; but such industries also included manufacture of carpets, tapestries, mirrors, hats and gold and silver lace, as well as the processing of tobacco, sugar, coffee and chocolate. Demand for all these luxury products was real enough, but also unsteady due to the shifting fortunes of an only modestly wealthy nobility which constituted their primary market and competition between state enterprises in different territories not infrequently resulted in at least temporary overproduction. This occasionally produced some rather unusual steps to guarantee sales of stocks that otherwise could not be moved:

3. Vierhaus, *Staaten und Stände*, p. 74.
4. It is not clear whether, as a group, such undertakings made a profit or even covered their own costs. Many of them, certainly, failed – chiefly, it appears, because in addition to a certain more or less predictable unreliability of their work force, they attracted more than their share of dishonest or incompetent businessmen more interested in quick profits than in building carefully on the advantage the state had given them. Lütge, *Deutsche Sozial- und Wirtschaftsgeschichte*, pp. 365–6.

Frederick the Great, for example, required Jews, upon marriage, to pay a certain sum to his Berlin porcelain factory, for which they received whatever the factory decided it needed to get rid of; under such circumstances, the well-known philosopher Moses Mendelssohn became the unwilling owner of twenty life-sized porcelain apes.[5]

Wholly state-owned industries were not a terribly important component of the entire manufacturing sector, since at most 60 of the more than 1000 manufacturing concerns existing in Germany in the late eighteenth century fell into that category and the profitability of many of these is suspect – except, perhaps, for the supervising officials who peculated funds from the budgets or subventions authorized for them.[6] But there were many more industries, representing a larger total product, which owed their origin or part of their continuing success to state assistance by means of subsidies, tax concessions, monopolies and other preferments. A number of these were industries producing essential goods – armaments, gunpowder, uniforms and other military equipment (of which some were government-owned and -operated); others were simply businesses governments were willing to support because of their contribution to the long-term economic and fiscal vitality of the state. An interesting case is that of mining, which ran the gamut from wholly state-owned to wholly privately-owned enterprises, with intermediate stages of mixed proprietorship. Since as early as the sixteenth century, the increasing exhaustion of easily accessible deposits of nearly all kinds of ores, but especially of all-important iron ore, had raised the expense of mining operations to levels which resulted in a slow but steady retreat of private entrepreneurs from the field. Deeper shafts had to be dug, requiring a new technology for ventilation and water removal, as well as a new smelting process with hotter furnaces to exploit the poorer ores now being mined. All these improvements came, indeed, in the course of the eighteenth century, but at a cost that was simply beyond the means of the small operations which, regardless of the location of ownership, continued throughout the period to dominate the business. State participation and proprietorship therefore tended to increase in the eighteenth century, as did the degree of its supervision of the whole industry whether private or governmental, eventuating in the larger territories

5. Engelsing, *Sozial- und Wirtschaftsgeschichte*, p. 89.
6. Aubin and Zorn, eds., *Handbuch*, I, 550.

in a real mining policy requiring new administrative agencies. Labour discipline was a major part of the new supervisory responsibility: experienced miners were valuable and were thus fairly well paid, but they were often also denied freedom of movement and became virtual hostages to their own highly prized skills.

As late as 1700, Germany still led the world in iron production, but by 1790 that leadership had been forfeited to greater increases in Britain, France and Russia. For much of the century and in addition to difficulties mentioned above, the mining industry, like the rest of society, encountered a particularly serious problem which became a cause for alarm in government and the whole industrial sector alike: a major and, for a time, increasing shortage of wood. Wood had so many common uses in heating, construction, farm implements and innumerable items of common consumption that it was always in steady and heavy demand. But considering that 4000 mature oak trees were needed to build a single medium-sized warship, or that some twelve tons of wood were required to produce enough charcoal to smelt one ton of ore of average quality, it is easy to understand why provision of charcoal became a serious bottleneck for all forges and foundries, making any increase in iron production all but impossible. A thriving import business in wood provided little relief. Only the introduction of new 'high' furnaces fired by coal (coke) began to address the problem convincingly and that was not until towards the end of the century. In the meantime, industry had suffered: the iron and other metallurgical industries, as well as glass factories and salt-works had to be closed periodically and even the construction mania of princes and prelates so characteristic of the age, and which was a major employer of masons and carpenters, was here and there interrupted temporarily.

One result of the wood shortage was a sharp increase of governmental interest in forest conservation. Forestry ordinances were nothing new: they were common in the later middle ages and increased in some areas after the Thirty Years War, especially in northern Germany in territories which the Swedes, in particular, had systematically deforested for their own needs and in order to sell wood to the Dutch or to Baltic port cities. But 'forestry police' became quite general by the early to mid-eighteenth century. It would seem simple enough to guard forest preserves through timely ordinances, but in fact it was not. Apart from problems arising from private property rights, attempts to limit destruction of woods and forests by large hunting parties offended a cherished social prerogative of the nobility and, even when successful, often aroused the ire of peasants whose fields and gardens were invaded by foraging wild life which quickly overpopulated the very forests from which hunting had been banished. It was also difficult to urge preservation of forest lands in a time of sharply rising agricultural prices, which put at least as much a premium on the production of grain as on that of wood. Nevertheless, the effort persisted, aided by the inevitable bureaucratic agencies which came into being to supervise it and by the end of the eighteenth century both remedial care and replanting were making real progress in reforestation, assisted by a relative decline in demand for wood by increased use of other materials, including the iron which was now available in growing amounts. The 'wood crisis' had passed.

Trade and commerce did not receive the same generous and enthusiastic attention and encouragement from governments and their Cameralist advisers as did manufacturing. The various German regimes tended not to see in trade anything approaching the net gains that might be expected from growth in the industrial sector. Behind this was the perception, strongly supported by the facts, that the foreign trade conducted by German merchants was primarily an import trade and therefore of negative value. Because the German territories for a long time could not equal in quantity or quality the goods produced by their trading partners and because they had virtually no direct access to the highly prized products of the overseas colonial world, any encouragement given to foreign merchandizing would be at odds with the strongly protectionist and bullionist emphases of German mercantilism. Commerce was therefore supported only as an adjunct to industrial policy – that is, insofar as it catered to exports. The fiscal interest of the state also dictated that both internal and border tolls and transit taxes be maintained; and while some territories in the later eighteenth century instituted a more unified and rationalized system of tolls which had some effect on easing traffic, no significant movement towards free trade either within or between the German states occurred. Otherwise, trade was viewed chiefly in terms of maintaining domestic price stability in agricultural products, especially in grains, whose movement was closely regulated. Governments were very chary of exporting grain surpluses, which they instead often bought up and stored for release in lean years and imported cheaper eastern European (mainly Polish) grains only for their armies or, on a larger scale, when harvests were unusually bad.

Until the early to mid-eighteenth century, the busiest centres of the inland export trade in Germany were the great international fairs at Frankfurt and Leipzig, but especially the latter, where buyers and sellers of all kinds of goods from all over Germany and western and eastern Europe negotiated their transactions. In the course of the century, both Vienna and Berlin became increasingly important as well. Of the coastal cities, Hamburg led all the rest in the volume of traffic, followed by Bremen; both lay to the west of the Danish peninsula and were the only German cities to share extensively in the new wealth of the transatlantic trade. As independent political entities, furthermore, they could rake in the profits of an essentially unrestricted traffic in foreign imports that was denied territorial cities under the protectionist regimen of mercantilist rulers. The Baltic cities fared less well, generally. The old Hanseatic League was all but moribund even before its last, poorly attended general diet in 1669; and its share of the carrying trade in the North and Baltic Seas was steadily eroded from the early seventeenth century onward by the growth of national navies in Denmark and Sweden and later in Prussia and Russia as well. The only city which enjoyed a steady prosperity was Danzig, which continued to build on its exports of Polish grain to western Europe, to Holland and then, increasingly, to England. Lübeck, however, lost to Hamburg a significant part of its middleman trade in colonial goods and wines from southwestern Europe; and Stettin, ceded to Prussia by Sweden in 1720, suffered from the diversion of traffic on the Oder to Berlin and eventually to Hamburg by means of a connecting canal between the Oder and the Spree completed between 1662 and 1669 by the Great Elector. Dealing very largely in bulk exports such as wood, grain and other agricultural products, none of these ports was able to maintain a favourable balance of exports over imports.

The two largest German states which were not landlocked – Brandenburg-Prussia and Austria – also made feeble efforts to capitalize on the colonial market. The Habsburg lands, of course, had no port cities in Germany at all; but they derived financial advantage from Trieste in the Adriatic – a free port after 1719 – which later in the century actually became the chief port city for Bohemia and parts of Austria proper after improvement of the overland connection between Trieste and the Austrian plain through the Semmering Pass. But the Oriental Company founded there in 1719 failed in 1737, echoing the fate of a similar joint-stock operation in Vienna which had lasted only from 1667 to 1683. The acquisition of the port city of Ostende in the Netherlands in 1714, initially hailed with great enthusiasm by Austrian officials who hoped to make it the centre of a thriving overseas trading operation, ultimately proved to be of little value when the chartered company established there had to be closed down because of opposition from Austria's British and Dutch allies, who wanted no new competition for their own trade.

Prussia had no better luck. After establishing the first German colonial settlement on the west coast of Africa in 1683, an African Company was set up in Königsberg to exploit what was hoped to be a lively commerce. Both the colony and the company (which was later transferred from Königsberg to Emden) were modelled on Dutch examples and were partly capitalized by the Dutch. Ironically, however, 'Gross-Friedrichsburg', as the colony was called, could not withstand competition from the Dutch themselves and was finally sold to them in 1721; the African Company, meanwhile, went bankrupt. An Asiatic Company founded in Emden in 1750 had no greater success and was shut down in 1765. While all of the enterprises discussed above were undercapitalized, they really had from the beginning no chance of success against the more experienced, better organized and richer foreign competition; funding them beyond the amounts they actually received would only have sent good money after bad.

Hidden behind the enormous variety of goods and service produced and transported into, out of and within Germany was a vast system of private and public finance which affected every aspect of the economy in important ways. As emphasized earlier, one of the problems bequeathed by the Thirty Years War was a terrible shortage of capital and especially of circulating capital – coinage – due to the loss of large amounts of precious metals, including coins, to foreigners; and it was at best a dubious mitigation of this situation that the entire economy was so wrecked that an absence of money was, for a time, easier to put up with as simple bartering became common in many areas. But there were private hoards of monetary assets in the hands of those who had managed to preserve and even increase their wealth during the war and it was from these sources – military enterprisers and suppliers, money-changers and -lenders and so on – as well as from some foreign banks that money began to recirculate. Much of this occurred through the borrowing of the territorial princes, who immediately returned the money to the economy in the form of reconstruction assistance or other subventions, as well as by their own court and governmental expenditures, luxury and otherwise. The money shortage was itself a chief reason why interest rates on loans had grown as high as 25 per cent in some areas near and immediately following the end of the war, leading to passage of an imperial law in 1654 capping those rates at 5 per cent – a return that proved unrealistic in some territories whose governments permitted rates to rise from one to three percentage points higher and, for Jewish lenders, as high as 14–18 per cent. Even though general economic growth remained at unimpressive levels for a long time after the war, the shortfall of coinage and therefore of credit, proved easier to overcome than had been feared; after 1675 rates sank to actual demand levels of 5 per cent or even lower and in most of the eighteenth century hovered around 5–6 per cent.[7] After about 1715, however and especially after 1750, stronger economic growth again caused worries about the money supply and the steadily increasing emphasis on achieving a favourable balance of trade during most of the eighteenth century was in part, at least, caused by the need for more precious metals as circulating coinage to keep pace with production increases and to prevent the depressive effect on industry that would otherwise result from deflation.[8]

The coinage raised concern for other reasons as well. With somewhere around 600 autonomous mints in the Empire, there was always a danger that the temptation to create instant wealth could lead unscrupulous princes to authorize a deliberate debasement of their coinage, with the added risk of a runaway imitation by others, leading to a re-enactment of the monetary crisis of the 'Kipper and Wipper' period. Quality control was therefore an area in which the diets of both the Empire and of the individual Circles were active with legislation that proved generally effective until the middle of the eighteenth century, when for their own reasons both Austria and Prussia began to abandon imperial currency standards. A different but equally important task of monetary policy was to assure the exchangeability of the bewildering variety of currencies against each other – a problem whose effects dampened the whole economy to some degree and for which, in spite of frequent contemporary complaints and demands for conformity to a common denominator, no completely satisfactory solution was found.

For those who could use them, however, there were answers of two kinds to both the above problems. The first involved settling large accounts – such as those common at the large international fairs – on paper, using credits based on known and reliable currencies. The second and more important was the private bank. By no

7. Ibid., 535.
8. Lütge, *Deutsche Sozial- und Wirtschaftsgeschichte*, pp. 369–70.

coincidence, two banks, important not just for their own activity but also because they provided models for others, were founded in the midst of the 'Kipper and Wipper' confusion: the Bank of Hamburg (1619) and the 'Banco publico' in Nürnberg (1621). The former was of special significance both because it was by far the biggest banking enterprise in a large and vital economic area and because it created the 'Mark Banco', a fictitious unit of value designed to provide a stable standard amidst the wild fluctuations of debased and manipulated currencies then existing. One of the strengths of this bank, like that of the smaller Nürnberg facility, lay in restricting itself to deposits and exchanges, or transfers. Lending or credit banks also existed, often mixed with wholesale merchandizing and industrial enterprises; but they were probably no more important than the numerous individual financiers, acting as bankers, many of whom had grown out of the money-changers of an earlier time. Of the various money centres of the eighteenth century, Frankfurt, home to such financier families as the Rothschilds, was the greatest.

The various government banks founded in Austria, Prussia, Bavaria and elsewhere in Germany were, on the whole, unsuccessful; with few positive features to attract either domestic or foreign deposits, they were disproportionately capitalized with state funds, bringing with them not only rigid supervision but also the ever-present danger of official monetary manipulation. Under these circumstances and with little domestic capital available anyway, no one much wanted to invest in them. Finally, primitive financial and stock exchanges existed in most of the larger cities, dealing less in equities than in financial obligations, including government 'bonds' (promissory notes) and often in merchandise and sometimes agricultural produce as well.

In the area of public or governmental finance (and disregarding such measures as the unilateral repudiation or reduction of debts or interest payments by which some rulers had helped to solve their worst fiscal problems right after the war), one may appropriately distinguish between 'regular' and 'irregular' sources of revenue. In the former category and generally quite prominent, were the cameral revenues – the income from domainal entrepreneurial farming (or from leases of it), including forests, fisheries, salt-works, lime and brick kilns, wines and other agrarian industries such as mining. The proportion of net income represented by these *cameralia* varied considerably over time and from territory to territory: in Prussia, it was just under 50 per cent in 1740 and about or a little above 40 per cent around the end of the century; the figures for Württemberg were about the same, but substantially less (about 25 per cent) in Bavaria.[9]

Taxes would also fall into the category of 'regular' revenues, including the 'contribution' of the estates, which was technically not regular because it had to be requested, but which in many territories had degenerated into a routine and even fixed annual grant. By the eighteenth century, indirect taxes had come to play a very important role almost everywhere, sometimes replacing the 'contribution' and therefore winning approval from the territorial estates. Princes also liked them because they allowed circumvention of the estates, while (in the case of excise taxes on luxury goods, especially) requiring the latter to become taxpayers themselves. Excise taxes on goods of common consumption were especially preferred, because both the tax rate and the number of potentially taxable items were susceptible to indefinite increases, limited only by the political and economic good sense of the ruler. Internal and border tolls and transit taxes were also common; so was the establishment of state monopolies on the sale of a few luxury products such as coffee, chocolate and tobacco, which really amounted to an excise tax since these were sold at artificially high prices set by the government.

'Irregular' revenues – the term can refer to both sources and steadiness of income – would include the loans contracted by princes for various purposes, but frequently simply as advances on annual revenues. Many such loans were arranged through the famous *Hoffaktoren*, the Jewish court factors who existed in almost all the important territories and whose financial skill and influence was of crucial importance to state finances. From 1698 to 1739, for example, the Viennese court was advanced two million florins a year, on average, from such sources; and Frederick the Great relied heavily on his court jeweller and others as 'monetary entrepreneurs' to cover some 20 per cent of the total expense of the Seven Years War. Probably the best known factors were the Rothschilds of Frankfurt, who attained the status of court bankers in Hesse-Kassel in 1795; but there was also the tragic case of Joseph Süss Oppenheimer – 'Jud Süss' – the Württemberg court factor who was caught in the middle of an ugly quarrel between estates and dukes and was executed in 1738 as a sacrifice to their reconciliation.[10]

Another not inconsiderable source of irregular income for a number of princes throughout the period was foreign subsidies. The

9.   Ibid., 396–7.
10.   Aubin and Zorn, eds., *Handbuch*, I, 565.

amounts and regularity of such subsidies varied greatly according to the perceived diplomatic or military utility of the different German territories to the foreign powers concerned. Nearly all of the larger territories received substantial sums at one time or another, while the princes of a number of smaller ones were almost permanent pensioners of big foreign states. The Great Elector of Brandenburg-Prussia is thought to have received almost three million talers from France and Holland in the years 1674–88 alone, while his famous great-grandson Frederick II could scarcely have fought the Seven Years War without large subsidies from Great Britain (or, for that matter, without the very different kind of 'subsidy' he extracted from the citizens of territories he occupied during the war). Vienna was not shy of accepting foreign money, nor were Bavaria and a number of western German states whose geographical position made their friendship useful to France, in particular. Finally, of course, there was the income derived from the famous *Soldatenhandel*, the trafficking in soldiers. Several territories engaged in this practice at one time or another; but there was one – Hesse-Kassel – which stood out above all others in a business which elicited much moral outrage from enlightened contemporaries, but which also lowered taxes and provided a generally very welcome employment for thousands of young men in a very poor country. Landgrave Friedrich II (1760–85), after receiving some 23 million talers in foreign subsidies for his participation in the Seven Years War, got another 21 millions for the almost 20,000 troops he dispatched to America to fight for Britain in the War of American Independence. This enterprise proved particularly remunerative, delivering a net profit of 12.6 million talers with which Friedrich and his successor, Wilhelm IX, were able to enter the banking business, lending money at between 2–6 per cent to German and foreign princes and states, including Great Britain, Denmark and Holland.[11]

In economic as in political terms, the territorial fragmentation of Germany makes summary generalizations for the entire country difficult and the differences between the economic situation of the various territories were at least as pronounced by the end of the period as they were in 1648. Some of them – especially those with economies large and diverse enough to be 'national' in scope – appear by 1780 and after to have had favourable balances of trade both with

---

11. Ibid. See also Charles W. Ingrao, *The Hessian Mercenary State: Ideas, Institutions and Reform under Frederick II, 1760–1785* (Cambridge, 1987), especially chapter 5.

other German states and with foreign countries; these include Prussia, Saxony and the German-Bohemian lands of the Habsburgs. For the whole of Germany, however, this was almost certainly not the case and especially not with the two biggest foreign trading partners, France and Holland. But trade, of course, is only one component of a larger balance of payments; and here, while the picture is somewhat less clear, it would again seem that Germany was a net importer of capital, chiefly in the form of loans from Holland, Britain and Switzerland which were not offset by receipts from foreign subsidies, tourism and so on. That there was growth almost everywhere over the whole period cannot be doubted; but it is hard to say anything very definite about overall levels of prosperity beyond confirming that while the gross national product was larger at the end of the period than at the beginning, its distribution was even more unequal and the numbers of both urban and rural poor as a percentage of the population grew steadily.

It seems clear, however, that within the business communities of at least the larger and economically more vigorous territories, a sense of growth and a new confidence in entrepreneurship was developing in the last third of the eighteenth century or so. A rather mild but gradually growing criticism of the restrictive and regulative policies of mercantilist governments was becoming evident and which stemmed less from any theoretical commitment to economic liberalism (which would not come for a while) than from an evolving sense that governments and their narrow-minded fiscal advisers and accountants were simply not as alert to new economic opportunities as were the financiers, merchants and manufacturers who were in the trenches fighting the daily battles of the business world. This developing attitude of self-sufficiency, though natural enough in the already long-independent mercantile communities of the more enterprising free cities, was not yet dominant elsewhere; but its evolution in the last third of the eighteenth century was both reflected in and assisted by the emergence not only of a literature devoted to business management, but also of special schools and academies which taught the principles, terminology and practical aspects of management. The latter appeared in Hamburg, Vienna, Leipzig, Mannheim, Frankfurt, Berlin and Cologne; significantly, all but the one in Vienna were established by the local merchant communities acting without government urging or assistance.[12]

In spite of the foregoing, it is not absolutely clear how much the

12. Aubin and Zorn, eds., *Handbuch*, I, 571.

various mercantile policies of governments had to do with what was, on the whole, a slowly but steadily improving economic picture for Germany throughout the 150 years discussed here. While the positive accomplishments of mercantilism have been emphasized so far, one must consider that in that time, especially, the economy was a much larger and more ponderous force than was any government and whether a different government policy – or indeed none at all – would have made a substantial difference in overall economic development, or its timing, is open to question. What seems beyond question, however, is that mercantilism as Cameralism – that is, as a system serving the fiscal needs of the territorial princes – was a considerable success. It more or less successfully funded their governing apparatus, their armies and wars and their lavish court establishments, with attendant palaces, parks, art collections, libraries, gifts, pensions and so on. The problem of whether and to what extent mercantilism as *economic* policy may have increased the overall social product is therefore complicated by the further question of the degree to which as *fiscal* policy it may have dampened economic development by steering it in the direction of taxability for purposes which were not as conducive to future growth as might have been the case had the taxes been left as investment capital in the private sector. It is certainly true that net investment in manufacturing and trade, as well as private saving, was small throughout the entire pre-industrial period, so that a great deal of the gross social product was used up in private consumption. It is equally true that tax monies were eventually recirculated through the economy. But at least some of the fact that Germany was capital-poor, as it clearly was, may have arisen from the existence of so very many princely and prelatic courts, all of them siphoning off social capital in the process of consuming comparatively large amounts of paid labour in economically unproductive services – including military establishments which by some estimates may have totalled over 600,000 men. That the various territories conducted highly protectionist policies not only against non-German countries but also against themselves was another dubious aspect of mercantilism, since in the name of territorial self-sufficiency it tended to waste social capital by subsidizing otherwise unprofitable enterprises. As in so many other ways in the history of this period, therefore, territorial division also cast a long shadow over the economic fortunes of the peoples of Germany.

CHAPTER TWELVE
The Structure of German Society, 1650–1800

Like most of the rest of Europe in the early modern period, Germany was a 'society of orders' (*Ständegesellschaft*) – a society, that is, in which the vast majority of the population belonged to groups differentiated from each other by sharply drawn legal and social criteria and organized in a hierarchy of prestige. The circumstances of birth, family and occupation (and inveteracy of one or both), education and political function, among other things, determined the individual's place in the social order, but almost always as a member of a group with recognizably similar characteristics. Identification with a group was important not only to the individual, who could scarcely locate himself in society without it, but also to government and to other groups, which essentially could not deal with individuals except as parts of the larger corporations which represented them. And while both upward and downward mobility was possible for individuals, a permanent hierarchy of social strata was considered part of a natural and divinely ordained order which defined both rights and duties for all and thus preserved social peace and equilibrium. Not the least of the functions of government at all levels was therefore to police the barriers which separated not only whole orders or estates from one another, but also the very important secondary stratification within those orders.

That complex secondary stratification is one reason why it is unproductive to deal with the German social structure in terms of the old, uncomplicated medieval division of society into clergy, nobility and commons – a categorization which still persisted here and there in the literature on the subject, but which most contemporaries well knew to be oversimple and misleading by now. Another reason is that while the clergy was still recognized as a distinct vocational group, the social prestige of its members had long since been determined as much or more by the particular offices held and by the criterion of noble vs. commoner status as by the social function of the group as a whole. Finally, to follow the medieval formula, which normally equated 'commons' with 'bourgeoisie'[1], would require eliminating the peasantry – fully three-quarters of the German population as late as 1800 – from the social order altogether. Recent historiography has adopted a scheme which makes more sense of the complex social structure as it was perceived and enforced by those who lived within it and which, while comprehensive, does not ignore the most basic traditional distinction between those groups which were privileged by law and custom and those that were not. By this scheme, German society of the early modern period breaks down into three main groups, each composed of several strata: the nobility, the bourgeoisie and the peasantry. In addition, various 'outsiders' and minorities existed, which were treated by special arrangements permitting them to live and work in society without becoming a fully integral part of it. The clergy, finally, always an 'honourable' group by virtue of vocation, was apportioned differentially among the three chief groups.

The nobility, which for many compelling reasons deserves to be dealt with first in this kind of analysis, was comprised of some 50,000 families with about 250,000 members in 1800. It was most importantly divided into those directly answerable only to the emperor (the 'immediate' or imperial nobility) and those subject to a territorial lord (the 'mediate' or territorial nobility). The former included all of the territorial princes, secular and ecclesiastical, as well as the Imperial Counts and Knights; the latter embraced virtually all others. The so-called 'high nobility' – those with imperial immediacy and the title of count or higher – included all the imperial nobility except the Imperial Knights, who together with the territorial nobles (further divided in some territories into 'lords' and 'knights') comprised the 'low nobility'. By 1700 or so, a further distinction was drawn between an 'old' and a 'new' nobility, which required the former to prove ancestral nobility prior to 1400; it arose primarily as a way of denying certain employments, especially in the church, to families of relatively recent noble origin. A special (but real) nobility was that possessed by some patricians of both Imperial Cities and a few of the oldest territorial cities. Ennoblement of commoners by

---

1. While the terms *bourgeoisie, bourgeois, bourgeoises* carry different historical connotations from the German *Bürgertum, bürgerlich,* and *Bürger,* the French will be used here as a matter of convenience.

emperor and territorial princes was possible and not rare and could be either 'personal' (for the lifetime of the individual only) or heritable; the older nobility successfully used its influence to keep the latter sort of entitlement to a minimum.

Within the nobility, at its various levels, rights of lordship (*Herrschaftsrechte*) were probably the most important single mark of status, ranging from the *Landeshoheit* of the territorial princes through the almost equal powers of the Imperial Counts and Knights on their tiny lands down to the local seigneurial rights exercised over their peasants by some territorial nobles, especially in lands east of the Elbe. With or without such rights, however, all nobles enjoyed certain privileges denied the rest of society: special judicial treatment, freedom from direct (and some indirect) taxation, hunting rights (defended with unusual ferocity against criticism from both peasants and princes) and other dispensations, not least of all a large measure of freedom from the annoying harassments of the princely 'police state'. But if the fact of privilege made of the nobility a unified aristocratic order, there was very little else that did and in the years from 1650 to 1800 there was a great and steadily growing variety of condition among nobles with respect to life-style, amounts and sources of income, location of residence, occupation, education and personal culture.

This increasing heterogeneity was to a large extent the result of forced adaptation to a long period of socio-economic crisis for the nobility, beginning in the mid-fifteenth century and continuing into the early seventeenth. During this period, several factors – loss of military employment, the celibacy required by economically necessary refuge in monastic establishments and other causes – resulted in both an extinction of numerous noble family lines and the self-derogation to non-noble status of families which could no longer meet the economic expectations of nobility. There seems to have been a slight further decrease even after 1650; by 1800, nobles had dropped to 1 per cent of the population from a number perhaps half again that large in 1500. The greatest saviours of noble fortunes after 1600 were clearly the territorial princes, from the emperor on down, whose courts, armies and governments employed literally tens of thousands of nobles for whom traditional sources of income – mostly from agriculture – were either inadequate or nonexistent.[2]

2. This included ecclesiastical states and foundations as well, where the cathedral chapters alone provided 1200–1400 positions for Catholic noblement, among whom the Imperial Knights were particularly strongly represented. Aubin and Zorn, eds., *Handbuch*, I, 589.

Throughout Germany, there developed a clear preference for nobles to fill positions in civil administration and military command and particularly the higher positions; they not only lent prestige to the princes' governments, but also provided them with a means of binding this highest social class more tightly to their thrones. Imperial Counts, as 'high nobility', were especially favoured for the most important court, ministerial and diplomatic offices. A steady pressure on princes from the older nobility to exclude both bourgeoises and the newly-ennobled from such employment reflected both its sense of entitlement to these posts and its increasing dependence on them.

By the eighteenth century, the number of nobles who derived all or the largest part of their income from state service of one kind or another was sufficiently large as to modify significantly the traditional picture of their class as composed of landowning rural magnates. Apart from the fact that in a number of areas a substantial proportion of nobles no longer lived in the country at all, many of those who remained there were quite poor. Figures given for Prussia in 1800, for example, indicate that as few as one-third of the nobles in the central province of Brandenburg, the Kurmark, lived in the country; for Silesia and East Prussia, the numbers were two-fifths and three-quarters, respectively. Probably one-third of the Silesian nobility and a quarter of the families in the province of Neumark, furthermore, could fairly be called poor.[3] For all that, it is probably not accurate to draw a very sharp distinction between a 'court nobility' and a 'country nobility' as yet. Members of the same family could very often be found in both places and while some figures show that as many as four-fifths of adult nobles in Brandenburg – an admittedly not altogether typical example – were active in the Prussian military or civil service as early as 1718–19, that did not necessarily mean either full-time or lifetime service: leaves of absence, dismissal, resignation or retirement often meant a return to rural life.[4]

Still, this *was* becoming a different kind of nobility in some important respects. Inevitably, life at or near the court – the centre of aristocratic *politesse* and of such high culture as the various princes could afford, according to their diverse means and desires – worked a change in behaviour, tastes and attitudes in the direction of greater

---

3. Diedrich Saalfeld, 'Die ständische Gliederung der Gesellschaft Deutschlands im Zeitalter des Absolutismus. Ein Quantifizierungsversuch', in *Vierteljahrschrift für Sozial- und Wirtschaftsgeschichte*, 67 (1980), 467.
4. Aubin and Zorn, eds., *Handbuch*, I, 577.

sophistication and refinement (if also occasionally of foppish superficiality and indebtedness through overindulgence in gambling and other expensive entertainments of court life). Foreign (especially French) words and phrases, fashions, manners and cultural standards achieved a general currency among the court nobility and from there later filtered down in varying degrees of purity to the literate bourgeoisie of the territorial cities. Employment in state service also gradually changed the way nobles thought about education. For a time after 1648, an enhanced self-awareness among the nobility led to a notable growth in the number of 'knights' academies' designed as finishing schools for young noblemen, in which a heavy emphasis on French, fencing, riding and dancing was usual. But since state service for the vast majority of nobles was real, not honorific and increasingly required juristic or other specialized knowledge, university training (often preceded by study at high schools whose educational emphases were different from those of most knights' academies) became generally acknowledged as a necessary supplement to (or even substitute for) the academies, many of which by 1800 had either disappeared or, while not abandoning their aristocratic features altogether, had taken on the character of more purposefully oriented vocational schools. On the other hand, the well established practice of sending noble sons on 'cavaliers' tours' to Italy, France, the Netherlands and elsewhere to round out their educations persisted throughout the period as an earmark of the class.

It is also true that life in the cities which housed the courts, garrisons or ecclesiastical establishments in which the nobles worked was very different from the relatively isolated existence of the rural manor. In particular, nobles were confronted with an urban bourgeois culture with which they had not previously been forced to reckon. For most, there was never any question of submerging themselves in that culture and especially not in its mercantile aspects, against which they were thoroughly inoculated by both law and tradition. But contacts between nobles and the upper strata of bourgeois society – the leaders of city administrations, the cultural elite, professional people and coworkers and subordinates in their own civil or military employments – were unavoidable and led to accommodations of various kinds, of which the most frequent and congenial occurred on the common ground of interest in scientific and literary culture. From the early seventeenth to the mid-eighteenth century there was a steady increase in the number of literary and cultural societies with mixed memberships of nobles and bourgeoises; to these must then be added the 250–300 German lodges of the Freemasons founded from the 1730s onward, as well as the 50–60 'patriotic and utilitarian societies' and the 400–450 'reading societies' (*Lesegesellschaften*) which sprouted everywhere into existence between 1750 and the end of the century. Equality of membership was observed in almost all of these; it was formally insisted on in the case of the secret meetings of the Freemasons and was publicly demonstrated in the reading societies. The number of people who at one time or another attended meetings of the Masonic lodges and the reading societies may have reached 40,000.[5]

It is clear from these and other evidences that by the last third or more of the eighteenth century a large and still growing percentage of nobles and especially of the influential court and bureaucratic nobility, were on fairly relaxed speaking terms with the higher bourgeoisie and particularly with the more highly educated, culturally productive elements of it – the so-called *Bildungsbürgertum*. But it appears equally obvious that this greater familiarity did not bring with it any real softening of class boundaries, much less any breakdown of them. The remarkable sociability of a court such as that of Karl August of Saxe-Weimar (1775–1828), where cultural luminaries such as Goethe, Schiller, Herder and others associated with the prince and the high court nobility in an atmosphere of companionable fellowship was highly unusual – though the example does serve to emphasize the importance of the dispositions of the prince in setting the tone for social relationships at court. Bourgeois officials rarely attained the highest ministerial positions and still regularly experienced the humiliation of being bypassed for promotion by less well qualified or experienced noblemen. In some territories, indeed – Prussia being the best but not the only example – the preference for nobles in state service after the mid-eighteenth century was even more pronounced than previously, leading one historian to speak of a 'refeudalization tendency'.[6] Marriages between noblemen and bourgeois women – especially rich ones – while not unheard-of, continued to be rare, though they were somewhat more common among the lesser and economically more poorly positioned nobility. The ennoblement of bourgeoises for achievements or services in everything from trade and finance to government, science, art and literature was already fairly common

---

5. The origin and history of these various types of societies is explored in detail by Richard van Dülmen, *Die Gesellschaft der Aufklärer. Zur bürgerlichen Emanzipation und aufklärerischen Kultur in Deutschland* (Frankfurt, 1986).
6. Vierhaus, *Staaten und Stände*, p. 206.

by even before 1700 and became more frequent in the course of the eighteenth century. But while this practice may have bled off some of the pressure for upward movement into the nobility – of which there was remarkably little throughout the period, however – it also tended to sharpen the distinction between noble and non-noble by implicitly discrediting the previous status of the newly ennobled by conferring social advantages not available to them earlier regardless of their achievements.[7]

The increasing acceptance by nobles of employment in the service of the territorial princes, as well as other causes of absenteeism from their landed estates, had long been criticized by some segments of both the bourgeoisie and the old, rural nobility as an abdication of responsibility, a surrender to princely autocracy, involving the sacrifice of the important principle that the nobility, occupying the 'middle position' in political life between prince and people, needed to maintain its independence from the former in order to protect the freedom of the latter – a chief legitimization of the special rights of the nobility. As the eighteenth century arrived and wore on, this criticism blended with and then gave way to two other types of critique: the first was simply an updated version of the venerable 'court- and noble-bashing' practised with such earnest delight by the humanists and which had never utterly lost its currency since their time. Directed against the luxury, extravagance and artificial social relationships of the courts and their now much larger complements of nobles, this kind of criticism is best exemplified in the book *The Master and the Servant* (1759) by Friedrich Karl von Moser, who was somewhat untypical of his fellow critics only in the relative gentleness with which he delivered his message. A second and much more serious criticism and one which occasioned a very vigorous debate in the last three decades of the eighteenth century, went to the very roots of the concept of nobility itself. A product of the enlightenment, which tended to predicate social distinction on the successful performance of useful social functions, this critique demanded that nobles justify their privileged position by actions beneficial to society – in other words, that they use their exalted and influential office for a social purpose more elevated than that of simply propagating their own privileges.

It was of great importance to the later history of Germany that its nobility, from the princes on down, withstood and survived this

7. Ibid., 209.

criticism with relative ease, and was able to enter the maelstrom of the Revolutionary era as a fundamentally cohesive, self-confident and socially esteemed class. The enlightenment itself was one reason. Its spirit proved capable of penetrating an increasingly well educated nobility almost as easily as it did the *Bildungsbürgertum* and representatives of the nobility were prominent official and unofficial advocates and executors of the various reforms in agrarian relationships, education, social welfare, religious affairs and other aspects of society associated with the 'enlightened absolutism' which appeared in a significant number of territories large and small after about the middle of the eighteenth century. Noble landowners were also among the forces encouraging various local reforms, including village schools and agricultural innovation. The favourable publicity given to them, as well as to reforming princes and ministers of state (most of them nobles) equalled or exceeded the bad press devoted to the misgovernment, corruption, moral dissolution and meanness more or less correctly identified among princes and nobles here and there and helped to discredit criticisms directed too broadly at the nobility as an entire class.

There is another important fact: in both reality and public perception, the German nobility was, on the whole, a *working* nobility, not a parasitic one and the life style permitted the vast majority of nobles by their income, regardless of its source, was generally modest and in more than a few cases downright frugal. Management of rural estates, for those who lived there, allowed neither languor nor laziness; and the court and bureaucratic nobles, regardless of preferment, were not much if at all less competent or hard-working than their bourgeois counterparts. In spite of its critics, therefore, the nobility retained its social honour as a genuinely functional class which for generations yet was to set the tone of social relationships in Germany. By combining the aristocratic tradition of lordship with dutiful employment in their courts, governments and armies, the territorial princes had given the nobility the reputation of a true service class and therewith a new lease on life. In doing so, they incidentally contributed a powerful reason for the long acceptance of the institutions of both nobility and monarchy itself in Germany.[8]

The clerical order in Germany comprised between one and two per cent of the population, varying by region, with a larger percentage

---

8. Ibid., 216.

of Catholic than Protestant clerics, due both to the differing administrative structures of the two and the larger number of Catholic conventual houses.[9] Both clergies can be dealt with in this context rather briefly, partly because their political importance as separate 'estates' had virtually disappeared in the course of the Reformation and Counter-Reformation and partly because in terms of the origins of its members it was sharply divided along the lines of noble vs. non-noble, which here as elsewhere tended to determine the location of individuals in the overall social structure. The German Catholic church is often referred to as an *Adelskirche* (a 'nobles' church') in this period, not because its clergy came mostly from noble families – in fact, they came very largely from bourgeois families, even in the higher territorial positions – but because of the existence of some sixty ecclesiastical territories with the rank of imperial estates, ranging from the three electorates of Mainz, Trier and Cologne through the various prince-bishoprics down to the prince-abbacies and -priories.

The elected prelates who governed these territories and especially those above the rank of abbot, came almost uniformly from the aristocracy, mostly the 'high' imperial nobility. At the same time, the governing councils (chapters) of these territories, together with their administrators, offered positions for well over 1000 people – again, mostly nobles. Many individuals within this high imperial prelacy were not ordained priests and viewed themselves primarily as secular administrators, leaving their spiritual duties to vicars-general of mostly bourgeois origin while they pursued a courtly-aristocratic lifestyle. Considering the further fact that Catholic monastic foundations well into the eighteenth century provided livings for very large numbers of noble sons and daughters – to the point at which some were almost nothing but welfare houses for the nobility – the term *Adelskirche* gains real meaning. In the Catholic territories, however, the higher clergy (excluding the prince-prelates themselves) were drawn chiefly from the upper bourgeoisie, with a sprinkling of peasants and nobles. The lower clergy came mostly from the petty bourgeoisie of artisans and shopkeepers, though many village priests were of peasant origin.

In the Protestant (mainly Lutheran) church, there were still bishops in sees such as Osnabrück and Lübeck and a handful of cathedral chapters as well, in which nobles were well represented.

---

9. Jeserich *et al.*, *Deutsche Verwaltungsgeschichte*, I, 247–9, and Aubin and Zorn, eds., *Handbuch*, I, 578, 589–90 are helpful on this topic.

But these were unimportant in a church which had become strongly oriented towards pastoral functions and in which the pastors, since the Reformation, had come to constitute almost a new class in themselves. Few nobles took up this calling, both because of its low pay and because of the abject dependency of most territorial churches on the princes who controlled them; and very few entered the pastorate from the lowest classes of either town or country because of the requirements for higher theological education which became universal by soon after 1650. Thus, many clergymen were recruited from bourgeois officialdom and to a lesser extent from artisan families; but a much larger proportion – as many as half, it would appear, in some territories – came from pastoral families themselves, thus establishing the rectory as a significant element of continuity within this social group. The highest internal standing in it was enjoyed by the court preachers and the superintendents and other high officials of the consistories – indicative again of the social importance of the court – who were among the very few bourgeoises considered acceptable as husbands for noble daughters. While by definition their profession was an 'honourable' one, the rural pastors, like the village priests in the Catholic church, were sometimes treated rather condescendingly by their urban colleagues, partly because of a penurious lifestyle which usually required them to become part-time farmers themselves. But they were a significant civilizing and enlightening influence in their districts and were at least as strong a force as any other in the improvement of village schooling, local welfare and agricultural improvement.

By 1800, almost a full quarter of the German population lived in cities of one or another size, representing a significant proportional increase relative to the rural population from both one and two centuries earlier. Some of the most spectacular growth rates were in those territorial cities which housed the residence and governing apparatus of the larger princes, while among the Imperial and Free Cities only the more important were able to hold their own and the rest declined in population throughout the eighteenth century. A few cities, indeed, actually lost their pretensions to imperial immediacy – Brunswick in 1671 and Magdeburg in 1680, for example – but the others, large and small, at least retained the dignity of full self-government throughout the period, while the territorial cities witnessed a fairly steady erosion of their administrative autonomy as they were more closely geared to the economic and political purposes of their princes. A few territorial cities were governed by powerful merchant and crafts guilds; elsewhere, in many cities of both kinds, government lay in the hands of a council and magistracy dominated by a small group of patrician families whose claim to rule was based primarily on inveteracy rather than sheer wealth, since while well-to-do they were not necessarily the richest families in the city. In some places – Nürnberg, for example – the patriciate ruled alone, while in others, such as Cologne, it shared the government with other elements of the community. Many of the territorial cities of more recent origin had no patriciates at all, resulting in a more open governmental structure and the same was true even of the Free Cities of Hamburg and Bremen, where the old council families not only admitted new ones to their circle but also imposed a requirement of legal training on the mayor and members of the council.

Any analysis of the social structure of the cities must begin by noting that not all urban dwellers were 'citizens', or *Bürger*. Citizens were those who had voluntarily acquired the so-called *Bürgerrecht* by taking an oath before the council, proving ownership of land and house and paying a substantial acceptance fee. All others were merely 'residents' (*Beisassen*) or 'guests', and they included almost half the inhabitants of most cities. Theoretically, citizenship (which was always local and non-transferrable) conferred an opportunity to participate in the city government through election to the council; depending on the constitution of the city in question, that might never happen, but the citizen was also possessed of such potentially burdensome 'rights' as military service, watch duty, construction of fortifications and other municipal chores. This, together with its financial obligations, explains why many people who could otherwise afford it chose to avoid citizenship, including most of those whose residence was temporary: wintering noblemen, foreign merchants, princely officials and so on. But the overwhelming majority of 'residents' consisted of those whose circumstances denied them eligibility for citizenship, chief among them journeymen, domestic servants and day labourers. But while the most fundamental social division among those who lived permanently in cities was between citizens and non-citizens, this distinction illuminates only the smallest part of the pattern of social stratification in the cities. That pattern, already well established by 1650, was composed of differentiations based on both wealth and occupation (the latter becoming more important with time) and it increased in complexity with the size of the city. The description which follows is based on the larger cities precisely because it permits an appreciation of that complexity.

The upper stratum of urban society consisted of a small patriciate (where it existed at all) and, just below it, a larger group of 'honourable' families (*Honoratioren*). Together, they comprised 3–6 per cent of the urban population. The patriciate was an 'urban nobility' in a more than merely figurative sense, since many of its members had attained formal patents of nobility and had a friendly relationship with the territorial nobility cemented by frequent intermarriage. While most families had risen to the patriciate through wealth originally acquired in trade and commerce, in some cities they had developed an 'aristocratic' prejudice against trade and closed themselves to new entrants from that source; in others, whether closed for other reasons or not, the patriciate continued to be active in commercial transactions. The *Honoratioren* consisted of the rich wholesale merchants, resident nobles, clerics, university-educated professionals such as jurists and physicians, permanently resident princely officials and, later on, some numbers of the new entrepreneurial elite. There were enormous differences in wealth within this group; the richest of them sometimes bought nobility, but with or without it engaged in a conspicuous consumption of which most of the blooded nobility must have been envious: impressive merchants' houses of baroque and rococo style were built in the busier trading centres, with elaborate gardens and sculptures, while substantial philanthropic endowments enriched the musical and theatrical life of such cities as Frankfurt, Hamburg and Leipzig.

Below this double-layered upper stratum was a 'middle class' – the bourgeoisie in the most essential sense of the term – which on average constituted perhaps just over 40 per cent of urban populations and which again can be divided into two sub-groups: an 'upper' middle class (*Grossbürgertum*) consisting of large retail merchants, brewers, the more prosperous master artisans, business agents, notaries and artists; and a considerably more numerous 'lower' middle class of small shopkeepers, commercial employees, subordinate officials, the generality of independent artisans and the so-called *Ackerbürger*, citizens who derived some or most of their income from out-farming. The distinction between the two groups was one of wealth, occupation and to some extent of outlooks and attitudes as well: unlike the great wholesale merchants, nobles and professional men of the *Honoratioren*, as well as the travelling businessmen of the upper middle class, whose horizons extended well beyond the walls of the home town, this petty bourgeoisie, or *Kleinbürgertum*, had a mentality almost entirely confined to its immediate surroundings, with a peevish self-interest in preservation

of status and elimination of economic competition and an entrepreneurial spirit which exhausted itself in the simplicities of local
supply and demand.[10] It was a profoundly conservative element in
society, which in the territorial cities welcomed the regulative order
of the autocratic state.

The guilds made up the numerically most important subsystem
within this middle class. Like citizenship itself, guild membership
was always local and could not be transferred into another city.
There were great differences in wealth between masters even of the
same guild; only a relative few belonged to the upper middle class,
usually because they had an income from trade in addition to their
artisan work, or because they worked in high-turnover specialties
such as bookbinding, gold- and silversmithing, confections and
innkeeping. In all cities there was a hierarchy of guilds, which
differed from place to place; the merchant guilds were nearly always
first in honour, however, followed by the crafts guilds in an order
determined by various factors such as length of existence, elegance of
product, or importance of product to the economy of the city,
especially in the export trade. In lowest rank were the manual-service
and agricultural guilds, including copyists, cobblers, tailors, spin-
ners, linen-weavers and clothmakers. While the guilds were fraternal
and mutual assistance organizations, there were fierce rivalries
between them and though masters, journeymen and apprentices may
have lived more or less amicably most of the time in the same
quarters, there was a well-understood and -observed social chasm
between them. As suggested earlier, there were some cities largely
governed by guilds which had successfully fought for representation
on the city council; but since council membership required much
unremunerated time, only the most prosperous masters could afford
it and with virtual heritability of such membership a small elite
analogous to the patriciate arose here.

The remainder of the people in the cities belonged to a 'sub-
bourgeois' stratum, consisting of those possessed neither of citizenship nor of an independent skill conferring a regular income. Its
numbers grew steadily throughout the period, from some 20 per
cent of the population in the sixteenth century to as much as 65 per
cent in some of the large cities in the late eighteenth century, with an
average figure for cities of all sizes of around 50 per cent. Among
those willing and able to work, the largest groups in this category
were composed of journeymen artisans and domestic servants (the

10. Vierhaus, *Staaten und Stände*, p. 201.

latter of whom alone comprised 16–20 per cent of the population of mid- to large-sized cities). Next in numbers and growing, were the wage labourers, of whom only a minority were part of the guild organization as piece-work artisans; the 17 per cent of Berlin's population consisting of such workers in the early 1780s was certainly larger than elsewhere, but it represented the same trend. The 'pure' (full-time and propertyless) industrial workers, on the other hand, cannot have exceeded one per cent or so of the urban population even by 1800.

Beneath this working population was a stratum of people either permanently or temporarily unable to work, or unwilling to work – the latter marvellously termed 'shy of work' in the parlance of the time. It included those disabled by birth, war or judicial maiming, the banished, the seriously retarded, many of the not dangerously insane, widows, orphans, neglected children and men discharged from various employments in military service; most of them begged sporadically or permanently. Begging, in fact, was shockingly common in this period, but that was only secondarily the result of an abysmally inadequate organized eleemosynary and social welfare system. Behind it lay the double social attitude that begging was acceptable as part of the ordinary tableau of daily life, neither unusually shameful nor socially dangerous and that nothing really permanent could be done about poverty anyway: 'the poor we shall always have with us' was a phrase which both reflected and justified the failure to expend social capital on the poor. Even in the enlightenment, social meliorism as a pragmatic philosophy was not strong at the popular level.[11] With few other means of looking after beggars, the authorities either tolerated them, shoved them into neighbouring territories or, in some cases, rounded them up to put as many to work as could. Generally not much more respected than beggars, though certainly not as poor as they[12], were those who belonged to the 'dishonourable' occupations, which only slowly

11. Begging was more evident in Catholic cities and states, especially the ecclesiastical states, than in Protestant ones, mostly because of differences in attitudes towards almsgiving. A contemporary estimate that between 12–20,000 of Cologne's population of 50,000 were beggars was doubtlessly exaggerated, but still says something about the impression mendicancy made and in any case is not far off other more recent estimates that beggars in the ecclesiastical states generally stood at a ratio of 1:4 to the rest of the population. Lütge, *Deutsche Sozial- und Wirtschaftsgeschichte*, pp. 382–3.

12. At least a few beggars were successful enough at their business to become 'street capitalists' as small-time money-lenders – 'loan-sharks', really, since their interest rates were exorbitant.

achieved greater acceptability: hangmen, torturers, jailers, gravediggers, herdsmen, animal renderers, street entertainers, pedlars, tinkers, scissors-grinders and others who roamed the land without fixed residence or attachment to a guild and who were therefore considered 'outsiders'. Probably 10–15 per cent of urban households were so poor as to pay no taxes at all; another 40 per cent or so either paid the pittance known as the 'have-nothing tax' (*Habenichtssteuer*), or were included in the lowest tax rate of the lower middle class.

While the percentage of the German population engaged in rural employments – the peasantry, loosely speaking – had shrunk by 5–10 per cent, depending on region, in the course of the seventeenth and eighteenth centuries, it still constituted three-quarters of the total in 1800. Its composition and circumstances were almost as varied and complex as those of nobility and bourgeoisie and the need to generalize in order to avoid what would otherwise be endless detail is even more imperative in its case than in theirs. One may first distinguish between peasants who were legally free and those who were not. The former constituted only some 4–8 per cent of the peasant population throughout the period, existed primarily in western (especially northwestern) Germany and many owned their own farms. The unfree, comprising the rest of the peasantry, were subject to legal constraints which bound them either to the person or the land of the owner, or both and which consequently limited their freedom of movement and of choice in various ways, as well as requiring regular or irregular dues, fees, ground rents and personal and family labour services for the lord. As a rule, in all of Germany west of the Elbe the effects of servile (unfree) status, however various in detail, were greatly less onerous than in the territories east of it, where the great entrepreneurial noble estates known as *Gutsherrschaften* were prevalent and where jurisdictional rights of lords were much less restricted than in the west.[13]

While personal freedom was probably the highest indicator of social status among the peasantry, it was not always a good measure of economic well-being, which depended more on the size and quality of land of individual farms and on the rights of tenure peasants had on that land. There were a number of different such

13. The proportion of peasants subject to the servitude of *Gutsherrschaft* varied from territory to territory, but was highest – over 60 per cent – in Mecklenburg, all of Pomerania and Silesia.

rights, varying considerably in characteristic frequency from one region to another and which embraced tenures ranging from heritability with (or without) right of divisibility, to lifetime tenure of the possessor only, to multi-year leases and finally to 'precarious' tenure, permitting eviction at the landlord's whim. In fact and regardless of which right legally prevailed, a strong tendency towards observance of heritability within the family, bringing with it guarantees for long-term investment of time and money in their farms by peasants looking to their families' futures, can be noted even by 1600. This drift became more pronounced as a result of the rural labour shortage caused by the Thirty Years War and in the later eighteenth century became a major objective of agrarian reform in a number of territories whose governments recognized the benefits of heritability for agricultural productivity and rural stability.

As this movement gained ground, furthermore, status distinctions within the peasantry based on the details of their differing conditions of servitude – always excepting East Elbia – as well as on the criterion of freedom vs. servitude itself, increasingly gave way to more materialistic distinctions, of which the size of farms was most important.[14] Since heritable tenure conferred rights of disposition of lands, buildings, livestock and implements which in practice were not much less than those of full ownership – often including mortgageability; and since the size of the farm determined the share of village common lands (woods and pasture, primarily) each peasant family could claim, the social standing of those with the larger holdings in the village community was correspondingly high. They tended to monopolize the important village offices and by frequent intermarriage such well-to-do families in some places came to constitute a virtual village patriciate, with a heritable monopoly on posts of local honour. This was especially noticeable in southwestern Germany, where there even developed groups reminiscent of the *Honoratioren* of the cities, consisting of mill owners, brewers, other prosperous peasants, pastors, governmental domains lessees and, eventually, even teachers.[15]

Just as not all urban dwellers were *Bürger*, not all who worked the

---

14. Nearly as important to this shift of emphasis was the tendency of landlords in most of western Germany to commute labour services, whose different kinds and amounts called attention to somewhat unequal degrees of servitude, to money payments, thus establishing an inequality only with respect to the cash value of services, not their legal origins. Jeserich *et al.*, *Deutsche Verwaltungsgeschichte*, I, 255.
15. Ibid., 256.

land were 'peasants' by contemporary usage. That term was reserved for those who possessed fields in the village *Flur*, the arable lands of the village district, as well as a share in the village commons, according to an inexact formula which differentiated between 'full', 'half-', and 'quarter-peasants'. The 'full' peasant (*Vollbauer, Vollhufner*) theoretically worked a 'full farm', defined as one whose return could by itself support a peasant family of average size. In fact, even some 'half farms' did that, so that a 'full farm' was in reality likely to be one which supported an extended family which included one or more farm hands or domestic servants. Still, numerous half- and most quarter-peasants did have to find part-time work for themselves or members of their families to scrape by and can therefore be reckoned as belonging to a peasant lower class of small farmers. Below them were the very numerous cottagers, or 'gardeners', (*Kätner, Kossäten, Kotsassen*), who usually possessed a home and garden, often on the edge of the village or on common meadowland; they characteristically derived a significant part of their income from artisanry, cottage industry or agricultural day labour, but were often able to improve their position by buying into small farming. Not all of them were poor and the line between them and the quarter-peasants, for example, was fairly fluid.

The cottagers were different from the rural artisans, who perhaps should not be included in the peasantry at all, since they made nearly all of their living from piecework as smiths, wheelwrights, or whatever and merely dabbled in agriculture. Both groups, however, were higher on the rural social scale than the so-called 'brink-sitters' (*Brinksitzer* or *Häusler*), who had small dwellings but no gardens or fields and who had to take wage labour in rural textile manufacturing or other branches of the domestic system. They, together with the full-time day labourers and the 8–12 per cent of the rural folk who worked as domestics, formed the lowest, propertyless rural stratum. While figures provided by different authorities vary slightly, it is clear that between the late sixteenth and late eighteenth centuries a major socio-economic revolution had occurred in much of rural Germany. While the total amount of arable land under cultivation in individual peasant tenures (as opposed to landlord demesne) remained relatively constant throughout the period, its apportionment among the peasantry had changed dramatically in the direction of smaller farms. The number of full peasants fell by around half, while the number of those with small to very small holdings nearly doubled and a significant part of the rural population increase, especially after 1750, joined the propertyless class, which by 1800 may have accounted for 20 per cent or more of the whole rural population. In large areas of southern and southwestern Germany, as well as in Westphalia, Lower Saxony and Schleswig-Holstein, there were still considerable numbers of large and medium-sized peasant farms in the eighteenth century; but by 1790 or so it had become obvious that agrarian Germany simply could not absorb its increasing population. The spectre of mass immiseration, representing the wholly new long-term social phenomenon of pauperism, began to emerge in many areas, sometimes bringing with it worrisomely higher levels of rural mendicancy and brigandage.[16]

As the above suggests, however, the economic situation of individual peasant families differed enormously. Genuine prosperity was possible for some, including not only the large peasants (*Grossbauern*) with farms large enough to require numerous hired hands, but also those living on or near the sea, rivers or canals, who may have taken part in coastal or riverine trade and occasionally in overland transport as well. To the extent that such part-time work was not essential to subsistence alone, it could produce an income adequate to support a comfortable existence; and the same could be true of the work of wives and children in the domestic system. In the vast majority of cases, however, the labour of the entire family unit was essential to survival, not to comfort. While for obvious reasons reliable generalizations of income and expenditure for the 'average' peasant farm are impossible, a study of one group of Lower Saxon farms of around fifty-five acres each for the year 1774 may not be far off the mark for small and medium-sized farms generally. It indicates that some 40 per cent of the gross product of these farms went to the landlord in the form of payments in cash, kind and labour services either for himself or for redistribution to the state (the larger part) and to local institutions such as church, school and poor relief; another 45 per cent covered all costs of operation and a bare 15 per cent could be considered net income to the peasant. Basic family expenses reduced this to a deficit of some 2 per cent, exclusive of any extraordinary one-time fees, dowries and outlays arising from

---

16. The issue of rural pauperism must be approached cautiously, however; one recent study of manorial labourers in Brandenburg has concluded that their standard of living, measured by food consumption (the chief household expense of most families), was much better than figures on wages and prices alone would suggest, since they received much of their income in the form of foodstuffs whose value was generally not reflected in statistics at all. See William W. Hagen, 'Working for the Junker: The Standard of Living of Manorial Laborers in Brandenburg, 1584–1810', in the *Journal of Modern History*, 58 (March, 1986), pp. 143–58.

accidents or sickness.[17] Extra work by some or all members of the household, inside or outside the home, was thus clearly a permanent necessity, emphasizing the importance of the family not only as the primary economic unit of pre-industrial society, but as a chief determinant of the individual's social status as well.

Oppressed though much of the peasantry was, however, it was not without recourse when its condition became suddenly or greatly worse. Peasant revolts were not uncommon in this period; but unlike the peasant 'wars' of an earlier time, they tended to be both sporadic and localized – generally as reactions against intolerable conditions in a specific time and place – and were accompanied by relatively little violence. Not all were strictly economic protests: events as dissimilar as occupation by foreign troops, sectarian religious quarrels, violation of local traditions and physical mistreatment by landlords (or, more often, by their overseers) could cause individual refusals to perform labour services, sometimes expanding to 'strikes' of whole villages and occasionally even abandonment of farms.[18] The omnipresent concern of political authorities to assure agrarian social stability actually led them to encourage peasants to seek judicial remedy for their grievances – an initiative to which peasants responded so enthusiastically as to create a serious new problem in itself: courts became clogged with peasant complaints against landlords, domains lessees and each other, many of them frivolous in the extreme and frequently caused by the ceaseless and self-interested prodding of unscrupulous rural lawyers. In many territories, this led not only to a cost-cutting reform and streamlining of court procedure, but also to both governmental and private efforts to instruct peasants in the rudiments of the law and of litigation in order to spare them (and the courts) the time and money otherwise sure to be expended on legally meritless grievances.[19] The various reforms of laws and regulations governing agrarian relationships instituted in the last decades of the eighteenth century were a further response of governments to the need for adjustments on the rural scene beneficial to the peasantry as the primary producer class and the backbone of a still overwhelmingly agrarian economy.

Aside from the major population groups already discussed – nobility, bourgeoisie and peasantry – Germany in this period also was (or

17. Aubin and Zorn, eds., *Handbuch*, I, 499–500.
18. Vierhaus, *Staaten und Stände*, pp. 193–4.
19. John G. Gagliardo, *From Pariah to Patriot: The Changing Image of the German Peasant, 1770–1840* (Lexington, Kentucky, 1969), pp. 44–6.

became) home to various not insignificant minority groups, almost all of which had two things in common: first, that religion played a role either in their reasons for settlement in Germany or in their identification as minorities within the general population; and second, that they had one or another kind of economic qualification which recommended them to the rulers of the territories in which they settled and without which permission to immigrate and remain would have been doubtful. Some of the earliest religious immigrants were Mennonites from the Netherlands, who before they gained official toleration in Holland in the late 1570s settled across northern Germany as far east as Danzig. Beginning at about the same time and continuing throughout the seventeenth century, were the immigrations of Dutch Calvinists, who settled in relatively sparse numbers in cities along the lower and middle Rhine, as well as in a number of coastal cities such as Emden, Hamburg and Danzig. They were active in trade as well as in high-quality artisan work – diamond-cutting, silk weaving and gold- and silversmithing, for example – but no group of them was of greater economic importance than the peasants who contributed their knowledge and experience to wetlands reclamation, especially along the lower reaches of the Vistula.

Of greater overall significance were the French Calvinists, the Huguenots, who fled by the tens of thousands into the Empire after 1685. The largest groups, totalling around 20,000, settled in Brandenburg-Prussia, especially in Berlin and Magdeburg; the remaining 40,000 of the early wave of immigrants were scattered in some 240 separate communities, with particular numerical strength in Hesse-Kassel, Württemberg and Bayreuth. With a largely urban background, they brought expertise not only in artisan production, notably in luxury manufactures, but also in wholesale commerce, finance and industrial entrepreneurship. For a long time, many of these Huguenot groups regarded themselves as a kind of social elite and refused real integration into the German population. This was made easier for them by the special privileges granted the larger communities, including separate churches, law courts, army regimental organization and freedom from guild membership and regulations and was reinforced by their own remarkable social insurance system of poor relief, health care and other charitable benevolences. In Prussia, as elsewhere, the prosperous Huguenots began to emerge from their self-imposed social and cultural isolation only after the Seven Years War, but thereafter became well-accepted members of their communities at both noble and bourgeois levels. The over 20,000 Salzburg Protestants driven from their land in 1731 also found homes elsewhere in Germany – over half of them in Prussia – and had less trouble adjusting to their new environment than the Huguenots because of fewer cultural and linguistic differences; they established themselves mostly in rural areas and were of real importance to agricultural improvement in northeastern East Prussia.

Jews, however, constituted the oldest and most significant of the minorities in the Empire. The emperor himself had once guaranteed the safety of the numerous Jewish communities in German cities and towns, but by 1600 that responsibility had largely been assumed by the territorial princes; only an unimportant assessment on Jews in Frankfurt and Worms persisted as a reminder of the original imperial guarantee. Forbidden to enter guilds or to practise ordinary trades and normally ineligible for *Bürgerrecht* except occasionally for fixed periods of time or on a revocable basis, they were forced to become money-lenders or -changers, pawn brokers, physicians and retail merchants and often several of these at once. They were allowed to charge higher interest rates on loans than Christians, however and the most successful of them achieved positions as *Hofjuden*, court factors, who financed princes and became provisioners of their courts and armies. These very wealthy Jewish families became an increasingly exclusive group through intermarriage, but avoided the pitfalls of excessive concentration of wealth in a very few hands by the distribution of business activity and therefore also of risk, among numerous family members. But the wealthy were a distinct minority of all Jews in Germany, most of whom lived by small-scale retailing or by practising the 'dishonourable' trades as pedlars, tinkers, second-hand dealers and so on. Many urban Jews were forced to beg and the generality of rural and small-town Jews were also poor.[20] The philanthropy of their more prosperous co-religionists helped out here and there, although some of the older, well established German-speaking Jews (such as the 500 or so proud families of the Frankfurt *Judengasse*, which constituted the self-appointed elite of German Jewry) often looked upon the unfortunate roving 'Beggar-Jews' with as much contempt as compassion.

The attitudes and behaviour of Christian Germans towards the Jews in their midst was more standoffish and cool than persecutive or violent. In a sense, of course, all special prescriptive or proscriptive legislation relating to Jews was at base persecutive; and there were incidents of violence against the persons and property of

20. Jeserich *et al.*, *Deutsche Verwaltungsgeschichte*, I, 260–1.

Jews, especially locally and during periods of acute economic crisis – as during the 'Kipper and Wipper' period. But the great importance of the court factors and of Jewish financial strength in general, as well as governmental fear and disapproval of civil disturbances of all kinds, combined to cast a generally protective shield around the Jews. Most of the Imperial Cities, to be sure, forced them to reside in rural locales outside the walls; but real ghettos were rare. Official persecutions were similarly infrequent, but did occur, as when the Habsburg government decreed the expulsion of all Jews from the hereditary lands in 1670–71; but those forced out of Vienna were invited elsewhere – especially to Brandenburg, where they received special legal status in the two cities (Berlin and Frankfurt on the Oder) where in 1700 most of the electorate's 2500 Jews resided. From the mid-eighteenth century onward, there was a slow general movement towards easing restrictions on Jews, much of it sponsored by an enlightened officialdom and carried out more by ignoring existing law than by new emancipatory legislation. A notable exception was Emperor Joseph II's Edict of Toleration of 1781, which conferred better civil rights on Jews in Austria and abolished their clothing insignia – in recognition of which, in 1788, they received the further 'privilege' of the first military obligation imposed on Jews anywhere in Germany. In Prussia, Frederick II tolerated Jews only in cities and distinguished between some 200 well-to-do Jews whom he favoured with heritable letters of protection and others who had such protection only for their own lifetimes. After his death, in 1791, full Prussian citizenship was granted to a Jew for the first time. Thus, while the trend towards emancipation was fairly clear by the later eighteenth century, its full implementation did not come until the nineteenth.

Some final comments about the general character of the social order and especially about social mobility, may be in order. First, as a *Ständegesellschaft*, German society was pervaded by a basic assumption that the circumstances of an individual's birth would determine his social position for the rest of his life. And while upward mobility both happened and was *known* to happen with enough frequency to deny the social structure the pristine character of a totally closed-caste society, there is very little evidence at any time in the period of a generalized ferment traceable to cheated expectations of upward mobility, *especially between whole orders*. There is a difference between the occurrence of mobility and the expectation of it. What was missing in Germany throughout the seventeenth and eighteenth centuries was even more the latter than the former and that was due to a number of mutually reinforcing factors. First, upward mobility, whether between whole orders or (much more often) between layers of one and the same order, was neither so common nor so rapid in the majority of cases as to suggest that it was easy. Ennoblement, for example, really did not happen as instantaneous fiat but as the cumulative result of years of hard work and notably meritorious achievement on the part of individuals, or of generations of accumulation of wealth and prestige on the part of families.

Secondly, for most of the period under consideration it is almost certainly true that far fewer people were worried about rising to a higher status than about sinking to a lower one; and that is a strong prescription for social conservatism, not for change. In both urban and rural areas, the numbers of the poor and very poor were clearly much greater in 1800 than in 1600 and the increase, while slow and uneven, was steady enough to be grimly obvious for much of the period. Many members of the already well situated upper middle class could certainly hope that, given time, their families might someday join the ranks of the *Honoratioren*, as indeed happened with some regularity. But a majority of the much larger numbers of the *Kleinbürgertum*, correctly perceiving themselves as the group from which a ubiquitous misfortune recruited the genuinely poor and destitute of urban society, strove far more consciously for preservation than for advancement. Guild masters, for example, saw their status receding as competition from rural industry, Free Masters and other sources increased; and their journeymen, almost permanently locked into the ranks of the labouring poor, entertained the hope of marriage to a master's daughter or widow – almost their only possibility of acquiring mastership – less as a matter of upward mobility than as a better guarantee against sinking into pauperism. To a considerable degree, the same was true of the rural cottagers, for whom a possible advance into the small peasantry was important not as a status symbol, but because it would put them one step further away from the 'brink-sitters' – an ironically appropriate term in this context!

The fact that the fear of losing status was more widespread than any dissatisfaction with barriers against advancement may not all rest on economic factors alone, but surely a very large part of it does. As a whole and for reasons already dealt with in earlier chapters, Germany was simply not a land of economic opportunity for most people in the seventeenth and eighteenth centuries. This meant, among other things, that wealth, to the extent it was increasing at all, was not increasing in large enough quantities among large enough groups of people to create upward-looking distortions in the traditional social order, while its decrease at the lower end, creating vast new numbers of the poor, only reinforced the commitment to preserve the traditional order among all those who were not poor. The territorial multiplicity of Germany also affected the social balance in several ways beyond its negative influence on economic growth. For one thing, much of the concentrated wealth that did exist and which might otherwise have demanded a reallocation or redefinition of social honour from the 'feudal' society of orders was in effect isolated from that society by political autonomy: the large and prosperous Free Imperial Cities had their own fully developed status systems which made invidious comparisons with 'feudal' society unnecessary; indeed, nobles from outside had lesser status within these cities than their own patriciates.

Every territory, in fact and regardless of the similarities between them, constituted a complete social system in itself; so, in a lesser sense, did virtually every city, town and village. It was these territorial and 'home-town' systems which constituted the real world of the German people in the early modern period: thus, the princely court was the social apex of the nobility's world, but not of the generality of bourgeois officials, who fitted more neatly and comfortably into the existing urban social categories of the capital or provincial city than into those of the court. There was really only one group which self-consciously attempted to transcend the localistic mentality described above. That was the community of intellectuals, or 'learned men' (a narrower group than the *Bildungsbürgertum*), who professed to see their whole society from 'outside of it', so to speak and who criticized its shortcomings through various literary devices. But their critique was characteristically mildly melioristic, not mordant and socially comprehensive rather than class-specific; and while most were of bourgeois origin, there were also nobles among them, so that they cannot properly be regarded as the 'cutting edge' of some sort of generalized bourgeois class consciousness.[21]

In general, the stratification within orders was more immediate and of far greater importance to contemporaries than the differences between orders themselves; mobility between orders was sufficiently

21. Indeed, the fact that many were wont to refer to themselves as members of a 'learned republic' (*Gelehrtenrepublik*) underscores their desire to escape identification with any traditional social class, including the bourgeoisie.

rare as not to play a role in everyday consciousness, but movement between strata was more regularly visible. Within each order, there were sore points of social discontent. By the late eighteenth century, for example, a new kind of 'crisis of the nobility' was looming in some places, the result of an inability of government service of all kinds to absorb the growing numbers of noble offspring who could not be supported by their family estates, but who were also denied access to bourgeois employments by law and the traditions of their class. The reforms of the early nineteenth century which abolished class-based occupational restrictions were probably even more necessary and welcome to the nobility than to the bourgeoisie. Within the cities, here and there, some serious quarrelling over political leadership occurred amongst patricians, *Honoratioren* and the upper middle class, as well as over more basic economic issues amongst guild masters, journeymen and other elements of the lower middle class; but the large numbers of the urban poor do not appear to have constituted a serious challenge to the social order, if only because there was so much fluidity in the alternation of their employment and unemployment, combined with a sharp status awareness about it, as to prevent the development of a specific underclass consciousness. Rural immiseration was also a serious and growing problem and it, like urban poverty, would not be alleviated until the industrial revolution and the scientific agriculture of the following century, among other things, provided an answer to the twin problems of underproduction and underemployment; but nowhere before the end of the eighteenth century did it threaten to breach the walls of the old social order.

Thus, while the social structure of Germany at the end of the early modern period could hardly be called flexible, much less progressive, it was also in no danger of collapse. Upward social mobility was possible on an individual basis – money, marriage and education being the best transitional means – but it was not calculable and therefore cannot even be called a general adaptive mechanism to relieve internal pressures.[22] But there were not many pressures anyway – at least not serious ones – and the confined and deferential mentality of nearly all social strata, together with an economic growth of such modest proportions as not to strain the seams of the social fabric, present the picture of a social order which, though rigid, was not yet dangerously brittle.

22.   Saalfeld, 'Die ständische Gliederung', pp. 459–60.

CHAPTER THIRTEEN

German Culture after 1648: Religion and Education

No survey of the development of German culture in the century and a half following the Peace of Westphalia can begin without first acknowledging the supreme importance of religion, which after the Thirty Years War and beyond all differences which separated the various confessions, remained the single most clearly identifiable concern of all individuals and groups in all territories and at all levels of German society. The primary purposes of religion – the glorification of God and the elevation and constant rededication of mankind to the service of the divine will – continued to be a chief mandate not only of the churches themselves, but of all institutions of social culture, including law, government, education, the arts and literature. In spite of various emergent political, intellectual and artistic currents which were slowly nudging it in a more wordly-minded direction, this was not yet a secular culture and it is impossible to understand the spirit of the age without first realizing that Germans still took their religions very seriously indeed.

It is true, of course, that after 1648 neither they (nor their leaders) accepted that seriousness as dictating a responsibility to exterminate the adherents of other confessions at whatever cost, including the destruction of their own civilization if need be. The high costs and terrible miseries of the Thirty Years War had done much to settle that. Furthermore, both the war itself and the terms of the peace which ended it had created new conditions which made the violent clash of religions less likely – above all through the two facts that the territories of the Empire were internally far more religiously homogeneous than ever before and that Protestant and Catholic states were geographically far less intermixed, now forming essentially separate blocs in north and south. At the popular level, especially, hostility between Protestants and Catholics (as well as between Protestants of Lutheran and Calvinist persuasions, often enough) remained high throughout the period[1]; but it was never again to be a cause for war or a more than very secondary influence on the conduct of foreign policy.

The toleration of religious minorities, while encouraged by both the Peace of Westphalia and the normally small size of such minorities as existed after 1648, varied from place to place: the Habsburgs tolerated some Protestants in Silesia and after 1691 allowed public worship to Protestants and Greek Orthodox Christians in Hungary, but expelled Protestants from Upper Austria and Styria in the 1730s and later (while resettling them in Transylvania for state economic reasons). The archbishop of Salzburg also expelled his Protestants in 1731. In Protestant Germany, the issue of toleration for Catholics was overshadowed by the open quarrel between Lutherans and Calvinists. This was a very serious problem in Brandenburg-Prussia, where the elector had to intervene to quiet bitter disputes between the majority Lutherans and his co-religionist minority Calvinists. Elector Johann Georg of Saxony, true to his long history of enmity towards Calvinism, had strongly protested the legal equality conferred upon it at Westphalia and his electorate remained the inviolate citadel of an unbending and unforgiving orthodox Lutheranism.

As even these few examples show, toleration was still almost nowhere regarded as either possible or desirable as a general principle of public policy. A few far-sighted individuals – the philosopher G. W. Leibniz, for example – hoped and worked for a broad-based solution which would include an eventual reconciliation and even unification of Catholicism and Protestantism. His efforts even found echoes of interest at the Vatican and in Vienna, where both Joseph I (1705–11) and Karl VI (1711–40) toyed briefly with such notions, but primarily for political reasons involving the imperial office. In the end, all schemes to eliminate intolerance by submerging it in religious universalism foundered on the rocks of the inveterate suspicions and hostilities of rulers and peoples alike.

On the other hand, the personal attitudes of princes could result in a degree of informal toleration: the restored Elector Palatine Karl

---

1. Riots and other minor disturbances in towns and cities of mixed religions, while not frequent, occurred throughout the period and there were evidences of serious discord within the religiously mixed Imperial Army as late as the 1790s. People would commonly refuse to buy clothing or other articles of ordinary consumption known to be made by artisans of a different faith.

Ludwig, Wilhelm VI of Hesse-Kassel and Duke Johann Friedrich of Hanover (a Catholic convert as of 1651), as well as Friedrich Wilhelm of Brandenburg himself, were examples of individuals who because their own religion differed from the 'official' one of their territories, or because of problems with the narrow-minded intransigence of their own church establishments, favoured toleration at least to the extent of leniency in the enforcement of legal proscriptions against minorities. All princes, furthermore, had an interest in minimizing the public expression of religious intolerance because it was a potentially potent cause of disruption of peace and order. Friedrich Wilhelm was not the only ruler who, while hoping for more permanent solutions (in his case, the reunion of Lutheran and Calvinist churches), had to settle for the much lesser result of simply keeping the opposing religions from mutual public verbal and physical abuse. While merely keeping the lid on religious quarrelling was hardly the same as toleration, it was helpful to the slow progress of mutual acceptance.

One problem common to both Catholic and Protestant Germany following the war was the reconstruction of ecclesiastical establishments with respect to lay and clerical discipline, physical plant and personnel. To some extent, the greater territoriality of churches in all Protestant lands worsened this problem by limiting the sources of assistance to their own territories; it was somewhat less severe in the Catholic states because of the supraterritorial (and even international) human and material resources on which they could rely. In this respect, as in all other religious matters, the small army of tireless Jesuits who had swarmed into Germany before and during the war was of particular importance; but so were the long organizational experience of the church itself and its continuing commitment to provide a vigorous and educated priesthood. In Protestant territories, the shortage of pastors apparent in so many places right after the war was gradually overcome by the revival of the universities which trained them. This had the positive result of producing a relatively high standard of education, since by the early eighteenth century virtually all ministers had studied for at least a year or two at a university, but also the negative one of creating an eventual oversupply of young theological graduates, who usually had to take poorly paid teaching positions in the urban Latin schools or the *Winkelschulen* while waiting – sometimes many years – for appointment to a church living. Their material lot often did not improve very much even then, since both the power of appointment to and patronage of the vast numbers of village churches usually lay with local noble landowners, many of whom could not afford to be generous with salaries or funds for church buildings or their upkeep.

In Catholic areas, the reconstruction of the church was an unremarkable process except perhaps in the one place where it proceeded furthest and most rapidly: the Habsburg territories and especially in Vienna itself, which now more than ever became the capital and showplace of German Catholicism in general. No territorial church employed as many Germans from all over the Empire as did that of the Habsburgs, whose role and reputation as the leaders of the church was further strengthened by the special imperial bond between emperor and ecclesiastical princes and by the chilly relations between Vienna and Rome for a half century or so after 1689, which encouraged the growth of a sense of self-sufficiency within the German Catholic church from the Emperor on down through the ecclesiastical hierarchy. From Vienna, too, radiated the powerful influences of exceptional homiletic preaching – sermons filled with imaginative imagery, striking language and piercing logic, all designed to reinforce with moral exhortation the message of faith and duty conveyed by a powerful and impressive ritual and liturgy conducted in the visually moving setting of richly ornamented churches and cathedrals. Abraham a Sancta Clara (Ulrich Megerle) (1644–1709) was only the most renowned of a group of chiefly Augustinian homilists who, true to the traditionally high rhetorical reputation of their order, both reflected and furthered the optimistic self-confidence of a church triumphant on its own soil; their published sermons are splendid examples of baroque literary expression in Germany. In Vienna, as elsewhere in the Habsburg patrimony, the government was deeply involved in religion, monitoring observance of the prescribed religious duties of its citizens and requiring its officials to lead or be visibly present in pilgrimages and processions; and although doctrinal controversy was rare and popular religious enthusiasm was easily kept within acceptable political bounds – facts which reflected the comfortability of a formulistic but relaxed faith – the future of Catholic belief was assured through the energetic educational activities and school development of the Jesuits, assisted by various of the now reinvigorated older orders and by the newly-founded Piarists.

The large measure of doctrinal agreement in Catholic Germany unfortunately did not exist in the Protestant territories, where theological squabbling within and between Lutheran and Calvinist churches reached new heights in the several decades following the war. It is a sad commentary on religious affairs here to note that even the most high-minded attempts to find formulas of concord (or even of peaceful coexistence) merely exacerbated the quarrelling. The Lutheran theologian Georg Calixt of Helmstedt, for example, represented a school which tried to reduce the sphere of necessary common belief to principles which had emerged in the first few centuries of Christianity, thus eliminating most of the subsequent doctrinal accruals which were the flashpoints of controversy between Lutherans and Calvinists; for his efforts, he reaped a whirlwind of denunciation and abuse from the academic strongholds of Lutheran orthodoxy in Wittenberg and Leipzig. Never before had orthodoxy been so narrowly defined or insisted on, or so jealously guarded against interpretational flexibility. Designed partly to protect public order by discouraging the emergence of disruptive religious enthusiasms and lunatic-fringe visionaries, this doctrinal rigidity tended to confine religious warfare to the professionals, the theologians, whose reciprocal slanders only occasionally became so publicly scandalous as to require intervention by the civil authority.

Against this backdrop of a puerile and peevish orthodoxy arose the immensely significant movement known as Pietism. Intensely Bible-centred and insistent on the necessity of individual spiritual rebirth, this movement appealed to many people for whom the achievement of justification before God by means of formulistic church teaching, while not wrong in the sense of incorrect, was simply not reassuring enough and which did not provide the emotional comfort and daily reminder of God's presence needed by so many after 1648, filled as the times were with continuing psychological trauma and material deprivation. In its emphasis on personal outreach to God and on Christian witness in the conduct of one's daily life in the community, there was nothing startlingly new about Pietism, which was not only reminiscent of similar initiatives of spiritual renewal that had arisen throughout the long history of Christianity itself, but was also adumbrated and encouraged by still active circles of believers which had more recently formed around the reformist teachings of mystics such as Johannes Arndt (1555–1621) in northwestern Germany, Jakob Böhme (1575–1624) in Silesia and Johann Valentin Andreä (1586–1654) in Württemberg. The strong influence of all three was visible in the educational background of the real founder of Pietism, the Lutheran pastor Philipp Jakob Spener (1635–1705), who accepted from all of them the central themes of personal conversion and the steady deepening of piety through Bible reading, self-examination and socially active brotherly love. Beginning in Frankfurt in 1670, Spener organized small groups of laymen into home Bible study groups – *collegia biblica* or *pietatis* – which later also met in the churches themselves. The movement rapidly overspread most of Protestant Germany, eventually affecting Lutheran communities as far afield as Switzerland and Scandinavia and assisted by the publication of Spener's *Pia desideria* in 1675. This treatise, reprinted many times, became a sort of primer for new societies, which characteristically were founded by laymen without special religious training.

There was, of course, a wide spectrum of belief within the Pietist movement and some individuals were much less inclined to accept the institutional church than others.[2] Theologically, however, neither Spener nor the majority of other Pietists deviated from 'correct' Lutheran teachings, nor did they directly or openly criticize the church establishment, within which they believed their own movement both could and ought to remain. But while this outer doctrinal conformity allowed Pietism easy introduction into many Lutheran territories, both its character as a lay movement and its emphasis on individual rebirth as something beyond the ability of church tradition, by itself, to accomplish eventually began to create suspicions about the tendencies of the movement among the stiffer guardians of Lutheran purity, many of whom had fallen so far away from Luther's own concept of the 'priesthood of all believers' as to insist that every word of Scripture was written by the Holy Spirit and that 'interpretation' of the Bible was therefore impermissible. Not surprisingly, perhaps, Spener first felt the full weight of such suspicions in Saxony, after he was called there from Frankfurt to become court preacher in Dresden in 1686. Things started off well enough; indeed, in light of Spener's own great popularity with the electress and in some other court circles, it appeared for a time that Saxony might become the permanent sponsor of a vigorous Pietist movement. But the practical implications of the new spirit of devotion soon proved annoying to the elector, who resented Spener's gentle but persistent criticism of his and his court's all-but-apostolic life style, as well as of the secularism of Dresden's magnificent high baroque culture in general. With a climate of disfavour also becoming evident in the theological fortresses of Leipzig and Wittenberg, Spener decided to leave Saxony; in 1691, he

2. As early as 1699–1700, Gottfried Arnold, sometime professor at the University of Giessen, had published a sensational history of the Christian church which took a very jaundiced view towards the ability of the Church after its very early history to produce or recognize genuine piety, which he found better represented among many of the so-called 'heretics' than within the orthodox establishment.

accepted an offer from Berlin, where he became pastor of an important local church and councillor in the Brandenburg consistory.

A whole new chapter in the history of Pietism began in Brandenburg when Spener's efforts were joined by those of his fiery younger disciple, August Hermann Francke (1663–1727), who had been forced out of Leipzig in 1690 amidst charges that he and his friends, including the well-known Christian Thomasius, were undermining the Saxon church. After a brief and unhappy stay in Erfurt, Francke was called to Brandenburg in 1692 to teach oriental languages and later theology, at the University of Halle – primarily through the influence of Thomasius, who had already fled to Halle from Leipzig in 1690. In the permanently friendly atmosphere of Brandenburg, the impulse of charitable social activism which was always a crucial part of the Pietist programme (and which Spener had earlier honoured in Frankfurt by the establishment of a workhouse for the poor and unemployed)[3] could now proceed at full speed. Most of this work fell to the energetic Francke rather than to the ageing Spener, though the latter's unflagging spiritual guidance lasted until his death. In 1695, Francke established a combination poor school and orphanage in Halle, to which he later added schools for more advanced instruction as well as a pedagogical institute for the training of future teachers. These initiatives were supported by some government grants, vigorous fund-raising from private sources and by Francke's own newly-established business enterprises, including a newspaper, publishing house, bookstore, pharmacy and light manufacturing.

His success in Halle encouraged in Francke the vision of a great 'universal seminary', from which trained and dedicated teachers and reformers would pour forth not only to Germany and the rest of Europe, but to the entire world. Things never got quite that far, to be sure, but an admiring awareness of his work was evident throughout Germany and beyond; his own commercial ventures reached as far as Russia and China, while branches of his orphanage were established in Nürnberg, Stockholm, London and Moscow and his personal correspondence was genuinely world-wide. Francke

---

3. This workhouse, designed to teach both permanently employable skills and a new work ethic, was imitated in a number of other large cities; almost all, however, eventually became victims of their own early success, since they tended to become catch-alls for too many other charitable and economic initiatives (as poor schools, orphanages, manufacturing enterprises and so on); and as their expenses increased, they were financially neglected or abandoned by the municipal governments which founded them.

enjoyed the steady support of King Friedrich I and, after his death in 1713, that of Friedrich Wilhelm I as well. Indeed, the most profound and long-lasting effect of Francke's labours came in Brandenburg-Prussia itself. His own pedagogical trainees permeated the Prussian school system, while his influence and that of Pietism itself were institutionalized in all the faculties of the University of Halle: young theologians and jurists, whether destined for careers as teachers, pastors, or officials, were henceforth for a long time cast in an educational mould shaped by a Pietistic work ethic and sense of Christian social responsibility. That responsibility stressed the inseparability of moral and material self-improvement and in that sense could be politically appealing to rulers and officials who shared the Cameralist conviction that the overall economic health of a country required not only that the appetite for consumption be curbed, but that an attitude towards labour as a social duty be encouraged. Pietism, with its pronounced puritanical tendencies and its emphasis on education and self-discipline as the surest means of producing a healthier, more highly skilled and more dutiful people, unquestionably harmonized with some of the most important political and economic currents of the time and, beyond that, helped to reconcile many people to their current state of penury by pronouncing it a virtue – even if an involuntary one.

Pietism was not everywhere protected or even tolerated; where it was not, that was almost always the result of its unacceptability on religious grounds to the established church, which might then use its influence with the civil authority to discourage it. Most Pietists did not hold unorthodox political or social views and were either accepting of or indifferent to forms of government, the formal class order and other structural elements of their society. Their belief that genuinely despotic government was abhorrent was in no way out of the Christian mainstream and while their spiritual individualism often led them to disapprove of state intervention in church affairs, with a correspondingly standoffish attitude towards the 'official' clergy, this brought with it less a separatism than a quiet and unobtrusive withdrawal to the privacy of their own prayer groups. Official protection was either freely given or successfully solicited in some territories – Prussia, of course, as well as Hesse-Darmstadt and especially Württemberg, where the Lutheran church was all but taken over by a pastorally-guided Pietism, subsequently producing an unusually impressive group of jurists, officials, poets and philosophers clearly bearing the stamp of the movement. Even in places where it was officially not approved, however, Pietism could and did survive, because it was in the nature of the movement that its adherents did not call attention to themselves as a separate sect they did not believe themselves to be – thus justifying the lovely name of '*die Stillen im Lande*' (the silent in the land) that was often applied to them.

The one offshoot of Pietism that did manifest separatist tendencies was the group which came to be known as the Moravian Brethren (or Herrnhuter), organized by Count Nikolaus von Zinzendorf (1700–60), scion of an aristocratic family from Lower Austria which had emigrated to Saxony during the Thirty Years War. A godson of Spener, Zinzendorf attended Francke's school from 1710 to 1716, later studied law at Wittenberg and eventually became an official at the Saxon court. Deeply concerned for the unity of all believers in Christ, but disappointed in early efforts to effect a reconciliation of the churches, Zinzendorf then not only set up prayer groups in his own home in Dresden, but also, in 1722, founded a separate religious community – Herrnhut – on his estate in Upper Lusatia. All witnesses to Christ were to be welcome there, though the original settlers were mostly Pietists from neighbouring areas as well as descendants of the Bohemian Brethren. The success of this community eventually led to new settlements elsewhere; and while the founder himself strongly opposed the separatist tendencies which inevitably arose, only in his native Saxony did the movement remain within the traditional church. Elsewhere – as in Prussia – it was recognized as a distinct Protestant sect, with some unique religious and secular practices.

Because of certain of his religious innovations, Zinzendorf himself was expelled from Saxony between 1736–47, a period the energetic reformer used to preach, to found new communities in Germany and to participate personally in overseas missionary work among native populations in the West Indies and North America – the first such organized endeavour of any Protestant denomination and one which was extended to Greenland and Russia as well. His marriage into one of the several Reuß families of Imperial Counts led a significant number of other families of the Protestant imperial nobility to join his movement, whose influence was also strong among the court nobility of several territories. Zinzendorf's religious convictions reflected the latitude of belief possible within the overall Pietist movement: his emphasis on sensualism as an important part of religious experience stood in some contrast to the more common Pietist reliance on the 'inner light' of reason and he was distrustful of excessive mysticism. He was no friend to the rigid Lutheran scholasticism of his day, but was far more tolerant of the established church than the Halle Pietists, for example: he accepted Luther's doctrine of justification, along with the entire Augsburg Confession and sought and received ordination as a Lutheran minister.

It was not the least part of the significance of Zinzendorf's movement that in founding actual communities it for a time gave continuing points of reference to a Pietism which, composed as it was of widely scattered groups of like-minded believers without any linking organizational structure, could have dissipated even more rapidly than it actually did. But like many such movements which are not oriented towards energetic proselytism and which fail to institutionalize themselves, Pietism gradually lost its forward impetus, especially after the death of the moving spirits of its 'glory days' of the late seventeenth and early eighteenth centuries. While its influence remained strong throughout the entire eighteenth century by virtue of the very large number of people in various classes, vocations and territories of Protestant Germany who had been touched by it, especially through the educational system, several factors were unfavourable to its continued vitality. The progress of the enlightenment was one of these, for while Pietism was not unfriendly to all tendencies of the former, there were certain of its premises it could not accept; and to the extent that active governmental encouragement was important to the maintenance of Pietist influence through institutional channels in schools and universities, an official shift in favour of 'enlightened' education could prove devastating in a very short time. This is what happened at Halle after 1740, when Frederick II quickly transformed the university, in all its faculties, from the foremost bastion of Pietism into the academic showplace of the Prussian enlightenment. The social base of the movement was also weakened by economic factors. While it is still unclear how deeply Pietism penetrated rural areas (except for pockets of noble support here and there), it seems likely that the urban middle classes, including artisans, were strongly affected by it. Of these, the upper bourgeoisie, which was of particular importance to the initial organization and continued sustenance of the movement, appears gradually to have lost sympathy with the puritanical, materially self-denying urges of Pietism and with its tendency to condemn the pleasurable aspects of a worldly culture which was becoming both more fashionable and more affordable by virtue of a slowly increasing prosperity. Finally, as in all subjective movements, especially after their abandonment by the guiding hand of the more respectable citizenry, the appearance of separatism, millenarianism and various incidents of bizarre and lunatic personal behaviour brought a certain negative notoriety and dubiety to some of the remaining groups.

Still, long after the currents whose confluence identified Pietism as a distinct movement had broken apart to run their separate courses, there were residues from the original stream which were of continuing importance to the development of German public life and culture. Both the advocacy and the concrete demonstration of an ethic of public duty and of labour as a social responsibility reinforced a similar message from other secular sources and invested it with an individual moral imperative. The emphasis on personal self-examination and its externalization in intimate discourse with others created a novel language of emotion and feeling which gave a new depth not only to autobiography, but also to biography and through it a new and more profound and critical understanding of human history itself. This new language was also specifically a German language, used both because of distrust of the impure importations of foreign cultures and because Pietism, after all, spoke within groups and about things which were themselves German and it thus contributed its share to enrich and legitimize the native language, especially for literary purposes, just as it was beginning to achieve respectability as a philosophical language at the hands of Christian Thomasius, Christian Wolff and others, whose work will be dealt with below. Without the Pietist impulse, finally, it is almost impossible to understand the emergence of the enormously important concept of *Bildung* in the later eighteenth century; this concept, referring to the intellectual growth of the individual through self-examination and self-improvement and to what he *becomes* rather than to what he *does* or to the information he possesses, transformed the whole educational ideal of German society and was fundamental to the development of literary, philosophical and even scientific movements well into the nineteenth century.

Religion in all its forms also continued throughout the period to be a powerful influence on the German educational system at all levels. Since the beginning of all true knowledge lay in the Word of God, the churches had long emphasized education as a primary vehicle for making the divine will known to man and the confessional struggles of the Reformation and Counter-Reformation had if anything given new urgency to formal schooling as a means of reinforcing religious conscience. As a result, religion remained the most important subject of instruction from beginning through intermediate stages of education. This was particularly noticeable in the rural or village (parish) schools, where the education of peasant children consisted almost entirely of reading and reciting the catechism and other simple religious texts and where the definition of literacy was exhausted by the ability to do this with even the most minimal competence; the limited evidence available suggests that rural literacy, in particular, remained very low throughout the period. Where the opportunity existed to pass beyond this basic level, as in the urban Latin grammar schools, religion still remained the substantively most important subject and it was not until students entered the universities that it was possible to choose a curriculum not primarily oriented towards religion.

All this should not be taken to mean that religious concerns were the only motivating and sustaining forces of education. The churches were quick to recognize the secular imperatives of human life which could and should be served by education; political authorities also recognized these imperatives and never more consciously so than in the period of reconstruction following the Thirty Years War, when well-known early Cameralists such as Seckendorff and Becher began to emphasize the theme (which became a standard refrain of nearly all of their successors) that improved education for all strata of the population was an important key to economic growth, greater general prosperity and enhanced fiscal yields. Initially and not surprisingly, it was in the smaller states and especially those of central Germany, where the first significant attention was given to school improvement; here, the traditions of pious, patriarchal rulership combined with the absence of expensive and distracting foreign policy and military concerns permitted princes in Gotha (Duke Ernst the Pious), Brunswick, Hesse, Hanau, Magdeburg and elsewhere, to promulgate comprehensive school ordinances and to provide for supervisory inspections and other means to insure the physical establishment of schools as well as adequate standards of curriculum and instruction. While these good intentions were incompletely realized, many other territories had similar laws on the books by 1700 or so; and these were even followed here and there by provision for compulsory schooling to an at least minimal level. Friedrich Wilhelm I of Prussia issued such a requirement in 1716–17; but it had so little effect that his son and successor Frederick II reissued it in amplified and amended form as the famous *General-landschulreglement* of 1763, which commanded school attendance of six hours a day for all peasant children between the ages of five and fourteen.

The fact that Frederick's ordinance even by the end of the century had not produced results strikingly better than those of his father's of almost fifty years before points to the very nearly insoluble problem of rural schooling in the early modern period – the problem at which the majority of educational ordinances were aimed, since urban and higher education, for all their imperfections, did not present the picture of dismal intractability represented by the village schools. The specifics of the problem were much the same everywhere and were very serious. While it is close to true that every parish had a school, that did not necessarily mean a separate structure or one in an even reasonable state of repair. Often enough, school convened in a rented room or in the home of the pastor, sexton or artisan to whom the unrewarding task of playing teacher fell. Schools often had no books and frequently neither did the children, whose parents resented not only the expense of books and of *Schulgeld* – the pittance they paid to the schoolmaster – but also the absence of their children from working farms where every hand was needed for the survival of the family. As a result, attendance was poor, irregular and often non-existent during the long growing season and was further reduced by the sometimes very great distances between outlying villages and the single parish school.[4]

The quality of teaching in village schools was generally poor and often downright awful: overworked pastors and sextons do not make model teachers, nor do tailors, blacksmiths, village brewers or other artisans to whom villagers turned because they could not or would not pay enough to support a schoolmaster who did not have income from another trade. Seminaries for formal teacher training were few even by 1800 and their products were in sufficient demand in the spiritually and materially more rewarding public and private urban schools to keep them out of the countryside. Examination systems for teachers, where they existed at all, were deficient and sometimes deliberately circumvented by officials desperate to fill unwanted positions; indeed, the whole system of school supervision and inspection suffered from irregular financial support and inconstant commitment on the part of the state. There really is no reason to doubt the sincerity of the widespread official and public desire to improve the village schools and the education they offered to rural children, who after all constituted the majority of all children. But

4. A report on the parish schools of Upper and Lower Austria in 1772 suggested that attendance averaged only 10–20 per cent. James Van Horn Melton, *Absolutism and the Eighteenth-Century Origins of Compulsory Schooling in Prussia and Austria* (Cambridge, 1988), p. 8.

the human and material resources required to attack the problem systematically, continuously and on a broad scale, providing buildings, books, trained teachers, an administrative support system and so on, could simply not be made available without a radical reordering of priorities such as was unthinkable in an economically marginal society with other important and often unpredictable demands on the meager stock of social capital.[5]

Some few well-to-do peasants whose farms lay close to a town or city might be lucky enough to send their children to urban schools, whose quality was decidedly better than those in the country. Here there were essentially two levels of formal instruction: the 'German schools' (primary schools) to which the youngest children were sent to learn the most basic skills of reading, writing and perhaps some arithmetic (along with Bible and catechism, of course); and the Latin schools, where a still heavy emphasis on religion was combined with teaching a command of Latin such as would permit admission to a university at the end of instruction, usually at about age sixteen. In the better schools, the two levels were combined in a single institution, often sponsored or licensed by the municipal authorities, or attached to a parish church or monastery. Fees were required from parents who could pay, though scholarships were available for some of the deserving poor. Besides these institutions, which were too few to satisfy actual demand, there were both licensed and unlicensed private Latin schools of varying but often mediocre quality, with transient teaching staffs in which theology graduates waiting for parish livings bulked large. Frankfurt and Leipzig, to cite but two examples, seem on occasion to have had as many as thirty or forty such private schools, some with 200–300 pupils; these would also include equivalents of the 'German schools' known variously as *ABC-*, *Klip-*, or *Winkelschulen*, which purveyed much of the usual

---

5. Adding to the overall problems of education was the unattractiveness of the teaching profession itself. The pay and social status of teachers were equally low. Village schoolmasters had the most miserable pay and prestige of all, but even teachers in the urban Latin schools, always alert to better livelihoods doing something else, tended to be transient; even headmasters often had to supplement their income by private tutoring and taking in boarders. At the universities, professors in the higher faculties were usually paid adequately, though not generously, but their colleagues in the lower faculty of arts and philosophy were paid much less well and were held in not much higher esteem than good schoolmasters. Status levels of teachers did improve markedly towards the end of the eighteenth century, largely because of changing attitudes towards education. That, in turn, was partly the result of the steadily improving quality of teachers, possibly produced by a recessionary environment which limited other and better employment opportunities for university graduates.

elementary educational fare, but with a pronounced emphasis on reading, writing and arithmetic – suggesting, perhaps, widespread parental dissatisfaction with the excessive time spent on religion in the officially-sponsored schools.

While no great wave of reform altered the basic curriculum of primary or secondary schools before 1800, there were two developments during the eighteenth century of more than passing interest, both of which pointed in the direction of a more utilitarian education. First, there was a tendency on the part of the more progressive Latin schools to add new and more 'modern' electives such as history, mathematics and French. This was done primarily to attract pupils from the upper strata of urban society which were not satisfied with the limited curriculum and rigid traditionalism of the Latin education; but even where this happened – and it was by no means everywhere – the new subjects were merely appended to a course of instruction which continued to be dominated by Latin and religion. Second, the very important pedagogical efforts of A. H. Francke inaugurated a whole new approach to the education of the young. In the 1690s Francke founded a complex of educational institutions in Halle, which included a poor school, a Latin boarding school, a pedagogical seminary, an orphanage and a girls' school. Greatly influenced by the pragmatic educational theory of Johann Comenius (1592–1670), Francke elaborated a curriculum which, while not abandoning all elements of received tradition, was designed to equip students to cope successfully with the real world of social relationships and work in which they would live. This education was as much utilitarian as academic and was strongly flavoured by Franke's Pietism, with its emphasis on practical social work. Whether destined for later university study or not, children could benefit from this curriculum; the Latin school, in particular, attracted students from all classes. The pedagogical seminary also gained a reputation for teacher training so impressive as not only to attract students from all over Germany, but also to procure preferred positions for its graduates in various places, notably Prussia.

What Francke had sowed were the seeds of what was later to become known as the *Realschule* – the 'school of reality' – which was to be a major component of the transformation of the entire German school system in the nineteenth century. In the eighteenth century, its time had not yet come on any broad basis; but it persisted as an idea and a renewable reality throughout the century. Francke's own institutions (and even some of the schools and orphanages founded in imitation of them) lost some of their vitality after his death in 1727, but their achievements were carried on and even improved upon, in the schools founded through the initiative of Count Zinzendorf and his Moravian Brethren, which enjoyed a universally high reputation. The vocational content of the education offered by Francke's and Zinzendorf's schools, never quite as strong as its more general social aspects, was considerably more strongly emphasized in a complex of schools established by Johann Hecker in Berlin after 1738. Hecker, a pupil of Francke and sometime teacher in his seminary, moved further away from Latin and more towards new mathematical and scientific methods of teaching and those methods were spread throughout a number of schools in Prussia and elsewhere.[6] Hecker's influence was evident not only in the Prussian *Generallandschulreglement* of 1763, which he helped to formulate, but also in the work of the reformer of German schools in Austria, the Augustinian abbot Johann Ignaz Felbiger, whose initiatives in Vienna after 1774 owed much to the school ordinance he had drawn up for Prussian Silesia after 1765 – a document based on many of Hecker's ideas.

Some mixing of social classes was evident in the student bodies of various schools. The Latin schools run by Francke and by the Moravian Brethren, like the broader Pietist movement itself, were intended not to be class-specific and that was more or less accurately reflected in their enrolments. To some extent, the same was true of the better Latin schools elsewhere, including the Jesuit *Gymnasien* of Catholic Germany, where in addition to the vast majority of pupils who came from the middling and upper strata of the bourgeoisie a smattering of lower middle class, patrician and even noble children could be found. The *Winkelschulen*, on the other hand, enrolled children from the lower bourgeois, artisan and even poorer classes almost exclusively, revealing the more general pattern of a class-determined education.

That pattern is even more clearly discernible in the two alternative educational paths preferred by the aristocracies of both town and country. The first ran through the Knights' Academies (*Ritterakademien*), noble boarding schools which enjoyed a new popularity after 1648 and until after the middle of the eighteenth century,

---

6. Hecker's *Realschule*, founded in 1747, was the first successful attempt to offer real vocational training to bourgeois and artisan families whose sons were not intended for the unversity and for whom the Latin schools were inappropriate. Hecker is noteworthy also for the introduction and dissemination of the method of teaching children collectively rather than individually in the classroom, an innovation which brought order to the schoolroom and immensely increased the learning time of all students. Melton, *Absolutism*, pp. 52–4.

where a very consciously class-based curriculum sharply different from that of the urban Latin schools was offered. The Latin grammar and religion which dominated the latter gave way in these academies to a combination of utilitarian subjects (including modern foreign languages, history, geography, rhetoric, some mathematics and natural science) and 'elegance training' in such social accomplishments as dancing, fencing, riding and general social comportment. Such institutions were the choice of much of the upper and lower nobility, as well as of many urban patricians and some of the most prosperous upper bourgeoisie.

The other (and no less common) path for the same privileged groups was private tutoring. This might last for only a few years, followed by enrolment in a Knights' Academy or a Latin school; or much longer, all the way up to the university level (and even beyond, since many tutors accompanied their charges to their new academic locales). The eighteenth century was the heyday of private tutors, among whom, for at least brief periods in their younger years, were many of the most famous figures of German philosophy, letters and religion. They were often recruited on recommendation from university professors or others who had acquired reputations in childhood education. Francke, Zinzendorf and their better-known disciples, as well as the Leipzig professor and fabler C. F. Gellert, were frequent recommenders of tutors in the early and middle part of the century, as in its later years were the authors J. J. Engel in Berlin and C. F. Weisse of Leipzig (the founder of children's literature in Germany and editor of the well-known children's magazine *Der Kinderfreund* – 1775–82). Long-term tutoring was generally conducted more along the academic lines of the Knights' Academies than of the Latin schools, following guidelines laid down in the numerous handbooks published especially for tutors.

Regardless of the kind of school attended, the educational process could be cut short at almost any point along the line. Apart from individual reasons arising from illness, gradual or sudden financial exigency, or poor performance, certain classes of pupils tended to abandon formal schooling at times determined by vocational factors. The poor, by necessity, normally left school to enter the work force after the very basic education offered by the 'German schools' or *ABC-Schulen*, while the sons of middling merchants or guildsmen often left the Latin schools to enter the family business well before the course was over. Even some noble children might not be formally tutored or otherwise educated up to university entrance level if the family either did not intend or saw little chance for a career requiring university training or the social polish of courtly life. In the village schools, needless to remark, attendance was frequently so irregular as to constitute a continuous interruption of education from the outset.

At the top of the pyramid of the educational system were the universities, of which, in addition to older ones, some twenty were newly founded between 1600 and 1800; most universities survived the whole period in reasonably good shape, the notable exceptions being the ten or so Jesuit-staffed universities of Catholic Germany, which were disastrously affected by the dissolution of the order in 1773. Only two universities – Cologne and Altdorf (Nürnberg) – were municipally-sponsored, the rest being princely creations (with the one exception of the purely ecclesiastical Benedictine university in Salzburg). All were small by today's standards: the largest, in the early 1740s, was Halle, with only 1500 students. The total number of students shrank – both absolutely and even more so as a percentage of the overall population – in the course of the eighteenth century, from 9000 in 1700 to around 6000 in 1800.[7] All the larger universities had four faculties: philosophy (or liberal arts), law, medicine and theology. The first was preparatory to and less prestigious than the other three, all of which conferred the doctor's degree and of which theology was at once the most ubiquitous and distinguished. Theology also had the largest enrolments (corresponding to the occupational demand for its graduates), while the medical faculties enrolled the fewest (a reflection, in part, of the backwardness of this field of study relative to much of western Europe).

Students generally entered the philosophical faculty between the ages of fifteen and eighteen for anywhere from one to four years and if successful would receive a bachelor's degree after one or two years and a master's degree after four. Since it was not necessary to have the master's (which qualified one to teach in the liberal arts faculties) before entering the higher faculties, many students did not wait that long – though minimum requirements of attendance in the arts faculty eventually existed everywhere. At the Protestant universities, well over half the students came from academically educated families, especially pastoral and official ones; the remainder were unevenly divided among aristocratic and patrician and upper

---

7. Charles E. McClelland, *State, Society and University in Germany, 1700–1914* (Cambridge, 1980), p. 28. Apart from a growing crisis of employment for university graduates towards the end of the century, this shrinkage was caused by state policies designed to restrict higher educational opportunities in the name of social stability and economic need. See Melton, *Absolutism*, pp. 115–19.

bourgeois families, with a small but noticeable contingent of scholarship students from the lower social orders. A very noteworthy exception to the norm was the University of Innsbruck, where a full third of the student body between 1669 and 1782 consisted of peasant sons. Whatever their origins (though clearly not unrelated to them), students tended to follow life styles which contemporaries identified as belonging to one of four characteristic types: rich and elegant fops; the *Renommisten*, who revelled in drinking, fencing and duelling; the so-called *Krassen*, who seldom got their noses out of their books; and finally the *Konviktoristen*, the scholarship students, for whom frugality and unremitting studiousness were iron necessities. To some extent, universities themselves were 'typed' in this fashion: Leipzig seems to have attracted more than its share of the fops, for example, while Jena was a clear favourite of the *Renommisten*; and Göttingen enrolled an unusually large percentage of nobles – some 14 per cent towards the end of the century.

The two universities which on an institutional scale were the real pathbreakers in German higher education during the period were Halle and Göttingen – the former in the first half of the century, the latter in the second half and for different reasons. Halle, by virtue of the remarkably profound and widespread influence of such giants as Christian Thomasius, A. H. Francke and the philosopher Christian Wolff[8], became the intellectual and pedagogical fountainhead of an energized and rationalized, but also humanized, Cameralism, embodying a governmental and administrative ethic of public duty and social service. Rooted in the optimistic meliorism which was a curious blend of Pietism and the natural law philosophies of the early enlightenment, this powerful new perspective was gradually absorbed into the teaching of other universities and into the practice of bureaucratic establishments, especially but not only in Prussia and eventually became perhaps the chief defining element of sound polity as that was understood in the old regime and even beyond. Göttingen, founded in 1737 chiefly through the efforts of the Hanoverian official and Imperial Knight G. A. von Münchhausen, made similarly impressive contributions. Through its close connection with England, whose king was also elector of Hanover and with the encouragement of Münchhausen himself, it became a major conduit for English influences of all kinds in Germany, but especially for 'liberal' political and constitutional ideas, which made it not only

8. See Chapter Fifteen for details on the work of Thomasius and Wolff.

the least orthodox and intellectually most stimulating university in Germany of the later eighteenth century, but a leader in the developing social sciences as well. Its unusually well-endowed library certainly enhanced the university's attractiveness, as did the strongly irenic policy adopted towards confessional differences among the student body and within its own theological faculty.

Göttingen was also instrumental in rescuing the study of the ancient classics from the neglect to which the intense pragmatism of curricula such as those which prevailed in Halle and elsewhere had led. This began with the efforts of J. M. Gesner, who abandoned the practice of reading the classics merely as instruments for the development of style and grammar and instead concentrated on their intellectual content to train the mind in taste, judgment and imagination. This novel approach was widely and rapidly disseminated through the pedagogical seminar he established – the first seminar of any kind in a German university. Gesner's work was soon joined by that of C. G. Heyne, the founder of classical archaeology, who taught at Göttingen from 1763 to 1812; they, together with such other scholars as J. J. Winckelmann, raised the reputation of humane letters to such renewed heights that by the end of the century the study of classical literature had come to be regarded as necessary to any higher education worthy of the name and an essential component of *Bildung* – that process of individual intellectual self-cultivation which was increasingly differentiated from mere 'education' by a new and self-confident intelligentsia comprised of literati, professionals and men-of-affairs generally.

It would not be appropriate to end this description of education in Germany without noting, as Rudolf Vierhaus has done, that much education in the widest sense of the term did not take place in formal classrooms of any kind. Church and Sunday school educated adults and children of all classes at all times; guilds passed along knowledge and professional skills, as did retail and wholesale businesses, banks and other enterprises to those who were apprenticed to them. The future Junker learned much while in service to the court as a page or to the army as a cadet; and all children, of course, picked up all sorts of knowledge at home, often including basic literacy.[9] Publications were another and increasingly important vehicle for education. The eighteenth century witnessed almost a publishing mania and almost all of the remarkable growth in the number of books and periodicals was in secular literature: the percentage of religious titles shrank over

9. See Vierhaus, *Staaten und Stände*, p. 158.

the century from one-third to one-twelfth of the total. Travel narratives, geographies, histories, current events and socially and vocationally informational materials bulked large, but there was also a vast literature on *Lebensklugheit* – the conduct of proper social intercourse in the widest sense – which reflected the aristocratic educational ideal of courtly comportment and which was as eagerly read by burghers as by nobles. In the last third of the century, there was also a notable increase in the publication of works specifically designed for popular education. Academies or societies of science in Berlin, Göttingen and Munich were involved in this effort, but so were many unaffiliated authors: Gellert's *Kinderfreund* was persistently (if also pleasantly) didactic and Rudolph Z. Becker's popular *Noth- und Hülfsbüchlein für Bauersleute*, published in several editions in the last two decades of the century, was but one example of a growing cottage industry of calendars, almanacs and newspapers – some of them funded by governments – intended to provide vocational and other useful information for a peasant readership.

In summary: while there were some not insignificant forward-looking developments on the German educational scene over the century and a half after 1648 and especially after 1700, the generality of students of the second half of the seventeenth century at all levels, from the 'German schools' up to and including the universities, would have found relatively little that was unrecognizable or disorienting in the educational system of a century later. To be sure, new subjects and emphases had in the meantime slowly crept into the secondary education of the Latin schools, in particular – some of it as the result of influences from the universities; and the important concept of the *Realschule* made a sporadic appearance here and there throughout the eighteenth century. At Göttingen, too, especially after 1770 or so, a rapid evolution of the philosophical faculty towards a more than just coequal dignity with the earlier 'higher' faculties was occurring through innovative work in history, Classical philology, political science, constitutional law and other fields, whose long-term effects were to change the whole shape of university education in the first half of the following century. Even at the level of peasant education, the degree of both private and public commitment to the ideal of an expansion and thoroughgoing reform of rural schooling, reflecting new attitudes towards the role of education in preparing the lower classes for a different kind of citizenship, was greater in the last quarter of the eighteenth century than ever before. And, if the sheer growth in the number and variety of publications is any indicator, it is even possible that a significant increase in the overall literacy rate occurred over the latter half of the whole period.

Still, in most important respects the realities of education even by 1800 ran much closer to the patterns of the mid-seventeenth than to those of the mid-nineteenth century. An only slightly modified traditionalism still reigned in the Latin schools and the Knights' Academies (though there were now fewer of the latter); the *Realschule* was in place only here and there; Göttingen, though in many ways a 'modern' university, was also a unique one; and while grand plans and theories for vast improvements in peasant education appeared regularly in books and journals churned out by eager educational reformers and were even realized in the form of a handful of model schools, concrete results on any general scale were scarcely in evidence during what in this as in most other areas of social life and culture remained the 'old regime'.

CHAPTER FOURTEEN

German Culture after 1648: Literature, Architecture and Music

One generalization on which historians are never likely to disagree very much is that German literature from the period of the Thirty Years War until the beginnings of an enormously vital literary revival around the middle of the eighteenth century was of undistinguished quality when compared with the better products of the literary art of much of western and southern Europe. There are a number of clearly discernible reasons for this. One may begin with the fact that Germany lacked not only a universally recognized high literary language and stylistic criteria appropriate to it, but also a single forum – a cultural 'capital' – in which such language and criteria could be discussed, debated and regularly reformulated and issued as standards which could act as a sort of 'floor' for poetic endeavour. The result was not only an unproductive scattering of literary energies which in a way paralleled the political fragmentation of the country, but also a retreat to the safer ground provided by imitation of known and respected foreign standards, including (for this period, especially) not only French but also the received traditions of Latin humanism which schools at all levels for a long time continued to teach as the first language of learned and literary discourse.

One must also consider the factor of audience, in that for most of the period a sharp distinction was drawn between a 'cultivated' and an 'uncultivated' readership and the most ambitious literary talents directed their efforts mostly at the former – whose tastes were chiefly conditioned by the standards of high (that is: courtly) society, where a distinct preference for foreign models in nearly all aspects of culture and behaviour prevailed. Patronage and literary reputation were also limited largely to these circles; and since scarcely a single author before the mid-eighteenth century lived even chiefly from sales of his works, those who wanted a substantial income from patronage knew very well which sorts of language, themes and styles to adopt and which to avoid. Some of the more interesting literature of the period, however, was produced by those authors for whom writing was quite secondary to their primary sources of income as clerics, teachers, officials or whatever. Their efforts, usually aimed at a relatively unsophisticated readership, were sometimes rough and uneven and obviously suffered from the authors' inability to concentrate full-time on their literary work; but they also often avoided some of the sterile, imitative homogeneity of the patronized 'court poets'. Finally, the emergence of a native German drama – a potentially very powerful medium – was unquestionably delayed by the almost total domination of the cultivated stage by the opera, most of it Italian or Italianate, whose librettos, even when written by Germans, were a far cry from genuine drama.

The fact that Germany was not home to a superior national literature did not go altogether unperceived by its literati, one of whom attempted early in the period to remedy its weakness by writing a comprehensive manual of style, based on ancient and neo-humanist Latin authors. This was the Silesian Martin Opitz (1597–1639), whose *Buch von der deutschen Poeterey* (1624), while not very original in itself, had the powerful effect of elevating the aims (and to a lesser extent the accomplishments) of German authors for many years; it set out a German metrical form, attempted to eliminate excessive Latin vocabulary from German writing and solicited a more widespread adoption of a standardized High German as a literary language. Opitz mocked the farcical doggerel knowingly spewed forth by German poetasters almost as self-punishment for their own incompetence and while his guidelines remained within the rather confined moralistic and didactic *raison d'être* of all literature of the time, they were eagerly seized upon and studied in many places, as was the volume of verse Opitz published in 1625 as an example of his own applied theories.

Very important to the dissemination of Opitz's standards were the several language and literary societies which sprang up in the first half or so of the seventeenth century. The earliest and most interesting of these was the 'Fruchtbringende Gesellschaft', or 'Palmenorden', founded by Prince Ludwig of Anhalt in Weimar-Köthen in 1617. Directly imitative of an earlier Florentine humanistic academy, its members took nicknames (and special coats of arms) related to the supposedly 'fructifying' objectives of the society: the founder was 'the Nourisher', while others were 'the Helper', 'the Useful', 'the Fragrant', and so on. Dedicated to improving the German language (and to purifying it from foreign influences), as well to higher literary standards generally, it had enrolled virtually all German literati of any significance, including Opitz himself, by even before the mid-century.

While the overall impact of the 'Palmenorden' on the quality of either language or literature was hardly revolutionary, it did spawn some important work – such as the detailed German grammar produced in 1663 by J. G. Schottelius ('the Seeker') of Wolfenbüttel; and it also invited imitation elsewhere in Germany, as in the 'Deutschgesinnte Gesellschaft' (Hamburg, 1643), whose members took the names of flowers; the rival 'Elbschwanenorden' (Wedel, 1658); and, in southern Germany, the famous 'Pegnitzer Hirten-gesellschaft' (Nürnberg, 1644). These three were all founded by well-known poets – Philipp von Zesen, Johann Rist, and G. P. Harsdörffer and Johann Klaj, respectively – who, while following Opitz in many things, also tried to go beyond him in others; none was immortally talented, but all did achieve respectability as typical baroque poets of the mid-century. A notable feature of the writings of both Harsdörffer and Rist was the employment of elevated language as a vehicle for the improvement of cultivated sociability – to inject elegance into conversational discourse – which sometimes (especially in Harsdörffer's case) led to a bloated floweriness of the sort which helped to define the baroque style.

That style, however, whatever its peculiarities, could embrace many genres. The Königsberg poetry professor Simon Dach (1605–59), for example, the central figure in a loose circle of north German poets, was a talented elegist whose own preference ran to mournful themes of resignation and human mortality, but who could also write happier poems, on commission, to celebrate births, weddings and other private and public events. Quite unlike the melancholic Dach was the Saxon physician Paul Fleming (1609–40), whose warmth, passion and energy gave freshness and excitement to a widely-read travel narrative and emotional depth to the sonnets he wrote to a lost love. Even satire – never a typically German genre – was respectably represented by the fine epigrammist Friedrich von Logau (1604–55), whose work did not receive adequate recognition in his own time, but who was sufficiently admired to be elected to the 'Palmenorden' as 'the Disparager' in 1648. Not a believer in writing by rule, Logau was no disciple of Opitz; he admired him personally, however and contributed his share to the latter's cultural patriotism by ridiculing German fondness for all things French, including the language. Also well known in their own time were two preachers who laced their writings and homilies with satire, comic stories and occasional earthy language: the Lutheran J. B. Schupp (1610–61) and the Augustinian monk and Viennese court preacher Abraham a Sancta Clara. The former got into trouble with the clerical establishment in Hamburg because of his rough style and sarcastic wit, but ultimately prevailed; the latter, an enormously popular preacher[1], could on occasion be downright vulgar, but obviously delighted his audiences with an inflammatory but witty style and his mordant commentaries on the behaviour and personalities of a host of public figures he disliked.

Not surprisingly, given the spirit of the age, a great deal of the literary production of the seventeenth century was either devoted to or strongly affected by religious concerns. The influence of a medieval mystical tradition (but also that of Jakob Böhme) was most clearly evident in the poems and hymns of the Catholic convert and priest Angelus Silesius (Johann Scheffler, 1624–77), but can also be glimpsed in the otherwise more personalized and down-to-earth pastoral poetry of the Rhenish Jesuit Friedrich von Spee (1591–1635). Protestant religious poetry was best represented in the hymns added to this traditionally important Lutheran musical genre by the Berlin cleric Paul Gerhardt, who employed Opitz's rules and a purified and simplified language to compose what resembled spiritual folk songs more than the typical versification of the baroque. His poetry already demonstrated something of the shift in the emphasis of worship away from the congregational and collective to the personal and individual – something which under Pietist influence became even more prominent in the later poetry of figures such as Gottfried Arnold and Gerhard Tersteegen (1697–1769).

Of the few literary works of the seventeenth century which have kept their interest for later generations, a handful of novels come first to mind. Two of them, almost predictably, were products of the Thirty Years War. The earlier was *The Wondrous and Veritable Adventures of Philander of Sittewald* (1642–43), written by the Alsatian Johann Michael Moscherosch (1601–69), who personally experienced many of the horrors of the war and was virtually reduced to starvation before finding refuge as a municipal official in Strassburg. His work, continuously critical of something, is almost more satire than novel and is both excessively episodic and capricious in the subjects it deals with and stylistically almost formless; but it contains

---

1. See above, Chapter Thirteen.

some remarkable descriptions of the devastation and demoralization brought by the war.

Even more realistic, historical and comprehensive in the pictures it paints of a society in cruel and endless war with itself was Hans von Grimmelshausen's *Adventures of Simplicissimus* (1669), which related the experiences of a peasant boy carried off by soldiers to grow up in the maelstrom of war. Much of the narrative is autobiographical and, like that of Moscherosch, its composition is somewhat whimsical and uneven. But there is real genius in the work; strongly influenced by translations of Spanish picaresque novels published earlier in the century, it established Grimmelshausen as the founder of the German 'rogue's novel' (*Schelmenroman*), a position strengthened by the three lesser but similar novels he published between 1670–72.

Much less impressive in quality, but abundantly produced, were the novels of heroic and gallant adventures which were the German version of a form of fiction popular all over Europe in the seventeenth century. Philipp von Zesen, mentioned earlier, was perhaps the best of a not very distinguished group of novelists of this kind, though he was not as prolific as Eberhard Happel (1647–90), who wrote numbers of romances in a heavy style which was perhaps alleviated for some readers by the inclusion of exotic locales designed to appeal to the intense geographical curiosity of the time.

Drama presented especially difficult obstacles for any author. To compete with opera for the stage was not easy, especially in a country where 'the stage' meant everything from stilted medieval morality plays to the productions of travelling troupes (primarily English) presenting barely understandable German translations of badly mangled English works (including Shakespeare) and from the elegant products of French and Italian playwrights to the horrible slapstick farces so popular among the lower classes.[2] The Silesian Andreas Gryphius (1616–64), one of the best poets of the period (and author of 'Tränen des Vaterlands anno 1636', a moving poetic description of the miseries of war), was also the best-known dramatist of the baroque. Well schooled in Holland and well read in Dutch drama, he had a serious intention of producing dramatic works of real quality. Whether from personal preference or because he knew his audience, he liked themes involving violence, martyrdom and the supernatural, accompanied by noisy sound effects and

---

2. Some real improvement in popular comedy did occur towards the end of the century, under Italian influence. Indeed, the first permanent stage for this genre – the *Hanswurst* as the German equivalent of the harlequin – was established in Vienna in 1706, but any claims it had to dramatic legitimacy were utterly ruined by the classical standards formulated by Gottsched in and around 1730; thereafter, it quickly sank back to its 'Punch and Judy' status.

exaggerated action and sentiment. His tragedies carried the message, perhaps reflective of his own unhappy youth, of the transitoriness and vanity of all worldly things and of the heroic quality of resigned endurance in the face of adversity. But he also wrote comedies, including the timely *Horribilicribrifax* (*c.* 1650), an updated bitter-comic version of the popular Renaissance satires on the braggadocio of the common soldiery. Gryphius's younger Silesian contemporary D. C. von Lohenstein (1635–83), perhaps believing that he had discovered the secret of his older countryman's success, indulged his own morbid taste for historical catastrophes, violence and sheer horror, together with absurdly exaggerated passion in words and deeds, to the point where his dramas lost their credibility even to critics and audiences normally accepting of much impossibility as part of the overall convention of the medium. He, together with the poet C. H. von Hofmannswaldau (1617–79), whose prose and poetry was so inflated by intellectual and emotional extravagance as to be both ludicrous and exhausting, really defined this last, already overripe phase of baroque literature.

While it is certainly arguable that a fairly steady growth in technical proficiency, ability to manipulate language and general literary self-confidence had accompanied even the worst excesses of the high baroque (which had some of the characteristics of a good experiment gone bad), it was almost inevitable that a corrective would be applied at some point. The first evidences of this emerged in a group of younger writers who, impressed by the great works of later seventeenth-century French literary figures (and especially the *Art poétique* of Boileau), moved to apply a fresher set of theories and standards than those supplied by the long-dead Opitz. With one or two exceptions – notably J. C. Günther (1695–1723) – their motives proved more admirable than their actual accomplishments, most of which came in the form of lengthy and tiresome odes and lyrics which were even less inspired than the poetry they strove to replace. More prophetic of future developments, and consistent with the mental climate of the early enlightenment, was the healthy influence of English naturalism which can be seen in the works of two poets born in Hamburg: B. H. Brockes (1680–1747) and Friedrich von Hagedorn (1708–54). In both, the typically baroque preoccupation with the sadness and evanescence of the world was replaced by appreciation for the beauty of the natural world (as in Brockes's still religiously-inspired works) or by a more secular and robust celebration of the pleasures of the world of man (as in Hagedorn's bright but unsentimental love songs, drinking songs and fables and poetic epigrams). In this new nature poetry, 'The Alps' (1732) of the renowned Swiss physiologist Albrecht von Haller (1708–77) occupies a prominent place; stylistically unpolished, its aesthetic and moral reverence for nature is profound and moving and it is notable for its depiction of peasant village life in terms that are both sympathetic and respectful.

To the extent that this more naturalistic literature adopted themes that were less aristocratically class-specific than the generality of baroque works (at least the secular ones), it was also a more bourgeois literature – which again points to the importance of English literary influences in the early eighteenth century. This was nowhere more obvious than in the huge body of publications loosely termed 'moral weeklies', which are dealt with below in greater detail. But it was also dramatically evident in the explosive popularity of Daniel Defoe's *Robinson Crusoe* (1719), which was immediately translated into German and, by inviting scores of German imitations, chased the overblown heroic adventure novels of the previous century into oblivion. Of these imitations, some short and others long, almost all were bad; but most were popular and none more so than Johann Georg Schnabel's *Insel Felsenburg* (4 volumes, 1731–43), one of the most widely read novels of the eighteenth century. No literary masterpiece, Schnabel's story is of shipwrecked travellers fleeing the Thirty Years War, who under the leadership of one of their number – Schnabel's hero – established on their island home an ideal society of distinctly bourgeois complexion. Unlike Defoe's book, whose appeal lies in its wonderfully executed story of the resourcefulness and dauntless perseverance of a single individual and which therefore deals primarily with personality and character, Schnabel's work, though similarly pervaded by bourgeois virtues, really stands in the utopian tradition of social criticism, containing – as Defoe's does not – an implicit rejection of his own society.[3]

The reaction against the excesses of baroque literature reached its culmination in the authoritative works of Johann Christoph Gottsched (1700–1766), who for some twenty years dominated the German literary scene as completely as had Opitz in his time. Very much a product of the intellectual climate of the early enlightenment, Gottsched caught up, combined and reformulated the various strands

---

3. Neither work has any real hint of the 'back-to-nature' theme falsely ascribed to them by a later generation; the heroes of both, on the contrary, tried as best they could to 'civilize' their primitive environments.

of stylistic restraint, naturalism and rationalism which had characterized earlier and largely unsuccessful efforts of individual imitators
of French classicism and reissued them as an aesthetic *diktat* in his
famous *Essay towards a Critical Poetic Art for the Germans*, published in
1730. At that time, Gottsched was a professor of poetry at Leipzig,
where he had lived since the mid-1720s and which he helped to
convert into the centre of German literature as well as a major fount
of enlightenment, alongside Halle. While his *Essay*, comprising a
detailed and practical guide to the writing of various types of
literature according to canons of carefully defined good taste, was
always the keystone of his aesthetic authority, Gottsched buttressed
his lordship of German letters by various other means, including
domination of the important Leipzig literary society to which he
belonged and his editorship of an important new literary journal
published between 1732 and 1744. And, like Opitz, he (and his
disciples) provided concrete examples of his theoretical prescriptions,
in this case by writing, translating and staging dramas – his favoured
medium – to serve as a sort of officially approved repertory for the
German theatre; a six-volume compendium of such plays, including
his own very popular (but also mediocre and very unoriginal) *The
Dying Cato* (1731), was brought out between 1740 and 1745.
Basically an optimistic utilitarian, Gottsched was deeply and
genuinely devoted to the rational and humanitarian ideals of the
enlightenment, which he attempted to advance not only in aesthetics
but in translating and popularizing such important works as Pierre
Bayle's *Historical and Critical Dictionary* and G. W. Leibniz's *Theodicy*
(originally written in French) and in other ways as well.[4]

There was, without doubt, much that was productive in the
Gottsched reform era, during which literature attained a previously
unheard-of pan-German capability of promoting the chief intellectual
and moral themes of the enlightenment and more elevated public
tastes and social standards. But there was a certain falseness and
superficiality in an aesthetic ideal which, while appropriately
commanding the imitation of nature, defined that nature – and
especially human nature – in so idiosyncratically narrow a fashion as
to frown upon the depiction of man as much more than an
intellectual automaton, invariably reacting rationally and without
occluding passions or enthusiasm to his environment. What was
absent in this ideal was emotion, sentiment and imagination – the
realities beyond reality which play so essential a part in inspiring and

---

4. See below, Chapter Fifteen.

defining man as he truly is, for good or ill. It was the recognition of this absence which underlay the growing discomfort of younger literary spirits with the Gottsched ideal and which, in overturning it, engendered movement towards a new literature of previously unimaginable range and quality. Discussion of that movement, which gained momentum from about 1740 onward, can be postponed for now, but it will be treated in detail below.

While it is certainly true that the German literature of the seventeenth and early eighteenth centuries bequeathed no very distinguished legacy to the future, the same cannot be said of some other areas of artistic endeavour. Architecture is one of these. In the century after 1648, Germany produced an impressive array of large edifices built in the baroque style, a number of which, indeed, are classic examples of it. The baroque originated in Italy as a significant modification of Renaissance classicism, in which the dignified symmetry and simplicity of line conveying an impression of quiet repose was deliberately distorted by means of curvatures, contrasts of colour and proportion, spatial illusions and other means designed not to calm or quiet but to excite and even disturb; the cool, static rationality of the classical style yielded to a fluidity, restlessness and boldness which spoke less to reason than to the imagination and exalted less order in itself than the ordering power of the will. Traditionally and with much good reason, the diffusion of the baroque style has been credited in part to impulses arising from the Catholic Counter-Reformation and particularly to the Jesuits, who recognized the need to utilize all forms of visual art as auxiliaries in the campaign to halt and then reverse the progress of the Reformation and who saw in the new style a means of stirring and committing popular imagery and emotions to their own religious vision.

With the progress of the Counter-Reformation and much deliberate cultural cross-fertilization, the baroque eventually became almost the official architectural style for new buildings and the remodelling of old in large parts of Catholic Europe; and as monarchical absolutism became as triumphant in such lands as had the church itself, the style was adopted on a very wide scale in the construction of palaces and other major princely edifices. In Germany, the new architecture was evident in the extreme south – Salzburg and Munich, for example – even before 1600, but it was not until after the Thirty Years War that it became common in a wave of new construction which had perforce been deferred during the war years and which reached its peak around 1700. By that time, the

Catholic territories were replete with baroque structures either finished or in one or another stage of construction or planning. These included not only some cathedrals and numerous monastic churches, but also dozens of small votive chapels and pilgrimage and parish churches, as well as secular structures ranging from the magnificent palaces of temporal and ecclesiastical princes down to lesser public buildings, military barracks and armories, rural manor houses and even the houses of some urban patricians. Northern and Protestant Germany was less hospitable to the baroque style than southern and Rhenish Catholic Germany; both Lutheran and Calvinist churches frowned on the lavish grandiosity and rich ornamentation which characterized the baroque, while the varieties of stone which were its chief building materials were more difficult to obtain than in the south. Still, a few major baroque edifices arose in the north: palaces in Kassel, Berlin and Potsdam, for example, and churches in Berlin and Wolfenbüttel (Brunswick). The most spectacular appearance of the new style towards the north was in Dresden, where Catholic cultural influences waxed strong after the conversion of Elector Friedrich August I (1694–1733).

Italian architects were ubiquitous in the early phases of baroque construction in Germany and many remained active well into the eighteenth century. But a wealth of native German talents soon became available and it was they who carried the weight of the flowering of the German baroque after 1700: J. B. Fischer von Erlach and Lucas Hildebrand in the Habsburg lands; J. M. Fischer and the two brothers Asam in Bavaria; Johann Dietzenhofer and Balthasar Neumann in Franconia (most notably in Würzburg); Maximilian Welsch in the Rhineland; M. D. Pöppelmann and Georg Bähr in Dresden; and Andreas Schlüter and G. W. von Knobelsdorff in Berlin and Potsdam. Every one of these was responsible for several notable buildings and, just as important, for the organization of space around and within them. In the case of palaces, in particular, it was important not only that the main structure itself be visually monumental from without and dramatically spacious and ornate within, but that it so dominate its surroundings as to suggest the obedient submissiveness of its entire external environment. Thus, formal gardens, paths, fountains, garden houses and arbours, portals and so on, were constructed and placed with a careful eye to the creation of a vast unity to which the palace, as the centrepiece, alone gave meaning. The open space required by such grandiose designs often did not exist in the middle of crowded older cities, which explains why so many princes (and prelates) built entirely new residences outside of them, or in suburbs, rather than simply remodelling existing palaces. Karl VI of Austria tried the latter alternative – the Klosterneuburg in Vienna – but the project was eventually abandoned and his daughter and successor Maria Theresia built the new palace of Schönbrunn instead. The Nymphenburg Castle in Munich was similarly removed from the centre of the old city. In both Karlsruhe and Darmstadt, whole cities were planned around new palaces.

But whether the new or remodelled baroque structures were ecclesiastical or secular, all were functional monuments intended to celebrate the glory and power of God or of his monarchical lieutenants on earth. Thus, while the elector of Brandenburg found many expensive ways of memorializing his elevation to a royal title in Prussia in 1700–01, none cost him more than the commissions for the new palaces and other edifices he conferred on Schlüter and Knobelsdorff; and it was no accident that in the Habsburg lands of central Europe the blossoming of new baroque construction coincided with the turning of the tide against the Turkish menace, the reconquest of Hungary, the more or less successful defence of the Empire against the aggressions of Louis XIV and the assumption of full responsibility for the future of the dynasty following the extinction of the Spanish line in 1700.

Like the great palace of Versailles in France, though mostly on a smaller scale, of course, the physical settings of the new German princely courts were designed as great multidimensional theatres within which the drama of an evolving absolutism could play itself out, with enough room to accommodate all the actors – officials, courtiers, mistresses, men- and ladies-in-waiting and other court functionaries, including thespians, musicians and singers – who created and sustained the magnificent illusion of a courtly society more important and real than reality itself. The larger ecclesiastical structures were no different in intent: the prelatic residences such as those built by the elector of Cologne in Bonn, the bishop of Bamberg in Pommersfelden, or the bishop of Würzburg, were no less grandly conceived than those of any secular prince and the great cathedrals and abbeys – 'baroque castles of Christ', as they have been termed[5] – were also in their own way ornate theatres within which the powerful history of the church militant and the moving drama of human redemption could be staged in awesome splendour.

Because of the significant delays which usually occurred between

5. Holborn, *A History of Modern Germany*, II, 176.

the approval of architectural plans and the completion of actual structures, baroque buildings continued to be constructed in various parts of Germany until late in the eighteenth century and the style even gained a temporarily renewed currency in a few places – Frederick the Great's Berlin and Potsdam, for example – around the mid-century. But by that time, there was little breath of originality in it and it was clearly receding in popularity almost everywhere. Much of the building mania of the princes, nobles and wealthy burghers which succeeded the dearth of construction during and after the Thirty Years War had exhausted itself by 1750 or so; this was especially evident in the larger and more expensive structures which, being now in place, made similar projects unnecessary for the foreseeable future. The construction which continued, whether public or private, was of generally smaller and more strictly utilitarian buildings to which the grandiosity of the baroque style was inappropriate.

In the princely courts themselves, furthermore, the earlier emphasis on pageant and elaborate formal ceremony and ritual as a stay against the uncertainties and confusion of confessional strife and civil and international disorder had begun to give way to courtly life conducted on a more human and personal scale. With the progress of the enlightenment and its confidence in reason and natural order, life was no longer cast in terms of heroic suffering and self-sacrifice, but of a reasonable and orderly elegance which replaced emotionality with intellectuality, ascetic spiritualism with aesthetic sensuality and public imagery with private intimacy. A new cultural style – the rococo – came to embody this perspective: lighter, brighter, smaller-scale and more playful (but not necessarily superficial or trivial) than the baroque, the rococo was primarily an interior decorative and ornamental style. It could be (and in Germany occasionally was) employed in basic architecture, but it appeared most frequently and effectively in the embellishment of windows, doorways, mouldings and pillars, as well as in gold and silver objects, porcelain table service and figurines, furniture, mirrors, tapestries, pictures and picture frames and so on.[6]

6. German painting for the whole period will be ignored here. It was undistinguished in comparison to that of the Low Countries, France and Italy in all genres and while there was a fairly steady production of landscapes, portraits and other pictures, their painters were more journeymen limners than genuine artists. The real talents of the portraitist Johann Heinrich Tischbein (1722–89) and his two nephews, J. F. A. and J. H. W. Tischbein, as well as of the latters' older contemporaries Anton Graff and Raphael Mengs, do not invalidate the generalization.

While the baroque impulse was already greatly weakened by the mid-eighteenth century, it received its formal death blow at the hands of Johann Joachim Winckelmann (1717–68), an enormously significant figure in the history of aesthetic theory in Germany. In his published works, beginning in 1755, he declared baroque art to be bad art, both directly and by contrasting it with a new aesthetic ideal based on a conception of ancient Greek art which he had developed from an idealized understanding of Greek civilization as a whole. This new ideal was central to a redefined 'classicism' which was to be of great importance to literary and philosophical movements of the late eighteenth century and about which more will be said below. In the area of the visual arts themselves, interestingly, it had little impact – partly, no doubt, because there was so little good native talent to influence and partly because except for hints and tendencies (or outright imitation of Greek models), the ideal itself was too elusive and cerebral for representational art – the very qualities, in a sense, that gave it influence on thought and feeling in philosophy and literature.

Besides architecture, music was the only one of the fine arts in which Germany could claim real distinction, especially after 1700 or so. Let it first be noted, however, that until the late eighteenth century such distinction did not much apply to the one area of musical composition and performance which attracted the strongest patronage and the most numerous audiences throughout the period – opera. Originating in Italy, this most thoroughly baroque of all forms of art began to find acceptance in Germany by shortly after 1600 – first at various courts and in some of the Imperial Cities of southern Germany, then gradually spreading northward. The originally rather small theatres built to accommodate opera became steadily larger and more luxurious: Dresden's opera house, constructed in 1667, could hold 2000 spectators; Brunswick's of 1691, 2500; and the most spacious of all, built at Ludwigsburg in 1750, had a huge stage across which whole squadrons of cavalry could gallop and was placed on the shore of a lake in such a way as to permit the spectators to view nautical productions. The last major capital to have a real opera house was Berlin (1741–2) and the last major city to build one was Frankfurt (1782). Italian influences on the composition and production of operas remained dominant throughout the period, reinforced by the widespread employment of Italians as court conductors, composers, dancers and vocalists. The only renowned German opera composers were the handful who, like the famous

Dresden court composer Johann Adolf Hasse (1699–1783), achieved a complete mastery of the Italian style; otherwise, German participation was limited to instrumentalists, a few well-known vocalists and translators and preparers of opera texts – including, in the late seventeenth century, a number of poets of the Hofmannswaldau school in particular. Attempts to create a native German opera proved abortive, but not for lack of effort; a German opera was the first production of the new Hamburg opera theatre in 1678 and for a number of years thereafter some of the best musical talent of northern Germany – including Matthison, Telemann and even the young Händel – became involved in the staging of German operas. But these works were hampered by the absence of a vital native dramatic tradition to build on, as well as by the prosaic tastes of the Hamburg audiences (further soured by the mordant attacks of the local critic Christian Wernigke [1661–1725], who exposed the ludicrousness and absurdity which was the very essence of nearly all baroque opera and which required a certain suspension of belief on the part of spectators as the condition of its enjoyment). German opera thus eventually disappeared from the Hamburg stage and the opera house itself was closed in 1738. The only other comparable undertaking, in Leipzig, failed in an even shorter time.

The most original German contributions to baroque music, though strongly influenced in style and tonality by various of the early Italian masters, arose primary out of the musical traditions of German Protestantism, anchored since the time of Luther in the hymnal chorale. By the early seventeenth century, the addition of the cantata – a composition containing not only choruses, but also solo arias, recitatives and instrumental interludes – had combined the affirmation of congregational or collective faith with a recognition of the individual's personal striving for redemption; and from there it was no huge step to arrive at the oratorio – a longer and more elaborate version of the cantata, with more singers, a larger and more complete orchestral accompaniment and more dramatic effect (though executed without action, scenery or costumes). The step was taken by the Saxon court composer and musical director Heinrich Schütz (1585–1672), who over the course of his fifty-seven active years in Dresden published four major oratorios, three of them in the single year 1666. Strongly influenced by the Italians Gabrieli (with whom he had studied) and Monteverdi and others, with whom he corresponded, Schütz founded an oratorical tradition that was continued by the gifted organist Dietrich Buxtehude in Lübeck, the composers Georg Philipp Telemann, Reinhard Keiser and Johann

Matthison in Hamburg and finally by Johann Sebastian Bach (1685–1750), Georg Friedrich Händel (1685–1759) and Joseph Haydn (1732–1809).

Bach, born in Eisenach into a Lutheran family with a long musical background, became a brilliant organist through study with various north German masters (including Buxtehude) and accepted several performing and supervisory positions before becoming cantor (music director) of the Church of St. Thomas in Leipzig in 1723, a post he occupied until his death. Profoundly pious and of venerable bourgeois dignity, Bach wrote both sacred and profane music; and while he was both known and honoured in his own time, he was not then regarded as the true genius a more distant posterity has seen him to be. There were many competent composers in his time, all of them technically proficient and well schooled in the rules and styles of their art and Bach himself introduced no new style or method which would automatically single him out as special. But he used what was already at hand in ways at once discerning, subtle and bold and his composition was reinforced by an encyclopaedic knowledge of music history and by a work ethic possessed only by those who see their work as a true calling, not just as a living. His compositions, suffused with a spiritual and ethical power which was not the property of the generality of musicians of his time, were intended to instruct the soul as well as to delight it; and unlike so many of his journeyman colleagues, Bach found it difficult to be frivolous and impossible to be trivial.

Bach's contemporary, Händel, came from an intellectually more sophisticated and somewhat more secular background and although he too was initially trained as an organist, he developed an early interest in opera and while still a young law student wrote and staged two of his own operas at the ill-fated German theatre in Hamburg. He then spent three valuable years in Italy, much of them with the masters Scarlatti and Corelli, and before long gained a reputation as a superior composer of opera after the Italian style. After a short stint as court conductor in Hanover, he left for England, where his previous German employer soon became the new King George I of England. For some two decades, his chief medium was opera; but he also wrote many excellent concerts and occasional pieces during this time and as the operatic fashion faded he turned to the oratorio, abandoning the stage for what soon became huge successes in the concert hall. His oratorios, composed in English and utilizing mostly Old Testament and ancient classical themes, were remarkable not only for the beauty, clarity and powerful spirituality of the lyrics, but for the dramatic impact of his elevation of the chorus to coequal status with the soloists. The thematic range of his oratorical compositions was impressive – from idylls to tragedies and from ethical and philosophical instructional pieces to profoundly touching religious subjects. Greatly admired on the continent, this German maestro (whom no less a figure than Beethoven regarded as the greatest composer of all time) was revered in England as a genuine national treasure and at his death was accorded the honour of burial in Westminster Abbey.

In Germany itself, the heroic age of baroque music, already showing signs of change in Bach's last years, was succeeded by the so-called 'pre-classical' period – an imprecise terminological catch-all for what was really a period of controlled experimentation. By the mid-eighteenth century, just as the rococo as a decorative style was responding to sensibilities which were more intellectual, secular and sociable, composers turned their efforts to the creation of a lighter, more convivial style of music appropriate to the smaller and more intimate gatherings characteristic of both princely courts and the private residences of nobles and the urban upper classes. This lighter but also brisker and brighter touch was accomplished by greater reliance on instruments such as the clavier, the flute and the violin, as well as by shortening compositions so as not to fatigue or bore audiences.

The new styles were not a degeneration from the baroque carried out by second-rate composers unable to match the achievements of their predecessors: Bach's own sons, the very gifted Carl Philipp Emanuel and the somewhat less original Johann Christian, belonged to this period; and even some of the lesser lights such as J. J. Quantz and Johann Stamitz had talent superior to many of their baroque counterparts. There was, furthermore, an identifiable aesthetic theory associated with the new style, first asserted by C. G. Krause in his *On Musical Poesy* published in Berlin in 1752 and continued in the theoretical writings of others. What most wanted was to rid the baroque style of much of the heaviness and intensity which made it more suitable to church services than to chamber concerts in more secular locales or, as in the case of the very important Austrian court composer Christoph Willibald Gluck (1714–87), to reform the opera by simplifying it and increasing its dramatic content at the expense of the long solos favoured by Italian composers, while at the same time unburdening it of the unnatural bombast and absurdly exaggerated pathos of which audiences were tiring.

It was only towards the end of the eighteenth century that the most impressive fruits of musical experimentation prior to the emergence of the Romantic school appeared in the works of Joseph Haydn (1732–1809) and Wolfgang Amadeus Mozart (1756–91). The former, who rose from an artisan family to become court conductor for the Hungarian grandee Prince Esterhazy in Vienna, achieved a remarkable mastery of homophonic music – the simultaneous combination of very different types of instruments into a single melodic voice – with which he and others had experimented for some time and, relying more heavily than most on the strengths of the clavier, produced sonatas of pristine quality. While primarily an instrumental composer, he was not uncomfortable with vocal music; he wrote decent operas and his oratorio *The Creation* (1798) – a composition which celebrated an almost Leibnizian universe of ordered beauty and joy – combined voice and instruments magnificently in what might properly be termed the culminating musical expression of the worldly-optimistic but also reverential themes which defined the German enlightenment. Two lengthy stays in England in the 1790s did much to spread his reputation, as well as to enrich his own musical experience; after his final return to Vienna, he spent his last ten (and very productive) years in honoured and materially comfortable circumstances.

Haydn had become very close friends with the young Mozart in Vienna in the 1780s, after the latter had left his employment as an organist in the court of the archbishop of Salzburg to try to gain wider recognition for a musical talent that has had few equals in history. This talent was discovered and cultivated from a very early age by his father through an unusually extensive musical education involving travel, performance and composition in much of western Europe. A somewhat prickly young man, who was perhaps too much consumed by his passion for composition to have much patience with the tedious tasks of a hired music-master, Mozart did not have an easy time in Vienna. In spite of numerous introductions to the world of courtly and aristocratic patronage and regardless of the friendship and assistance of admirers such as Haydn, he never acquired the steady financial support always needed by composers (and other artists) of this era if they were to have the secure environment so important to the free development of their art. That this fact certainly contributed to his early death is especially tragic because the extraordinary quality of the work he completed gave such shining promise of things yet to come. Mozart's compositions are so varied and exciting as to prohibit their description in a short space. He was a brilliant instrumentalist, who learned much from

Haydn and then took what he learned in new directions; but while his symphonies and other occasional pieces will always compel admiration, his operas stand as his real masterpieces, as much in dramatic quality as in musical novelty: his imaginative new uses of the orchestra, his employment of several vocalists singing in simultaneous melodic harmony while venting individually different feelings and his ability to use music not only to set general moods but even to describe separate scenes and the human individuality of characters drawn from all ranks of society – each of these was remarkable in itself, but the combination of all was stunningly impressive.[7]

It is important to understand that while it was impossible for Haydn, Mozart and indeed all of the composers discussed above to avoid putting some part of their personal, subjective relationship to the world into their work, it was not really part of their intention or their ideal to do so. For them, the world was an objective reality, consisting of a mixture of divine, natural and human forces and it was their task to describe that world. This still left them with a variety of musical approaches, of course, since the multiple fusions of those forces suggested different combinations of voice, instruments and melodic and harmonic devices as vehicles for the expression of the reality they saw. But the personal feelings of the composer were always secondary to the greater importance of an extrinsic truth; and that is why even a Mozart, for all of the frequent moodiness of his work, must be regarded as one of the last great innovators of the baroque era, a man who in both attitude and basic style was closer to the traditions of a Händel, or even a Bach, than to the unfettered and sometimes explosive subjectivism of Beethoven and others of the Romantic school. The world in which he lived was certainly a less stylized and more informal and convivial one than that in which the great Bach had grown up; but it was still the world of the old regime.

---

7. If there was a 'German' opera of the eighteenth century, it was surely and uniquely that of Mozart, who did indeed borrow some things from Gluck, but who stood very far from the Italianist Hasse (who was still living when Mozart arrived in Vienna). Mozart wrote only two of his operas in German, however: *The Abduction from the Seraglio* (1782) and his last, *The Magic Flute* (1791). His final and unfinished composition, the moving *Requiem* (also 1791), was written in Latin, befitting the Catholic influence of his upbringing, his creative environment and to a certain extent his own beliefs.

CHAPTER FIFTEEN
The Early Enlightenment to 1750

In broadest perspective, the enlightenment grew out of the long process by which, since the Renaissance, the worlds of nature and of man began to be understood and analyzed not as reflections of a divine will which had frozen them in eternally immutable immobility in a single act of creation, but as dynamic entities, parts of an ongoing creation which had the capability of change and development according to their own natures.

Underlying this evolving conception of the human and natural worlds was a reconstitution of the concept of natural law which tended to return it in the direction of its origins in the ancient classical world, before its modification by medieval Christian thinking. In this reformulation, natural law was the law by which God had willed His creation to be ruled and was itself pure reason. Man, endowed by divine will with his own nature which included the faculty of reasoning, was capable of understanding the plan of the universe – the laws of its operation – by careful study of the phenomena of the created world. The applicability of this idea to the study of the physical world was obvious. The entire 'scientific revolution' began in astronomy with Copernicus in the sixteenth century and was advanced in the same field well into the seventeenth by the work of such figures as Tycho Brahe and Johannes Kepler – both of them court astronomers in Prague – and Galileo Galilei and was provisionally capped by the publication of the comprehensive *Mathematical Principles of Natural Philosophy* by the great Isaac Newton in 1687. Careful observation and cataloguing of data, aided by a rapidly growing array of more accurate instruments of observation and measurement and by an increasingly sophisticated application of mathematics and of mathematical method, yielded spectacular results which were as important in the development of physics as in astronomy itself. With the exception of Kepler (and Leibniz, who discovered the calculus independently of Newton), Germans played no very distinguished role in these and the other great discoveries in chemistry, medicine and other areas which cast the world in such a new and revolutionary light. But, after all, no single people could claim a monopoly of the creative thinking which made up the scientific revolution or, for that matter, the whole movement of intellectual illumination of which it was a part. This thinking was pan-European in its occurrence and thanks to the 'German art' of printing the educated public in Germany quickly became party to both the new discoveries and to the new philosophies which arose from them. The establishment of state-sponsored academies of science in various territories from the end of the seventeenth century onwards assisted in the dissemination of ideas, as did many of the very numerous private reading and philosophical societies.

Although Germany was more onlooker than participant in the process of unlocking the secrets of the physical universe, this was much less true in the rational exploration of the world of human experience and institutions. In the now prevailing theory of natural law, man's own institutions, including the laws he made for himself, were but emanations of his will designed to serve his own needs, including social existence, according to his nature; and while they would necessarily vary with his circumstances and would be more or less appropriate according to the greater or lesser degrees of his understanding, all could by rational analysis be reduced to what all had in common – the first principles of natural justice, or the natural laws of society – through which divine justice itself could be understood. It would then be possible to deduce new and more appropriate laws and institutions which, being in greater harmony with natural law, would incorporate a larger measure of natural and divine justice.

The most important element in this concept was its refutation of the long-standing theological explanation of human institutions as direct ordinances of God and its insistence that divine intentions could best be known through an analysis which started with human nature itself and which then proceeded to understand the conventions of man's social existence as derivatives of that basic nature. Both the Dutch jurist Hugo Grotius (1583–1645) and the English philosopher Thomas Hobbes (1588–1679), while differing strongly in their definitions of human nature itself, had agreed that all positive law and government could be traced to the attempts of an inborn faculty of reason to satisfy human self-interest – that is, the needs which arose from human nature itself. Whether that self-interest necessarily embraced others and was illuminated by an at least primitive inherent sense of right and wrong, as Grotius believed, or was a pure selfishness, unrelieved by any moral sensibility and led in the direction of sociability only through reason, as Hobbes believed, was less important than the sheer force of the argument common to both: man was the author of his own institutions.

The works of both Grotius and Hobbes, but especially of the former, were widely known and discussed in Germany and helped to shape the thinking of the earliest and most important seventeenth-century writer on political philosophy, public law and the philosophy of law, Samuel Pufendorf (1632–94).

Born to a Saxon family which had produced several generations of Lutheran theologians, Pufendorf had the kind of professional career not altogether unusual for one of his training: he taught at the universities of Heidelberg and Lund (Sweden), occupied various high official posts in the Swedish government and in 1688 was called to Brandenburg, where he spent the last years of his life as jurist and court historiographer. His most notable early work, published pseudonymously in 1667, was a shrewd analysis of the German imperial constitution and of the German political scene in general. In it, he mercilessly pinpointed the nature and historical origin of its numerous weaknesses; sharply criticized the disintegrative policies and ambitions of the Habsburg emperors, the greater princes and the Catholic church; likened the constitution to a monster; and proposed certain reforms which might give the Empire greater strength and viability by reconstituting it as a true federation. In several other works, most of them published after the imperial critique, Pufendorf laid out a comprehensive set of ideas in all areas of political and juridical scholarship, insisting on strict separation of church and state in all matters of law. He also introduced a sort of cultural and historical relativism into his thinking about constitutional and positive law, asserting that no single form of government or code of laws could be termed appropriate for all times and peoples, since their particular needs would vary with their own differing circumstances.

In his political philosophy, Pufendorf began with a set of assumptions about human nature which closely paralleled those of Grotius rather than Hobbes, and drew consequences from them about government and its relationship to human rights which were therefore very different from those of the English philosopher. For Hobbes, all sense of right and wrong was utterly absent in human nature in its original state; as a result, human beings lived in the absolute and mortally dangerous anarchy of a 'war of all against all'. To escape this condition, reason had taught them the need for a common set of rules to safeguard each against all others. To obtain those rules, they had created government by agreeing to subject themselves to a common authority (whether monarchy, aristocracy or a democratic assembly), which then dictated those rules to them as 'rights'. In that agreement of common subjection, they had created a one-way contract with that authority which Hobbes conceived as both inviolable and irrevocable as a matter of logic: unable themselves to postulate any common definition of right or wrong, the people had clearly decided that any rules were better than the anarchy of none and for any one, several, or all to resist that government and its laws – no matter how tyrannical they might appear – was to court a relapse into anarchy, the worst possible condition. Hobbes therefore recognized neither any responsibility of government beyond the most basic protection of life, nor any right of rebellion on the part of the citizenry.

Pufendorf, on the other hand, believed to find an at least dimly perceived sense of morality and mutual obligation among even the most primitive human beings, which meant that the original 'state of nature' was already a more or less sociable one. If that were true, then no inescapable brutishness of universal anarchy existed at all and government, instead of arising as a necessity for mere survival, was created as a two-way contract between a people desirous of living better and a government which accepted certain duties towards the people as the condition of its empowerment to govern. Pursuing this logic, Pufendorf accepted the theoretical right of the people to demand change or removal of their government if it violated the terms of its contract in any one of several possible ways. More importantly, however, he demonstrated the most profound reservations about the translation of this theoretical right into the concrete act of rebellion or even lesser acts of civil disobedience. While some of this reluctance may have reflected professional prudence, given the nature of his employment, the greater part of it arose from Pufendorf's practical sense that rebellion could easily prove destructive to even the most noble motives and goals of those who engaged in it and often enough created conditions worse than those they sought to correct. Nevertheless, his insistence that government had a contractual duty to advance the welfare of the people and that definite implications were to be drawn from this not only for the education and training of rulers, but also for the organization and operation of their administrations – implications he examined in detail – added a new and powerful secular reinforcement to the older ideal of the 'Christian state', and one that remained strong in several generations of academics, officials and students and practitioners of law, among whom Pufendorf's ideas were widely known and respected. He also wrote extensively on international law, in which, building on Grotius, he derived an axiomatic equality of all nations from the prior principle of the equality of individuals, all of whom had a right to ask from others the same respect they held for themselves. He condemned aggressive war as contrary to self-interest and therefore to natural law, but acknowledged that its occurrence was an expectable (and to a degree admissible) result of the absence of a universally accepted authority for judging disputes among nations. But moderation in war, as in victory, should be dictated by both long-term self-interest and awareness of the problematic quality of self-serving definitions of right and wrong.

Among the academics of the next generation strongly influenced by Pufendorf's ideas (and those of Grotius and Hobbes) was Christian Thomasius (1655–1728), a native of Leipzig, who after studying both philosophy and law eventually settled in his home city as a lawyer and copublisher of a learned monthly journal. He gradually incurred the increasing displeasure of the Saxon authorities by his attacks on the stiff orthodoxy of the Lutheran church, the university and the government – involving, among other things, a vigorous defence of A. H. Francke and of Pietism – as well as by his denial of the divine origins of princely sovereignty. Eventually threatened with both censorship and prosecution, he fled to asylum in Berlin in 1690 and thereafter was permitted to lecture at Halle in an academy which soon thereafter became a university, largely by his own efforts. He remained at Halle as a respected lecturer and writer for the rest of his life. A less profound thinker than Pufendorf, he also spoke to a different audience and with a more direct message designed to bring about observable social change through the exercise of practical reason. He transformed Pufendorf's still largely custodial view of the duties of government to the people in a more actively remedial and ameliorative direction, while at the same time rejecting any governmental interference in the realm of individual conscience. His advocacy of religious toleration was only one evidence of a strong empirical and utilitarian streak which became more pronounced as he grew older and which caused him to oppose the persecution of witches and heretics and the employment of torture as part of the judicial process – practices he had once accepted. His early sympathy with Pietism also disappeared later in life, partly because of its excessive mysticism and otherworldliness.

Thomasius's adoption of German as his preferred language for teaching and writing was a sensational innovation; but it came less from a glowing patriotic love for the language than from a desire to liberate his students, higher education and the educated public at large from the sterile Latin (and French) scholasticism and pedantry he found so appallingly inimical to a rational and realistic grasp of the true problems of human life. He was no enemy of foreign cultures and in the French, in particular, he found many traits and tendencies he was prepared to commend – as long as it was done in German. With Thomasius's concrete and down-to-earth approach to law, administration, moral and religious matters and so on, he brought into his teaching a distinctly 'bourgeois' flavour – an optimistic, workmanlike philosophy to underpin the specialized education of the students who sat in his classes. In his some thirty-five years as a professor at Halle, he trained hundreds of students – many of them nobles – who later became officials or holders of other positions of public responsibility in Prussia and elsewhere in Germany; through them, Halle became as important an influence on the development of public administration in eighteenth-century Prussia and Germany as it was, through Francke's Pietism, on the reformulation of the responsibilities of public service as an individual moral imperative. The first German chairs in Cameral Science established by Friedrich Wilhelm I in Halle in the year of Thomasius's death were fitting memorials to a man whose life was spent teaching others to honour and serve an enlightened ideal of 'public interest' whose character Thomasius himself had done so much to define.

One generation beyond Thomasius was the imposing figure of Christian Wolff (1679–1754), whose teachings and writings, more than those of any other individual, really defined 'enlightenment' for most eighteenth-century Germans – not least because he was the first important systematic philosopher to write extensively in German, thereby fully legitimizing it as a philosophic language.

Born in Breslau as the son of a well-educated tanner, Wolff's early education was a fertile mixture of Lutheran teachings and Catholic classical scholasticism, which he later broadened and deepened at Jena with studies in theology, law and mathematics. After a few years in Leipzig as a collaborator on a learned journal, during which time he began correspondence with the famous Gottfried Wilhelm Leibniz, he was called to Halle in 1706 to teach mathematics and natural science and, a few years later, philosophy as well. Through occasional writings on mathematics and science, but especially through three major works on logic, metaphysics and political theory (published in 1719, 1720 and 1721, respectively and of which one bore the imposing title: *On God, the World, the Human Soul and All Things in General*), Wolff built a massive doctrinal edifice representing the first thoroughly non-theological ontology (or system of apprehending being and reality). Both his reputation and the number of his students grew rapidly; he received invitations to join academies of science in Berlin, London and Paris (which he accepted) and to take up professorships in Wittenberg, St. Petersburg and Jena (which he refused). But neither his European reputation, his friendship with Thomasius and Francke, nor his own sincere Lutheran piety were able to shield him from the persistent attacks launched on him after 1721 by the suspicious theological faculty at Halle, which convinced Friedrich Wilhelm I that Wolff's conviction that men could live happy and virtuous lives by the cultivation of reason alone smacked of atheism. The king, hardly a model of cool and refined rationality himself, expelled Wolff from Prussia in 1723 and forbade the use of his writings a few years later. Wolff easily obtained a new professorship in Marburg where, by employing Latin rather than his theretofore usual German in many of his works, he signalled his intention to appeal to an ever broader European audience. By 1730, Friedrich Wilhelm had changed his mind about Wolff and invited him back to Prussia – an offer the latter perhaps wisely refused; but the philosopher quickly accepted the reappointment to Halle proffered by Frederick II immediately after his new reign began in 1740. There he remained, at the height of his reputation and influence, until his death in 1754.

Wolff's philosophical system, which was derived in varying degree from Lutheran and Catholic scholasticism, Calvinism, Descartes and Leibniz – among others – was based on an almost boundless belief in the ability of human reason to understand and accommodate itself to the inherent rationality of nature, thereby creating conditions under which an uninterrupted progress towards perfection would be possible. That progress was identical with human happiness and also corresponded to the will of God, whose entire creation was so shaped and ordered as to be useful to man – if he would but understand it correctly (that is, rationally). The formation of society was itself a dictate of reason, arising from the recognition of individuals that the rights and duties flowing from the law of reason and the obligation of self-perfection could best be realized within the framework of mutual assistance provided by community. The state, as the active agent of community, had a responsibility both to the security of the citizenry and to its welfare; and while Wolff explicitly denied the state any power beyond that necessary to fulfil this responsibility, the list of activities he either mandated or permitted to the government was so vast as to leave few areas of individual or community life untouched by public authority: moral enlightenment and physical security, education, employment, entertainment, health and hygiene – these and many other particulars fell within the proper sphere of state regulation. His abstract desire to protect individual rights and freedoms, genuine though it was, was simply over-whelmed in practice by his limitless enthusiasm for the potential of a truly enlightened government to lead (or push) the citizenry towards perfection. This emphasis, together with Wolff's embrace of most of the standard police and economic practices of the German territorial governments of his time and his prudent restraint on the question of the right of resistance to bad government, appealed to many princes, officials and academics as a philosophical justification not only of much of what they were already doing, but also of new interventionist initiatives which in the name of reason would permit reform, circumvention or destruction of 'irrational' traditions by 'enlightened' princes who, coincidentally, would thereby also contribute to a significant increase in their own power. Unintention-ally, for the most part, Wolff's teachings therefore became a significant underpinning of the appearance of 'enlightened ab-solutism' in Germany and were not without influence elsewhere in Europe as well.

While the direct influence of Wolff on his own time was certainly greater than that of his partial contemporary Gottfried Wilhelm Leibniz (1646–1716), the latter's comprehensiveness of interests and philosophical profundity far exceeded Wolff's. Leibniz is still honoured today as an almost universal genius who, along with Descartes, Hobbes and Spinoza, was one of the towering philosophi-cal system-builders of the intellectually explosive seventeenth century. Unlike Wolff, furthermore, Leibniz was an active and important administrator and public official – first in Mainz and then, for his last forty years, at the courts of Brunswick and Hanover. This career, while allowing him time for thinking and writing, also scattered his energies and his projects, with the result that no comprehensive corpus of his work was available for contemporaries;

most of his writings, indeed, did not appear publicly in his own day and a significant part was in the form of an immense and far-flung correspondence to all corners of Europe and beyond. Leibniz's interest in increasing human knowledge was joined by the desire to use such knowledge to increase human happiness. At various times in his life, he devoted himself to mathematical and scientific research and to projects as diverse as improved law codes, the reunification of Protestant and Catholic churches (and, that failing, the reconciliation of the Protestant confessions), the establishment of an international network of learned academies and general peace through the rule of international law. A few such projects achieved concrete results: his efforts were responsible for the founding of the Berlin Academy in 1701, for example, as well as for a similar society in Russia after his death; he wrote what almost amounted to a constitution for the electorate of Mainz; and his mathematical work led to the independent discovery of calculus. His vast and erudite correspondence also contributed significantly to strengthen the intellectual bonds between an international community of scholars in almost all areas of human learning and to meld their separate efforts into a common European enlightenment. While he was celebrated throughout Europe, however, this prophet was, sadly, without honour in his own land in the last years of his life; his own ruler, Elector Georg Ludwig of Hanover, did not appreciate his accomplishments and ignored him both before and after his accession to the English throne as George I in 1714, while even the Berlin Academy Leibniz had helped to establish turned its back on him following the accession in 1713 of Friedrich Wilhelm I, a man with neither interest in nor understanding for intellectual concerns.

It is impossible to comprehend the variety of Leibniz's achievement in a short space. His political ideas were diffused throughout so voluminous and differentiated a literature that no one could use them as a single coherent source, but in the important points they show much similarity with those of Pufendorf – a thinker for whom Leibniz had an only limited respect. Both thinkers had a considerable influence on Wolff and all three, while committed to an ideal of good government which admitted the original human rights of the citizenry, as well as the latter's inherent right to change or abolish a bad government, were respectful of traditional social and political institutions and conventions and very chary of change brought about by any but evolutionary processes. All, furthermore, assigned to government the leading role in the educational process by which the individual was to be guided towards happiness and self-fulfilment in society.

Leibniz, however, had a special significance to the unfolding of the German enlightenment because he, more than any other single figure, provided a philosophical bulwark against the empiricism and materialism which were making rapid progress in intellectual circles in western Europe and which eventually defined much of the difference between the German enlightenment and that of France and England. In his famous *Monadology*, published only after his death, Leibniz rejected the notion, first evident in Hobbes's work, that man's mind or spirit was as purely the product of a physical, mechanistic universe as was his body – a notion which easily led (as in John Locke's 'sensationalism' and among a large group of subsequent English and French thinkers) to the conclusion that ideas of all kinds, including moral ones, were derived entirely from man's own sense experience and ratiocination, not from divine principles placed in his mind, before birth, by God. Horrified by this view of morality as little more than a relativistic and self-serving utilitarianism, Leibniz hastened to restore to man a divinely-implanted love and sense of harmony which, together with reason, motivated and enabled him to commune with and progressively understand the mind and plan of God. He saw God as active not simply in the laws of a physical universe long ago created, but as a continuing personal presence in every individual and an active partner in the realization of His own plan. Such divine immanence was rejected by many western European thinkers on the grounds that the existence of evil in the world was incompatible with the reality of a transcendent God. But Leibniz challenged that argument in his *Theodicy* of 1710, wherein he propounded his famous explanation of the world at any given time in its history, including the present, as the best *possible* one God could have created, given His overall plan; evil, while real, was therefore not evidence that God was not personally present in creation, as the materialists asserted, but was another proof of the complex nature of the evolving divine plan itself and perhaps in obscure ways even a stimulus to the process of man's self-perfection.

The importance of Leibniz's arguments is not that they converted anyone to a system of specific beliefs, but that they reinforced an already existing climate of opinion among German thinkers with a sophisticated – even intellectually dazzling – philosophical underpinning. Germans were already convinced that religion carried an indwelling truth, quite apart from the study of nature and its laws to which, for the materialist, the continuing existence or 'meaning' of God was irrelevant because unnecessary. A personal and transcendent God was accepted emotionally as axiomatic in Germany, along with a firmly anchored conviction (clearly evident in the work of all the German philosophers discussed above) that the institutions and conventions of the human world, no matter how presently imperfect, were in some sense reflections of the ongoing presence of a divine spark in man. Since movement towards perfection in every aspect of human existence was accepted both as a human capability and a commandment of God, social, political, intellectual and moral meliorism as a mind-set was therefore almost universal among major and minor German thinkers throughout the enlightenment. But improvement was seen as an evolutionary process, revealing itself as a perpetual refinement of existing beliefs and institutions, not as a revolutionary one requiring their destruction and replacement. Thus, the virtual absence in Germany of radical critiques of the church, the clergy, the fundamental structures of society and government and so on, had much to do with the profound individual religious convictions of those who might otherwise have delivered such critiques. Leibniz defended this faith with a brilliant and comprehensive argument suited to the philosophic spirit of the age, one which was sufficiently impressive to insulate the mainstream of German thought from the sharp turn western European philosophy took from the late seventeenth century onward.

Leibniz's influence on Germany was further enhanced by the fact that the more or less equal contributions he made to the fields of theology, law and history appealed to the learned community as an unexampled display of that baroque humanistic tradition of knowledge which defined the 'high learning' of the period and which was anchored and perpetuated above all in the structure and curriculum of the universities. This was a strongly synthetic tradition, reflecting an iron belief in the unity of all knowledge, and it was on the whole unfriendly to the introduction of new specialized knowledge that could not easily be integrated into or harmonized with existing disciplines. Theology, as the greatly more comprehensive field of study it was in that time, was really at the core of this. Both the undiminished prestige and influence of the theological faculties and the continuing importance of theology as a subject of intense theoretical and practical debate made it always necessary to attempt to create connections between traditional metaphysics and whatever new knowledge or speculation was produced. Pietist influences had, if anything, increased the requirement that religious referents be integrated into intellectual discourse of almost whatever kind.

It is fair to say that for purposes of acceptability the attempt was generally more important than the result: both Leibniz and Wolff made only dubious efforts to provide such linkage for the new natural sciences, yet the work of both – in spite of the latter's problems with the theologians in Halle – found honoured acceptance in the universities. Nor was the relationship between the purveyors of old and new knowledge a completely one-way street: many theologians accommodated themselves more or less easily to the new understanding of natural law, as demonstrated in numerous high-spirited and optimistic attempts of the first half or more of the eighteenth century to justify divine revelation itself by showing its 'rational' content. Similarly, there was sufficient latitude in the old faculties to permit significant advances in many increasingly specialized branches of knowledge. The study of history, archaeology and classical philology could proceed comfortably within theological faculties, for example, as could that of history, philosophy and eventually even economics and political science in the law faculties – especially after Pufendorf, Thomasius and others had begun to abandon Aristotelian paradigms in political questions in favour of natural law rationalism, thus raising the study of public law (including Cameral and Police Science, as well as political theory in the proper sense) out of the inferior realm of 'practical philosophy' which was assigned to the less prestigious liberal arts faculties.

While enlightened ideas could and did progress within the framework of the existing university system, however, their direction and impact was inevitably conditioned by this necessity of accommodation to the traditions and assumptions of the older and still dominant disciplines, chief among them theology. It was not until later in the eighteenth century that a separate and distinct 'philosophical faculty' could be formed as a partner of coequal dignity alongside those of theology, law and medicine; and until that happened, philosophy itself, in its various branches (including the natural sciences), could not define a purpose for its own existence and development that went significantly beyond that of handmaiden to the older disciplines in a system of higher education still designed far more for the transmission of received knowledge and the preservation of a static socio-intellectual order than for innovation and reform.

It was of inestimable significance to the character of the entire German enlightenment that in its early stages the universities, especially of Protestant Germany, were the primary vehicles of its propagation and dissemination to the socially important classes, who took from their education not the potentially revolutionary message that their society was irrational at its core and in all of its basic assumptions, but instead the gently melioristic message, both conservative *and* progressive in its implications, that enlightenment could (and should) take the rough edges off a society which in all fundamental respects already enjoyed balance, good order and the possibility of future perfection.

The nature of enlightenment's integration into and symbiosis with an already entrenched tradition of higher education therefore had much to do with shaping this message; but there were other influences as well. Pietism, for example, helped to reinforce both the conservative and the progressive tendencies referred to above – the latter because of its emphasis on an active welfare policy, the former because, setting its hopes for that policy chiefly on individual spiritual rebirth, it was uncritical of the existing social and political order. It is also true that the thinkers and writers whose work defined the German enlightenment differed sharply from their western European counterparts in one important respect: nearly all were professors or officials (or both, since professors *were* officials, after all, even when they had no governmental administrative responsibilities) and were therefore financially dependent on and professionally answerable to the political authority which appointed them. The 'private' philosophers – men outside the universities with independent fortunes, untouchable sinecures, or rich and benevolent patrons – who were so important to the evolution of the enlightenment in France or England scarcely existed in Germany; neither, therefore, did the more objectified 'outsider' perspective which made mordant criticism of any and all institutions and practices of public life possible. Such criticism was not altogether undangerous even in those countries, of course, since legal censorship existed and writers could be and were persecuted on occasion, especially in France. But since professors in Germany could lose their livelihood for reasons far more trivial than those for which they could legally be prosecuted, prudence dictated much caution in both teaching and writing. It is also arguable that the nature and sheer burden of professorial duties – including composition of innumerable and exhaustive instructional texts, public lectures and the time-consuming tradition of formal disputations – removed much of the intellectual leisure time which plays such an important role in creative thinking and added another reason for them to become what so many of them in fact did become: able, intelligent and pleasantly discursive interpreters and popularizers of an enlightenment viewed as a long-term process of moral and material improvement without unpleasant or socially disruptive side-effects.

Yet while such practical considerations cannot be dismissed as causes for the comparatively tentative and conservative character of the early (or later) enlightenment in Germany, the root causes were more fundamental. The unique combination of strong individual religious piety, parochial and familiar political and social experience, a formal educational system which accepted and supported the status quo while approving and advocating non-structural ameliorative change, and the variety of political, cultural and professional vocational alternatives available in the territorially diverse Germany of the period created among German intellectuals an attitude towards their society which, though not uncritical, was fundamentally accepting and even admiring of its basic features. Advancement for intellectual merit was a regular phenomenon in Germany and in spite of censorship and a number of incidents of individual persecution, there is little evidence that many of the major or minor figures of the German enlightenment chafed under restrictions they regarded as unacceptable – or, differently put, that they had a strong but repressed desire to say or write things they were not already permitted to say or write. Furthermore, they could observe before their very eyes the progress of some of the greater rationality in government and social improvements they advocated in their classes and in their writings – a point regularly insisted on when they drew comparisons between the practical reality of their spirit of enlightenment and that of France, for example. Thus, while the German enlightenment clearly marched off to a drumbeat different from that of western Europe, the perfection of man and his world was no less the ultimate destination of the former than of the latter.

The powerful and eventually dominant influence exercised by the enlightenment on the German public mind even before the mid-eighteenth century occurred at several levels and by different means. In formal academic instruction, Christian Wolff's philosophy, laid down in a large body of systematically executed instructional literature, steadily pervaded the universities of Protestant Germany and came to dominate them more or less absolutely from the late 1730s onward as his own students began to take up teaching positions throughout the university system – eventually even in Catholic Germany. Since a university education was increasingly a requirement for professional and public service careers of all kinds, the cumulative effect of this education was considerable, giving an enlightened cast to the world view of a steadily growing proportion of the socially important classes. Nor can the continuing influence of

Thomasius be forgotten. His work, to be sure, did not constitute a formal system of knowledge as did that of Wolff and he therefore left no 'school' to propagate his ideas. But his interests had always lain less in the organization of knowledge than in its utilization for individual and social improvement. He represented a spirit of practical action which not only bridged the gap between academic learning and daily practice, but also called both for the intellectual honesty to pass beyond superstition, intolerance and received prejudices of all kinds and for the moral courage to act on the new understanding achieved. As a mental disposition, this spirit continued to ripple through universities in Halle and elsewhere for many years and to influence both the substance and the teaching methods of the Cameral and Police Sciences in particular.

Yet while the universities were unusually important to the dissemination of the enlightenment in Germany, printed media of several kinds were of even greater significance. First, there were the published writings of both major and minor thinkers, which appeared as separate works, as articles in learned journals, or as part of the published proceedings of the private scholarly philosophical societies and state-sponsored academies of science which were founded in various territories from the late seventeenth century onward. Second, there were the reviews, essays and other occasional pieces which filled the increasing number of journals – over 200 of them by 1720 – which were intended for the general public rather than a scholarly readership. Nearly 40 per cent of these were of the historical and political type, dealing in past and current affairs; they were not vehicles of political criticism, of course and strictly speaking were not even genuine news publications, though they devoted some attention to uncontroversial institutional innovations in the territories, strange and unusual happenings in Germany and elsewhere and so on. Their subject matter did not for the most part include philosophical issues in the narrower sense directly; but in tone and approach to their topics they did reflect the rational and didactic emphases of the early enlightenment. Much the same could be said of a third category of literature – belles-lettres – which, as seen in the previous chapter, fell under the almost dictatorial authority of J. C. Gottsched beginning in the 1730s. Gottsched, of course, developed a poetic theory which in its own way was as rigid, comprehensive and rationally systematic as was Wolff's philosophy – and not coincidentally so, since Gottsched was essentially a Wolffian himself, who once published a lengthy popularized version of Wolff's system. There was, in fact, so much continuity between

231

Gottsched's theoretical approach to literature and the general themes of the whole early enlightenment itself that both the older established language and literary societies of the seventeenth century and the score or more of new ones founded between 1700 and 1750 became about as much philosophical as poetic clubs and as such contributed their own share to the diffusion of the enlightenment.

Of special significance because of its popularity among the educated bourgeoisie, in particular, was a fourth type of publication: the 'moral weekly'. Established in unabashed imitation of Addison and Steele's London weeklies (the *Tatler* and the *Spectator*, which appeared between 1709–14), the German moral weeklies achieved a very considerable total readership in their heyday, especially between about 1720 and 1750. The first of them, *The Rationalist*, was founded in Hamburg in 1713 and as many as 500–600 may have appeared at one time or another before their popularity all but vanished after 1760 or so – though many of that number were simply retitled reprints or refurbished versions of earlier ones. A few, like Bodmer and Breitinger's *Discourses of Painters*, established in Zürich in 1721, *The Patriot* (Hamburg, 1724) and *The Citizen* (Göttingen, 1732) had fairly long publication histories and something approaching a mass readership by the standards of the time: *The Patriot*, for example, often had a press run of 5000 copies and was also reprinted elsewhere in Germany. Even Gottsched, never to be left behind in any literary enterprise, founded two short-lived weeklies in 1725 and 1727.

The moral weeklies served several important purposes at once. One was simply to inform – to satisfy people's curiosity about the world they lived in by reporting on current events of the most varied kind, though avoiding really controversial issues, especially in the areas of politics and religion, in order to avoid the kind of censorship that closed down *The Rationalist* after only 100 issues. Another major purpose was to educate and elevate the readership by encouragement of self-cultivation through reason, leading towards a life conducted according to the highest standards of rational morality. False beliefs and practices of all kinds were repeatedly denounced: superstition, harsh and unfeeling treatment of children at home and in school, mean-spirited treatment of servants and other social inferiors, boorish and offensive manners and so on. The fashionable upper-class pastimes of gambling, duelling, idleness and extravagant consumption were identified and pilloried as the vices they were, while the covetousness, pride and ignorance which underlay them were exposed and condemned. Some weeklies, most notably the *Discourses of Painters*, also paid special attention to the improvement of the quality of German language and literature. Nearly all the weeklies blended the rational and worldly optimism of the early enlightenment with a strong commitment to traditional Christian ethics; and while they favoured freedom of thought and expression, they combatted such currents of radical free-thinking as might lead to atheism or other socially destructive notions.

The human being envisioned by these weeklies as their ideal was thus to be rational, moral, 'patriotic' (in the sense of humanitarian and philanthropic) and cosmopolitan (meaning not intellectually and morally parochial). But that also meant a man with the self-assurance to move easily and comfortably in any and all situations and social circles – a man whose relaxed confidence in his own knowledge, abilities and behaviour would protect him from the folly of pride and haughtiness, at one extreme, and servility and obsequiousness at the other. The unhappy consequences of improper behaviour representing both extremes were regularly depicted in caricature and satire in the weeklies. And here, no doubt, lay the greatest appeal of these publications to a partly noble, but more largely educated bourgeois readership consisting of individuals eager to learn the worldly facts, the social behaviour, the language and forms of discourse and the mental disposition necessary to social and vocational advancement in any context – including especially that of the princely courts to which so many of them aspired, but not excluding home, counting-house and coffee house. Nowhere was the influence of the concrete and down-to-earth wisdom of Christian Thomasius more obvious than in these weeklies, which sought to disseminate the very kinds of 'political' sagacity Thomasius did much to define and explain in his own *Short Outline of Political Prudence*, published in 1710. As vehicles for the propagation of practical enlightenment at the semi-popular level, the moral weeklies were of almost unexampled importance in the early enlightenment.

The weeklies eventually outlived their appeal, due in part to their own success: the somewhat unrefined writing style that had originally brought a certain sprightliness to many of them began to be perceived as inelegant by a public that had become better instructed partly by their own efforts. Worse yet, they had become boring through the exhaustion by constant repetition of themes which, to the extent they were eventually not perceived as irrelevant, were carried in a more interesting and sophisticated manner in other media, including the more carefully written journals whose numbers began to explode after the middle of the century. As a group, their paid circulation, never large to begin with, dwindled to the point of unprofitability, followed by collapse. But as was true of all publications, whether books, journals, newspapers, pamphlets or whatever, the moral weeklies circulated among a much larger circle of readers than the small number who actually bought them. Estimates of total readership of the weeklies, as of all the printed media, are impossible; but the more important question is that of the extent to which enlightened ideas, in their German form, reached the literate public. And here, in contrast to many usual textbook depictions of an intellectually backward and uninformed Germany, the sheer flood of publications purveying the cardinal themes of the enlightenment, even in its early stages, must lead to the conclusion that the proportion of the German reading public exposed to those themes was very large indeed. While different from that of other places in its tendencies, the enlightenment in Germany was therefore, from its beginnings, both real and pervasive and no less historically influential than anywhere else in Europe.

CHAPTER SIXTEEN

The Legacies of Westphalia and Beyond (1648–1685/99)

Like a great earthquake whose aftershocks continue well after the main event has ended, the Thirty Years War bequeathed a mixed legacy of disturbances, hostilities and opportunities which persisted as a source of division and conflict in Germany for a number of years after 1648. Not surprisingly, many serious problems originated with the foreign participants in the war, who in single-minded pursuit of their own interests remained indifferent to the fervent desire of the Germans to be rid of them. The Dutch, for example, continued to garrison various German towns in East Frisia and along the lower Rhine for years, while Spain, still at war with France, was understandably reluctant to remove its troops from such strategically important fortifications as Frankenthal and did so only in 1652. The marauding forces of Duke Karl of Lorraine – a Spanish ally not included in the general peace – also created mayhem in various areas along the Rhine until his own Spanish paymasters, disgusted, removed him from the scene.

Some of the worst problems were caused by the Swedes; even after the basic issues of compensation and withdrawal of forces had been successfully negotiated by the Nürnberg 'Execution Diet' (April 1649–July 1651), Sweden refused to evacuate all of Eastern Pomerania until May 1653 (and then only because of imperial threats and financial concessions by the new owner, Brandenburg) and did not abandon its attempts to overawe the free city of Bremen until late 1654. German princes, however, were also not blameless for the troubles of the time. Emperor Ferdinand III continued to help his Spanish relatives in the Netherlands and in Italy in violation of promises made at Westphalia; and the elector of Brandenburg in the early summer of 1651 used military force in an unsuccessful but unsettling attempt to increase his already disproportionate spoils from the peace by adding parts of the duchy of Berg to his share of the Jülich-Cleves inheritance agreed upon in 1614.

Disgruntlement, dissatisfaction and disruption were evident in other quarters as well. For one thing, the chronic resentment of the lesser princes against the elevated political position of the electors had once again flared up, a circumstance which in certain respects favoured the plans of Emperor Ferdinand, who played upon the fears of the electors to persuade them to elect his eldest son Ferdinand as Roman King – and thus his automatic successor – in May of 1653. To court the other princes' favour, however, the emperor in 1652 had also agreed to convene a full diet, at which he hoped to push through a series of important programmes. But by the time it met (late June 1653), Ferdinand's earlier refusal to accept Brandenburg's claims to some Silesian territories – a bitter disappointment to the latter, especially in view of his help in the election of the emperor's son only a month before – had converted Friedrich Wilhelm into an opponent of the imperial agenda. Sufficiently influential to squelch several key parts of that agenda, the elector also gave ear to the 'Grand Design' of his minister Georg Friedrich Waldeck, who proposed nothing less than a great league of chiefly Protestant princes, under Brandenburg's leadership, which with the support of France would aim at the exclusion of the Habsburgs from the imperial throne and a reform of the Empire on a federative basis.

While in the end nothing came of this plan, Ferdinand was fearful of 't and with his own legislative programme in ruins, he dismissed the obstreperous diet in mid-May 1654. His undoubted anxiety about Waldeck's plan came partly from the knowledge that it was only the most recent (and most threatening) example of a tendency towards independent association among various princes of the Empire. That tendency, most noticeable among the less powerful estates, was produced by the desire for security in the uncertain political climate of post-Westphalian Germany; and while it was by no means an unambiguously anti-Habsburg movement, it was both politically centrifugal, from the imperial standpoint, and fraught with the danger that foreign 'protectors' might be invited to join it. Even ongoing attempts at closer cooperation among the estates of some of the imperial Circles, otherwise regarded as a good thing, could look suspicious in this context, as could any attempt at union across Circle boundaries – such as that undertaken by the three spiritual electors of the Electoral Rhenish Circle with the members of the Upper Rhenish Circle in the spring of 1651. And when a foreign power was added to the equation, as in the Hildesheim Union of February, 1652, embracing the Guelph duchies of Brunswick, Hesse-Kassel and Sweden (through Bremen and Verden), the problematical character of such separate associations was greatly increased.

In the event, however, only one such league was to have any real future. In December, 1654, Cologne, Trier, Münster and Neuburg joined in a Rhenish alliance which was given real direction only in the following year when the imperial archchancellor, Elector Johann Philipp of Mainz, joined and adopted it as the means of realizing a patriotic plan to keep war out of the Empire. Such war had by now become quite possible, since the French government, having once again put its domestic house in order after the long agony of the Fronde (1648–53) and newly strengthened by an alliance with Oliver Cromwell's England, was at last in a position to act forcefully to prevent further assistance to Spain by Ferdinand III. On another front, an initially successful Swedish war against Poland, begun in 1655, presented immediate dangers to both Brandenburg and the emperor and could widen to include other German states as well. Johann Philipp, however, like most Germans, identified Austria, with its Spanish connections, as the greatest danger to peace in Germany and had long entertained the idea of constructing a league of German princes powerful enough to deter the Habsburgs from pursuing a dynastic foreign policy which would endanger the rest of the Empire. The unexpected death of Ferdinand's eldest son and heir in mid-1654 at once raised the possibility that Austrian policy could be powerfully influenced by electoral threats to deny the imperial succession to a Habsburg – a possibility strengthened by the fact that Ferdinand's second son, Leopold, was still too young for election as Roman King. For almost three years, France's Cardinal Mazarin, Johann Philipp and the other electors toyed with various alternatives to replace Ferdinand, until the emperor himself died in April of 1657.

Since Leopold had still not attained his majority and no other candidate had been agreed upon, an interregnum of some fifteen months now ensued, during which both French and German agents of Cardinal Mazarin lavished threats and inducements on the electors in an attempt to deny the imperial crown to the House of Austria. Their efforts failed when Leopold was elevated to the emperorship in July of 1658 – but not before Johann Philipp and his league, assisted by Brandenburg, extracted a firm and formal promise from Leopold that he would give no further assistance to Spain. To guarantee fulfilment of that promise, Johann Philipp quickly expanded and recast his alliance, eventually adding to its original signatories the members of the Hildesheim Union, as well as Trier (1662) and, finally, Brandenburg (1665). This new Rhenish Federation (*Rheinbund*), formed in August 1658, also invited France to join in its capacity as a guarantor of the Peace of Westphalia. The members agreed to refuse passage through their territories to any imperial troops intended for the Netherlands and to establish an army of 10,000 men in case of war, of which 2400 would be supplied by France. Since most of the fears which had moved the German princes to create this federation were laid to rest by the termination of Franco-Spanish hostilities in the Peace of the Pyrenees in November 1659, its subsequent history was uneventful. The fact that the federation was never tested in its intended role as a German balancer, or peacekeeper, was probably fortunate for most of its German members, whose admirable patriotic intentions would likely not have spared them the baleful consequences which frequently await those who set goals unattainable except by the help of outsiders with interests very different from their own.

It is also true, however, that the likelihood of an Austrian challenge to the blockade proposed by the Rhenish princes against the movement of imperial troops to the Netherlands had been considerably reduced by the diversion of Habsburg interests to the northeast caused by the beginnings of the so-called First Northern War in 1655. In 1654, the Swedish count palatine of Zweibrücken, Charles, had ascended the throne of Sweden following the abdication of Gustavus Adolphus's daughter, Queen Christina. In the summer of 1655, the newly-crowned Charles X invaded Poland, reviving the by now traditional Swedish attempt to gain control of Poland's Baltic coastline. Emperor Ferdinand, friendly for both religious and strategic reasons with King John Casimir of Poland and always suspicious of Swedish motives, was particularly alarmed by Charles's surprise attack; but so was Friedrich Wilhelm of Brandenburg, whose territories abutted Swedish Pomerania and who saw danger in the suddenly intensified Swedish military activity next door. He also saw opportunity, however, because if he chose his options correctly, he might be able to achieve full sovereignty over the duchy of Prussia which he currently held only as a fief of the Polish crown, with annoying restrictions on his powers of lordship. To this end, he first allied with Sweden, a decision whose initially bright promise faded to dangerous disappointment by 1657: in that year, Charles X's Transylvanian ally George II Rakoczi was forced to a humiliating peace, Denmark had pounced on Sweden in the Baltic and Austrian troops were on the march towards northwestern Poland. Sweden's setbacks caused Friedrich Wilhelm to abandon his alliance with Charles in September 1657 and then, in November, to ally with Poland in return for concession of full sovereignty in Prussia and of the small Polish territories of Lauenburg and Bütow, both of which bordered on Eastern Pomerania. By February of 1658, he had also – albeit hesitantly – allied with Austria.

An unexpected revival of Swedish energies against Denmark in the early months of 1658, together with Austria's reluctance to invade Sweden's German territories from fear of violating the terms of the Peace of Westphalia (thus offending the German electors and their allies just before the imperial election and perhaps even inviting French intervention), led to a temporary paralysis of the war effort against Sweden. This was only overcome in the second half of the year, after the election of Leopold as emperor and after the Swedes, pressing too far their advantage over the Danes, united their enemies and added a possible new one in the form of a Dutch fleet which appeared in the Baltic as a hedge against Swedish maritime hegemony there. Friedrich Wilhelm, leading an army of 30,000, marched through Holstein to Jutland, but could not confront the Swedish forces on the Danish islands. France's Cardinal Mazarin, meanwhile, fearing a total Swedish defeat and a concomitant strengthening of Habsburg influence in northern Germany, not only secured the neutrality of Swedish Bremen and Verden (with the help of the Rhenish Federation), but also dispatched envoys in a vain attempt to separate Brandenburg and Poland from their Austrian ally, and in May 1659 reached agreement with England and the Dutch on a mutual commitment to help end the war. Before these efforts could produce results, however, Austria, carefully weighing the conse- quences of open war with France against the opportunity to rid northern Germany of a Swedish presence (and a French ally) once and for all, proposed to its allies an invasion of Swedish Pomerania. The province was indeed overrun in the summer of 1659 and the key city of Stettin was put under siege while allied forces defeated Swedish contingents on the Danish islands. But the balance of risk for Austria changed dramatically for the worse with the Peace of the Pyrenees in November; war with France had suddenly become a dangerous probability instead of a mere possibility and with Sweden still far from broken and strong pressures for peace being brought not only by England, Holland and France, but also by Poland and Denmark, the belligerents now moved towards a peace whose negotiation was eased by the death of the bellicose Charles X in February 1660.

By the terms of the Peace of Oliva signed in May of 1660 between Austria, Poland and Brandenburg, on one side, and Sweden on the other, the Swedes (thanks largely to France) were permitted to keep all their German possessions of 1648, but in both reality and perception were now a much weakened force in the entire northern theatre. Austria, though delighted that one of its enemies was thus diminished, was also unhappy witness to the enhancement of the power and prestige of France that was so evident both in the way the war was ended and in those peace terms by which it had successfully protected its Swedish client. Brandenburg, on the other hand, was a net winner by any standard, for while the momentary hope of absorbing all of Pomerania had vanished at Oliva, the acquisition of Lauenburg and Bütow was not meaningless; neither were the achievement of sovereignty over Prussia and the considerably increased diplomatic and military prestige which had accrued to the elector by virtue of his shrewd policies and an impressive military role which had greatly exceeded any played by Brandenburg in the Thirty Years War.

While armed conflict within the Empire ended at Oliva, however, relations between the princes, electors and the new emperor remained anything but cordial. Almost no one was happy about the renewed visibility of Habsburg armed forces in northeastern Germany in the late 1650s and that was especially true of the members of the Rhenish Federation, whose own ties to France, however, were a source of concern to some non-members. Various princes continued to feed their jealousy and resentment against the electors, whose preeminence and powers had recently been publicly reemphasized in the election of Leopold I and in the electoral capitulation they had successfully extorted from him. But even some of the electors – Saxony and Bavaria, most notably – had turned unfriendly to Leopold soon after the election. To calm the princes' fears and suspicions, Leopold decided to convene a general diet, which met at Regensburg in early 1663 and, because it refused to dissolve, remained in permanent session as the 'Eternal Diet' thereafter. The most urgent item on the emperor's agenda, far more pressing than the hardly unusual political disarray of the Empire, was an appeal to the princes for immediate help against a large Turkish army which had surged into Austrian-ruled Hungary after a successful conquest of Transylvania and which was making steady progress towards Vienna.

In view of the Empire's overall churlishness about virtually all proposals initiated by the Habsburgs, its response to Leopold's appeal was swift and remarkably generous, a fact explained by the profound and permanent fear of the infidel menace on the part of all European Christians. The diet authorized the call-up of the Imperial Army, while Bavaria, Saxony and Brandenburg sent separate corps and the Rhenish Federation, approving the diet's decision, also provided its own army of 13,000 men – 6000 of them supplied by its French 'protector'. These auxiliary forces were of major importance in the victory achieved against the Turks by the imperial general Raimondo Montecuccoli at St. Gotthard-on-the-Raab in early August of 1664. This battle stopped the Turks' advance, but by no means shattered their power and the terms of the treaty of Vasvar (Eisenburg) negotiated shortly thereafter were not notably favourable to Austria: a twenty-year truce was agreed upon, but the Habsburgs had to recognize a Turkish puppet as prince of Transylvania, consent to Turkish occupation of the fortress of Neuhäusel (which commanded the approaches to Austria) and concede a number of commercial advantages to the Ottomans. Though criticized in some quarters for its acceptance of these terms, Vienna was keenly aware of both its own military weakness and the strength of the Turks; it also faced intrigues and incipient revolt among the Hungarian nobility and, finally, needed a quick peace in the east, even if a questionable one, in order to cope with the possibility that Philip IV of Spain, no youngster, might soon die, leaving as his heir a sickly infant whose own early demise would open up the explosive issue of the future of the entire Spanish Habsburg inheritance.

Philip IV did indeed die in 1665, but although the Spanish question lingered in the background, no immediate international complications arose from it. While in 1666 Leopold strengthened his claims to an eventual Spanish inheritance by marrying Margaret Theresa, Philip's second daughter by his first wife, Johann Philipp of Mainz continued his efforts to keep the Empire from being plunged into crisis over the Spanish issue by urging agreement on it by France and Austria. Minor disturbances of the peace also continued to plague Germany, indicative of the opportunistic atmosphere created by the chronic state of tension between emperor and estates and the estates among themselves. This situation was often aggravated by foreign conflicts or alliances, as when Prince-Bishop Christoph Bernhard of Münster attempted to take advantage of an Anglo-Dutch war in 1665 to improve his territorial holdings at Dutch expense, while at the same time Sweden, with English approval, once again tried to force the free city of Bremen into territorial status. Brandenburg, together with France (a Dutch ally), forced Münster to back down in April 1666 and Elector Friedrich Wilhelm then allied with the Brunswick duchies, Denmark and Holland to force the Swedes to lift their siege of Bremen and once and for all to recognize it as an Imperial City in September 1666. While Brandenburg got generally good publicity in Germany for its peacemaking efforts, the same was not so true of France, which to many Germans (including some in the Rhenish Federation) began to appear excessively meddlesome, arrogating to itself the role of senior partner in the affairs of the Empire. As early as 1663–4, the appearance of French arms in Germany even as assistance against the Turks had created uncomfortable feelings here and there; and such sentiments became more widespread, soon thereafter, by the intervention of French troops to help Johann Philipp of Mainz quell disturbances in Erfurt (a dependency of Mainz) and of Franco-Swedish arbitration to settle a quarrel between the Palatinate and a group of it neighbours, chief among them Mainz itself. France's active role in the Münster affair described above created further anxiety.

All such old fears were minor compared to the new ones occasioned by the French invasion in force of the Spanish Netherlands in 1667, opening the so-called War of Devolution. King Louis XIV, married since 1660 to Philip IV's eldest daughter, Maria Theresa, had long looked at the crisis-ridden Spanish Habsburg Empire as ripe for the plucking and since Philip's death in 1665 his diplomats had negotiated with the senior advisers of the feeble child-king Charles II for an outright cession of the Spanish Netherlands, as well as with the Dutch for the possibility of partitioning them. When all such efforts proved futile and on the legal pretext that he was entitled to them as an inheritance through his wife, Louis invaded the Netherlands in the spring of 1667. The French were intelligent enough not to rely on the structure of old (and, for this circumstance, unreliable) commitments in the Rhenish Federation to protect their eastern flank against the possibility of Austrian or other German intervention and instead made separate new treaties with Mainz, Cologne, Münster and Neuburg. There was much for France to gain in a successful annexation of the Spanish Netherlands, including not only the elimination of a long-standing strategic headache on its northeastern frontier, but also the economic advantages which could come through commerce, including colonial trade, especially if the river Scheldt were opened (it had been closed at Westphalia, at Dutch insistence, to eliminate competition for

Amsterdam from the port of Antwerp). Such potential economic gains for France, however, immediately raised the hackles of other maritime states: England and the Dutch composed the war they had been fighting since 1665 and, together with Sweden, formed a Triple Alliance whose diplomatic pressure was then brought to bear on Louis.

In spite of the easy and complete military victories he had achieved in the Spanish Netherlands (as well as in the Franche-Comté, which was overrun in the spring of 1668), Louis consented to the Peace of Aachen in May 1668, by whose terms he retained only a handful of fortress towns in the southern part of the Netherlands. That he was prepared to accept such modest terms, however, was the result of a diplomatic triumph for which he had been angling for several years: in January 1668, Emperor Leopold, desperate in the face of French military successes he could do nothing about and fearing even worse for the future, disregarded the advice of many of his advisers and signed a treaty with Louis agreeing to a partition of the Spanish inheritance. By its terms, upon the death of Charles II (expected at any time because of the boy's frail health), France would receive the Spanish Netherlands, the Franche-Comté, Navarre, Naples, Sicily and the African territories; Leopold would inherit all the rest.

Of all his opponents from the late war, Louis was particularly annoyed with the Dutch, who had repudiated a pact with him to join the Triple Alliance; their republicanism and Calvinism also rendered them odious to this most absolute and Catholic monarch. Soon after the Peace of Aachen, therefore, Louis resolved to attack them. A successful conquest of this proverbially prosperous land could yield economic advantages even more attractive than those he had sought in the last war, and eliminate one source of future resistance to French acquisition of the Spanish Netherlands. As usual, French agents prepared the diplomatic ground carefully. King Charles II of England proved easy to detach from the Triple Alliance, since his private policy had always been aimed at friendship with France and by the secret Treaty of Dover of June 1670, which provided him with subventions and other assurances, he agreed to a common attack on the Dutch. The Swedes, even more greedy for subsidies than was Charles, joined Louis as soon as he promised more money than they were already receiving from Holland and agreed to attack any German prince who helped the Dutch. Christoph Bernhard of Münster, seeing a chance to revive his territorial claims against Holland, also signed up with the French, as did Elector Maximilian

Heinrich of Cologne (thus opening up Cologne's dependency of Liège as a corridor from France through the Spanish Netherlands to the United Provinces). Like Maximilian Heinrich, who was under the strong influence of the Francophile Wilhelm Egon von Fürstenberg, Johann Philipp of Mainz was also led by internal circumstances into adopting a position favourable to France: his own chapter had elected the pro-French Lothar Friedrich von Metternich as his coadjutor (and presumed successor); and while John Philip had worked to terminate the Rhenish Federation in 1668 from fear of France, he now felt obliged to promise to work for the neutrality of the Empire. Several other important Rhenish territories, chief among them Württemberg, the Palatinate and Trier pledged neutrality; so too did a nervous and uncertain Emperor Leopold, in November 1671, against Louis's assurances that neither the Empire nor the Spanish inheritance would be affected by the war.

When the attack against the United Provinces began, on land and sea, in the spring of 1672, the only prince to offer an alliance to the Dutch was Friedrich Wilhelm of Brandenburg, who was concerned about both the exposed position of his Rhenish provinces of Cleves and Mark and the threat to his Dutch co-religionists and to Europe's commerce that might result if Holland fell to France. This alliance, which called for the Dutch to pay half the costs of an army of 20,000 supplied by Brandenburg, did not last long: a defensive pact between Friedrich Wilhelm and Emperor Leopold in June 1672, which called only for vigilance against a French attack on the Empire, convinced the Dutch to stop paying subsidies to a prince who now appeared unwilling to enter a war on their behalf. That unwillingness was increased by the ease with which Friedrich Wilhelm's small forces in Cleves were scattered by the much larger French army on its way into Dutch territory and in June 1673, the elector found it politic to make peace with France. By that point, however and especially in the face of what for a time appeared to be an unparalleled disaster for the Dutch, Leopold had decided that neutrality was a potentially more dangerous course than intervention and in the summer of 1673 he sent the capable Montecuccoli with a large army to the lower Rhine. Soon reinforced by new allies such as Saxony and Denmark, as well as by the stiffened resistance of the Dutch themselves, the Austrian intervention altered the war very much to the disadvantage of France, whose troubles mounted steadily thereafter: the Empire formally declared war on Louis in the spring of 1674 (partly as a response to French occupation of the so-called 'decapolis' of Alsatian cities the previous summer) and by mid-year France's allies Cologne and Münster had defected, while a grand alliance consisting of Austria, the Dutch, Spain, the duke of Lorraine, Mainz, Trier, the Palatinate and Brandenburg had come into being. Of the larger German territories, only Bavaria and Brunswick-Hanover maintained neutrality throughout the war.

One result of the unexpected downturn of French fortunes was a demand from Louis XIV that his Swedish ally (from whom nothing had so far been asked in return for the large French subsidies) relieve some of the military pressure on France in the west by invading Brandenburg. In the spring of 1675, the Swedes reluctantly complied, forcing Friedrich Wilhelm to force-march his troops home from the Rhine. The Brandenburgers defeated the main Swedish force at Fehrbellin in July and thereafter attacked the Swedes in Western Pomerania. In spite of its heavy losses elsewhere[1], Sweden's stiff resistance in Pomerania was not fully overcome until 1678. In the west, meanwhile, a see-saw war had finally settled into a stalemate, permitting France to play on the war-weariness of all the allies – and the selfish interests of each – to detach them from the coalition by separate treaties, raising the price for peace with each subsequent negotiation. By 1679 the various separate instruments were combined into a comprehensive settlement at Nymegen. Louis XIV did not gain his original goal in the war – the conquest of Holland – since the Dutch lost no territory and even gained some commercial concessions from France. But he kept a number of things gained elsewhere during the war itself: from Spain, the Franche-Comté, conquered in 1674, and permission to exchange the forward bases in the Spanish Netherlands conceded to him in 1668 for a single (and considerable) strip of territory along his northern frontier, running south and east from Dunkirk in the east to the Meuse; and from the Empire, the Alsatian towns overrun in 1673. The final settlement also contained a nasty surprise for those princes who had successfully expelled Sweden from all its German possessions: all were required to return whatsoever Swedish territories they had taken – a requirement which was particularly painful to the elector of Brandenburg, whose heroic efforts (and strenuous protests) shattered against the rocks of Louis XIV's insistence and the wall of indifference of his former allies, including the emperor. It says much about the extent of Friedrich Wilhelm's

---

1. Brunswick-Celle, Osnabrück, Münster, the Dutch and Denmark had all pounced on the hapless Swedes; Bremen and Verden were overrun by the first four, while the Danes occupied both Wismar and the island of Rügen and even set some forces ashore on the Swedish mainland.

disgust with Vienna, in particular, that in October 1679, less than four months after signing away his conquests from Sweden, he accepted a ten-year subsidy treaty with France, in which (though largely tongue-in-cheek) he promised Louis not only a degree of military cooperation, but also opposition to the election of another Habsburg as emperor.

Given his gains from the settlement of Nymegen (which had also witnessed a good deal of dissension among his opponents), there was really nothing in the whole so-called Dutch War to discourage Louis XIV from supposing that further territorial acquisitions along France's frontiers might be possible, especially if they were carried out piecemeal, without an alarmingly large display of brute military force (from large armies which grew steadily throughout the late war) and were accompanied by the usual techniques of combined blackmail and subsidies. Under the particularly strong influence of his war minister Louvois and primarily on military and strategic grounds, Louis decided that his fragmented eastern border with the Empire needed to be tidied up, unified and annexed to France. All along that border, side by side, existed numerous enclaves of French and foreign territory; the latter were now to be combined with the former, thus imposing full French sovereignty on all. In 1680, Louis established a series of special law courts (*chambres de réunions*) whose single purpose was to justify the annexation of such foreign districts by establishing their legal dependency on various towns of the area which, by virtue of Nymegen, were already French. The courts arrived at their unsurprisingly pro-French determinations with appropriate alacrity and by 1681 the French army had seized numerous towns and territories previously belonging to Liège, Trier, the Palatinate, Zweibrücken and other princes along the upper Rhine, as well as the great Imperial City of Strassburg.

Immediate uproar and bitterness resulted in Germany from these so-called 'reunions' (and especially from the loss of Strassburg); but Louis's advisers had correctly assumed that no German or other European state would challenge their larcenous acts by war. The imperial diet, to be sure, roused itself to a rare demonstration of solidarity in 1681 in passing a new imperial military law designed to augment the defences of the Empire by increasing the size of the peacetime Imperial Army to 40,000 men (with provision for expansion in time of war) and by strengthening the imperial military administration. Since this was a completely defensive reorganization, however, and one from which no experienced observer had reason to expect any very remarkable results in any case, it made little impression on the French. Some diplomatic commotion also arose elsewhere in reaction to the reunions. William of Orange, stadholder and military chief of the United Provinces since early in the Dutch War, formed an alliance with Sweden (angry because Zweibrücken had lost reunions to Louis) in 1681 and both Spain and the emperor joined it before the year was out. Within Germany, William also had his hand in the initiation of a separate union of several small princes and counts from the Franconian and Upper Rhenish Circles, which with the addition of the emperor (and eventually Hanover, Saxony and Bavaria as well) became known as the Laxenburg Alliance (1682).

While many of the conditions for another large war were thus in place, two circumstances combined to prevent it, at least for the time being. First, Louis still had some clients within the Empire working against war, chief among them Friedrich Wilhelm of Brandenburg who, now that relations between France and Sweden had soured over Zweibrücken, entertained hopes that continued friendship with Louis might be manipulated into an attack on Swedish Pomerania with the latter's permission. Second, a new and massive offensive by the Turks, which carried them to the gates of Vienna by the summer of 1683, profoundly changed the complexion of international affairs in southeastern Europe and required such immediate and large-scale military attention as to make a new war in the west almost unthinkable. Consequently, when Louis, after tentatively nibbling at Luxemburg in 1682, invaded it in force in June of 1684, only Spain made a feeble and unsuccessful effort to defend it and was forced to agree to its annexation by France in 1685. Brandenburg, meanwhile, preaching caution for reasons that were only partly selfish, had led a movement which resulted in the Regensburg Armistice of August 1684, an agreement by which the imperial diet permitted France undisturbed possession for twenty years of all reunions occupied before 1 August 1681, reserving their ultimate disposition for later negotiations. But while this truce postponed a clearly belligenic problem in western Europe, events were soon enough to prove that the haughty Louis XIV was entirely capable of raising even more serious problems and long before the term set for the armistice had expired. More will be said about this in the next chapter.

In the meantime, however, the Turkish threat which had prolonged the respite from war in the west had occupied the urgent attention of much of the Empire. More or less constantly at war along various sectors of the vast perimeter of their empire since the 1640s, the Ottoman Turks had most recently concentrated their attention on Hungary, encouraged by ferocious quarrelling among the Hungarians themselves: Catholics supported by Vienna were pitted against Protestants (Calvinists, chiefly), as were greater against lesser nobles and pro-Habsburg factions against those which favoured an independent Hungary with a weak Magyar king. The various anti-Habsburg groups, with occasional support from France and steady backing from the Turks and their puppet government in Transylvania, engaged in conspiracies and intrigues which reached the level of virtual civil war in the 1670s; by 1682, one of their leaders, Imre Tököly, had been proclaimed king by the Upper Hungarian diet. With Habsburg power and influence in Austrian Hungary nearly destroyed, the Turks decided that the time was favourable for an attack on Austria itself. Moving against little resistance from an ill-prepared opponent, their armies, under the command of Kara Mustafa Küprülü, crossed the Austrian border and by mid-July 1683, had surrounded Vienna itself with a force which, including auxiliaries, numbered perhaps as many as 200,000 men. The Viennese court, issuing appeals to all of Christian Europe for help, moved to Passau, leaving the defence of the city in the hands of some 12,000 troops and a small group of valiant leaders, including the mayor, the military commander and the bishop of Vienna. While the city lay under siege for two months, a large relief army was quickly being assembled elsewhere. An alarmed Pope Innocent XI was responsible for part of it, since it was his intervention which persuaded King John Sobieski of Poland to interpret his alliance with France loosely enough to permit him to lead over 25,000 Poles against the Turks; and while some French clients among the German princes delayed, using the occasion to pressure the emperor for a quick agreement with Louis XIV on the reunions, others – among them Saxony, Bavaria and various estates of the Franconian and Upper Rhenish Circles – made haste to assist. On 12 September the combined Polish and German armies, formally commanded by John Sobieski but under the field leadership of Duke Karl of Lorraine, confronted the Turkish host in a savage day-long battle from which, at nightfall, the latter fled in disorder.

With Vienna saved, the Polish king removed his army and many of the south German auxiliary forces also withdrew. The troops now remaining in and around Vienna were too few and too poorly supplied to take immediate advantage of the Ottoman defeat, though the Habsburgs had now clearly set the reconquest of Hungary as the highest priority of their foreign policy. The first major enablement towards that goal was the so-called Holy League of March 1684, engineered chiefly by the pope, which linked the emperor, Poland, Venice and later (1686) Russia in a common offensive against the Turks on several fronts. Initial progress was not rapid and the failure of a first attempt to conquer Budapest provided proof to Vienna that it was impossible to present a strong face to Louis XIV in western Europe while conducting a tough campaign in Hungary. By accepting the Regensburg Armistice with France in August 1684, however, the emperor created conditions in which, for several years, the military energies of his own lands as well as those of several German allies could be focused more or less exclusively on the southeastern front. Significant forces were contributed to the Hungarian campaign by Bavaria and Saxony and eventually by Brandenburg as well, while large numbers of German troops from other territories served in a Venetian army which successfully carried the war to the Turks in Greece. John Sobieski, meanwhile, harassed the Ottomans in the principalities of Moldavia and Wallachia.

In Hungary, the first major success was Karl of Lorraine's conquest of Budapest in late 1686, and for about three years thereafter the imperial forces registered one victory after another: Karl won a great battle near Mohacs in August 1687, clearing the way to Transylvania and the lower Danube, while armies commanded by Elector Max II Emanuel of Bavaria (the 'Blue King') and Margrave Ludwig of Baden ('Turkish Louis'), pushing southward, took Belgrade in 1688 and moved further into Serbia. In 1690, however, the Turks mounted a determined counter-offensive to save Transylvania as a strategic bridgehead north of the lower Danube and forced Ludwig to shift most of his army to meet the new threat. The Ottomans quickly reoccupied all of their lost territories south of the Save, including Belgrade; but they were stopped at the Save-Danube line, which henceforth became the frontier and northernmost extent of Turkish dominion in that area. Ludwig, meanwhile, had decisively defeated an enemy army at Zalankemen in August 1691, a battle which permanently settled the future of Transylvania. By this time, however, a new war in the west had already forced the recall of many German troops to the defence of the Rhine frontier; even Margrave Ludwig left for the western front in late 1691 and the entire war in Hungary slowed down and assumed something of a see-saw character thereafter, especially after 'Turkish Louis' was replaced by the much less able Elector Friedrich August of Saxony. The latter's election as king of Poland in 1697, however, elevated the remarkably talented Prince Eugene of Savoy to the leadership of the imperial army and he promptly celebrated his new command by destroying the last effective Turkish army in Hungary at Zenta in September 1697.

Although the great war in western Europe to which the Habsburgs themselves had committed significant resources was at this very moment drawing to a close, Vienna chose not to exploit its favourable position against the Turks and instead, along with the other three members of the Holy League, began negotiations with the beleaguered Sultan Mustafa II. To a certain extent, that choice was made in deference to the wishes of Austria's maritime allies England and Holland, who were increasingly disturbed by the disruption of seaborne commerce in the Mediterranean which had resulted from the Turko-Venetian naval struggle there; but it was also conditioned by a realization that in the face of the somewhat surprising indifference of the Balkan peoples to their own 'liberation' from the Turks, further conquests in southeastern Europe would not be easy. Furthermore, the steadily increasing likelihood that the heirless Charles II of Spain might die very soon, producing a succession crisis of major proportions, convinced the emperor that peace was now as advisable in the southeast as it had been in the west in 1684 – a view with which the maritime powers heartily agreed. The final Peace of Karlowitz (January 1699) brought results for Austria which entirely justified the strenuous efforts and the sacrifices made over the previous fifteen years: all of Hungary except for the Banat of Temesvar fell under Habsburg rulership, as did Transylvania and Slavonia up to the Save-Danube frontier. Throughout the years of fighting, the political reduction and integration of the new lands proceeded step by step, unhindered by the objections of the Magyar estates whose power, to the extent it had not virtually disappeared already (as in Turkish Hungary), was broken by the imperial armies of conquest. After the fall of Budapest in 1686 and the victory at Mohacs the following year, Emperor Leopold had prepared a new constitution for Hungary, by which the previously elective monarchy was replaced by one that was henceforth hereditary in the male Habsburg line; it was immediately activated through the coronation of Leopold's elder son Joseph in December 1687. The Transylvanian diet, meanwhile, recognized the superiority of the king of Hungary, though the country retained its own prince; and even after he renounced his title in favour of the Habsburgs in 1697, the principality remained technically independent of Hungary, keeping its own diet and some vestiges of home rule in an arrangement which placed it under the *de facto* authority of a governor and council appointed by Vienna.

It is almost impossible to overstate the significance of the reconquest of Hungary for Europe in general and for the Habsburg dynasty in particular. The victories won against the Turks in this relatively brief period for the first time, and forever after, removed from the hearts and minds of European Christians the terrible fear of a Turkish penetration of central and even western Europe – a fear whose depth and immediacy since the fall of Constantinople in 1453 is difficult to appreciate or even to imagine today. The repulse of and successful offensives against the Ottoman Empire amounted almost to the lifting of a universal paranoia – the breakthrough of brilliant sunshine on a scene hitherto always darkened by clouds feared as the harbinger of an all-destructive storm just over the horizon. The Habsburgs, of course, had for a long time lain under the darkest of these clouds and had repeatedly suffered from the smaller storms which rippled along the front of the tempest behind them. This period of triumph, celebrated for many years in song, story, verse, the visual arts and perhaps above all in the surging power and majesty of the baroque architecture of the time, not only removed a challenge to the Habsburg inheritance more serious than any it had faced since the Bohemian rebellion in 1618, but also added vast new resources to the dynasty which were immensely important to its long-term survival in a Europe where perpetual peace and harmony among nations were not expected to prevail for as long into the future as even their most ardent advocates could see. Hungary and Transylvania, to be sure, were never as fully integrated into their inheritance as the Habsburgs would doubtlessly have liked and on occasion may have appeared to cause more trouble than they were worth; partly because of them, the Habsburg lands as a group never really coalesced into even a unified territorial state, much less the nation-state of a later era. But the organization and external unity now given to a massive area of central and southeastern Europe both strengthened Austria and stabilized an important flank of Europe as a whole; in doing so, it also, for many years, gave a better balance to the entire European states-system. No one, perhaps, in view of its modest and far-off gains, took much notice at the time that one of the signatories of the Peace of Karlowitz might have a rather interesting future in southeastern Europe and possibly elsewhere as well; Russia, after all, was too remote to worry about in the euphoria of the moment.

CHAPTER SEVENTEEN
Germany in the Maelstrom of War, 1685–1721

While the attention and energies of the emperor and most of the German princes were riveted on western Hungary and the difficult initial campaigns against the Turks which followed the lifting of the siege of Vienna, Louis XIV, not content with the added security he had gained on his eastern frontier with the Empire through the terms of the Regensburg Armistice of 1684, remained alert to new opportunities to strengthen his position in the east. One such opportunity arose in 1685, when the Elector Palatine Karl died without a direct male heir, causing his title and territories to devolve upon the Catholic duke of Jülich and Berg, Philipp Wilhelm of Neuburg. With no hope of gaining Philipp Wilhelm as a client (since his daughter was Emperor Leopold's third wife), Louis tried instead to acquire part of his territory by asserting a legal claim to certain of Karl's lands and other property on behalf of the newly expired elector's sister, duchess of Orléans and Louis's own sister-in-law. Anticipating a determination in his favour, Louis agreed to allow both the imperial diet and the pope to sort out and pronounce on the legalities of the issue.

One reason, no doubt, why Louis expected a favourable hearing in Rome, at least, is that in the same year, 1685, he had demonstrated the depth of his Catholic faith in what he believed to be a notable act of piety – the revocation of the Edict of Nantes. That edict, issued by his grandfather Henry IV in 1598, was the legal basis for the toleration enjoyed by the large minority of French Calvinists, or Huguenots; with its revocation and with the persecutions which both preceded and followed it, thousands of Huguenots were forced to flee the country. While Louis probably did not see this action in other than domestic terms, it turned out to be one of the worst blunders of French foreign policy during the whole of his long reign, instantly turning virtually every Protestant ruler and territory in Europe against him. An almost immediate result was the collapse of the 'northern system' of alliances so carefully constructed and nurtured in previous years. Friedrich Wilhelm of Brandenburg, outraged by Louis's action, headed the list of defectors from French clientage. Already correctly suspecting that the Regensburg Armistice had significantly lessened his usefulness to France and that there was no longer any chance of gaining Louis's support for an attack on Swedish Pomerania, the elector not only granted refuge to expelled Huguenots by the Edict of Potsdam in November 1685, but in quick succession also renewed his alliance with Holland and formed a new one with Charles XI of Sweden for the defence of Protestantism; between January and April 1686, furthermore, he reached agreements with the emperor whereby Leopold was promised 8000 Brandenburg troops in Hungary and the elector's support for Habsburg claims on the Spanish inheritance and help against any new French offensive actions against the Empire.[1]

Just as significant as an indicator of rising German suspicion and hostility towards France as Brandenburg's about-face was a new alliance, formed in July 1686, by the emperor, Bavaria, most of the estates of the Franconian Circle and some other southern and southwestern princes. Known as the League of Augsburg, it was soon joined by Sweden and Spain and later by other German princes as well. But while this new union was originally conceived simply as an extension or renewal of the Laxenburg Alliance of 1682 and was therefore entirely defensive and pacific in purpose, it was not interpreted as such by Louis XIV's advisers, who saw in it the beginnings of a sinister coalition which would strike at France as soon as the war in the southeast permitted a large-scale transfer of forces from Hungary to the west. In this context, the increasing success of imperial arms against the Turks was anything but comforting, suggesting that the moment of confrontation might not be too far off. A certain urgency now became detectable in the several policies adopted by the French. One of these – the hasty construction of new fortifications on the extreme eastern frontier – was directly threatening to the Germans, who were now also

---

1. Leopold, in return and against Brandenburg's abandonment of old claims to certain Silesian territories, abdicated to the elector the small district of Schwiebus, which lay between Brandenburg and Poland. Friedrich Wilhelm did not know that Austrian money had purchased the secret agreement of his own son and successor to return Schwiebus after the Great Elector's death.

subjected to vigorous French diplomatic pressure to convert the stipulations of the Regensburg Armistice into a definitive treaty, once and for all assuring Louis of his precious reunions. An attempt was also made to capture Elector Max II Emanuel of Bavaria for the French camp by unspecific but alluring hints that friendship with Louis might someday bring him the kingdom of Naples and Sicily from the Spanish inheritance and perhaps even elevation to the emperorship.

But if anything was needed to sour his potential clients in the Empire while deepening the hostility of his enemies, Louis's intervention in the succession to the electorate of Cologne provided it. In June 1688, Elector Maximilian Heinrich died and his coadjutor since January, Wilhelm Egon von Fürstenberg, presented himself for election. An almost slavish Francophile, Fürstenberg had earned the contempt and hatred of the Habsburgs during the Dutch War, but had been rewarded for his services to France by elevation to the see of Strassburg and, in 1686, to a cardinalate. He had dominated Maximilian Heinrich while he lived and had been chosen coadjutor because of that domination and by virtue of French influence. Even that election had been protested vigorously in many quarters, including not only Vienna and in Holland, but in various of the electoral capitals as well and Fürstenberg's coadjutorship was not confirmed by the pope. Elector Max II Emanuel of Bavaria was particularly disturbed by these events, because he saw Cologne (and its various dependencies) slipping out of the control of his Wittelsbach family for the first time since 1583; his own younger brother, Joseph Clement, earlier chosen as titular bishop of Freising and Regensburg, had already been advanced as an alternative candidate in Cologne. When, in July, the Cologne chapter failed to produce the required two-thirds vote in favour of Fürstenberg and he was rejected by the chapters of Liège, Hildesheim and Münster, he seized the government of Cologne, invited French troops into his territorial fortresses and disregarded a papal proclamation of Joseph Clement as the legitimate elector.

It is far from clear that the actions now undertaken by Louis XIV were intended to provoke the great war which followed; but it is clear that by ordering his troops to march on the fortress of Philippsburg just after learning of the fall of Belgrade to the imperial army, he meant to intimidate the Empire at a fleeting moment of advantage which would disappear as soon as German troops returned to the west from the Turkish wars he feared might now end at any time. Simultaneously, however, Louis issued a mildly conciliatory manifesto in which, among lesser items, he promised to abandon his claims on the Palatinate inheritance for a money payment – but only on the conditions that the terms of the Regensburg Armistice be made definitive and permanent and that his creature Fürstenberg be admitted to the Council of Electors as the rightful ruler of Cologne. Rebuffed in these demands by an Empire which found itself in rare unanimity against him, Louis then unleashed military forces which quickly overran the Rhenish electorates and even penetrated Swabia and Franconia, all the while extorting 'contributions' in the best traditions of the marauding hordes of the Thirty Years War, but with even greater discipline and efficiency. With unusual alacrity, his enemies gathered their forces against him. In the north, Brandenburg, Saxony, Hesse-Kassel and Hanover formed the so-called Magdeburg Concert in October 1688 and made immediate preparations to send troops to the middle and lower Rhine, while in the south the emperor, supported by the League of Augsburg, undertook to defend the upper Rhine. The imperial diet declared war on France in early 1689 and by May, the emperor, England and the United Provinces had combined to form a great alliance made possible by the assumption of the English crown by William of Orange as the result of the Glorious Revolution in 1688. By the time Savoy and Spain joined the alliance – within about a year – a massive coalition confronted France on all sides, on both land and sea.

In this suddenly and unexpectedly dangerous situation, Louis, following the advice of his ungentle war minister Louvois, ordered a strategic withdrawal of his forces all along the front, leaving only a handful of garrisoned strongholds in the north to slow the advance of the enemy. Under orders to destroy whatever might prove useful to the foe along their line of retreat, French troops executed this command with systematic and brutal punctilio, blowing up castles and fortresses, burning towns, murdering citizens and destroying crops, farm buildings and livestock. No German area through which the French passed was untouched, but the devastations of this 'scorched earth' policy were particularly severe along the middle Rhine and in the Palatinate, where such relatively major cities as Heidelberg, Worms, Speyer and Mannheim were virtually burned to the ground. This was a fundamentally stupid policy, since it proved to be both militarily insignificant and diplomatically disastrous: with one stroke, it utterly shattered whatever illusions might still have existed in the Empire that France was a friend of Germany, a defender of the imperial constitution or of the Westphalian settlement and a 'protector of German liberties', and introduced a degree of emotion and bitterness into the war (and the years beyond) reminiscent of the early, confessional phases of the Thirty Years War.

The campaigns of this Nine Years War (sometimes called the Palatinate War or the War of the League of Augsburg) can be summarized rather briefly. The allies, energized by their anger and determination, quickly eliminated the forward fortifications the French had left behind in their retreat, but thereafter were unable to push on into France itself. For the rest of the war, while some significant fighting took place in northeastern Spain and in northern Italy, the main action took place in the flat terrain of the Low Countries, where siege after dreary siege eventually produced the same stalemate that developed on the other fronts as well. On the sea, the French navy more than merely held its own against England and the Dutch, until the disastrous engagement at Cap la Hogue (Normandy) in 1692, where the loss of fifteen capital ships crippled Louis's Atlantic fleet for the remainder of the war. By even before that time, however, the solid front of France's adversaries in the Empire had begun to crack under the strain of various quarrels and special agendas. While Emperor Leopold, successfully exploiting the national outrage against France, had easily persuaded the electors to crown his son Joseph as Roman King in early 1690, some of his major German allies began to become restive thereafter. Max II Emanuel of Bavaria, for example, constantly wooed by the French, was kept in line only by Habsburg agreement to appoint him stadholder of the Spanish Netherlands, thus keeping alive his hopes for an eventual share of the Spanish inheritance. Other serious problems arose in the north: Johann Georg IV, elector of Saxony since 1691, began toying with the idea of an independent 'third force' alliance, an idea found tempting by Denmark, Sweden and a few of his fellow German princes, including Ernst August of Hanover. The latter, an astute and able ruler with ambitious plans for the whole Guelph (Brunswick) inheritance[2], had for some time already been pestering the emperor to elevate his territory to the rank of an electorate, but had received no encouragement from him. Now, with worrisome rumours of a new non-aligned association circulating in Vienna, Ernst August took the dramatic step of signing an actual alliance with France. This instantly produced the result he had doubtlessly hoped for: an agreement with Leopold in March 1692, whereby Hanover would (and in December did) become the ninth

2. See below, Chapter Eighteen.

electorate of the Empire; in return, Ernst August promised not only to send an auxiliary corps to Hungary, but also to support Habsburg claims to the Spanish inheritance and, on behalf of his house, forever to vote for the Habsburg candidate in imperial elections.

The creation of the new electorate, while politically prudent for Leopold, was constitutionally quite questionable on procedural grounds and led to a storm of protest from the electors of Trier, Cologne and the Palatinate[3], as well as from the older Guelph line of Brunswick-Wolfenbüttel, which in its jealousy of Ernst August undertook to form and lead a new princes' league to dispute the latter's new title. While this and other silly quarrels unquestionably had a negative effect on the Empire's conduct of the war against France, it proved not to be a totally disabling one: Saxony, at least, had returned to the allied fold and 'Turkish Louis' of Baden – supreme commander of German forces along the Rhine since 1693 – had successfully stopped French advances into southwestern Germany. Imminent danger also had the positive effect of temporarily revitalizing cooperation between the six militarily most exposed western Circles, which by shortly before the end of the war produced the so-called Frankfurt Association Recess, an agreement for a league which would henceforth maintain a common army of 60,000 in wartime and 40,000 even in peacetime. Reminiscent of the Rhenish Federation of Johann Philipp of Mainz (whose nephew Lothar Franz von Schönborn, also elector of Mainz, was an important presence here as well), this league was regarded by the emperor and some of the larger princes with much the same suspicion they had entertained towards the earlier one. None had any need to worry, as things turned out; the new association played no politically important role now or in the future, though its armed forces did valuable duty for many years, garrisoning imperial fortresses and acting as guardians of the Rhine frontier.

In view of the apparently unalterable military stalemate which developed rather early in the war on all fronts, Louis XIV had begun to entertain thoughts of ending the struggle, especially after the death of his always bellicose war minister Louvois in 1691. Sporadic negotiations with several of his opponents began in 1692; but not until 1696, when Savoy was detached from the allied cause, did the

3. All three were Catholic, of course; and part of Ernst August's case for the elevation of Hanover as a new and Protestant electorate was based on the accession of a Catholic line in the previously Protestant Palatinate in the person of Johann Wilhelm of Neuburg in 1685, leaving only two Protestants (Brandenburg and Saxony) in the Council of Electors.

solid front of the coalition crack open far enough to allow Louis's diplomats to destroy its unity by playing on the special interests of its individual members. Louis recognized William of Orange as King William III of England and promised to abandon his support of the exiled Stuart pretender, James II; at the same time, he restored to both Holland and Spain all lands taken by French forces since the Peace of Nymegen, gave trade concessions to the Dutch and consented to a private treaty between them and Spain whereby the former were permitted to garrison several major fortress-towns in the Spanish Netherlands to serve as a more emphatic barrier against future French aggression.

The emperor was not a party to these negotiations, by which all of his major allies ended their struggle with France at the Peace of Ryswick in 1697. Leopold and his German confederates had hoped that France would be forced to give up all her reunions, including the Alsatian towns and Strassburg; but the latter were conspicuously missing from the concessions Louis had made in the treaty and the emperor, now shorn of powerful friends, had insufficient leverage to alter these terms. He was therefore forced to join the peace, both for himself and the Empire, in October, leaving the 'jewel of Alsace' and the other towns and territories in French hands. Other terms provided some compensation, however: Lorraine, occupied by French troops for some thirty years, was now restored to its own duke and Louis agreed to give up all French bridgeheads on the right bank of the Rhine, to abandon support of his puppet Fürstenberg in Cologne (which now fell definitively to Joseph Clement of Bavaria) and to exit the dispute over the Palatinate succession in return for a money payment to his sister-in-law. While the Empire had therefore not suffered as much as it might have at Louis's hands, its territory was nevertheless diminished, in the end; and although the imperial negotiators tried hard and honestly to forestall the Alsatian losses, their failure led to accusations in some quarters that the Habsburgs, while conquering Hungary for themselves, had uncaringly abandoned German lands to a foreign despot.[4]

4. The anger this issue aroused was magnified among some Protestant princes by the so-called Ryswick Clause negotiated secretly between Leopold, Louis and the Elector Palatine Johann Wilhelm, whereby various changes favouring the Catholic church introduced by the French during their occupation were to be maintained after the peace. Viewed by Protestants as a gross breach of the religious provisions of the Peace of Westphalia, this clause (finally repudiated by Emperor Karl VI in 1734) was a source of acrimony for many years, especially in view of its expansion and ruthless enforcement by Johann Wilhelm in his own largely Protestant territories.

The rather unusual magnanimity Louis XIV had shown in the terms offered at Ryswick – terms which gained him surprisingly little in return for the staggering costs of the war he had fought – clearly originated in his awareness that the future of the Spanish Habsburg inheritance was about to become the major issue of European politics. The sickly Charles II of Spain, only a step from death's door for all thirty-five years of his pitiful reign, was clearly about to cross that threshold in the near future and Louis wanted his international agenda cleared of lesser distractions to allow him to deal single-mindedly with what, if he were lucky, might become the greatest prize of his entire foreign policy. Louis had never believed that he might acquire the entire Spanish empire, but he had long regarded a partition of the inheritance between himself and the Austrian Habsburgs as eminently possible and had negotiated a secret treaty to that effect with Leopold in 1668. Since the tumultuous events of subsequent years had rendered that agreement nugatory, Louis attempted to get a new partition treaty with Leopold after the Nine Years War. The emperor, however, now much stronger and more confident than in his time of troubles of thirty years before and convinced that one of his sons both should and could rule over all of Spain's possessions, resolutely refused all French partition proposals. Charles II's Spanish advisers similarly resisted the idea of partition, but believing that a war between France and Austria ending with exactly that result would occur if an undivided Spain were delivered into the hands of another Habsburg, sought and found an alternative in Joseph Ferdinand, son of Elector Max II Emanuel of Bavaria (and stadholder of the Spanish Netherlands) and a great-grandson of Philip IV of Spain. Holland and England, on the other hand, agreeing with France (chiefly for commercial reasons) that the Spanish territories should be partitioned, reached an understanding with Louis XIV in the autumn of 1698 whereby Spain's Italian possessions would be divided between Leopold (Milan) and France (Naples, Sicily and Sardinia), while Joseph Ferdinand as king of Spain would get everything else. Spain responded by declaring Joseph Ferdinand inheritor of the whole empire – but the young prince's sudden death in early 1699 terminated this possibility. France, England and Holland then reconvened to set new terms for their earlier bargain: Spain, together with its overseas empire and the Spanish Netherlands, would now fall to Karl, Leopold's younger son, and France would receive all the Italian territories (with the prospect of trading Milan to the duke of Lorraine in exchange for his duchy).

But since Leopold immediately rejected this solution, the final disposition of the Spanish inheritance remained as cloudy as before.

Ironically, in view of the liberties others were taking with his legacy, it was Charles II himself who finally clarified the situation, but who in doing so also started a chain of events which in the end produced results exactly the opposite of what he and his advisers intended. Still hoping desperately to prevent any sort of partition, Charles, virtually on his deathbed, made what was perhaps the only truly significant decision of his pain-wracked life: in late 1700, he declared Philip of Anjou, grandson of Louis XIV and a great-grandson of Philip IV, sole heir to the Spanish crown and all its possessions, trusting that the power of France would guarantee the integrity of the inheritance. Shortly thereafter, on 1 November 1700, he died. Louis XIV, though caught by surprise, quickly decided to repudiate the partition treaty he had negotiated with England and Holland earlier in the same year and threw his full support to Philip. Had Louis proceeded cautiously and tactfully in this support, it is possible – even probable – that the two maritime powers, in view of their profound abhorrence of a new war (and in spite of William III's personal fulminations), might have consented to this arrangement, especially had Louis given formal assurances that the crowns of France and Spain would never be united. But such was hardly Louis's style; far from making such a concession, he reaffirmed Philip's rights of succession to his own throne and by several other actions alarmed precisely those powerful merchant groups in London and Amsterdam on which his hopes for Philip's peaceful accession depended.

The first military actions, unsurprisingly, were taken by Leopold, who in spite of the recognition given to the new king, Philip V, in Madrid and the other power centres of the Spanish empire, dispatched an army commanded by Eugene of Savoy across the Alps to secure Spain's northern Italian possessions for the House of Austria. In September 1701, the emperor, Holland and England formed the so-called Grand Alliance by a treaty which accepted both the eventuality of war and the principle of partition: the emperor was promised Milan, Naples and Sicily, while the two maritime states were permitted to seize and retain whatever Spanish colonies they could. No mention was made of sovereignty over the Spanish Netherlands, or indeed over Spain itself, though the clear assumption was that the latter, at least, would pass to Leopold's younger son Karl. Though William III of England, an energetic advocate of the alliance and an implacable foe of Louis XIV, died in March of 1702, this brought no change to the structure or purposes of the alliance in either England or Holland, both of which declared war on France in early 1702. In one fashion or another, most of the German states joined the anti-French coalition. Elector Friedrich III of Brandenburg, seeking to elevate the duchy of Prussia to the dignity of a kingdom, had already sold his loyalties to Leopold in return for the emperor's permission to do so[5], while Elector Friedrich August of Saxony (King Augustus II of Poland since 1697), deeply involved in a serious regional war in the Baltic, chose an offensive and defensive agreement with the emperor over an alliance with France once the latter had proved unable to assist him diplomatically in his own war. The elector of Hanover, now linked to England by the parliamentary Act of Succession of 1701 which would elevate him to the English throne upon the death of Queen Anne (1702–14), also joined the allies, as did Leopold's brother-in-law, Johann Wilhelm of the Palatinate. The various princes of the western imperial Circles who in 1697 had formed (and subsequently renewed) the Frankfurt Association also abandoned an initially neutral position and in March of 1702 joined the Grand Alliance; and when the imperial diet declared war on France in the autumn of the same year, authorizing the call-up of 120,000 troops, virtually all of Germany was in arms against Louis XIV.

There were, of course, the usual interesting exceptions. Duke Anton Ulrich of Brunswick-Wolfenbüttel, still feeding his resentment against the new electoral dignity of the younger Hanoverian line, allied with France, but fled his country after an imperial execution carried out by Prussia, Hanover and Brunswick-Celle; his ally, the duke of Saxe-Gotha, quickly drew the consequences and thereafter meekly accepted allied subsidies for the use of his troops. The duchy of Holstein-Gottorp had also signed on with France in October 1701, but changed sides under a new ruler the following year. Far more significant were the defections of Bavaria and Cologne. Elector Max II Emanuel, still bitterly disappointed about the death and failed candidacy of his son for the Spanish throne and angry over the emperor's hostile reaction to that candidacy, had now set his hopes for new titles and territories on the suddenly increased importance of his position as stadholder of the Spanish Netherlands. Encouraged in his vague ambitions by the French, he had quickly recognized Philip V and had invited French troops to occupy the

---

5. See below, Chapter Nineteen. With his coronation in January 1701, Elector Friedrich III became King Friedrich I of Prussia.

fortresses of the Netherlands. For a time, the elector obscured his ultimate loyalties by haggling for advantage with both sides, but he clarified his position suddenly and dramatically in September 1702, by capturing the Imperial City of Ulm, strategically vital to control of the upper Danube valley. His brother, Joseph Clement of Cologne, meanwhile, nourished his own grievances against Austria for its earlier opposition to his election as prince-bishop of Liège and, encouraged by Max II Emanuel, had handed over his military strongholds in both Liège and Cologne to the French.

In the general continental war which now got underway in earnest, many German troops fought outside the Empire itself, subsidized by English and Dutch money. While these forces certainly contributed to the overall war effort against France, their removal from Germany also weakened the Imperial Army, which fought as best it could in southern Germany and along the upper Rhine under the command of the still able but now old and more cautious 'Turkish Louis', margrave of Baden. The Habsburgs put most of their own troops in Italy, the theatre of war of most direct interest to them. The first German campaigning, undertaken by a combined force of Prussians, Hanoverians and Dutch, was designed to push French forces out of Cologne and went very successfully. But a more ominous scenario soon developed in the south, where Max II Emanuel, after some initial failures, managed to establish such a strong position on a long stretch of the Danube that Louis XIV decided to send his main forces to Bavaria to mount a combined assault against Vienna itself. Eugene of Savoy, who had earlier left his campaigns in Italy to wage a successful political struggle to improve the conduct of policy in Vienna, succeeded against strong opposition in England and Holland in persuading the talented and perceptive commander of the allied army in the Netherlands, the English duke of Marlborough, to shift the bulk of his forces to southern Germany. On 13 August 1704, the combined armies of the two military geniuses met a slightly larger Franco-Bavarian force at Blenheim, near Höchstädt, in an unusually long and bloody battle from which they emerged victorious.

How important this battle was can be seen from its dramatic results, which amounted to nothing less than the liberation of all of Germany from the armies of France and its allies. The French not only retired beyond the Rhine, but were also cleared out of Trier and the Mosel valley by Marlborough as he made his way back to the Netherlands. Max II Emanuel fled Bavaria for Brussels and for the next ten years his German territories were governed by Austrian administrators who treated them as spoils of war, extorting payments and requisitions in cash and kind. Later, with the approval of the other electors, both Max II Emanuel and Joseph Clement were deprived of their electoral and princely rank and placed under the ban of the Empire. While outright annexation of all or most of Bavaria was discussed in Vienna, it was rejected for several reasons. First, the serious peasant revolts against Austrian authority which occurred in 1705, though harshly suppressed, suggested that an attempt to assimilate such a hostile territory, especially in wartime, would not be wise; second, such a large increase in the German base of Habsburg power might negatively affect the attitude of the maritime powers towards Austrian claims on the Spanish inheritance, an issue yet to be settled definitively; and third, the old mistrust of imperial intentions among the German princes, which had already been reactivated here and there by the Austrian occupation of Bavaria, could not be allowed to grow into an active hostility of such proportions as to affect the war against France. Vienna therefore chose not to absorb Bavaria, but to weaken it and in a way designed to gain support rather than to alienate it: the Habsburgs did take the small 'Inn Quarter' for themselves, but also handed off other bits and pieces to various of Bavaria's neighbouring ecclesiastical states, restored imperial immediacy to the city of Donauwörth and grandly returned the Upper Palatinate to the Elector Palatine. The fate of the rest of Bavaria was left to a later time.

Except for one final (and unsuccessful) French offensive into southwestern Germany in 1706–7, no more military action of any significance occurred in Germany for the rest of the war. The defection of the duke of Savoy from his alliance with France in 1703 was of no great help, but the addition of Portugal to the allied ranks permitted an Anglo-Portuguese expeditionary force to attack in Spain itself. Prince Eugene's forces also expelled the French from Italy in 1706, allowing Emperor Joseph (who had succeeded his father in 1705) to occupy Naples in 1707. In the Netherlands, the advantage gained by Marlborough by the battle of Ramillies in 1706 was made permanent by the great triumph at Oudenaarde in July 1708 – a victory in which Eugene, by leading a German army to assist Marlborough, returned the favour done for him by the great English commander in 1704. With the conquest of the fortress city of Lille at the end of 1708, the way for an invasion of France itself was cleared. In the spring of 1709, Louis XIV, worried about the increasingly disastrous course of the war, offered terms for peace, including abandoning his support for Philip V, which might easily have resulted in a return of Strassburg and all of the Alsatian reunions to the Empire, as well as other concessions favourable to Germany. It was understandable, in light of their long experience with Louis, that the allies wanted more far-reaching sacrifices from him, including a promise to help them expel Philip V from his Spanish possessions if he should refuse to give them up. But Louis rebuffed this humiliating demand and the war resumed. The allies continued to push forward; but a very costly victory at Malplaquet in late 1709 revealed that the French had lost neither the will nor the ability to resist and new negotiations were begun. This time, Louis promised to return all of Alsace to the Empire and even offered subsidies to help the allies drive his grandson from the Spanish throne; but since he again refused the demand that he participate militarily in that effort, the war continued.

As was frequently the case in this era, events having nothing to do with battlefield decisions were chiefly responsible for bringing this long and exhausting war to an end. In England, parliamentary elections of 1710 resulted in a victory for the Tories – a 'peace party', in effect – which made it possible for Queen Anne to indulge her intense dislike for the Whigs and specifically for the duke of Marlborough, who though neither Whig nor Tory had enjoyed the support of the previous Whig government. The unfortunate duke was recalled to England and disgraced; his successor in the Netherlands was told not to cooperate closely with his allies and secret negotiations were initiated between England and France. At this moment – April 1711 – Emperor Joseph died unexpectedly, without male issue, leaving his Habsburg crowns to his younger brother Karl. With the latter's election as emperor in October, the allies were confronted with the certainty that if current assumptions about the disposition of the Spanish crown became reality, the newly crowned Karl VI would rule a Habsburg empire as vast as that of his great ancestor Karl V in the mid-sixteenth century. England viewed this eventuality as no more palatable than a future union of the French and Spanish crowns and so arrived at the position that Philip V be allowed to keep the Spanish crown against a renunciation of any future claim on the French throne. This proposal became a chief basis for the numerous separate agreements which were finally combined into the great Peace of Utrecht signed by France, Holland, England, Savoy, Portugal and Prussia in April 1713.

By the terms of this treaty, Philip V, forever excluded from the French succession, was confirmed as king of Spain and kept his colonial empire; but he was forced to cede Milan, Naples and

Sardinia to Emperor Karl VI, Sicily to Duke Victor Amadeus of Savoy and Gibraltar and the island of Minorca, along with trade concessions in the New World, to England. The Dutch obtained a renewed entitlement to garrison barrier fortresses in the Spanish Netherlands[6], as well as control of the mouth of the Scheldt. From France, England gained territories in North America and the Caribbean, as well as recognition of the Hanoverian succession soon to occur. Prussia secured international recognition of its claims to the Orange succession lands (from the inheritance of William III) of Lingen and Mörs in extreme northwestern Germany and Neuchâtel (Neuenburg) on the Franco-Swiss border, as well as part of Gelderland, on the lower Rhine, from Spain. Louis XIV, meanwhile, ceded all conquests on the east bank of the Rhine, but retained such earlier gains as the Franche-Comté, the 'Flanders line' awarded him at Nymegen, and Alsace, including Strassburg. The Empire, more or less forgotten in the scramble of self-interested negotiations to which the emperor himself was not a party, had therefore not obtained the concessions which were of greatest importance to the exposed western Circles that had made so many sacrifices in so many wars against France.

Those sacrifices, sadly, were not quite yet at an end. Emperor Karl refused to accept the Peace of Utrecht, but only secondarily because of the Alsatian issue; dissatisfied with the disposition of the Spanish inheritance, Karl decided to continue the struggle. Fought entirely along the Rhine, this war did not go well and was finally and mercifully ended by a treaty between France and the emperor at Rastatt in March 1714. This agreement accepted most of the terms of Utrecht, except that Eugene of Savoy (who negotiated the treaty with the French Marshal Villars) was able to add the Spanish Netherlands to Karl's share of the Spanish inheritance. This change was directly related to the long-deferred decision on the future of Bavaria, which was also decided at Rastatt. Both Max II Emanuel and Joseph Clement had taken refuge in France and during the haggling over the Spanish issue the former had persuaded Philip V to cede the Spanish Netherlands to him. He believed he might purchase Austrian agreement to this by abdicating Bavaria to the Habsburgs and actually made this proposal to Vienna. The idea died a quick death – not because the Austrians rejected it, but because all the other powers did: England and Holland had no wish to see a French

---

6. These rights were also granted the Dutch by Karl VI after he received the Netherlands from Spain at the later Peace of Rastatt (1714).

puppet installed in the Netherlands and France opposed it on the grounds that the House of Austria, already strengthened by its recent gains in the southeast, would with the addition of Bavaria become an overmighty power in central Europe as well, with the ability to overawe and control the whole Empire in its own interest. Vienna's economic and territorial gain in acquiring the Spanish Netherlands, on the other hand, would be largely offset by their geopolitical exposure and removal from the nucleus of Austrian power in the southeast. In the end, then, the Netherlands were given to Karl VI and a disgruntled Max II Emanuel was reinstalled with all his former dignities in a completely restored Bavaria. It was a great easement to virtually all of the eternally suspicious princes and estates of the Empire that the emperor did not get his hands on Bavaria; that fact, indeed, had to serve as their chief consolation for the permanent loss of Alsace, whose fate was unchanged both at Rastatt and at the Empire's own nearly identical peace with France signed in Baden in September 1714.

While the great wars in the west were therefore ended for the foreseeable future, to the great joy and relief of the financially exhausted states which had fought them, another war continued to unsettle the Baltic world. This so-called Second (or Great) Northern War was not conducted on the scale of the wars of Louis XIV and intruded on the last of those wars only sporadically and in minor ways; but it had some results for Germany that were not unimportant. The origins of the war lay in the fact of an overextended Swedish empire which had been won at the expense of various of its Baltic neighbours, and which Sweden's own human and financial resources were becoming too weak to defend, especially in the face of the growing strength of some of her opponents, notably Russia. Large French subsidies had for many years hidden the steady depletion of the Swedish crown's own resources, a development which was most apparent in the alienation of crown lands and their revenues into the hands of the Swedish nobility. Charles XI (1660–97) launched a determined and largely successful effort to reverse this trend, but in doing so created deep resentments in Swedish society which in the province of Livonia boiled over into a serious but fruitless revolt. These internal troubles, placed in the context of what was already a long history of military confrontation between the Baltic powers, set the stage for a more or less coordinated attack on the Swedish empire in 1700 by Poland and Russia, already linked by an alliance of 1699, and Denmark.

For several years, the war these allies conducted against the young and energetic Charles XII (1697–1718) seemed to have been an almost nightmarish mistake. Within less than a year, Charles (styled 'the Lion of the North') forced Denmark to give up its attack on his allies, the dukes of Holstein-Gottorp, and to forsake its own alliances; repulsed a Polish offensive against Livonia and reduced the rebellious nobility there to obedience; and, most remarkably, destroyed a Russian army much larger than his own in Estonia, at Narva, in November 1700. For the next several years, Charles concentrated his military attention on Poland. His astonishing successes against the Saxon-Polish armies of the hapless Augustus II allowed him to proclaim a new king of Poland in 1704 – the Polish grandee Stanislas Leszczynski – and in September 1706, by occupying Saxony itself, to impose on Augustus the humiliating Peace of Altranstädt, by which the chastened Saxon elector renounced both the Polish crown and his Russian alliance. After remaining for a year in Saxony, Charles decided to shift his forces to the east to meet a growing threat from the Russian tsar, Peter I (1689–1725). In doing so, he gave great relief to Austria, which for a long time had worried about his intentions, but never more so than when he had crossed Silesian territory in the course of invading Saxony. Had Charles accepted offers of an alliance with Louis XIV which were desperately urged upon him by French diplomats, Austria and the entire allied war effort in the west could have been seriously threatened. But the maritime powers spent as much effort to strengthen Austro-Swedish relations as did the French to rupture them; furthermore, Charles, fancying himself a protector of Protestantism, already had a profound dislike for Louis and his anti-Huguenot policy and after he extracted promises from Emperor Joseph to respect rights granted to Silesian Protestants at Westphalia, the dangers of either a pro-French or an anti-Austrian policy disappeared.

While Charles was occupied in Poland (and Saxony), Tsar Peter, recovered from the disaster at Narva, had slowly been extending his annexations along the Baltic coast at Sweden's expense: after conquering Ingermanland in 1703, his forces soon overran Estonia, Livonia and Courland as well. With the intention of delivering a knock-out blow, Charles decided to carry a campaign into the Russian heartland, towards Moscow; but he could find no large Russian force to fight and as time went on and his supply lines lengthened, he decided to turn south to augment his army by the addition of Cossacks from the southern Ukraine. There, at Poltava, the Russians finally caught up with him and virtually eliminated his already diminished forces in July 1709. Charles fled to Turkey, where for several years he worked to establish an alliance between Sweden and the Ottomans which, from his standpoint, was designed to divert Russian energies southward, away from the Baltic where he hoped to revive Sweden's sagging fortunes. He failed in this project and did not return to his northern kingdom until 1714.

The disaster at Poltava led almost immediately to a renewed cooperation among Sweden's enemies in the Baltic: Denmark resumed its attacks on Holstein, Augustus vacated the Peace of Altranstädt and again mounted the Polish throne and Tsar Peter continued his march down the Baltic coast. King Friedrich I of Prussia momentarily considered joining the war against Sweden in 1709–10; but a rebuff by the tsar, together with Prince Eugene's personal plea not to remove troops from the western front, persuaded him to continue his policy of neutrality. As it became clear that Sweden's north German possessions were likely to come under attack, thus involving some members of the Empire in a war which would detract from the common effort against France, both the emperor and the maritime powers made strenuous efforts to secure neutrality for all of northern Germany. These initiatives collapsed in the summer of 1711, when an army of Russians, Saxons and Poles marched through Prussian territory to attack Stralsund and through Mecklenburg to besiege Wismar, while Denmark made preparations to invade Bremen. The return of Prussian troops from the west after the Peace of Utrecht now for the first time allowed Prussia, under its new King Friedrich Wilhelm I (1713–40), to abandon its neutrality by stages. By agreement with the tsar, the city of Stettin, conquered by the Russians, was delivered over to Prussian occupation for the duration; but after Charles XII made it clear that he would never concede the city to Prussia permanently, Friedrich Wilhelm entered into a treaty with Peter whereby Prussia recognized Russia's conquest of Estonia, Karelia and Ingermanland and Peter assented to eventual Prussian annexation of both Stettin and the southeastern part of Swedish Pomerania.

Not until the spring of 1715 did Prussia actively enter the war, however and then only in response to an attack on Prussian troops ordered by Charles XII, who had returned to the Baltic from Turkey in late 1714. Hanover, originally stirred to action by Denmark's designs on Bremen, had occupied Verden in 1712; three years later, by agreement with the Danes, Hanoverian troops also occupied Bremen and in the same year (1715) war was declared on Sweden. The accession of the elector of Hanover to the English throne as

George I in 1714 gave new harmony to the interests of the two countries, both of which would benefit from access to the Weser and Elbe rivers; and, since the presence of large Russian forces in Mecklenburg and Denmark was discomfiting to both (as indeed it was to all of Sweden's other enemies), a strong desire to bring the war to a beneficial end now existed. Quarrelling among the allies delayed the final treaties, which were negotiated individually with Sweden; even the death of the remarkably obstinate Charles XII in 1718 did not bring immediate results. But by the time the last treaty was signed between Sweden and Russia at Nystadt in September 1721, Sweden had already conceded Bremen and Verden to Hanover (1719), Stettin and nearly half of Western Pomerania to Prussia (1720) and had concluded a peace essentially without gains or losses with Poland and Denmark (also 1720). At Nystadt, Russia was granted Livonia, Estonia, Ingermanland and much of Karelia; and her intrusion into Europe, already soberly noted by the other northern powers, was before too much longer to become an important fact for much of the rest of Europe as well.

Though the princes and peoples of Germany had paid dearly for the right – especially in the last two of Louis XIV's wars and to a somewhat lesser extent in Hungary and in the Baltic area – they were clearly more in control of the destinies of the Empire by 1713–14 and 1721 than at any time since about 1630, when foreign powers had begun to take charge of the course of the Thirty Years War. The Ottoman Turks, a hitherto persistent menace on one flank of the Empire, had been pushed back and permanently contained far to the south and east in a determined effort which was all-German, not just Austrian in nature and which was recognized as such at the time. The overmighty France of Louis XIV, while not humbled or even really defeated by the great coalitions which had faced it, had none the less failed to establish the hegemony over Europe it had sought and in the attempt had so weakened itself diplomatically and financially that for over seventy-five years after Utrecht it was able to play at the game of power politics on a not much more than equal level with the other great powers of Europe – and especially England, whose rise to international power and influence after 1688 was nothing short of spectacular. It is probably not quite correct to say that a genuine 'balance of power' had been established on the continent even by 1713, especially if that term is understood to mean a distributive equilibrium of power recognized and accepted as such by statesmen and diplomats generally. But it is clear that Louis

XIV's policies themselves had created a new alertness and sensitivity on the part of nearly all other states towards future initiatives of a similar kind, from whatever source, which might be likely to disturb the general peace of Europe; such initiatives, being now more obvious, were also more risky and therefore less probable. The Empire itself, though slightly diminished in territory after the trials of the period, on the whole benefited from the greater international watchfulness which resulted from them, since its great human and material resources in the heart of Europe, though politically fragmented, were recognized as one of the important keys to the political balance and repose of the whole continent; any great disturbance in its own inferior balances, regardless of the source, would ripple outwards as shocks to the greater system of which it was a part.

The German imperial system itself was not an altogether stable one, of course, and contained princes and territories of greatly varying resources which could turn their energies for or against each other, the Empire and various foreign powers. They could also be steered in those directions, responding from necessity, ambition, or sheer greed to the threats and inducements of powers greater than themselves. But even this disturbing characteristic of the German system was considerably attenuated for some time after 1715 or so, assisted in particular by the relative decline of France and the ungraceful exit of Sweden from the ranks of the major states. With one of the major foreign disturbers of the German peace contained and the other forever restricted to a relatively unimportant regional role, the many lesser conflicts yet to come in the eighteenth century did not have to take on the character of almost superhuman efforts to defend Europe as a whole against the awful threat of universal hegemony. That was a boon to all nations, but to none more than to Germany.

CHAPTER EIGHTEEN

Austria and the Larger German States to 1740

Although the Habsburg government in Vienna had accepted the treaties of Utrecht and Rastatt reluctantly, Emperor Karl VI (1711–40) had much reason none the less to congratulate himself and his two predecessors on the outcome of the several decades of crisis, both internal and external, which had so seriously threatened the integrity and cohesion of his dominions. Whereas many well-informed Europeans on several occasions in the previous forty years had had good grounds to predict a diminution or even collapse of the Habsburg monarchy, it actually emerged from the pacification of the War of the Spanish Succession and its subsequent adjustments as the largest state in both population and territorial extent in all of western and central Europe. It had not only salvaged as much of the Spanish inheritance for itself as could reasonably be expected, including both the Spanish (now Austrian) Netherlands and the strategically important Italian territories, but had also solidified its control over nearly all of historic Hungary, virtually neutralizing its ancient Turkish enemy in the process. And while it is true that there was still some grumb‚ling in the Empire about the losses of imperial territory to France, and that Karl had been forced to accept the longest electoral capitulation ever demanded of a candidate for the imperial throne as the price of his election, his relations with the imperial estates, benefiting from the diminished tensions of a more peaceful Europe, were generally good.

But while no fair-minded observer could deny the tenacity and dedication with which the Habsburgs had defended their interests throughout the long period of wars in west and east, he might well be excused for questioning how much of their ultimate success on both fronts had really derived from their own efforts. There were, in fact, good grounds for raising such a query; taken together, they could suggest that Austria's real strength may actually have lain in its relative military weakness, which made it appear more threatened than threatening to its neighbours or to the balance of power in Europe. By attaching itself to separate coalitions aimed against its principal foes – France in the west, the Turks in the east – it was able to pursue its goals successfully with divided forces which, otherwise unaided, could not have achieved the same results. The Habsburgs' allies were often unhappy with the reduced Austrian commitment this division of effort occasioned in the theatres of war of greatest concern to them; indeed, the diversion of large military forces to Hungary from 1703–11 to quell a very serious Magyar rebellion was a source of much rancour between Vienna and its Anglo-Dutch partners, who became convinced that the Habsburgs were drawing out the revolt by their unreasonable terms for peace and who showed their displeasure in part by their insouciance towards Austrian interests in the west in the negotiations which led to Utrecht.[1]

Thus, while the overall strength of the coalitions masked Austria's own military weaknesses, it also obscured the deficiencies of government and finance which underlay that weakness. At the top and however different their personalities, the emperors who presided over the Austrian inheritance in the period 1658–1740 – Leopold I, Joseph I and Karl VI – were not extraordinary individuals in either positive or negative senses. Leopold (1658–1705) was scholarly, sedate, cautious and bland, while his older son Joseph (1705–11) was more spirited, active, impatient and a bit lusty; Karl seems to have been rather more like his father than his brother. All liked hunting, all were accomplished musicians and fairly generous patrons of the arts and all – but especially Leopold – carried more than a bit of that almost maddeningly serene faith in the protection afforded the dynasty by divine Providence that was so characteristic of its leaders. All took their duties seriously, by the standards of the time (though those standards did not necessarily include assiduous and meticulous attention to the details of daily government business), and while all could be called competent, the term 'talented' does not spring to mind. Leopold and Joseph were shrewd in their choice of good advisers and administrators – Karl less so – and that was important in a government which was still more personal than bureaucratic in nature; but while all were consistent in the beneficial practice of

---

1. See Charles W. Ingrao, *In Quest and Crisis: Emperor Joseph I and the Habsburg Monarchy* (West Lafayette, Indiana, 1979, pp. 1, 159–60.

rewarding loyalty and good service, they were unfortunately almost as consistent in their reluctance to punish (or even recognize) laziness or incompetence in their servants and tended to keep appointees in their posts far longer than their performance merited, often for life.

The structure of the government and administration was in many respects similar to that of many other German states of the time – which, given the enormously greater size and complexity of the Habsburg dominions and the much more active role Vienna was forced to play in German and European affairs, was a decided disadvantage. While states as small as Sweden and as powerful as France had already made great strides towards more rational and efficient administrative systems, Austria's remained frozen in the patterns of a barely emergent renaissance state. The emperor theoretically determined his policies with the assistance of a Privy Council; but its membership had already become so large by Leopold's reign that it was seldom convened except for ceremonial occasions. Leopold and his two successors actually met and advised with a much smaller body of these councillors which, with minor modifications in organization and a brief disappearance under Joseph, was dubbed the Privy Conference and which included the most important persons of the court, including the presidents of the three chief Austrian administrative bodies: the Court Chamber, the Austrian Court Chancellery and the Court War Council. The Court Chamber was supposed to be the central treasury and accounting office for the whole monarchy and was responsible for supervising the regalian revenues of the crown. In fact, it had almost no authority over Bohemia or Hungary and until Joseph's reign shared its responsibilities in Inner Austria and the Tyrol with independent offices in Graz and Innsbruck. The Chamber was vastly overstaffed and stupefyingly inefficient, overseeing a score of disbursement offices whose accounts were chaotic. Since the administration of both Bohemia and Hungary (and after 1714 of the Austrian Netherlands and the Italian territories as well) was conducted by entirely independent chancelleries with their own subordinate financial agencies and since a jealous non-cooperation characterized their relations with each other and with the Chamber, nothing even faintly resembling a comprehensive overview of the monarchy's finances was possible: income could not be predicted (or even properly accounted for), budgeting was a wild guessing game and the bloated and incompetent fiscal administration lost or consumed a high percentage of its own revenues.

The Austrian Chancellery had some of the same weaknesses as the

Chamber, since its responsibilities for judicial and political administration did not extend beyond the Austrian hereditary lands proper and even there, until 1709, had to be shared with the separate offices in Inner Austria and the Tyrol mentioned above. It was somewhat better organized for its business than the Chamber, however, especially after the appointment of a second Court Chancellor in 1705 permitted a slow evolution towards the separation of judicial from political matters. The latter included all the diplomatic correspondence of the monarchy (except, for some years, that with Moscow and Istanbul, which by an arguably defensible logic was conducted by the Court War Council), so that something resembling a foreign office existed well before 1700. Still, the persistence of independent chancelleries for different dominions reveals the basic character of this polyethnic dynastic state as a congeries of separate and distinct relationships between ruler and territories. This character was never questioned by Leopold and was accepted in a resigned fashion by Charles, under whom its territorial diversity increased still further; Joseph chafed against it and may have dreamed of a more strongly unified territorial state, but even he could do little about it during his short and war-ridden reign.

It is not surprising, on the other hand, that just as the Austrian Chancellery had developed at least some of the characteristics of a functional ministry for all the foreign affairs of the single Habsburg ruler, so the War Council (and its steadily more important associated agency, the General War Commissariat) supervised military strategy and supply for the entire monarchy from a very early date. Diplomacy and war, after all, were the twin instruments of policy by which the fortunes of the House of Austria would wax or wane in the face of continuous challenges from the chancelleries and armies of the rest of Europe; furthermore, the functions of recruitment, provisioning and strategic planning were universally accepted as the unique responsibility of the crown in all territories. The War Council was staffed by military professionals and its president – Raimondo Montecuccoli and Prince Eugene were the most illustrious – was a key minister. Here, as elsewhere in the government, there were some problems of divided or overlapping competence and military policy could not be discussed without continual reference to the work of other administrative bodies and to the revenues which flowed capriciously into Vienna from various sources. Nevertheless, the War Council was in many respects the most efficient and centralized agency of the government.

As previously suggested, however, no single problem was more crucial, or chronic, than government finance. There were many reasons for the permanently desperate shortage of money, but none was more important than war itself, because to the high direct costs of military campaigning must be added various indirect costs whose amounts can scarcely be guessed at. For example, even fiscal and administrative reform designed only to decrease waste and increase the efficiency of current collections, difficult under the best of peacetime conditions because of local privilege and vested bureaucratic interests, became almost unthinkable in wartime; Joseph did a little of it by cutting personnel and initiating better bookkeeping practices, but the results were hardly dramatic. Similarly, all planning to increase revenues through general economic growth by government encouragement of agriculture, trade and manufactures was not only nullified by the higher priorities of war, but was also subverted by the capital sums removed from the economy by heavy taxation or, as in Hungary, by direct war damage. Even in peacetime, the curious (but for the time not unusual) belief that it was unnecessary for the court and government to economize – to 'save up for a rainy day' – diverted considerable monies to relatively unproductive uses, including the undiminished importation of luxury commodities unavailable from domestic sources. Leopold, to be sure, commissioned a survey of the entire economy with the approach of peace in 1698, but the results were spotty and in any case told the government no more than it already knew from the work of the early Austrian Cameralists about the baleful effects of the confusion of weights, measures and coinages, the heavy burdens of internal and external tolls and tariffs, bad overland and riverine transport and so on. Renewed war soon removed any chance of acting on such information in any case.

Emperor Joseph showed some genuine interest in various initiatives to encourage the mercantile economy, but simply could not afford the subsidies, tax remissions and other means necessary to implement them. He did experiment on a small scale with agricultural reform, by dividing some crown lands among peasants to farm not as serfs but as tenants, with fixed rents and no labour services; but in spite of its encouraging results, the experiment did not survive his reign. Certainly the most important improvement in agricultural production during the whole period came as the result of peace, primarily in Hungary, when a great wave of settlers – mostly Germans – poured into the country after 1711–12 to reoccupy the vast farmlands laid waste and depopulated during the long Rakoczi rebellion. Some attempts to standardize weights, measures and

275

currencies got underway after 1714, accompanied by the establishment of regional commissions here and there to encourage commerce. But the major economic initiative of Karl VI's reign – the Ostend Company and its associated projects[2] – fell victim, by stages, to the hostility of the maritime states and his own obsession with the Pragmatic Sanction (about which more will be said below); thereafter, Charles lost interest in economic reform and innovation for the rest of his reign.

In the absence of any fundamental changes in either the fiscal administration or in the economy which underpinned it, the crown was forced to rely on its traditional sources of income, as well as on a series of imaginative alternatives. To the former category belonged the revenues from the crown lands, tolls and tariffs, state monopolies and indirect taxes, as well as the 'contributions' of the estates. These grants involved interminable annual negotiations for sums almost always smaller than the government requested and from which the estates' own variable (but always considerable) expenses for assessment and collection, and other things, were subsequently deducted; in Hungary, furthermore, the principle of obligatory contribution by the estates was not even accepted until 1715. Among the alternative sources of income may be reckoned not only the large subsidies paid by England and the Dutch for the conduct of operations against France, but also the money contributed by Rome for the crusade against the Turks in Hungary (much of which Innocent XI wisely sent directly to commanders in the field, circumventing the notorious inefficiencies of the Court Chamber in Vienna). Making war pay for itself is always a good idea and the Habsburgs correspondingly shifted some of the costs of their campaigning onto the local population, including Hungarians as their country was slowly cleared of the Turks, the inhabitants of the Spanish Netherlands during the late stages of the War of the Spanish Succession and the people of Bavaria for the period of its occupation during the same war. The confiscation and sale of rebel estates in Hungary and Croatia, especially in Leopold's reign, followed essentially the same principle; but the sale of some crown lands

2. It was originally planned that the trade of this Netherlands company with the East and West Indies would be shared with the Adriatic coastal cities of Trieste and Fiume, which were declared free ports in 1719 in an attempt to compete with Venice. These ports were then linked to the Austrian plain – Vienna and Wiener-Neustadt – by an improved road over the Semmering Pass and to Hungary by a new road (the *Via Carolina* or *Karlsstraße*) built somewhat later. Even after the abandonment of the Ostend project, these overland routes brought tangible benefits.

became necessary as well. Jews were a favourite target for the enhancement of the fisc: in 1670, Leopold sold the Jewish quarter of Vienna, including the right to expel Jews, to the city council for 100,000 guilders and forced loans were later extracted from Jews living in the Habsburgs' own lands as well as in the Imperial Cities. On the other hand, the same 'benevolences' were on occasion demanded from wealthy Austrian nobles as well, while at one point every officer at court was forced to loan the equivalent of two years' salary to the treasury; Joseph even squeezed a substantial 'free gift' out of the notoriously tight-fisted Austrian clergy. The prerogatives of the German imperial crown were not without some utility in fund-raising: Ernst August of Hanover was happy to pay Leopold 750,000 guilders for his new electoral title in 1692, while Joseph, after meticulous research into the 'reserved rights' of the emperor, presented a startled group of Imperial Counts, Knights and Free Cities with an array of feudal dues and fees all had supposed long since extinguished by inveterate neglect.

The court experienced near panic in 1703, when its credit was all but destroyed by the sudden death of the *Hofjude* Samuel Oppenheimer, an expert and honest financier and chief military contractor for the General War Commissariat, whose high personal reputation almost alone had ensured a steady supply of new money to his bank. The disappearance of new depositors after his demise forced the government to establish its own Giro Bank in 1704; but its abysmal failure to attract deposits – chiefly because the Court Chamber could not put enough seed money into it – led in 1705 to an agreement with the Vienna City Council to set up a new City Bank which merged with and assumed the debts of the failing Giro Bank. Perceived by the public as more trustworthy than its predecessor, this institution by 1711 had assumed the significant total of some twenty-four million guilders of state debt – the approximate average of the Court Chamber's annual expenditures in this period.[3] In 1714, an additional state bank (*Bancalität*) was founded and charged to manage all state debts and to act as a central treasury. A new 'Privy Finance Conference' supervised both banks; but this reform had merely juxtaposed the *Bancalität* and a newly re-constituted Court Chamber as separate, independent and competing agencies, whose mutual and continual abrasion nullified most of the benefits expected from the reorganization.[4]

3. Ingrao, *In Quest and Crisis*, pp. 26–7.
4. Jeserich *et al.*, *Deutsche Verwaltungsgeschichte*, I, 500.

None of the subsequent (and minor) reforms of Karl VI's reign changed the essentially dreary picture of Habsburg finances, which were again put under pressure by Karl's foreign policy, if not as seriously so as under his predecessors. But no financial exigency was permitted to diminish the grace and splendour of the court itself or of the great city of Vienna which was home to it. The unshakeable sense of mission to all of Christian Europe which explains so much of the self-perception and self-confidence of the Habsburg dynasty was grandly displayed in a court and city where the most heterogeneous cultures from all corners of Europe came together in dazzling magnificence.[5] The court itself was the scene of elaborate fêtes and operas (one of them composed by Karl himself) arranged in the Italianate high baroque style by such well-known poets as Zeno and Metastasio, which were performed in impressive new theatres like the one built at the Carinthian Gate. The seat of the court, the famous Hofburg, was enlarged and remodelled, while throughout Vienna the many great aristocrats who chose to spend most of their time (and money) in the capital commissioned the construction of elegant urban palaces from the most renowned baroque architects, who set them down in the midst of a city made resplendent by many new ecclesiastical structures and by the fountains, statues and architectural decorations created by a small army of artists and craftsmen imported from many parts of Europe.

In all of this, however, the intense attention of the court and of the high society which filled and surrounded it to the Catholic faith and its devotional forms never faltered. With the partial exception of Joseph, who had a more 'enlightened' and secular tutelage than his father or younger brother (and who had a rather strong dislike for the Jesuits), the emperors were devout in belief and observance and imposed an orthodox regimen on their surroundings – testimony to the still indissoluble tie between dynasty, state and church. The reverse side of this coin, of course, was a continued loathing of Protestantism. Even in his moments of greatest need, Leopold had never been comfortable with his Protestant alliances and he showed

---

5. The mysterious combination of the vowels A E I O U, first used as part of his emblem by Emperor Friedrich III (d. 1493), was still popularly cited in reference to the 'universal' mission of the House of Austria. Friedrich himself had interpreted the vowels to mean, in German, 'Alles Erdreich ist Österreich untertan' (All the world is subject to Austria) or, in Latin, 'Austriae est imperare orbi universo' (Austria is to rule the whole world); a no less confident, though more bemusing later Latin interpretation ran 'Austria erit in orbe ultima' (Austria shall be the last on earth). Hans Kohn, *Prelude to Nation-States: the French and German Experience, 1789–1815* (Princeton, N.J., 1967), p. 159.

little of his characteristic indecisiveness in his dealings with the Hungarian Protestants, even when it would have served him politically to be more cautious and moderate. Karl, for his part, not only persisted in a vigorous prosecution of Protestants in Bohemia, but also lent his approval (and some troops) to the expulsion of Protestants from Salzburg in 1722–3 and decreed similar expulsions from his own provinces of Carinthia, Styria and Upper Austria in 1723–5.[6] It need hardly be remarked, in view of the strong hold of the church on so much of the cultural and intellectual life of the country and aside from the many achievements in music, architecture and the visual arts encouraged by the ecclesiastical establishment, that obscurantism was more typical of the Austrian lands than enlightenment; the spirit of rationalism was not yet at home in a country whose own rulers were inclined to ascribe its past and future fortunes as much to the intervention of divine Providence as to their own efforts.

In political matters, the earliest success of Karl's reign was the final settlement of the long Rakoczi rebellion in Hungary (1703–11) by a peace which restored the outward obedience of the Magyars at the expense of the confirmation of many rights and privileges in government, administration and finance which together assured Hungary a special position within the Habsburg dominions that endured as long as the monarchy itself. The Hungarians did for the first time agree to the establishment of a permanent standing army under the direct command of the king – a significant concession, but one whose impact was limited by the estates' continued exemption from direct taxation and by their right to determine annually how much money they would give to support the army. An opportunity to seize the last part of historic Hungary not yet under Habsburg rule – the Banat of Temesvar – arose in 1716, when Vienna joined a war already in progress between Venice and the Ottoman Empire; by the victorious Peace of Passarowitz of 1718, Vienna received Temesvar and some other small territories as well. This peace represented the high water mark of Habsburg conquests of Ottoman territory; some of them were to be lost again before Karl's death.

6. The unyielding stubbornness of Habsburg rulers until Joseph II on the question of religious toleration in their own territories was certainly due to more than just personal fanaticism; in their inheritance, more than in any other perhaps, religious differences were still linked to political disobedience and to the very real dangers of separatism that could arise from it. Hungary is the best example for this period, but the Bohemian rebellion in 1618 and the perils it engendered for many years thereafter were far more than just curiosities of history in the Habsburg dynastic memory.

Two other issues, in particular, dominated the foreign policy of Karl's reign. The first arose from Spain's dissatisfaction with the disposition of her former Italian territories after the War of the Spanish Succession. Egged on by Elizabeth Farnese, wife of Philip V, who wanted some of these lands for her son Charles ('Baby Carlos'), Philip and his chief minister Alberoni adopted an aggressive policy in the Mediterranean which an alliance between England, France and Holland sought to counter but also to appease because of their maritime traffic in the area. Karl, who joined this alliance in 1718, was persuaded to make some adjustments in Italy, recognizing the succession of the Spanish Infante to Tuscany, Parma and Piacenza, and trading Sardinia to Savoy in exchange for Sicily. Alberoni's fall from power led to an agreement between Spain and Austria on this basis in 1720. The second issue revolved around the perennially vexing issue of the succession to the Habsburg inheritance. In 1713, Karl had issued a unilateral declaration stipulating that upon his death all his territories should pass as an undivided whole to any sons, successively by age and, in the absence of any male heir, to his daughters, also by primogeniture.[7] Since a female succession was unprecedented, Karl made it a chief priority of his reign to obtain the formal agreement of the diets and estates of his own lands to it and thereafter the assent of as many of the states and sovereignties of Europe as possible – the goal, of course, being to assure the peaceful transmission of his various dynastic titles and to avoid the always dangerous circumstances surrounding disputed successions. The urgency of Karl's efforts was intensified by the death of his only son, an infant, in 1716 and the birth of two surviving daughters, Maria Theresia and Marianne, in 1717 and 1718, respectively.

Except for Hungary, where protracted negotiations were required before the diet gave its assent in 1722–3, the confirmation process in his own lands went smoothly and in 1724 Karl ceremoniously reenacted and published his declaration of 1713, together with the ratifications delivered by his own dominions. This document, known as the 'Pragmatic Sanction', dominated and conditioned Karl's relations with the rest of Europe very nearly until his death in 1740. After 1720, Austria's relations with England, Holland, France and Spain were chilly because of hostility towards the new Ostend

---

7. In so doing, Karl overturned an earlier family pact of 1703 which provided that if both Joseph and Karl died without male heirs, Joseph's daughters (who were still living in 1713) would inherit before any Karl might have.

Company; but differences between France and Spain allowed Vienna in 1725 to reach an agreement with Madrid whereby Karl obtained both recognition of the Pragmatic Sanction and various privileges for the company in Spanish ports. Offended, the other three maritime powers concluded a new alliance, also in 1725, which now included Prussia as well. Karl countered this in the following year with a Russian alliance which brought another important guarantee for the Pragmatic Sanction, but he also assuaged the maritime powers with a promise to halt operations of the Ostend Company for seven years. In this improved atmosphere, Prince Eugene also coaxed the king of Prussia into giving his agreement to the female succession. Spain, disgusted with Karl and fearful of isolation, returned to its old alliance with England, France and Holland, but Madrid's truculence on various Mediterranean issues persuaded the English to work at pacification through Vienna instead; in March 1731, in return for a guarantee of the Pragmatic Sanction from both England and Holland, Karl agreed to abandon the Ostend project altogether and to allow Spain actually to occupy Parma and Piacenza in Italy. By 1732, the imperial diet had also ratified the Pragmatic Sanction, with the notable dissent of Bavaria, Saxony and the Palatinate.

In 1733, the death of King Augustus II of Poland occasioned a new election, with all the usual opportunities for foreign interference and influence-peddling. The French candidate, a Polish nobleman named Stanislas Leszczynski, was elected, but was immediately challenged by the Austro-Russian nominee, Elector Friedrich August II of Saxony, son of the newly deceased king. The ensuing war, which saw only minor military action (mostly in Italy), pitted Austria and Russia against France, allied with Spain and Savoy in Italy, and with Bavaria, the Palatinate and Cologne in Germany. Since nobody was interested in a major war, a preliminary settlement was arranged at Vienna as early as October 1735, which was modified only slightly in the final peace of November 1738. The Polish crown was awarded to Friedrich August, who mounted the throne as King Augustus III; his rival Leszczynski was transferred to the duchy of Lorraine, which was to revert to France upon his death. The previous duke of Lorraine, Franz Stephan, who in 1736 had married Karl VI's daughter Maria Theresia, was made duke of Tuscany as part of a larger agreement that finally settled the more than three decades of unrest in the Mediterranean and by which Parma and Piacenza reverted to the Habsburgs, Naples and Sicily went to Spain and Savoy received a small strip of contiguous territory in northern Italy. For Karl VI himself, this War of the Polish Succession was a success perhaps less for the victory of his candidate in Poland than for the fact that it harvested a host of guarantors for the Pragmatic Sanction, including Poland, Saxony and all signatories of the treaty which ended it. Even the loss to the Turks in 1739 of all territories gained in the Peace of Passarowitz, with the important exception of Temesvar, through a disastrous war entered chiefly to honour his obligations to his Russian alliance of 1726 could not erase the satisfaction with which Karl contemplated the certainty of the undisputed succession of Maria Theresia to his inheritance. Considering the demoralization of his army, his empty treasury and the still haphazard character of his government (not to mention the hardly novel practice of governments to disavow their own most solemn promises and covenants when it was in their interest to do so), Karl was probably more confident than he had any right to be when he passed from the scene on 29 October 1740, leaving the destiny of his lands and his dynasty to his twenty-three-year-old daughter and to a scrap of paper called the Pragmatic Sanction.

If the mood of Karl VI at the conclusion of the War of the Spanish Succession was one of mild disappointment that he had not gained more from the war, that of Elector Max II Emanuel of Bavaria (1679–1726) had to be one of sheer relief that he had not lost everything in it. In supporting France and Spain, he had put his chips on the wrong number; after two successful years, the disastrous defeat at Blenheim in 1704 forced him to retreat beyond the Rhine and from there to the Spanish Netherlands, abandoning his electorate to his wife, who turned it over to Austrian occupation for the remainder of the war. He was lucky to get it back in 1714. Max Emanuel was no inveterate Francophile, nor was he the first of his family to sell his foreign policy to Louis XIV: his father Ferdinand Maria (1651–79), needing money, fearful of a renewal of war along the Rhine and in the Netherlands and disgruntled by unkept Habsburg promises from the time of Leopold's election in 1658, had begun to tilt out of the Habsburg orbit well before he accepted a formal subsidy treaty with Louis in which he promised to observe a policy of armed neutrality – a promise he kept throughout the Dutch War in spite of enticements and threats to do otherwise. But Ferdinand Maria was a far more cautious ruler than his son and successor and was much more modest in both self-image and lifestyle. Max Emanuel, modelling his personality and comportment on the character and achievements of his grandfather Maximilian and on the grand style of Louis XIV, pictured himself as the baroque prince *par excellence*, dashing and brave as a soldier, an easy-living and generous patron and philanthropist and a mover and shaker in high politics.

For the first twenty years of his reign, Max Emanuel believed his ambitions best served by friendship with Vienna: he broke with his father's pro-French policy, made a defensive alliance with the emperor and soon married Maria Antonia, Leopold I's only daughter by his marriage with Margaret of Spain – from which a possible expectancy to the Spanish Netherlands arose. In the 1680s, he played a spectacular role in the Turkish wars, beginning at the siege of Vienna, during which he won admiring appellation as the 'Blue King'. But he gained nothing tangible from those wars and while he supported Leopold in the Nine Years War, their relationship slowly soured. In 1691, the sickly Charles II of Spain appointed him stadholder of the Spanish Netherlands and named his son Joseph Ferdinand to succeed him on the Spanish throne; and while Max Emanuel's highest hopes were dashed by the early death of Joseph Ferdinand, he declared against Austria in the Spanish succession controversy in order to salvage his claim to the Spanish Netherlands. This was the origin of the disasters which befell him until 1714, after which he wisely chose prudence over ambition in foreign policy for the rest of his reign. His successor, Karl Albrecht (1726–45), maintained a largely secret pro-French orientation which brought minor diplomatic clashes with Austria on several occasions, but no major confrontation until after the succession of Maria Theresia in 1740.

The vicissitudes of Bavarian foreign policy, sharp though they were, did not much affect the nature of the electorate's government. Ferdinand Maria continued the strongly personal and absolutist methods successfully pursued by the great Maximilian, ruling through a Privy Council of his own appointees, to which all other central agencies for military, financial and religious affairs were subordinated as its executive organs. The so-called *Rentmeister* – the local officials responsible for administering the crown's domains and regalian revenues – were also empowered to act in matters of local police and to supervise trade, industry, agriculture, schools and the church. The Privy Council was essentially servile under Maximilian's commanding leadership, but gained increased power and influence under his somewhat less capable successors; in particular, the indecisiveness of Ferdinand Maria and the minority of Max II Emanuel, as well as the latter's long absences from the country later, provided the council with both the opportunity and the necessity to develop the kind of steady leadership which was especially evident during the tenure of the powerful vice-chancellor Kaspar von Schmid. In Bavaria, as elsewhere, the council's growth in membership tended to favour the conduct of important business by a smaller group which Karl Albrecht in 1726 formally designated as the Privy Conference, initially with only four members; towards the end of his reign, this body took on the more modern shape of a council of heads of executive departments – a cabinet, virtually.

The elector's relationship with his estates was almost an absolute ruler's dream. For many years, the prince had not dealt with the diet at all, but only with a small committee deputed from it, which was composed of eight nobles, four prelates, four burghers and an additional group of four 'accountants'; known as the *Landschaftsverordnung*, this group proved far more tractable than the full diet. After repeated petitions from the committee, however, Ferdinand Maria agreed to convoke a plenary diet in 1669. When it met, for the first time in fifty-seven years and for the last time in the old regime, only about two-thirds of those eligible to attend appeared at all; the assembly meekly voted the elector some 372,000 guilders a year for nine years and agreed to assume most electoral debts. After empowering the *Landschaftsverordnung* to grant another small sum if necessary and to request another diet if the amount proved insufficient, the diet promptly disbanded. Some days later, the elector and the committee agreed that they needed no diet to decide what was financially necessary for the future and Ferdinand Maria authorized the group to choose its own members as vacancies occurred. In spite of its often self-effacing posture towards the prince, however, the committee did exercise real influence on the government and during periods of Austrian occupation in 1704–14 and again in 1742–5 it stoutly represented the country 'beyond the court'. The permanent financial crisis of the electorate bolstered the committee's influence, as shown in 1721, when it once again gave a general guarantee of the elector's indebtedness and in 1729 when it assumed responsibility for redemption of a large specific debt. The elector, to be sure, generally held the trump cards over the committee and more than once brought it to heel by threatening to convene a full diet, whose authority would displace that of the committee; but relations between the two were generally cordial and mutually respectful: the committee continued to meet each year, grant the taxes requested by the government, raise grievances and supervise the financial apparatus of the estates.

The Bavarian economy, while overwhelmingly agrarian, was not an unhealthy one and could support a reasonably active government as long as the latter was prudent in managing its resources and was careful to see that its expenditures did not exceed the level of overall economic growth. Such growth was slow – partly because over half the arable land of the electorate was in the hands of tax-exempt churches and convents and partly because government attempts to encourage the economy were half-hearted and mostly unsuccessful. The chief financial agency, the Court Chamber, established one investigative commission after another and repeatedly urged both tax reform and the limitation of ecclesiastical land ownership, but with no significant results. The fiscal administration, furthermore, was chaotic: there were essentially three parallel fiscal systems, one directed by the Court Chamber, another controlled by the estates and a third (from 1671–1751) in the form of a tax farm responsible for collecting most of the indirect taxes; all were separate and all were riddled with malfeasance and corruption. The widespread sale of public offices also did nothing to increase the efficiency of financial or other administrative agencies.

Ferdinand Maria's policies bear little responsibility for the financial disasters which befell his country after 1700; he, in fact, was able to raise significant new revenues from taxes, state monopolies and French subsidies. There was enough money to create a new standing army of a few thousand men to replace the larger one disbanded, at the estates' insistence, at the end of the Thirty Years War, and to introduce baroque art, music and architecture to Munich, whence it quickly spread to other parts of the country. Encouraged by his vivacious wife Henrietta Adelheid of Savoy, Ferdinand Maria was a generous (but not profligate) patron, during whose reign several prominent building projects were undertaken, including a new Italian opera house, the Theatine Church of St. Cajetan and the beginnings of the Nymphenburg palace. Ferdinand Maria's prudent policies were unfortunately not observed by his two successors, whose military and political adventurism nearly ruined the country by straining its fiscal resources to the breaking point. Only with the accession of Elector Max III Joseph in 1745 did a chastened and very nearly bankrupt Bavarian government once again begin to live within its means.

In considerable contrast to Bavaria, where the great war and its aftermath contributed to the establishment of a comfortably secure absolutism, the influence of the estates of Saxony in almost all governmental affairs increased in the few decades following the Peace of Westphalia, chiefly for monetary reasons. The expenses of the elector's court and bureaucracy mounted steadily and the lively interest of Johann Georg II (1656–80) in arts and literature added still more costs. The diet, dominated by the landowning nobility, was not unfriendly to the purposes for which its prince constantly requested money and its relationship with him was more often cordial than not; but the brunt of the responsibility for keeping it that way rested more with him, since the diet (which as early as 1661 had been granted the right of assembly on its own initiative) remained firm in its demands for consultation and accountability. The general tax burden of the electorate increased considerably throughout the seventeenth century, especially for commoners, but its negative impact was partly offset by the vigorous growth of the commercial and industrial economy from the 1650s onward; Saxon products, indeed, were a significant part of Europe's overall trade and were prized for quality from Russia to England and Portugal and from Venice to Stockholm.

Still, and in spite of an administrative apparatus relatively more efficient than in many other places, money remained a problem and one which got worse with time. There were several causes for this. The first was the establishment of a permanent standing army in 1682, replacing the old militia system, or *Defensionswerk*; this was the work of Johann Georg III (1680–91), who personally led his new army to help relieve the siege of Vienna in 1683 and who died as a courageous and capable commander in the war against France in 1691. Another cause was the assumption of the Polish crown in 1697 by Friedrich August I (1694–1733), which brought real international significance to Saxony and its ruler and introduced a sort of golden age of arts and architecture into a country which was already the cultural leader of Germany. The new responsibilities of the king-elector prompted a major reorganization of the central government in 1704–06, resulting in a considerably improved conduct of business through the establishment of a Privy Cabinet with functionally differentiated departments for internal affairs, foreign policy and military matters. But that all of this would be monumentally costly became apparent in the Second Northern War, when the early misfortunes of the Polish king were visited upon Saxony in the form of a Swedish occupation of the country in 1706 that may have cost as much as twenty-three million talers. It is certainly no accident that an urban excise tax on a wide range of goods, services and property, already in effect in more than a hundred cities and towns in 1703, was imposed on all the rest in 1707.[8] A third reason for Saxony's fiscal problems, especially from the 1690s on, was an almost complete absence of planning for future economic development. The government never seemed to understand the necessary relationship between economic growth and safe increases in fiscal yields, or to figure out how or when or where government intervention might make a positive difference. In the face of steadily increasing fiscal demands, therefore, Saxony moved into the middle decades of the eighteenth century economically more fragile than the beauty of its countryside, the elegance of its urban culture and the industriousness of its inhabitants might otherwise have suggested.

A brief glance at a few other relatively important territories will further illustrate the diversity of political, economic and other developments possible in the variegated landscape of separate sovereignties in the Empire after 1648. In the Palatinate, brutally devastated by the Thirty Years War, the return of Karl Ludwig (1649–80), son of the exiled Winter King Friedrich V, inaugurated a period of strict absolutist rule dedicated to the reconstruction of the electorate. By his energetic policies of economic encouragement, educational improvement and religious pacification, the country made slow but steady progress towards recovery. The standing army and military administration he founded were costly, but were funded by permanent taxes on wine, fruit and meat, as well as by savings realized from sharp reductions in court expenditures. Unfortunately, an economy which in the early 1670s contained taxable capital and property little more than a quarter of their value in 1618 was further shaken by the French invasions and other costs occasioned by the Dutch War and was not improved by the dramatic increase in outlays for the court and army which occurred during the short reign of Elector Karl (1680–85), the last of the Simmern line of Calvinist rulers. His successor, Philipp Wilhelm of the Neuburg line (1685–90), cut expenses by drastically reducing the number of officials, but the benefits disappeared in the flood of expenditures brought on by the Nine Years War and its renewed and terrible devastations. As the

8. This excise was largely imitative of one imposed earlier in Brandenburg by Elector Friedrich Wilhelm (see below, Chapter Nineteen), and in fact was proposed to Friedrich August by his field marshal H. A. von Schöning, who had been a close friend of Friedrich Wilhelm. The reasons for its acceptance by the Saxon towns were also similar to those of the cities of Brandenburg. This new tax lessened but did not eliminate the elector's dependence on grants by the estates, which continued to produce more revenue than the excise.

first Catholic elector, Philip William also initiated an unwise policy of open favouritism for the Catholic minority of the country, a policy continued and intensified by his heir Johann Wilhelm (1690–1716), who ignited a long and nasty quarrel with his Calvinist consistory as well as with Lutherans demanding religious equality. Since many Calvinists chose to flee the country, taking portable skills and assets with them, this was a further economic blow to the electorate, whose sad history throughout almost the entire seventeenth century resulted in its reduction to virtual insignificance for most of the eighteenth.

The duchy of Württemberg, like the Palatinate, emerged from the Thirty Years War very much in need of reconstruction, a task pursued with great energy by Duke Eberhard III (1628–74) and during the brief reign of his son Wilhelm Ludwig (1674–7). But the generally cordial relations between these two dukes and the Württemberg estates began to sour under the regency of the Duke-Administrator Friedrich Karl (1677–93), who in the face of the total defenselessness of the country against military attacks by France in the late 1680s and early 1690s transformed the militia into a regular army. The estates – unique in the Empire as a unicameral body which included no nobles[9] and whose deputies represented only some sixty towns and secularized monasteries – vigorously opposed this action and eventually carried their case before the Aulic Council in Vienna. Such protests had as little effect on Friedrich Karl as on Eberhard Ludwig (1693–1733), who succeeded his regent-uncle and who introduced the duchy to absolute rule. The diet, which at one time had exercised what almost amounted to a budgetary right, was soon ignored almost altogether in favour of small and pliable committees of its deputies to which the duke transferred the functions of the diet beginning in 1699. He further reduced the influence of the estates by creating a 'Conference Ministry' in 1717, thus bypassing the older Privy Council which had many ties with the estates. By 1724, he was even able to secure a weary diet's recognition of his standing army. Eberhard Ludwig also encouraged the development of the early enlightenment and a spirit of religious tolerance, which included the settlement of exiled French Huguenots

---

9. Almost the entire nobility of the duchy had long since achieved immediacy as Imperial Counts or Knights and therefore had neither need for nor entitlement to territorial representation.

and Piedmontese Waldensians; these policies arose partly from the duke's own convictions, but partly also as a crafty attempt to undermine the powerful influence of the orthodox Lutheran territorial church from which the estates derived much of their support. The deliberate encouragement of Pietism by his cousin and successor Karl Alexander (1733–7) served much the same purpose. Under both dukes, but especially under Eberhard Ludwig, most of the trappings of the typical small baroque court came into being: construction of parks and palaces (Ludwigsburg was begun in 1704), guards regiments, hunts, festive balls, opera, chamber concerts and mistresses. Thus, Württemberg, while not a major player on the German political scene, provides another example of a state which, for all its peculiar features, had much in common with the history of all the German territories, large and small, in this period.

Hanover provides a final example of the unusually rapid progress of absolutism. In this Guelph duchy, which was known as Calenberg-Göttingen until its elevation to an electorate in 1692, Duke Johann Friedrich (1665–79) and his brother and successor Ernst August (1679–98) decreed comprehensive reorganizations of the government in 1670 and 1680, respectively, which had the effect not only of reserving a host of the most important affairs of state to the exclusive competence of the prince, but also of reducing the Privy Council from a single advisory and policy-making body to a series of four administrative colleges which increasingly operated as functional ministries, separately dealing with finance, judicial matters, war and ecclesiastical affairs. The estates, for their part, were relegated almost exclusively to those rights and duties connected with the administration of their 'contribution'. Even more than Johann Friedrich (whose motto 'I am emperor in my own country' conveys something of the tenor of his regime), Ernst August exalted the position of the crown within the governmental apparatus: he removed himself entirely from the deliberations of the Privy Council in both its plenary and collegial sessions and ruled alone, from his 'cabinet', with the assistance of only two cabinet secretaries. It was he who also notably strengthened the finances of the duchy by a consumption tax, approved *pro forma* by the estates in 1686, which applied in both urban and rural areas to a number of both luxury items and daily necessities.

In foreign policy and military affairs, Ernst August cooperated closely with his brother Georg Wilhelm, ruler of the neighbouring Guelph duchy of Lüneburg-Celle; together they raised armies which eventually reached the impressive size of 30,000 men and whose active participation in wars against the Turks, the French, and rebel forces in Hungary earned them the gratitude of the Habsburgs. Using this, as well as a timely bit of extortion based on a threat to defect from the allied coalition during the Nine Years War, Ernst August persuaded Emperor Leopold to confer an electoral title on him in 1692. His son Georg Ludwig (1698–1727) inherited not only his father's new dignities but also, upon the death of his uncle Georg Wilhelm in 1705, the duchy of Lüneburg-Celle, which was then integrated into the new electorate. As the result of events of the Second Northern War, both Bremen and Verden were added to this now rather considerable territory in 1715. By that time, of course, Georg Ludwig had become King George I of England and, like his son George II, spent most of his time there after 1714. While both king-electors maintained an active interest in their German possessions, the internal government of the electorate was conducted by regents drawn from the native nobility, of which a few families monopolized the most important official positions. At the provincial level, the estates, dominated by the nobility and divided into seven separate corporations corresponding to the several duchies and counties which comprised the electorate, ruled the countryside in a generally mild but also socially self-protective and therefore unprogressive fashion. Such opportunities as might have existed in the eighteenth century for further economic and political development and unification would have required the energetic leadership and undivided attention of a strong executive authority; but any possibility of that was packed up in the baggage which accompanied Georg Ludwig on his journey to his other and royal home in England in 1714.

Several features in the above sketch of the history of a few of the German states in the three-quarters of a century or more following the Peace of Westphalia invite special commentary, much of which could as easily be applied to a score or more of territories which cannot be dealt with individually here. It should be clear, first of all, that much, though not all, of the striving for princely absolutism in the territories was related to the desire to achieve sufficient political power to command the financial instruments without which the free conduct of policy by the ruler was impossible. An increase in political power meant enhanced control of both the sources of revenue and the apparatus by which it was assessed, collected and accounted for, with the possibility of greater freedom to increase the former and to reform the latter in the direction of higher efficiency. The larger income thus realized (where that occurred) was generally returned to the economy in one of three ways: first, in programmes to expand the economic base of the country, which had a very spotty history (depending on the territory in question) and which themselves were ultimately designed to enlarge the fisc; second, as expenditures on what one might call the emotive infrastructure of princely rule – the palaces, parks, public edifices, the visual, literary and musical arts, cultural events and so on – which powerfully reinforced the image-building of princes and were far more important to such degree of absolute rule as was actually realized than is perhaps commonly appreciated; and third, in outlays for standing armies and permanent military administrations which were almost invariably established in the second half of the seventeenth century in all territories of any size.

These armies were of particular importance to the princes, not necessarily because of what they could achieve in the field with them (some were small, after all and often ill-trained and inexperienced), but because of how they could employ them in their chancelleries: as bargaining chips for alliances which might protect their countries in the jungle-like climate of international relations of the time, or which could yield other tangible benefits such as a new income in the form of subsidies. Internationally, the Europe of the seventeenth and eighteenth centuries was a shopping mall for diplomatic engagements, in which allegiances almost always had a price tag. That, of course, explains the remarkable permutability of alliances in the period, especially for the smaller states and territories of Europe, whose only permanent interest was survival. In the Empire, the defection of some territories to the side of Louis XIV at various times can in a few cases be explained by greed or ambition – Bavaria comes to mind here – but it was far more often the result of fear or prudence. Certainly geographical proximity to the war zones of the greater powers explains the desperately shifting policies of many German territories (not excluding Bavaria) in this respect; but a foreign policy based on altruism (which would include almost any truly permanent alliance) was simply forbidden to any prudent German territorial ruler, who had no choice but to recognize that, next to sheer survival, whatever policy served to strengthen his ability to deal with the next crisis was probably best. As far as loyalty to the emperor was concerned, no even cursory glance at history would encourage any territorial prince to confuse his own interests with those of the Habsburg family and, indeed, might well suggest that supporting France could on occasion serve the Empire's interests better than allegiance to Vienna.

Still, the realities of international politics made the pursuit of a truly independent foreign policy very difficult for all territories of the Empire outside of Austria. No matter how much they twisted and turned, or how often they changed patrons, clientage to someone was the almost inevitable fate of most of the princes. But there was one territory in which a grimly determined and ultimately successful effort was made to escape the trap of clientage and to achieve a position in which a truly independent foreign policy could be pursued primarily on the basis of its own strength alone. That territory was the kingdom of Prussia, which deserves the following chapter to itself.

CHAPTER NINETEEN

The Northern Sparta: Brandenburg-Prussia, 1640–1740

It is natural that historians have shown great interest in the early development of Brandenburg-Prussia, since after all it was this state which under the 'Iron Chancellor' Otto von Bismarck united most of historic Germany in the new German Empire of 1871. But even without that event, there would be much reason for special attention to Prussia's history in the seventeenth and eighteenth centuries because of certain unique features of its development in the context of the German world of its time. After 1640, in particular, a combination of unusual challenges and opportunities, together with a couple of strong rulers who largely eschewed those seductive comfortabilities of rulership which ensnared so many of their counterparts elsewhere in Germany, resulted by the mid-eighteenth century in the elevation of this electorate and kingdom to a position of power not remotely approached by any territory of the Empire besides Austria.

There was very little to foretell the phenomenal rise in the fortunes of Brandenburg-Prussia at the time of the accession of Elector Friedrich Wilhelm – the 'Great Elector' – in 1640. The twenty-year-old elector himself was certainly not ill-prepared for rulership; a large man and physically tough and vigorous, he had not only received a good standard princely education, but had spent several invaluable years with his relatives in Holland – especially the stadholder Frederick Henry – where he learned much about war, politics and the economic foundations of power from the practitioners of the most modern agricultural and commercial techniques of the time. The best background imaginable, however, was no preparation for the spectacle of the wrecked and divided inheritance which confronted him. His possessions were geographically scattered across northern Germany from the Rhine to beyond the borders of Poland and all had suffered – some very severely – from the devastations and depredations of the Thirty Years War; some, like the recent inheritance of Pomerania, were still occupied by foreign troops. The total population of his territories had dropped by over 50 per cent from their 1618 levels; and, of course, the war continued. Friedrich Wilhelm, whose army consisted of fewer than 5000 undependable mercenaries, immediately perceived the uselessness of the Habsburg alliance to which his indecisive and unimaginative father had remained stubbornly committed and in 1641 arranged an armistice with Sweden; this brought not only peace but a gradual reconciliation with Sweden and the other chief enemy of Austria, France, both of which (for their own reasons and with some concessions on his part) were prepared to help the elector gain compensation at the Peace of Westphalia. In return for abdicating to Sweden his title to the western part of the duchy of Pomerania from an inheritance of 1637, Friedrich Wilhelm received the eastern part of it, as well as the secularized bishoprics of Kammin, Minden and Halberstadt and an expectancy to the archbishopric of Magdeburg, which finally fell to him in 1680.

While this was a very respectable increase in territory for an electorate whose own military efforts had done little to deserve it, the gain was not without drawbacks. One of these became evident as early as 1650, when a border dispute with Sweden in Pomerania forced Friedrich Wilhelm to request the committee of the Brandenburg estates for money to increase the tiny army that had survived his early purges of incompetents and his cost-cutting after Westphalia. With perfect parochial indifference to the fate of Pomerania, but not to the possibility of a war the elector might start there, the committee refused. Understandably worried by this refusal, especially in view of the disproportionate importance of Brandenburg to his overall fiscal resources, the elector decided on the unusual step of consulting a plenary diet. By demanding approval of a general excise tax he knew would be unpopular and after much debate over many sessions, he was able to manoeuvre the diet into a famous compromise in 1653; in return for abandoning his excise, confirming the privileges of the nobility as local seigneurs and promising both to submit treaties to the estates for ratification and not to employ Catholics in his service, the elector won a grant of some 500,000 talers over a period of six years. With this money, he raised the nucleus of the army which enabled him not only to enter the First Northern War in 1655, but more importantly, to impose illegal taxes and requisitions by which the army was sustained and steadily augmented, reaching a size of 27,000 men by 1660. Such taxes yielded 700,000 talers in 1655–6 and for a time, in 1659, almost 110,000 talers per month from Brandenburg alone. The Rhenish territories – Cleves and Mark, primarily – were squeezed for an additional one and a half million talers during the war. All protests by the estates were ignored by the Elector and his military commanders during a period which resembled military dictatorship.

The grant of 1653, then, was the foundation on which Friedrich Wilhelm raised a military force whose very existence from the time of the First Northern War was sufficient to assure the at least grudging cooperation of the Brandenburg estates – especially because Friedrich Wilhelm, like his successors, was careful to honour his promises regarding the one capital concern of the nobility: their rights and privileges as local landlords. Nor should it be forgotten that while the sovereign responsibilities of the prince, as he interpreted them, inevitably brought conflicts with his noble estates, a strong community of interest between him and them as patrimonial seigneurs conferred a degree of mutual respect and even deference observable right down to the end of the Hohenzollern monarchy in 1918. The military crisis of the First Northern War also provided Friedrich Wilhelm with the means of anchoring his princely authority in Cleves-Mark by challenging a host of privileges insisted on by the estates there. Here, unlike Brandenburg, a spirit of cooperation had long existed within the sophisticated and prosperous mixed group of nobles and burghers which made up the estates, whose strong sense of independence was buttressed by close ties with the Dutch and the Neuburg dukes of Jülich-Berg. In 1649 and again in 1653, the elector had granted sweeping concessions to these estates which severely limited his own sovereignty, including even their right to negotiate independently with other states. As in Brandenburg, Friedrich Wilhelm violated various of these privileges between 1655–60 and after the Peace of Oliva he threatened the estates with military occupation if they did not agree to curtail their 'liberties'. Since good relations obtained between the elector and the Dutch after Oliva and between him and the Neuburg house after 1666, Cleves-Mark no longer had protectors to turn to and agreed to a compromise in which the estates retained some rights with respect to taxation and freedom of assembly, but gave in on the more important political and military issues. Soon enough, the estates were voting regular and substantial contributions to Friedrich Wilhelm's army and by the end of his reign in 1688, Cleves-Mark, while still privileged relative to other parts of his dominions, had been administratively integrated into the single state the elector was trying so hard to build.

Friedrich Wilhelm's problems in the third major area of which his inheritance was composed – the duchy of Prussia – were at least as severe as those in the Rhine provinces and took even longer to overcome. By 1640 the Prussian estates already had a long history of acquiring and defending a multitude of special privileges by the device of appealing against the actions and decisions of their own dukes to the king of Poland, the feudal overlord of the duchy. Upon his investment with Prussia in 1640 and because of the difficulties of his situation elsewhere, Friedrich Wilhelm had confirmed all these privileges, though here too he overrode many of them during the First Northern War (and was even reluctantly supported by the estates in doing so). But the grant of absolute sovereignty over Prussia obtained from the Polish king in 1660 precipitated a political crisis: the Prussian estates argued that their traditional constitution, including the location of sovereignty over the duchy, could not be changed without a concurrence involving their participation and that of the king of Poland. Friedrich Wilhelm sent representatives to negotiate with a special diet, but after two years of wrangling the Prussians still insisted on a package of privileges far in excess even of those earlier demanded in Cleves-Mark and emphasized their determination by a direct appeal to King John Casimir of Poland. In 1662, his patience exhausted, the elector led 2000 troops to Königsberg and there arrested a chief leader of the opposition, the merchant and city magistrate Hieronymus Roth. This decisive act broke the deadlock and in May 1663, in return for his confirmation of such of their privileges as were not incompatible with his sovereignty – a vague formula, indeed – the estates recognized Frederick William's sovereignty. Further trouble arose in the course of a loosely organized noble conspiracy centring around C. L. von Kalckstein, an old foe of the elector, which resulted in a refusal of the estates to grant requested taxes in 1669. This conspiracy was not fully dissolved until Kalckstein, spurning the generous treatment originally accorded him by Friedrich Wilhelm, fled to Poland to stir up more trouble; kidnapped on the elector's orders, he was returned to Prussia, where he was tortured and executed in 1672. A final episode of intransigence occurred in 1674, when the city of Königsberg refused to allow the elector's troops to collect taxes; on this occasion, Friedrich Wilhelm ordered his soldiers quartered in civilian homes until the taxes were paid. There were no major disturbances in Prussia thereafter.

An important feature of the Prussian opposition to princely authority was the remarkable degree of unanimity between the noble estates and those of Königsberg, reminiscent of that which also existed in Cleves-Mark for a long time. Recognizing their cooperation as a serious obstacle, Friedrich Wilhelm sought to divide them by separate fiscal treatment: after 1680, both small towns and noble estates were required to pay a direct land tax, while Königsberg was put on the entirely different footing of an excise tax. This device was so successful in exploding the solidarity of the estates that after some years of rapidly decreasing effectiveness they disappeared altogether after 1705.[1] In this clever policy the elector was doubtlessly relying on earlier experience with excise taxes in Brandenburg. What he had always desired was a major source of steady military revenues such as was not guaranteed by the grants of the estates – their *Kontribution*. Thinking to get at that part of the income of the Brandenburg nobility which was derived from their demesne lands and which could not be taxed directly, he proposed a general excise tax on a wide range of items for both nobility and towns as a replacement for their *Kontribution*. The nobility, which completely dominated the urban deputies in the estates, decisively rejected it for themselves, but in order to escape it agreed to it in principle for the towns. The elector proceeded cautiously, first offering it in 1667 only to some towns as an optional way of paying their 59 per cent share of the *Kontribution* and only later (1680 and 1682) imposing it on all others by decree. The excise was not unwelcome in many towns, partly because as an indirect tax it was less visible and painful than the annual direct hit of the *Kontribution* and partly because it tended to equalize the tax burden between ordinary burghers and the governing patricians whose control of assessments allowed them to shift the weight of the *Kontribution* onto the backs of lesser citizens. For the elector, the excise provided not only a dependable income, but also the promise of larger sums for the future through increases in both tax rates and the number of consumer items to which the tax could be applied. Above all, however, he was essentially liberated from dependence on the grants of the estates, especially since the nobility continued to vote its annual *Kontribution* more or less on cue from the government.

1. In the 1660s, the initial response of all the estates to a permanent general excise had been strongly negative, but after its imposition on Königsberg the nobility petitioned repeatedly to be included in it in order to restore the estates' unity and strength by a uniform taxation which could then be resisted by all in common. The elector wisely rejected all such petitions.

In the early 1680s, when the excise became compulsory for all towns, new officials were appointed to collect it; these Tax Commissioners (*commissarii locorum*, later *Steuerräte*), took their place alongside a group of other officials at several levels who together comprised the General Commissariat (*Generalkommissariat*), which was not only the most important administrative and financial agency of the monarchy, but also the one organ of the central government which existed in and therefore tied together all of the scattered provinces of which Brandenburg-Prussia was composed. The institution consisted originally of individuals appointed in each district (*Kreis*) of every territory during the Thirty Years War to coordinate troop movements and supply and to take charge of the money granted by the estates for military purposes (chiefly the *Kontribution*). Quite often, the government chose for this position as District Commissar (*Kreiskommissar*) the same man appointed District Director (*Kreisdirector*) by the district estates to supervise collection of certain other non-military taxes voted by the territorial diet.[2] By the end of the war, the District Commissars in each province had been subordinated to a Chief Commissar (*Ober-kriegskommissar*) and in 1655 a single General Commissar was appointed for the entire state – at which point the famous General War Commissariat (*Generalkriegskommissariat*) was born. Since the lessees of the crown lands were also integrated into this nexus as Crown Bailiffs (or Crown Commissars [*Ämterkommissare*]), all rural areas acquired a degree of local military and financial supervision; the establishment of the Tax Commissioners in the early 1680s then brought the towns into the system as well. The General War Commissariat supervised all matters of logistics and military administration, but it had the equally important task of raising military revenues from sources other than the *Kontribution* and thus became an active force for (and the state's chief instrument of) financial and economic intervention and innovation. It invented a graduated poll tax, a stamp tax and a special impost on most state servants equivalent to half of their first year's salary; but it also sought to create new wealth by establishing commissions to evaluate and improve commerce and industry. The Commissariat thus

2. By the later years of the century, the two positions were almost uniformly united in the same individual, who continued to be chosen by the elector from a list of nominees supplied by the district estates. Throughout the old regime, therefore, this official (whose titles were merged into the single one of Rural Commissioner (*Landrat*) in 1702) had a dual character as a representative of the central government and of the local estates.

became the fiscal and economic spearhead of the administration as a whole.

In addition to the military revenues which have so far dominated the discussion, the Elector had another source of income in the so-called civil revenues; these were managed by the Court Chamber (*Hofkammer*) and consisted of receipts from the crown lands and from the various tolls, tariffs, fines and profits from coinage and wholesale monopolies to which the sovereign was entitled. Of these, the potentially lucrative domainal yields[3] were far less than they should have been for most of Friedrich Wilhelm's reign, due to a combination of theft, mismanagement, bad record-keeping, lack of a system of translating payments in kind into cash equivalents, and, finally, leases of very long duration which did not allow for adequate accountability or for inflation of land rents. Only after 1683, when the East Frisian Baron Dodo zu Knyphausen was appointed to look into these and other civil revenues did a dramatic reform take place, including a system of fixed-rent leases based on the cash value of natural produce. By the end of the elector's reign, furthermore, Knyphausen's improved bookkeeping enabled him to begin drawing up the first comprehensive budget of all civil revenues and expenditures.

Apart from the increased energy with which the ordinary mercantilist measures of the time were pursued – regulation of exports and imports, guild controls and so on – only three initiatives really distinguish Friedrich Wilhelm's economic policies from those of many other German rulers. The first was his attempt to develop colonial trade; doomed from the start by persistent undercapitalization and competition from the larger and more experienced overseas operations of the great maritime states, the enterprises founded for this purpose either failed or sputtered along in permanent unprofitability until all were terminated early in the reign of King Friedrich Wilhelm I.[4] The second – a happier story – was the construction of a canal linking the Oder and Spree rivers, which enabled barge traffic from eastern Saxony (Lusatia) and Silesia to reach the Elbe and Weser valleys of northwestern Germany. Berlin profited from the transshipments made there, as did the elector's coffers from the transit taxes which were now collected by his officials instead of by the Swedes waiting at the mouth of the Oder

---

3. The crown lands may have embraced as much as one-third of all agricultural land in the monarchy, with some 30 per cent of the total peasant population.
4. See above, Chapter Eleven.

in Stettin. Finally, the immigration and resettlement policies of the elector were of considerable importance to the economy and were better organized and administered than in most other territories. This was particularly evident in the example of the 20,000 Huguenot refugees he welcomed in and after 1685, for whose relocation the General War Commissariat established a new agency, the French Commissariat. With many excellent artisans, as well as knowledgeable commercial and industrial entrepreneurs, the Huguenot community made economic contributions out of all proportion to its numbers and even provided several units of well disciplined troops for the elector's army.

This army was by far the largest consumer of revenues; its size was always greatest in wartime, of course, but its peacetime strength grew steadily as well: from 1800 men in 1653, it swelled to 27,000 by the end of the First Northern War; it was then reduced to 12,000, but grew again to 45,000 by the end of the Dutch War; thereafter it was cut by half, but increased slowly to 30,000 by 1688, the year of the elector's death and the beginning of the Nine Years War. An overwhelming percentage of its costs were paid from the military revenues of the crown, with some help from foreign subsidies; very little came from loans. This meant that a military power now second only to Austria in Germany had paid for its rise to that position almost entirely from its own resources. That it could do so was due partly to the prudent foreign policy of the elector, who chose his conflicts carefully and was not embarrassed to be duplicitous or to appear less than heroic when belligerency promised either no gain or gain disproportionate to the costs or risks of achieving it. At first glance, the net profit ascribable to Friedrich Wilhelm's own foreign policy may not appear very impressive: all of the territorial gains of his reign were arranged at Westphalia more by the machinations of other interested parties than by the force of his own diplomacy, while his one great territorial conquest by force of arms – Swedish Pomerania – was taken away at Nymegen by Louis XIV. But the outcome of the First Northern War provides a better clue to the final harvest of his closely interrelated foreign and domestic policies, for his attainment of full sovereignty over Prussia in 1660 merely symbolizes the real purpose and direction of his reign and its true achievement: the imposition of a genuine *working* sovereignty over all his dominions that would give them the character of a single state, if indeed a still geographically divided and imperfectly unified one, and would enable him to pass on to his son and successor an army and the outlines of an administration sufficiently strong and developed to keep it that way. Looked at from this perspective, foreign and domestic policy were simply different aspects of a single *military* policy which served the higher goal of state-building.

It is probably too harsh to aver, as some historians have, that the greatest accomplishment of Elector Friedrich III (1688–1713) was that he did not succeed in destroying the legacy of his father. But there is more than a little truth in the accusation none the less.[5] Friedrich was very different from his father (with whom he was not close); he had an undistinguished intellect, a malleable will and an insecure and somewhat neurotic personality. To mask his own deficiencies, he surrounded himself with a pomp, ceremony and elegance which would have both angered and embarrassed the Great Elector – not least because of their expense. Perhaps the best act of the early years of his reign (rooted more in weakness than in wisdom, however) was to turn the government over to the capable and strong-willed Eberhard von Danckelmann, a well trusted adviser of his father and his own former tutor, who by 1692 had in effect become an uncontested prime minister. Danckelmann, a very important figure in the rise of Brandenburg-Prussia, honoured the Great Elector's commitments to Leopold I and to the great anti-French coalition in the Nine Years War and wisely used the considerable subsidies received from his allies not just for military purposes but for long-term administrative and economic development as well. Unfortunately, his strong Calvinist attitudes and his strict financial management eventually brought him into conflict with the free-spending and luxury-loving court and especially with Friedrich's second wife Sophie Charlotte, who also resented his commanding position in the state and his opposition to her husband's project to acquire a royal crown. The elector also allowed himself to be persuaded that Danckelmann was responsible for Brandenburg's failure to realize any gains from the Nine Years War. Brought up on false charges in 1697, the faithful minister was removed from power and imprisoned.

Danckelmann's fall also led to the dismissal of a number of other able officials who had survived the Great Elector, including Knyphausen, and inaugurated a shameful era of almost fifteen years in which the court and government were dominated by self-seeking and dishonest favourites and flatterers, chief among them a trio of

---

5. A recent attempt at a strongly positive reevaluation of Friedrich and his reign is both uneven and unconvincing. See Linda and Marsha Frey, *Frederick I: The Man and His Times* (N.Y., 1984).

counts – Wartenberg, Wartensleben and Wittgenstein. Expenses for the household soared, while the favourites looted the treasury and falsified accounts. By the later years of the War of the Spanish Succession (to which Friedrich had committed himself partly from vanity), the shortage of money – aggravated by plague and famine in some provinces after 1708, as well as by the war itself – had become so acute that the military budget depended entirely on the subsidies of the maritime allies, meaning that the government had virtually lost control of its own foreign policy. At this point (1710), Crown Prince Friedrich Wilhelm instigated an investigation which revealed the malfeasance, mismanagement and larceny of the regime of favourites; the three corrupt counts and many others were dismissed and the crown prince assumed virtual control of the government until his father's death in 1713.

Friedrich III's notorious pursuit of a royal title to cap his dignities was consistent with the emphasis on external display that characterized his entire reign. Having already observed the assumption of the Polish crown by his Saxon neighbour Friedrich August I in 1697 and aware that his fellow Elector Georg Ludwig of Hanover was likely someday to inherit the English crown, the jealous Friedrich, urged on by his wife and his sycophantic ministers, conceived the idea of elevating the duchy of Prussia to the status of a kingdom. Since it lay outside the Empire, he could have accomplished this by unilateral declaration, but he was worried that no one would recognize his new title. So he approached Emperor Leopold for a prior assurance of recognition and after lengthy negotiations (which by no accident were concluded on the eve of a new war) he promised an alliance to Leopold, while the latter, no doubt pleased by such a cheap bargain, promised Friedrich a small subsidy and recognition of his new dignity. Friedrich rang in the new year with elaborate preparations for his coronation, which was celebrated in Königsberg on 18 January 1701.[6]

While there was obviously much that was not admirable about Friedrich's reign, it did have some redeeming features. For one thing, the support given by him (and his father before him) to the overthrow of James II in England by William of Orange in 1688–9 and to the anti-French coalition in the War of the Spanish Succession, resulted in the acquisition by devolution or subsequent purchase of

---

6. From the time of Friedrich's coronation as 'King in Prussia', the entire Hohenzollern inheritance is and hereinafter will be referred to as 'Prussia' and the numeration of its rulers will follow that of the royal, not the electoral title; the former duchy of Prussia now becomes 'East Prussia'.

some small territories from William's Orange inheritance, including Mörs and Lingen (1702), Tecklenburg and Neuchâtel (Neuenburg) (1707) and part of Gelderland (1713). Thus, to the real but intangible benefits which accrued to Prussia from the stellar performance of its troops in such battles as Blenheim, Turin and Malplaquet were added the concrete ones of additional territory. Furthermore, while Eberhard von Danckelmann's harsh disapproval of 'frivolous' court expenditures was doubtless consistent with both his Calvinist morality and his scale of financial priorities for the state, it must not be forgotten that those expenditures included significant outlays for the new streets, statues, palaces, churches and other architectural adornments which brought baroque beauty and magnificence to a Berlin badly in need of them. The great Andreas Schlüter, appointed court sculptor and architect in 1694, would not have remained in Berlin without such expenditure; nor would either the Academy of Arts or Leibniz's project for an Academy of Sciences (1701) – both strongly supported by Sophie Charlotte – have been realized. Finally, Friedrich himself deserves credit for his support of the new University of Halle (1694) and of the Pietist movement of Spener and Francke, to which neither some Calvinist courtiers nor the Lutheran territorial church of Brandenburg were originally very sympathetic. So while Friedrich's pursuit of pomp over power did little to advance the military and political capabilities of Prussia, it brought no permanent harm even in those areas, while yielding some lasting gain in others.

Friedrich I's successor, Friedrich Wilhelm I (1713–40), was as little like his father as his father had resembled the Great Elector. Born in 1688, he was brought up by a French nurse, a French tutor and the proud and high-minded Count Alexander von Dohna. From the first two he learned to speak French fluently, though he always wrote it (and his native German) badly, with a forceful and colourful disregard for grammar and spelling; from the latter he absorbed a deep Calvinism, from which two lifelong attitudes were developed: an unyielding distaste for loose living, luxury and foppery (which included all cultural refinement) and a powerful sense of a ruler's accountability to God for the discharge of his public duties. Almost like an old-testament patriarch, he fully accepted the responsibility of guiding his subjects to their own welfare (which it was also his duty to define); but he expected obedience as their duty to him and to God and a violent temper frequently made its appearance when they did not respond instantly and without reserve to his commands. The symbol of his reign was not the sceptre, but the heavy walking-stick he carried, with which on more than one occasion he pounded the unfortunate persons of able-bodied beggars, idlers or drunkards he turned up during frequent walking tours of his capital. His behaviour in private towards his own family was as gruff and violent as any he demonstrated publicly.

That the frugality with which he managed his own finances as crown prince would later become public policy was first evident in the last three years of his father's reign, when Friedrich Wilhelm essentially ran the government; but it was not fully implemented until after Friedrich I's funeral – an elaborate and expensive affair ordered by a son out of respect for the tastes of his father. Immediately thereafter, draconian cost-cutting in the court and household was initiated: overall expenditures dropped by three-quarters within a year, while two-thirds of the court officials were either cashiered or sent off to the army. The coronation ceremony in Königsberg was a penurious and perfunctory affair, much unlike the lavish and incredibly expensive celebrations of 1701. The new king also proceeded immediately to extend the reform of the civil revenues he had begun in the last years of Friedrich I's reign, when a policy of short-term (mostly six-year) leases of the domains had been adopted as a way of taking advantage of rising prices and of easing the process of replacing incompetent lessees possessed of lifetime or hereditary contracts. Under the supervision of the careful and capable Ernst von Kameke, who was placed in charge of all civil revenues, the domains were also declared henceforth inalienable, indivisible and ineligible for lease by nobles. An immediate and dramatic rise in domainal income occurred and continued throughout the reign. In 1713, Kameke was put at the helm of a new administrative body, the General Finance Directory, which replaced the old Court Chamber, while the several earlier treasuries for the civil revenues were combined into a single new agency, the General Finance Chest.

Military revenues also increased significantly, due not only to an expansion of the excise tax and an annual 'allodification' fee of forty talers imposed on possessors of noble estates to free their lands from feudal tenure, but also to a new general land tax in East Prussia which for the first time applied to nobles' demesne lands as well as those farmed by their peasants. The activities of the General War Commissariat, directed for many years by the intelligent and hard-working F. W. von Grumbkow, expanded steadily; much of its work involved supervision of its subordinate provincial agencies, the

War Chambers (*Kriegskammer*) which had grown up around the Chief Commissars of an earlier time. These, in turn, directed the activities of the Rural Commissioners (*Landräte*), some aspects of the work of the Crown Bailiffs (the domains lessees) and above all the rapidly expanding duties of the Tax Commissioners in the towns – a point which requires some explanation. Because of their great importance to the expansion of the industrial economy on which Friedrich Wilhelm set his hopes for higher revenues from the private sector, the towns and their governments were subjected to a more intense governmental scrutiny than ever before, carried out by special commissions whose reports convinced the king that the administration and finances of the towns, as mismanaged by their self-serving and traditionalist oligarchies, required fundamental reform. The crown began to replace these previously elective town governments with smaller bodies of paid officials, appointed for life; by 1740, this reform was both general and nearly complete. The central government assumed the often considerable debts of the towns, but also took control of the rural properties they owned, putting them out on short-term leases whose return was used to defray town expenses; proceeds from the excise were granted, sparingly, to cover such deficits as remained. The Tax Commissioners, however, became almost municipal viceroys in this arrangement, vested as they were with very extensive powers and responsibilities: they inspected weights and measures, fixed prices on necessities, looked after orphanages and hospitals and, in short, exercised or supervised all functions of local police (in the very broad contemporary meaning of the term). And since their duties included industrial labour discipline, regulation of competition and quality control of manufactures, they more than any others were the front-line troops of the mercantilist general command in Berlin.

It was the same concern for efficient management of the fiscal and economic resources of the country as a whole that led to the most important single administrative reform of Friedrich Wilhelm's reign. The General Finance Directory and the General War Commissariat were really parallel agencies, both charged with producing as much revenue as possible for the crown; yet because the economic basis of the growth they sought lay in different sectors – the one chiefly agrarian, the other primarily industrial – the peculiarities of mercantilist practice often put them at loggerheads, resulting in lawsuits between the subordinate officials of the two agencies and other problems which increased costs and slowed the work of both. The king – a dangerously nasty individual on occasion – grew furious and took it upon himself to provide a solution. It came, in 1723, in the form of an amalgamation of the two hitherto separate bodies at both central and provincial levels; thus arose the General Supreme Finance, War and Domains Directory (or General Directory) at the centre and, in the provinces, the War and Domains Chambers to which all local officials mentioned above henceforth reported. During Friedrich Wilhelm's reign, the General Directory was divided into four departments, each with a directing minister, or vice-president (as well as a fifth minister for judicial matters who 'floated' among the four) and a number of subordinate councillors; all departments always met together, but each had different responsibilities, based partly on territories and partly on functions, which it was required to present as the agenda for the whole group on a particular day of each week. All vice-presidents and their departmental councillors were collectively accountable for all discussions and decisions of the entire body. The king himself assumed the presidency of the General Directory, for symbolic reasons, but seldom attended its meetings. The work of the provincial chambers was conducted along roughly similar lines and the principle of collective responsibility applied there as well.

While the benefits of this important reform became rapidly apparent in a more efficient and less contentious conduct of administrative business, another and equally significant development was occurring in the policy-making area. Since shortly before 1700, the Privy Council – the chief advisory body of the crown – had been divided into smaller bodies for the separate discussion of foreign affairs, justice and certain other matters of royal prerogative. Friedrich I, in the sense that he had still advised with and made decisions in these groups, was a prince who ruled 'in council', as contemporary usage had it. Friedrich Wilhelm, however, early developed the practice of retiring to his own suite (or 'cabinet') to consider the memoranda of advice and information sent to him by his subordinates and of conveying back to them the decisions he made all by himself by means of 'cabinet orders' dictated to one or two well trusted cabinet secretaries. This special kind of 'cabinet government' represented a high degree of personal royal absolutism and became a distinct earmark of the Prussian system under both Friedrich Wilhelm and his son and successor. It originated in the former as a response to the system of favouritism, corruption and ministerial collusion which had contaminated his father's government for many years, but in a broader sense was also indicative of the deep suspicion he had throughout his reign that with few exceptions his administration at all levels was shot through with laziness, graft and malfeasance and which led him to see moral failure or wilful disobedience (summed up in his oft-used term 'chicanery') as the cause of whatever difficulties or delays arose in the execution of his policies. He particularly distrusted the nobles in his bureaucracy, suspecting them of harbouring a private aristocratic agenda; from this, he developed the practice of appointing an unusually large number of commoners to positions in the civil service. He was a harsh and often unreasonable taskmaster, who worked his officials hard and paid them poorly – apparently in the belief that prosperity and idleness went hand-in-hand and that together they formed a veritable devil's workshop.[7]

In general, there was nothing very remarkable about Friedrich Wilhelm's economic policies, which simply intensified and systematized much of the governmental restriction, regulation and selective encouragement of industrial enterprise characteristic of mercantilist practice everywhere. Two matters, however, received the particular attention of the royal government. The first was the reconstruction of a whole section of northern East Prussia, known as Prussian Lithuania, which had been severely devastated in the Second Northern War and in the same period (1708–10) ravaged by a terrible plague. The population of the area, which included the cities of Tilsit and Memel, had plummeted in three years from 600,000 to 350,000, leaving some 11,000 peasant farms deserted. Resettlement and restoration was begun under Friedrich I, who attracted some colonists from Switzerland and other parts of Germany; but Friedrich Wilhelm made this effort of 'Rétablissement' into one of the high priorities of his reign, to which he contributed substantially from his private treasury. Progress was slow, but with an occasional quick success, as when some 11,000 of the 20,000 Salzburg religious refugees were settled in the region in 1731–2.

A second major object of official economic concern was the grain trade. The government had long maintained grain storehouses, or magazines, to insure adequate supplies for the army; but the number of such magazines was greatly increased under Friedrich Wilhelm, who in good harvest years ordered the purchase and storage of large amounts of grain in order to keep prices up, and in bad years sold them off to keep prices and supplies at reasonable levels. This policy

---

7. In so doing, Karl overturned an earlier family pact of 1703 which provided that if both Joseph and Karl died without male heirs, Joseph's daughters (who were still living in 1713) would inherit before any Karl might have.

lent a degree of stability to the economy as a whole, with the even more important effect of reducing the incidence of sharp fluctuations in fiscal yields. Duties imposed on grain imports in 1721 – directed primarily against cheap Polish grain – and the total prohibition of such imports in 1732 were related to this policy, which aimed at an essentially absolute control of grain supplies (and prices) as the most important variable of the entire economy. But while economic growth did occur in Friedrich Wilhelm's reign, how much of it was due to governmental intervention is not clear, since the active encouragement of the manufacturing sector was accompanied by a deliberate neglect of commerce, especially the import trade, and by the withdrawal of much circulating coinage to fill the king's huge reserve war chest. The absence of war and of its costs, direct and indirect, for most of the reign was probably the greatest single boon to economic expansion.

Friedrich Wilhelm's economic system, like that of his predecessors, was geared to the fiscal needs of the state, but even more fully so. As in their time, too – war or no war – the chief claimant on government funds was the army, which by 1740 grew to a size of 83,000 men; as the fourth largest in Europe by that time, it consumed just under three-quarters of the entire budget.[8] That figure would have been even higher, and tax yields lower, without the military exemptions granted to those who could prove engagement in productive activity (including a large proportion of the urban population). Furthermore, military labour was released into the civilian economy by furloughing long-term peasant soldiers to work their farms and cottage industries for some nine months of the year. This was facilitated by the so-called 'canton system' introduced by the king in 1733 to replace the problem-ridden practice of recruitment of troops by company captains. Under the new system, the country was divided into roughly equal military districts (cantons), each supplying recruits – chiefly peasants – for a particular regiment. To avoid building expensive barracks, the majority of troops on active duty were lodged with families in the various

8. One of the king's regiments – the famous 'Potsdam Giants' – was specially funded from a Recruit Chest established early in his reign, which took its revenues from unusual sources such as royal pardons or other acts of grace, some of the first year's pay of newly appointed army officers and 'donations' from successful candidates for civil service positions. The 'Giants', all six-footers or more, were Friedrich Wilhelm's special plaything; recruited from all over Europe (sometimes as gifts from other rulers), they received special uniforms and treatment, but were not subjected to the harsh realities of war until Frederick II, in one of his first acts as king, disbanded them as the idiosyncratic and costly indulgence they were and dispersed them among other units.

garrison towns, where they paid bed and board from their own wages and, by their other expenditures, brought enough economic benefit to these towns to be regarded as welcome guests.

The tendency to replace foreigners and mercenaries with native soldiers, already noticeable in the Great Elector's reign, was much intensified under Friedrich Wilhelm I. The majority of the common soldiery came to consist of native Prussians, mostly peasants, who during furloughs remained under the control of the local army commander, rather than their landlords; gradually, a sense of belonging to a 'national' community appeared among them, giving rise to a certain *esprit de corps* not found in the more cosmopolitan armies of other countries. Nearly all positions in the officer corps were now reserved for native noblemen from families for which such positions became both a right and a duty: at least one son from every noble household was expected in his teenage years to enter cadet companies for training, then to spend a period of active duty with troops in the field and thereafter to remain on call for as long as he was able to serve. The increasing identification of noble status with service to the state – especially in the military, but also in the civilian administration – began in earnest in Friedrich Wilhelm's reign and proceeded still further under Frederick II. Both the state and the crown derived benefit from that identification, but so did the nobility, which in this way developed a strong claim to represent the permanent interests of the state – a claim that was to have important ramifications for the social and political history of Prussia and of Germany far into the future.

The high costs of the military establishment and of the civil service which supported it left little money for other purposes. If there was any liberality in Friedrich Wilhelm at all, beyond his generosity to the army, it appeared in the favour he showed to various religious projects, including Pietist institutions such as those of A. H. Francke in Halle and elsewhere and church construction where it was urgently needed – as in the 'Rétablissement' of Prussian Lithuania. His sense of religious duty also underlay the compulsory schooling ordinances he issued in 1717 and 1736, as well as his order of 1734 that no illiterate child should be presented for religious confirmation. But almost no money was made available for the books, teachers' salaries or school buildings without which these decrees would (and

9. The king reserved some of his most colourful vituperation for lawyers (and judges), whom he variously referred to as 'clowns', 'dogs', 'dumb devils', 'gallows-birds', 'arch-do-nothings' and 'councillors of confusion'.

largely did) remain nugatory. He had very little concern for higher education and the universities except as training schools for preachers and civil servants (but not for lawyers, whom he hated)[9] and he had neither interest in nor understanding of such higher intellectual pursuits as philosophy, whose most eminent contemporary German representative – Christian Wolff – he drove from the country at the urging of his theologians. The underfunded Academy of Arts meanwhile sank to the level of a drawing school and not even the strongly pragmatic orientation of the Academy of Sciences could attract the king's attention or his money.[10]

For a king as strongly military-minded as Friedrich Wilhelm, his foreign policy was surprisingly pacific. The only war he fought was the Second Northern War, which he was dragged into by circumstances and which was a very safe war for him by the time he entered it. The territorial acquisition of the eastern half of Swedish Pomerania, with Stettin, was the last he made. He did pursue one diplomatic initiative very stubbornly: a Prussian succession to the duchies of Jülich and Berg, based on a treaty of 1666 with the Neuburg dukes which was later disputed. Though Friedrich Wilhelm reduced his claim to Berg alone and made various concessions to have it honoured – including an alliance with Austria eagerly solicited by Vienna – all his support eventually evaporated and nothing came of his claim. It is possible that apart from a certain apparent lack of skill and judgment in diplomatic and international affairs which may have led to an insecure and overcautious foreign policy in general, Friedrich Wilhelm was also simply too stingy to put his army and his treasury at risk in military ventures made dubious by his own ignorance of how to protect them by diplomatic engagements. But while he gained very little from European power politics, especially in the later years of his reign, his domestic accomplishments were immense. The most obvious of these was his army, more than double the size of the one he had inherited and much better equipped, trained and officered; less visible, but equally important, were three other achievements: an economy and fiscal system which could be counted on to yield a steady annual revenue of some seven million talers; a war chest of nine million talers; and, above all, a crown which not only commanded an unprecedented degree of authority within all its territories, but also could make its will effective through an administrative machine which, for its time, was perhaps the most rational and efficient in Europe and certainly

10. Vierhaus, *Staaten und Stände*, pp. 289–90.

the best in Germany by a wide margin. That Friedrich Wilhelm himself was possessed of no grand vision of what further purpose might be served by these accomplishments seems clear; what a successor might do with them as his legacy remained to be seen.

CHAPTER TWENTY
The Austro-Prussian Dualism,
1740–1763

The not unexpected death of Friedrich Wilhelm I in May of 1740 conferred his crown on his eldest son, Frederick II, who guided the destinies of the kingdom of Prussia until 1786. Considering the circumstances of his childhood and youth, it would not have been altogether surprising had the young king renounced the model of rulership established by his father to lead a life of cultural refinement and easy courtly amusements for which he had shown much affinity as a youngster. Such interests had earned him the suspicion and contempt of his father, whose view of the responsibilities of rulership explicitly forbade time-consuming and expensive indulgence in the 'frivolities' of high culture and who was morbidly afraid of raising an effeminate sensualist as a successor. His harsh and clumsy efforts to discipline and toughen the crown prince led to an increasing estrangement between the two which reached its nadir in Frederick's unsuccessful attempt to escape father and court during a royal tour in 1730. Imprisoned in Küstrin for a time thereafter, where he was forced to observe the execution of his friend and co-conspirator Katte, the prince began to alter his behaviour (and to some degree his thinking as well) to conform to his father's expectations; indeed, his education in economic and governmental matters really began during his confinement at Küstrin. He eventually obtained his father's pardon, attained a measure of genuine reconciliation and later received a regimental command in Ruppin (the latter in part as reward for accepting an unwanted marriage to a woman he largely ignored during his lifetime and who bore him no children).

While his subsequent career certainly demonstrates that Frederick's 'conversion' to the stern dictates and duties of a kingship conceived along the lines of his father's own rule was anything but superficial, it also never forced him to abandon a deep and genuine devotion to music, literature and the philosophical movements of the early enlightenment, in all of which he found spiritual refuge and solace from the staggering challenges and burdens of his official duties for the rest of his reign. He initiated his extensive correspondence with many of the leading lights of European high culture, including Voltaire, in the mid-1730s and had begun to write down some of his observations and opinions on international relations and political life even before he succeeded his father at age twenty-eight. Yet his practical education for rulership and military command continued in these years and was given some sense of urgency by the chronic ill health of Friedrich Wilhelm in the last several years of his reign. He showed particular interest in foreign affairs in the few years before his accession to the throne and appears to have been influenced by his father's growing hostility to the Habsburgs, based on a long history of both real and imagined slights, deceptions and unfulfilled promises from Austria to the House of Hohenzollern The most recent of these unkept promises was Vienna's failure to support Prussian claims to the duchy of Berg; Friedrich Wilhelm was stubbornly pursuing this claim at the time of his death and for the first few months of Frederick II's new reign it was also the chief business of his foreign policy. But with the sudden death of Emperor Karl VI in October 1740, Frederick drastically changed the whole direction of Prussia's policy through the formulation of a bold plan of attack on the Habsburg province of Silesia; and when he sent his troops across the Silesian border in mid-December, he inaugurated a new era in the political life of the Empire and, indeed, of Europe itself.

While legal arguments supporting old Prussian claims to some parts of Silesia were quickly produced to justify the invasion, its real causes lay partly in Frederick's own (and later self-admitted) desire to win instant glory for himself and his house and partly in the more concrete wish to strengthen the Prussian state by acquiring at least part of one of Austria's most populous and prosperous territories. But timing – the exploitation of a favourable moment – was also of capital importance in the selection of the target. The young and wholly inexperienced successor to Karl VI, his eldest daughter Maria Theresia, now presided over a group of hereditary lands which were in even greater than usual disarray by reason of an empty treasury, old and witless advisers and an army which had emerged both weakened and demoralized from an unsuccessful war against the

Turks that had ended in 1739. Various ruling houses, including those of Bavaria and Spain, were raising claims as heirs in the male line of succession to various parts of her dominions and an anti-Habsburg war party in France was agitating for active support of such claims – especially those of Elector Karl Albrecht of Bavaria, who had assurances of French assistance for just such a case as this by a secret treaty of 1727. Frederick, for his part, commanded a superb army with a full war chest at its disposal and he was keenly aware of the difficulties and confusion which threatened the Austrian court at this very dangerous moment. In calculating his risks, therefore, he had good reason to think that his surprise attack, which quickly overwhelmed the weak Austrian forces in Lower Silesia, would force Maria Theresia to grant terms which, under the circumstances, might seem reasonable: cession to him of various Silesian territories in return for a money indemnity, his vote for her husband Francis at the next imperial election and his formal guarantee of the integrity of the rest of her inheritance.

Maria Theresia's surprising response to this offer – given against the advice of nearly all her advisers – astonished much of Europe and instantly signalled the extraordinary strength of character which distinguished her entire subsequent reign. Anchoring herself in dynastic pride and in her faith in God and unutterably offended by the immorality of Frederick's surprise attack, she refused his terms and resolved to fight, thus discouraging other possible aggressors and encouraging assistance from at least some of the states which had earlier guaranteed her lands by ratifying the Pragmatic Sanction. One traditional ally on which she set her hopes was England. George II (1727–60), whose continuing concern for Hanover was well known, was alarmed by the bellicosity of his Prussian neighbour and was therefore sympathetic to Austria; but because of the peculiarities of England's 'mixed monarchy', George was less in control of British foreign policy than was his *de facto* prime minister Robert Walpole – a fact Maria Theresia and her advisers never seemed quite able to grasp. Walpole, with a majority in the House of Commons forever suspicious that their 'German' king would not hesitate to subordinate English interests to those of Hanover, was at this time chiefly worried about the possibility that France might join Spain in an Anglo-Spanish maritime war that had erupted in 1739; he therefore shied away from providing direct aid to Austria against Prussia (whose friendship he also valued) and urged compromise on Maria Theresia, promising only as a non-belligerent to supply such minor assistance as England had earlier pledged in support of the Pragmatic

Sanction. Other possible sources of aid for Austria – Saxony and Russia for example – decided in favour of neutrality for the moment.

The Silesian war became European in scope and far more dangerous for Austria when the war party in France, led by the duke of Belle-Isle, overcame the objections of the cautious and superannuated prime minister, Cardinal Fleury, and convinced Louis XV to enter into an agreement with Karl Albrecht of Bavaria, promising subsidies and joint military operations in support of the elector's claims to Austrian territories and to the German imperial crown. A first major Prussian battlefield victory over Austrian forces at Mollwitz in April 1741 led the French also to commit themselves to an alliance with Frederick II in June, promising recognition of Prussia's conquest of Lower Silesia against Frederick's renunciation of all claims to the Jülich-Berg inheritance and his pledge to vote for Karl Albrecht at the impending imperial election. George II of England, seeing Hanover threatened on east and west, now hastened to negotiate the electorate's neutrality, also on the basis of a promise to vote for Karl Albrecht. As combined French and Bavarian forces began to gather from mid-1741 on, Maria Theresia's desperate position was eased somewhat by the promise of help she single-handedly wrung from the Hungarian diet by her personal appearance before it (her infant son Joseph in her arms) and by a truce with Prussia arranged by the Convention of Klein-Schnellendorf in October 1741 – a secret and only temporary agreement for which Frederick II's suspicions about the intentions of his own French and Bavarian allies was largely responsible. Nevertheless, Franco-Bavarian forces, now strengthened by the addition of Saxon troops[1], penetrated Bohemia towards the end of the year, capturing Prague in late November; and Prussia, renouncing the truce of October, reentered the war before the end of the year. Karl Albrecht of Bavaria, now the self-appointed king of Bohemia, was elected emperor as Karl VII in January 1742 – an event greeted with little enthusiasm in the Empire and from which the new emperor and his home territory were to reap crushing debts and other misfortunes, but no military or political benefits during the short reign of the only non-Habsburg to wear the imperial crown between 1438 and the dissolution of the Empire in 1806.

1. Elector Friedrich August II of Saxony, who was also King Augustus III of Poland, had weighed both pro- and anti-Austrian alliances since the war began, his principle of choice relating primarily to territorial gain, including especially such as would enable him to link Saxony and Poland by a common border. By late 1741, he decided to ally with France in return for assurances of various prospective conquests from Austria – some of which worried Frederick II and helped push him towards the Convention of Klein-Schnellendorf.

While Karl VII was celebrating his new dignity in Frankfurt, however, he was losing Bavaria to a powerful Austrian assault; this was the beginning of a significant reversal of Vienna's military fortunes, which continued with the failure of a Prussian-Saxon advance on Moravia and increasing Austrian pressure on French forces in Bohemia. Frederick, now feeling the pinch of an emptying war chest, plagued by troop exhaustion and worried that recent Franco-Bavarian defeats might result in a separate peace with Austria, proved amenable to negotiations towards which both he and Maria Theresia were being pushed by a British government that was eager to separate Prussia from its French ally, against whom direct military action was being contemplated in London. Maria Theresia, though reluctant to make peace, was convinced to do so by the prospect of increased English assistance against France, as well as by a timely Prussian victory at Chotusitz in May 1742; a preliminary peace in June was made definitive in the Peace of Berlin of July, by which Frederick exited the war in return for possession of most of Silesia. Since both England and Holland had now entered the war against France as auxiliaries of Austria, Saxony, fearing isolation, also made peace with Austria a few weeks later. The so-called Pragmatic Army of the Anglo-Dutch allies, moving into western Germany, registered successes against French forces from mid-1743 on; these, together with Vienna's own slowly growing strength and its new alliance with the fickle Saxon elector, seemed to promise a complete turnabout in Austria's once-desperate position and the likelihood of the deposition of the Wittelsbach Emperor Karl VII.

Frederick II, though now a neutral observer, was increasingly alarmed by Austria's new-found vigour and began to fear for his own title to Silesia; thus, after contracting a new alliance with Louis XV in June of 1744, he renewed his war with Austria by a sudden attack on Bohemia in August. For a time, this appeared to be a mistake: his army, beset by illness and logistical problems, stalled in Bohemia and was eventually forced to retreat back to Silesia; worse yet, his luckless Bavarian ally Karl VII died in January 1745 and was succeeded by his son Max III Joseph, who abandoned his father's ambitions and ill-fated policies and made peace with Austria in April, renouncing all claims to Austrian territory and to the imperial crown. Frederick, fearing desertion by his war-weary French ally, was now forced to wage a desperate defensive war against combined Austrian and Saxon armies, but did so with such brilliant success throughout the second half of 1745 that Austria, anticipating the total collapse of Saxony and urged along by England, reluctantly agreed to end the war in December; the Peace of Dresden reconfirmed Prussian possession of Silesia against Frederick's recognition of Maria Theresia's husband as Emperor Franz I, a position the latter had obtained by majority vote of the electors in September.

While the German issues of this War of the Austrian Succession were now settled[2], the larger struggle of which they were a part continued. France, allied with Spain, fought an increasingly difficult maritime, colonial and continental war against a somewhat ungainly coalition which included Austria, Britain, Holland and Sardinia. Most actual fighting ended in 1747. By that time, Holland, never happy about the war to begin with, was talking peace with France, while Louis XV was worried that negotiations between Spain and Britain which had been continuing since late 1746 might lead to Madrid's defection as an ally. French finances were bad, furthermore, while Britain's naval superiority was ruining French maritime and colonial trade. Such factors, together with Louis XV's own war-weariness, came together at Aix-la-Chapelle (Aachen) in late 1748 to end a war in which nearly all participants had by now lost interest. By the terms of the treaty hammered out there and which were largely dictated by England and France, territorial changes were few, mostly at minor expense to Austria's Italian possessions: Parma went to Spain and some pieces of Lombardy were awarded to Sardinia as the price of an alliance contracted in 1743. Significantly, both France and Britain insisted on writing a guarantee of Prussia's conquest of Silesia into this treaty, even though Frederick II was not even a party to it – certain evidence of the desire of both powers to court the favour of a state whose impressive military achievements since 1740 marked it as a major player in the game of international politics for the future.

While it would seem obvious that Austria, shorn of most of the rich and strategically important province of Silesia, as well as of some less important Italian territories, was a heavy loser in the late war (and was in fact so regarded by a pained Maria Theresia herself), the situation of the Habsburg inheritance in 1748 was not a deplorable one, especially by comparison with what many observers had confidently predicted would happen in the darkest days of 1741: the collapse of the monarchy and the wholesale partitioning of its

2. German historiography often treats these German issues separately by reference to three 'Silesian Wars' – the first (1740–2) ending at the Peace of Berlin, the second (1744–5) at Dresden and the third, terminating at Hubertusburg, as essentially coextensive with the larger Seven Years War (1756–63).

territories among a host of greedy neighbours. In some respects, indeed, the most important result of the war was the survival of the House of Austria. That result, however, was due about as much to the restraint shown by Austria's enemies at one or another point in the war (by France in 1741–2, for example, or by Prussia after 1745) as to Vienna's own efforts, heroic though they were. This fact was recognized in Austria even as the war proceeded and from 1745–6 onward, several changes in the administration of military and financial affairs were undertaken, whose importance lay perhaps less in the relatively minor immediate benefits they brought than in demonstrating how much deeper and more extensive any reform aimed at fundamentally strengthening the monarchy would have to be.

Such reform began in earnest in 1748, based on the plans of Count F. W. Haugwitz (1702–65), the able administrator of Austrian Silesia (that small part of Silesia left to Austria after the Prussian conquest), who had learned much from the reorganization imposed on the rest of the province by its new Prussian masters. What Haugwitz proposed and first carried out in Silesia was nothing less than the elimination of the estates' participation in all internal political and fiscal affairs, which henceforth were to be directed and administered by agencies and personnel appointed by and responsible to the central government. While the right of the estates to vote their 'contribution' remained, it was made clear not only that the amounts so voted were to follow the government's recommendations (meaning that they increased substantially, supposedly to make up for the increased costs of functions now assumed by the crown), but also that refusals to vote the suggested sums would not hinder their actual collection. Landlords retained various seigneurial privileges, including judicial ones; but the overall effect of Haugwitz's scheme was to abolish almost all those characteristics of the dualistic *Ständestaat* which had denied the central government direct administrative contact with its own subjects, had kept its revenues low and unpredictable and, in short, had crippled its ability to augment or even to tap its own human and material resources to anything resembling the degree necessary for its security in the persistently menacing international climate of the eighteenth century.

Given the great political differences and the distances which separated Hungary, Transylvania, the Netherlands and the Italian territories from the Austrian–Bohemian lands, the reformers wisely chose to concentrate their chief efforts on the latter alone – the nuclear provinces of the monarchy, so to speak. A fundamental reorganization of the administrative structure in these areas was instituted in order to accommodate both old and new responsibilities assumed by new direct agents of the crown. At the local level, a total of some forty-seven so-called District Offices (*Kreisämter*) were established, each headed by a District Officer (*Kreishauptmann*) with a small staff of subordinates. Originally restricted primarily to military and logistical tasks, as well as to keeping the peasantry in a proper state of taxability, the District Officers' functions grew rapidly throughout the 1750s and 1760s and they eventually became the virtual governors of their districts. They reported to a group of new provincial boards in German Austria and Bohemia, eleven in number, which were eventually known as *Gubernia*; these boards, in turn, reported to a new central agency in Vienna, the *Directorium in publicis et cameralibus* (or *Directorium in internis*), which took over much of the work of the old Court Chamber and completely replaced the two hitherto separate chancelleries for Austria and Bohemia.[3]

Accompanying this administrative reform, which was of vital importance to Austria's future attempts to mobilize resources from the local level upward, were certain other changes of equal significance. First, most judicial functions were segregated from administrative ones, chiefly to insure greater efficiency in both; a new and rationalized chain of appeals split the provincial courts from the *Gubernia* and capped the entire system with a new high office of justice, the Supreme Judicature, in Vienna. Second, beginning as early as 1742, the direction of foreign affairs was consolidated and improved by the creation of what amounted to a single foreign office for the monarchy – the House, Court and State Chancellery; this step meant, among other things, that relations with the Empire would henceforth be handled with the same cool objectivity that applied to all other foreign countries and demonstrates a weakening of Vienna's sense of a special German imperial mission. Third, the formation of a new Directory of Commerce provides evidence of a more determined attempt to invigorate the economy as a whole; its work, however, while beneficial, brought no revolutionary results to an

---

3. There was a very strong functional similarity between the *Directorium in internis* and *Gubernia* in Austria and the General Directory and the provincial War and Domains Chambers in Prussia; the District Officers, on the other hand, combined most of the functions and powers of the two chief local officials in Prussia (the Tax Commissioner and the Rural Commissioner). On paper, at least, the new Austrian administration was therefore even more centralized than that of Prussia. The similarities were no accident, representing Haugwitz's tribute to the Prussian system.

economy which remained stubbornly backward in many ways. Finally and most important, the entire tax structure of the Austrian-Bohemian lands was reformed, primarily to raise the annual sum of fourteen million guilders per year which Haugwitz set as the cost of creating and maintaining a standing (peacetime) army of 108,000 men to provide the minimum adequacy of military security. The annual votes of the estates were replaced by ten-year grants – thus destroying the last vestiges of the estates' rights and duties with respect to recruitment, outfitting and provisioning of the army – and a new land tax was imposed which, while burdening the peasantry more heavily than landlords, for the first time subjected both nobles and clergy to this form of direct taxation. Various personal taxes were collapsed into a single and much fairer income tax, while indirect taxes on non-essential goods were raised and a new tax on investment income was imposed; and, as part of a strengthened mercantilist programme, numerous provincial, corporate and private tolls and duties were replaced by new protective tariffs and import prohibitions on the monarchy's frontiers.

The overall impact of these reforms, carried out with whirlwind rapidity, can scarcely be overestimated: they virtually transformed the Austrian state from an old-fashioned *Ständestaat* – an aristocratic republic in which the monarchy was forced to beg, wheedle and cajole its resources from the often refractory (and always stubbornly independent) estates – into a much more resolutely and confidently governed state with the ability to formulate and execute something resembling a unified national policy. Instead of a kaleidoscopic congeries of more or less independent territories and provinces, the Habsburg monarchy could now be looked at as a single state composed of Austria, Bohemia and (in spite of the continuing peculiarities of its position) Hungary, with dependencies in the Netherlands and in Italy which took on increasingly secondary importance to the integrity of the compact bloc of central European lands. As might be expected, the reforms were attended by vigorous protest from several sources, including not only representatives of the noble and clerical estates, but some high-ranking personnel within the government as well; the former were angered both by the new taxes and their exclusion from the political process, while the latter – also nobles – disliked not only these changes but also some unanticipated bureaucratic difficulties which accompanied the reform. Chief among these was the tendency of the *Directorium in internis* to absorb so many and functionally diverse other offices (including, by 1757, the Directory of Commerce, the General War

Commissariat and the Board of Coinage and Mining) that it became unwieldy and noticeably less efficient. Under the new strains of the Seven Years War (1756–63), the dangers of administrative confusion not only prompted some disaggregation of this overburdened super-agency, but also led to Haugwitz's ouster, on honourable terms, from his important position as chief of the *Directorium*. By late 1760, a new figure enjoyed ascendancy in the government: Wenzel Anton, Count (later Prince) Kaunitz (1711–94), who, like Haugwitz, was to make a deep impression on the Austrian state and about whom more will be said elsewhere.

No such fundamental reorganizations as those which occurred in Austria took place in Prussia in the first fifteen years or so of Frederick II's reign. Unlike Maria Theresia, for whom war had meant drastic reform as the only alternative to destruction, Frederick (who was actually at war for less than three full years of the period 1740–56) could afford the luxury of only fine-tuning the governmental and administrative system he had inherited – a system whose considerable merits were saluted by Austria's attempts to imitate it. Soon after his accession, however, the king created a fifth department in the General Directory to direct commerce and manufactures, giving early expression to his strong interest in the development of the non-agrarian sectors of the economy – an interest soon even more emphatically emphasized by his invasion of Silesia. Some later changes came about because of Frederick's experiences in and conquests from the war itself; thus, in 1746 he created a sixth department in the General Directory for military administration to grapple with financial and other problems that had not existed in the peacetime army of his father, but which quickly surfaced in his own larger army on its wartime footing. To coordinate Silesian affairs with those of the rest of the kingdom, as well as for certain treaty reasons, the province was not administered through the General Directory, but was directly governed by the crown; and the principle of religious toleration Frederick enunciated at the outset of his reign became essential to the political integration of the majority Catholic population of Silesia, whose inhabitants by the 1780s constituted a full quarter of the total population of the monarchy.

The years of peace following the end of the Second Silesian War were a period of slow but steady growth of the Prussian economy, which allowed Frederick to refill his depleted treasury and to undertake various schemes of economic improvement, including the drainage and resettlement of marshlands in the Oder valley. The absorption of East Frisia (*Ostfriesland*) by succession in 1744 brought some 100,000 new subjects under the king's rule, though attempts to exploit the province's geographical position by launching an overseas trading operation (the Asiatic Company) in Emden proved disappointing and were later abandoned (see above, Chapter Eleven). These peacetime years were probably also the happiest and relatively most carefree of Frederick's reign, during which he indulged his interests in music, literature and philosophy at the many soirées and other entertainments he arranged for small groups of acquaintances at his beautiful but modest palace of Sans-Souci in Potsdam. Such diversions, however, did not diminish his attention to his domestic duties or his alertness to foreign affairs. As his Political Testament of 1752 shows, he was sharply aware of the continuing geopolitical awkwardness and vulnerability of Prussia's international position: exposed to potential enemies in the east (Poland and Russia), the north (Sweden) and the south (Saxony and Austria), Frederick could not afford to regard his borders as eternally secure, or to ignore such favourable opportunities as might present themselves for new conquests to rationalize and further strengthen those borders. He knew, however, that such opportunities were not now his to create and that, for the moment, it was enough to keep the peace and hold fast to what he had.

For Maria Theresia and her advisers, on the other hand, keeping the peace was not a high priority at all; regaining Silesia *was*. They had turned over this province to the 'robber baron' king of Prussia only with the greatest pain and reluctance, recognizing that in doing so they had lost one of the richest nuclear lands of the Austrian-Bohemian inheritance, a sacrifice for which no adequate compensation – or indeed any compensation at all – had been received.[4] This disagreeable fact was one reason why Vienna believed it could not rely on a reconstitution of its old alliance system with the maritime powers as the basis for a war of revenge against Prussia: Britain had at all times in the late war evinced an unwillingness to offend Prussia, had used its military forces exclusively against France, had constantly pressured Austria by threats of withholding subsidies to compromise with Frederick and, as a final insult, had reneged on its promise to secure compensation at the peace table for such losses as Austria might suffer. The British, for their part, were equally unhappy with Austria over various issues, while the Dutch, reluctant

4. Bavaria might have provided more than enough compensation, had Austria been able to annex it permanently during the darkest days of the Wittelsbach Emperor Karl VII; if that had happened, it is arguable that the recovery of Silesia would not have been a compelling cause for war after 1748.

and stingy allies to begin with, absolutely could not be counted on as effective partners in another war. Vienna's other alternative – albeit a revolutionary one – was to seek reconciliation with its ancient enemy France. This strategem would aim at separating France from Prussia and under optimum circumstances at an alliance between Vienna and Versailles, backed by an Austrian promise of eventual territorial gain for France in the Austrian Netherlands. The shrewd and perceptive minister Count Kaunitz, in particular, had long since decided that this remote Habsburg possession, difficult and expensive to defend against France and of small intrinsic economic value, had little importance compared to the possible recovery of Silesia. Maria Theresia had independently reached much the same conclusion and in 1750 she sent Kaunitz to Versailles to discuss some sort of understanding with Louis XV. The latter gave the Austrian minister a polite hearing, but nothing else: old suspicions, as well as Louis's unwillingness to abandon his most powerful ally in Germany (in spite of the mutual personal dislike that existed between him and the Prussian king), combined to send Kaunitz home empty-handed. It was significant, however, that the French court, while not responding positively to these Austrian overtures, had not absolutely rejected them, either; and in spite of episodes of Franco-Prussian collaboration on various minor German imperial issues in the early 1750s, Kaunitz's wise advice to wait upon further events was accepted by Maria Theresia, who showed her continuing confidence in him by appointing him chancellor in 1753.

In 1754, as renewed hostilities between France and Britain over maritime and colonial issues once again erupted, the British government, fearful that the war would extend to the continent, sought protection for George II's electorate of Hanover by offering a new subsidy treaty to Maria Theresia, expecting her to commit herself to the defence of the Austrian Netherlands against France. But she and Kaunitz had no thought of replaying the late war; if a new conflict broke out on the continent, they would not divide their forces but would employ all against Prussia alone. By a reply which set very expensive terms for a renewed alliance with Britain, Vienna in effect rejected it and the British did not pursue the matter further. From this arose two consequences: first, Austrian negotiators once again appeared in Versailles to see if the French, in view of the escalating British threat, were now prepared to be more accommodating to the notion of an Austro-French rapprochement; and second, the British, fearing a revitalization of the Franco-Prussian alliance of the late war which could find Prussian troops marching into Hanover at a moment's notice and after unsuccessful negotiations with Prussia for a guarantee that it would not attack the electorate, found in Tsaritsa Elizabeth of Russia a new guarantor for Hanover: in September 1755, against hefty subsidies, the Empress agreed to maintain a large army in Livonia, ready to march as needed against Prussia. Frederick II, now seeing himself in worst case as open to attack on three fronts (Russia on the east, Saxony and Austria on the south and an army of Hanoverians and English, Dutch and mercenary German auxiliaries to the west) and with little help from a France preoccupied with naval and colonial conflict, made haste to escape this trap: in January 1756, he concluded an *ad hoc* accord with Britain, known as the Convention of Westminster, which contained a pledge of mutual neutrality as well as an agreement to combine their forces to resist attack on Germany by any foreign power.

Britain was thus reassured and Frederick had relieved himself of the nightmare of a three-front war without – as he believed – abrogating his existing treaty of alliance with France, since that agreement was purely defensive in nature and in any case did not apply to any war which originated outside of Europe (as the current Anglo-French war had). But Louis XV was in no mood to accept legalistic arguments, or to forgive the acid-tongued and presumptuous Prussian king for the sin of making agreements of any sort with a Britain which had by now replaced Austria as the arch-enemy of France's interests; and so, in spite of continuing misgivings which had stalled negotiations with Austria for months, Louis signed a defensive alliance with Vienna in May 1756 (the First Treaty of Versailles).[5] But this was only a half-victory for Kaunitz; to be sure, he had assured Austria of a new continental ally in case of a Prussian attack, but he had not gained France as an active partner in the offensive war against Frederick both he and his empress-queen so much wanted to start. Without France, he was unwilling to move, even though Elizabeth of Russia was almost indecently eager to assist in such an attack.[6] Two possibilities remained, however: if Prussia

5. This was the only genuinely revolutionary aspect of the so-called 'Diplomatic Revolution' of 1756, which in other respects merely confirmed the new priorities of foreign policy which had emerged in both France and Austria; for the former, the struggle against British colonial and seaborne commercial supremacy and for the latter the assurance of continued great-power status by the recovery of Silesia and the reduction of Prussian influence in Germany.

6. Elizabeth, who hated Frederick, had signed the subsidy treaty with Britain in 1755 with every expectation of using the money to launch an attack on Prussia, her eventual goal being to detach East Prussia and later to exchange it for Polish territory contiguous to Russia. Until her death, she fuelled the emotional engine of the anti-Prussian coalition even more than Maria Theresia herself.

could somehow be lured into attacking Austria, then France would be forced to send armies to fight Prussia regardless of Louis's desires in the matter; or, on the other hand, perhaps Versailles would agree to an offensive role if, in return for the recovery of Silesia, Austria would abdicate all or most of the Austrian Netherlands to France. Negotiations on the latter possibility were in fact progressing throughout the summer of 1756; but they were rendered irrelevant by Frederick II's sudden attack on Saxony in late August, initiating the first military actions of what was to be known in Europe as the Seven Years War and in Germany as the Third Silesian War.

Whatever long-range dreams Frederick may have entertained about further territorial conquests, it seems clear that his attack on Saxony was prompted primarily by defensive considerations: he had many bits and pieces of both diplomatic and military intelligence which indicated purposeful war preparations within a loose but steadily coalescing group of powers which intended Prussia no good and his strike at Saxony (also no friend of Prussia) was merely the first strategic step of a campaign directed against Austria, but ultimately aimed at halting or reversing the process of alliance-building among his enemies. In this larger aim, he was woefully unsuccessful; by May 1757, through the (Second) Treaty of Versailles, France, Austria and Russia had agreed on the specific terms of their individual contributions to a joint war against Prussia, as well as on a spoilation of Prussia which, if realized, would reduce that kingdom to the level of a second-rate electorate. Sweden, seeking to increase its north German coastline at Prussian expense, quickly joined the now perfected coalition and, in contrast to the previous war, French and Austrian diplomats were able to evoke a military response against Prussia from the Empire by a majority vote of its diet early in 1757. Frederick's only allies were a distant England, as well as several German states linked to England by political ties or treaties – Hanover, of course, but also Hesse-Kassel, Saxe-Gotha and Brunswick. For a time, however, it appeared that these allies would be of little or no help, especially after their 45,000-man defensive 'Army of Observation' subsidized by George II in Hanover was boxed in by superior French forces and was forced to disband by the Convention of Kloster Zeven in September 1757.

Meanwhile, Frederick's own campaigning had not gone well. To be sure, he speedily overwhelmed the Saxon army and thereafter incorporated it into his own, subjecting the electorate itself to substantial contributions and requisitions for the remainder of the war; but his initially successful advance on Prague was stopped short in June of 1757 and while he was then forced to evacuate Bohemia, the inept manoeuvres of another Prussian corps under his brother August Wilhelm left Silesia itself open to invasion. Austrian troops soon occupied both Lower Silesia and Lusatia, a Russian army forced its way into East Prussia, Swedish forces advanced into Prussian Pomerania and an Austrian raiding party was even able to occupy Berlin for a short time, extorting contributions from the astonished citizens of the Prussian capital. All of this unsettling news came to a Frederick who in the meantime had marched northwestward from Bohemia to meet an additional threat from a combined army of French and German imperial troops in Thuringia; there, in November, after several unsuccessful attempts to force a battle, he routed this joint force in the short but subsequently much celebrated battle of Rossbach, by which his title as 'Frederick the Great' became secure. Thus temporarily secured on his western flank, Frederick hastened back to Silesia, where the Prussian military situation had continued to deteriorate and, after recombining and strengthening his troops both morally and materially, won a major battle against superior Austrian forces at Leuthen in early December, a victory which led to the recovery of all of Silesia.

The campaigning of the spring of 1758 began under bright auspices for Prussia, especially since the rise of William Pitt as leader of the British war effort had resulted in a reversal of the earlier minimalism of England's efforts on the continent: Pitt not only repudiated the Convention of Kloster Zeven and ordered the reestablishment of a new and larger Army of Observation, well subsidized and brilliantly commanded by Prince Ferdinand of Brunswick, but also authorized the payment of large and badly needed subsidies to Prussia. The subsequent actions of this new army effectively neutralized French forces in western Germany, removing them as a threat to Prussia for the remainder of the war. But Frederick's own campaigning throughout 1758 produced a mixed picture of victories and defeats. By the end of the year, on the positive side, he remained in control of all his own territories except for East Prussia, continued to occupy Saxony and had essentially disposed of Sweden as a threat; but this result had been achieved at a terrific cost in money, men and equipment. Such losses became more than ever apparent throughout 1759 and 1760, when the king's earlier field force of 150,000 men was reduced to around 100,000, standing against enemies whose armies were somewhat more than double that size. By 1761, both sides were engaged in what amounted to a war of attrition, but with somewhat different objectives: Frederick, fighting a desperate defensive campaign under the guise of the offence, hoped by merely surviving to encourage such signs of war-weariness as had become visible in Versailles and Vienna (though not in St. Petersburg, where the warmongering Tsaritsa Elizabeth remained as grimly committed as ever to Prussia's destruction), while his opponents, sensing the increasing exhaustion of his resources if not his determination, kept up a pressure which was often tactically bungled but strategically sound. As the year went on, no objective observer, including Frederick himself, would have predicted that Prussia could escape an early and disastrous fate at the hands of its enemies. Saved so far as much by the disruptive jealousies and military ineptitude of his Austrian and Russian adversaries as by his own heroic efforts, Frederick also became joyless witness to the fall of the energetic William Pitt and the rise of the diffident and conciliatory Lord Bute in the British cabinet in the late summer of 1761, bringing a further cooling of relations with his only major ally that had begun with the accession of George III the previous year. With a number of the very territories from which he drew men, money and supplies under enemy occupation in the hard winter of 1761–2, it appeared that Frederick and with him Prussia, were doomed.

At this moment, however, occurred one of those fantastic twists of fate which occasionally make nonsense of even the most inarguably certain historical predictabilities. On 5 January 1762, Elizabeth of Russia died, bringing to the throne her unstable nephew Peter III. Peter distrusted Austria, hated France – and literally worshipped Frederick the Great (whose role he assumed as commander of the army of toy soldiers he played with as crown prince, even as his country was fighting Prussia). In May 1762, Peter not only signed a peace by which all Russian conquests were restored to Prussia, but in June also entered into an alliance with Frederick by which a part of the Russian army was put at Prussia's disposal. Frederick, in return, gave a tongue-in-cheek promise of future support for an effort to assert the rights of Peter's relatives in Schleswig-Holstein against the king of Denmark. This absurd Russo-Prussian agreement lasted just long enough for Frederick to make a single but effective use of Russian troops against Austrian positions in July 1762; but Peter's wife, a princess of Anhalt-Zerbst, removed her imbecilic husband from the scene by murder in the same month and, after assuming the throne herself as Catherine II, repudiated the new alliance. With no interest in a war against Austria for Prussian interests, however, Catherine also had no desire to reenter the war against Frederick and therefore confirmed the peace made in May. As a reinvigorated Prussia now registered further military successes and through diplomatic pressure effected a declaration of neutrality from the imperial diet, a disgruntled and disgusted Austria, faced with an already concluded preliminary peace between France and Britain in November and with no prospects against Prussia more promising than an expensive and exhausting stalemate, agreed to negotiate a peace. A final treaty, mediated by Saxony, was signed at Hubertusburg, near Leipzig, in mid-February of 1763; by its terms, the territorial *status quo ante bellum* was confirmed, including the full restoration of Saxony and Prussian ownership of Silesia. Frederick's only concession was his agreement to vote for Maria Theresia's eldest son Joseph as Roman King, clearing the way for the latter's automatic succession to his father's imperial throne in 1765.

Though this war had exacted a toll on his kingdom which was to dominate its economic life for years after peace was concluded, Frederick carried away from it gains incalculably important to Prussia's future. Not the least of these were the images formed of him and of his state in the minds of Germans and other Europeans, who had perhaps admired the boldness and cunning of the young king in his original conquest of Silesia, but who were far more deeply impressed by the mature qualities of determination and stoic steadfastness in the face of repeated adversity he and his armies had demonstrated in this much longer and more bitter war. This produced a respect and admiration that was both greater than and different from that ordinarily given to a great soldier[7] and which was coloured by the reputation he had already acquired as an enlightened or 'philosophical' ruler. There is no doubt that Frederick's personal renown blended with the known strengths of his government and administration to produce the picture of a state considerably more

7. In the narrower military sense, indeed, there is no reason to think of Frederick as a genius, however unusually alert, competent and clearheaded he may have been. He lost half the battles in which he held immediate field command (and not always against larger forces) and as a tactician was perhaps only somewhat superior to the average of his time. His overall strategy, furthermore, was essentially handed to him by geography and the nature and number of his enemies – though he was at least shrewd enough to recognize the dictates of his circumstances; and, like many other Prussian general officers, he reacted to his defeats with an energy and determination which were not the property of most field commanders in other armies of the time. He also kept the loyalty of his troops better than most commanders, being keenly attentive to their food and quarters while sharing their privations and dangers.

powerful than its population and resources, left to themselves, would otherwise justify. Still, in more concrete terms, the importance of his retention of Silesia should not be underestimated: this was the great and now permanent material gain without which Prussia's role as an independent force in European international politics was barely imaginable, at least for the time being; in this sense, it was the factor which permitted Prussia finally and truly to escape the perils of clientage to one or another great power and was for that reason perhaps the finest gift Frederick could possibly have offered up on the altar of his father's memory.

CHAPTER TWENTY-ONE

The Development of Prussia and Austria, 1763–1790

While Frederick the Great's achievements through the end of the Seven Years War had elevated him to a position of respect in European public opinion unique among the sovereigns of his time, they had also left a deep and ineradicable impress on his personality. Stressed to the limits of psychological and physical endurance by the continuous challenges and dangers of a long and bitter war he almost lost; and driven for many years thereafter by the different but equally demanding tasks of reconstructing his seriously damaged country and of defending its newly-won political position in Europe, Frederick lost most of the exuberant lightheartedness he often displayed earlier in his reign. Physically gaunt, preoccupied by the constant pressure of crushing responsibilities and often irritable (especially during painful episodes of the gout which plagued his later years), the king developed a strong misanthropic bent which was particularly evident in his behaviour towards his bureaucrats, the majority of whom he suspected of laziness, graft or one or another kind of obstructionism. An extreme reserve in all his personal relationships, perhaps resulting from the self-protective secretiveness he developed in childhood as a shield against his father's insults and rages, made him an increasingly isolated and emotionally lonely figure in whom unremitting service to the state and to the welfare of his people as he understood them swept all other human considerations aside and led him to presume wilful indolence in all who did not work as hard as he.

And work hard he certainly did. Never was there a monarch who believed more strongly in his right to rule than did Frederick, but never, also, was there one who tied that right more absolutely to public duty. Frederick genuinely believed in a social contract theory of government, derived from the natural law constructs of the early enlightenment and in that respect he broke sharply with the religiously-inspired patriarchal and patrimonial concept of rulership which had prevailed as recently as his father's reign. Frederick's view was that a prince had the right to govern and to be obeyed, but only on the iron condition that he in turn respect the right of his subjects to be governed in their own best interest. In the end it was the monarch who defined that 'best interest', of course; but that merely put an extra premium on his personal enlightenment, reinforced by accurate information, good judgment and dedicated hard work. That there was no hint of popular sovereignty in this doctrine cannot be surprising, given the times; more noteworthy is the fact that Frederick acted out his view of himself as but 'the first servant of the state' on every day of a hard and self-denying life. On the other hand, there is no evidence that Frederick defined the public welfare to which he was committed in the progressive terms of forever increasing levels of popular enlightenment or material well being; that notion, not strong in the German enlightenment in general (or elsewhere, for that matter, until somewhat later), was discouraged not only by Frederick's increasingly dim view of human nature, but also by the generally abysmal level of popular education and the stubbornly backward condition of the economy, which would hardly have led anyone to predict the advent of a spiritual or material welfare state anytime soon. Frederick's 'welfare' had much more to do with physical, spiritual and economic *security*, a goal which at this fundamental level could realistically be achieved by governmental control, guidance and encouragement. His foreign policy, after allowing for the youthful dalliance with 'glory' in the first years of his reign, was essentially directed towards the same objective in political terms: for him, no philosophical considerations dictated an obligation to be passive, or pacific, in a dangerous world where inattention to self-interest was an invitation to aggression by others. If Frederick's own aggressions mark him as no saint, he also did not live in the company of saints; what made him different from other rulers was not the lesser degree of his moral rectitude but the greater degree of his successes, which were the result of a sober analysis of Prussia's vulnerabilities, his sharp eye for opportunities and his remarkable personal qualities as a ruler. To the latter must be reckoned considerable self-restraint, because except for the initial conquest of Silesia, there was little adventurism in his foreign policy, which from as early as 1742 became primarily defensive and security-oriented.

331

In spite of his gains, however, neither Frederick nor his immediate successors accepted the equality of their kingdom with the other great powers that was conceded in public diplomacy. In population and overall resources, Prussia simply could not stand comparison with Britain, France, Russia or Austria. For that reason, a strong emphasis on raw military strength had to continue. Far from demobilizing the army after 1763, Frederick augmented it: by the end of his reign, it numbered between 190–200,000 men, though as a proportion of the total and greatly increased population of the country (less than 4 per cent of a 1786 population of nearly 5.5 million) it was no larger than in 1740. This military force was about equal to that of France, but smaller than that of either Austria or Russia; it seldom accounted for less than 80 per cent of the state's budget, but in view of the furlough system which in peacetime liberated nearly half the troops for agricultural or industrial employment for much of the year, the costs were bearable. While the formal training of officers was still inadequate – even a new War Academy founded by Frederick in Berlin in 1765 took only a handful of students – the experiences of the Seven Years War brought about a permanent separation of military command from administration through a highly centralized system of recruitment and supply which in removing all such responsibilities from field commanders professionalized the army as never before.

The economy which supported this army and all other government expenditures, was not greatly different in character from that of Friedrich Wilhelm I's reign; Prussia remained a very predominantly agrarian country, in which for a long time grain, wood and woollens remained the chief exports. More even than his father, however, Frederick was convinced that manufacturing was the wave of the future – which accounts for much of his interest in annexing Silesia, a province which eventually accounted for nearly half of the import-export trade of the entire kingdom. Silesia's fine linens, woollen goods, pottery and glassware were well regarded all over Europe. Of greatest long-term significance, however, was the Silesian mining industry which under the direction of the Saxon expert F. A. von Heinitz after 1777 became the most modern industry in Prussia; the value of its output of coal, iron, lead, cobalt and other minerals equalled that of the country's entire agricultural sector by 1800. In general, Frederick adopted a strong protectionism in industrial policy; this was standard mercantilist practice, of course, but for Frederick it was also a means of insuring the livelihood of his subjects, including both bourgeois entrepreneurs and noble families whose estates produced not only grain, flax, wool and other basic agricultural goods, but also a host of processed commodities such as flour, lumber, lime, bricks and alcoholic spirits. Tax remissions, outright gifts of money or buildings and grants and monopolies were used to encourage new industries, especially in the decade of vigorous reconstruction after 1763, and the government itself owned (and monopolized) several manufacturing enterprises, including porcelain, tobacco and silk, as well as parts of a rapidly expanding shipbuilding industry in Stettin. To encourage the movement of goods, Frederick largely abolished internal tolls, repositioning them at the frontiers instead and as early as the 1740s built both the Plauer and Finow canals to round out and improve connections between the Oder and the Elbe, with the important manufacturing complexes of Brandenburg, Potsdam and Berlin in the middle; soon after the annexation of West Prussia in 1772, another new canal linked the Vistula to the Oder, via the Netze, thus providing cheap and direct east–west transportation from East Prussia to the central provinces. In light of the devastated condition of the economy after the Seven Years War, its ability to generate a surplus of exports over imports of some three million talers by the early 1780s was a considerable achievement.

Frederick's special interest in manufacturing implied no neglect of agriculture. For some years after 1763, when basic reconstruction was the highest priority, the king authorized low interest loans, outright gifts of money, tax concessions, grants of seed grain and lumber and loans of military draft animals to assist both peasants and estate owners to reinvigorate the rural economy; later, when expenses arising primarily from reconstruction nevertheless threatened to dislocate many noble families by submerging their estates under a mountain of unpayable debts, Frederick organized the so-called *Landschaften*, rural credit institutes restricted to the nobility which permitted owners to mortgage estates up to half or more of their assessed value to pay off indebtedness and initiate improvements.[1] As an agricultural innovator, Frederick had considerably more

---

1. The *Landschaften* were so good a source of ready cash that some nobles used mortgage money simply to buy up other estates, touching off a lively land speculation in the last decades of the century. When tight restrictions on bourgeois ownership of such estates were relaxed after Frederick's death, commoners entered the market and by 1800 owned some 10 per cent of all noble estates in the monarchy. Robert M. Berdahl, *The Politics of the Prussian Nobility: the Development of a Conservative Ideology, 1770–1848* (Princeton, 1988), p. 82.

success on the royal domains than on private aristocratic estates, since reforms commanded for the former could only be recommended for the latter; only in the important policy of protecting peasants from displacement by landlords seeking to expand their dominical lands at the expense of peasant tenancies were Frederick's efforts on noble lands largely successful. Of the domainal reforms, perhaps the most important were the conversion of most peasant farms into hereditary tenancies and the contractual limitation and regulation of labour services; together, these measures provided new incentives and opportunities for agricultural improvement and, when combined with edicts ordering consolidation of strip fields and the partition of village common lands among individual peasants, resulted in the creation of thousands of more productive farms of desirable medium size. While various complications prevented the outright abolition of serfdom even on the royal domains, servitude was not allowed in the peasant colonies established on the reclaimed marshlands of the Oder valley (1747–53) and the Netze district (after 1772); these resettlements of free peasants drawn from other parts of Germany and Europe were a significant achievement of Frederick's reign, augmenting Prussia's population by some 250–300,000 souls in over 1500 new villages and outlying farms. Frederick paid even more attention to grain policy than did his predecessors and especially to the storage of reserves which assured consumers and producers a relatively steady price for grain and flour in both good and bad harvest years; ten times larger in 1786 than in 1740, these reserves not only provided bread at normal prices during a particularly serious inflation of the early 1770s, but also reduced price volatility in other sectors of the economy which always accompanied sharp fluctuations in food costs.

While the 'contribution' of the noble estates and the urban excise tax continued to provide the bulk of the state's income, supplemented by domainal and regalian income, such sources were wholly inadequate to defray the enormous costs of Prussia's war effort between 1756–63, estimated at 100 million talers. Even with nearly three-quarters of that sum covered by a combination of English subsidies (16 million) and forcible exactions from occupied Saxony and Mecklenburg (50 and 8 million, respectively) Frederick eventually had to rely on such expedients as debasement of the coinage and the issuance of promissory notes. But since he recognized the importance of financial credibility, he paid off his notes very quickly and as early as 1764 was able to restore the currency to the peacetime value originally set by the important Coinage Ordinance of 1750, which by permanently fixing the silver content of the Prussian taler had equalized its real and nominal value; since it had subsequently become the standard for all German states which used the taler, the restoration of its integrity was indispensable to the favourable balance of trade Prussia once again achieved by the early 1770s.

Still, financial administration was not one of the most regularized facets of the Prussian government, largely because Frederick deliberately maintained a variety of treasuries (including the famous *Dispositionskasse* established in 1763) to afford him a financial flexibility beyond what the ordinary budgetary process allowed (and which, not coincidentally, left him as the only person with complete knowledge of the state's finances). He always kept a separate war fund, essentially untouchable for ordinary purposes, which contained some 50 million talers in 1786 – more than double the annual revenues of 23 million; and while he was aware of the deflationary impact of hoarding such huge monetary reserves, he regarded doing so as an indisputable necessity. Aside from a persistently under-capitalized State Bank, founded in 1765, whose impact on the economy was slight, the only major fiscal administrative innovation of Frederick's reign was the establishment of the Excise and Tolls Department in 1766; better known as the (French) Regie, this institution comprised some 200 Frenchmen headed by the tax farmer de Launay and was charged with collecting various indirect taxes, most notably the urban excise. During the late war, Frederick's military commissars had unearthed all sorts of hitherto hidden sources of revenues among Saxons and Mecklenburgers unlucky enough to suffer Prussian occupation; after the war, the king decided that French contract professionals were better suited than his own officials to extract similar revenues from his own subjects. While it is doubtful that any very significant increase in revenues resulted from the substitution of this for older agencies, the Regie earned the intense dislike of the Prussian people through its ungentle and intrusive procedures as well as the resentment of the regular bureaucracy which more or less correctly interpreted the king's creation of the new department as a vote of no confidence in its own honesty and efficiency.

But Frederick's reliance on the Regie was only one example of his increasing uncomfortability with much of the administrative structure he inherited from Friedrich Wilhelm I. The General Directory and its provincial boards, while competent enough in many matters of routine administration, had been designed for a state very different in size and responsibilities from the one that emerged triumphant from the Silesian wars; they moved too ponderously and mechanically for Frederick's taste and as early as the 1740s he had begun to remove certain functions from the General Directory by creating new departments that soon became almost separate ministries. His experiences in the Seven Years War and with the highly successful direct administration of Silesia reinforced this tendency to rely on individual ministers with specialized responsibilities, who reported only to him. By the end of his reign, war, churches and schools, mining, forestry, justice, the economy and most of the state's finances were essentially separate and independent of the General Directory. Structurally, this represented a decentralization and even disorganization of the bureaucracy whose potentially adverse results did not appear during Frederick's reign because he, being the author of the changes, knew how to deal with them; only under his uninitiated successors did the disadvantages of the new system become clear.

Frederick's relationship with his administrative personnel was, on the whole, a suspicious and antagonistic one and was not eased by the king's stiffness in personal relationships generally. There were individuals he clearly valued, trusted and conferred with frequently; but he himself regarded these as exceptions in a pattern otherwise characterized at best by routine and mediocre performance and at worst by laziness, malfeasance and corruption. It might be suggested that his own hostile attitudes and punitive actions, widely publicized throughout the bureaucracy, were not helpful in infusing a spirit of willing self-sacrifice into his officials and instead promoted a sense of dread which discouraged initiative on the principle that correct but uninspired performance was least likely to attract unfavourable attention. Bypassing the traditional agencies in favour of the more 'personal' ministerial system described above also tended to create something of a siege mentality among the staffs of the older boards, who conspired with each other in self-protective actions not conducive to a vigorous pursuit of their official duties. Still, if indeed Frederick was correct in believing that few of his officials approached his own almost superhuman devotion to the needs of the state, there is no reason to think of his bureaucracy as a whole as anything but dedicated and at least reasonably efficient by the standards of the time; fear of the king and his notorious 'fiscals' (special administrative control agents, or spies) was not the only motive driving an educated and well trained body of officials, most of whom were steeped in the public service ethic created by the combined influences of Pietism and Wolffian philosophy and, among the nobility, by the steadily stronger linkage between aristocratic status and service to the state. Frederick did prefer nobles in the higher civil service positions – as ministers and board presidents, for example; but that merely reflected the social realities of the time, according to which the nobility was the governing class and was accepted as such by the bourgeoisie (for whom, in fact, deference and obedience to aristocratic superiors may have come more naturally than to one of their own class).[2]

Frederick almost certainly entertained ideas for a thoroughgoing restructuring of the Prussian administration, but it was clear to him that war, military and diplomatic watchfulness and financial considerations forbade the disruptions such reform would occasion. To a considerable extent, indeed, the same qualifications existed on all other kinds of reform. In education, for example, the appointment of the able and intelligent K. A. von Zedlitz as head of the Spiritual Department in 1771 brought a flurry of administrative reforms designed to improve the quality of education by raising and testing the qualifications of teachers, introducing the *Abitur* examinations to prove readiness for university-level study and by the formation of special 'school boards' attached to all the chief provincial administrative agencies. Zedlitz also took a keen interest in model schools and new curricula and managed to find subventions for some of them. But a complete reformation of the educational system and especially of the still very deficient system of village schools was impossible for lack of the massive funds necessary for buildings, instructional materials and teacher training and salaries. In the end, therefore, most of Zedlitz's reforms remained spotty and incomplete, or on paper, and brought few changes to distinguish Frederick's Prussia from that of his father.

Legal and judicial reform was a different matter. Though not without interruptions, improvement in this area was pursued with a dedication which reflected Frederick's strong personal belief in the importance of law as the most fundamental institutional element of a well-governed state – the place where enlightenment itself could be codified as a permanent guide to welfare for both officials and

---

2. The king's preference for nobles in the higher positions of the army officer corps was even more marked, but here was justified by the concept of aristocratic 'honour' supposedly lacking in the bourgeoisie. Virtually all non-noble officers commissioned out of necessity in the later stages of the Seven Years War were either dismissed or assigned to garrison duties after the war. Some access to commissions in fortress garrisons was available to sons of domains lessees, who also might later be knighted and placed in regular regiments.

citizens. The king's commitment to a kind of 'rule of law' was real enough, with the qualification that it had to be *his* law, executed by a judiciary obedient to his intentions. Then, in all matters of justice, it would be possible, as he himself put it, for the law to speak and the monarch to be silent. The one well-publicized instance in which he grossly violated this ideal again illustrates how little confidence he had in his own officials, especially when he suspected the intrusion of 'chicanery' into state business: he intervened to overturn a verdict favouring a nobleman in a case involving a quarrelsome peasant, the miller Arnold, incorrectly assuming that the judges had been swayed by social prejudice. That the facts of the case were entirely on their side was little consolation to the several innocent jurists subsequently clapped into prison for a year by the enraged Frederick. The possibility of direct royal intervention thus compromised the full independence of the judiciary, as did even more strongly the continuing judicial competence of many administrative agencies – the provincial War and Domains Chambers, for example – especially in cases relating to fiscal and police matters, which Frederick regarded as too important to be left to an impartial justice.

In spite of all this, the progress made in judicial reform was real and significant. The work of Samuel von Cocceji (1679–1755), who had begun his service under Friedrich Wilhelm I, was notable in several respects: he not only streamlined procedure (as in the *Codex Fridericianus* of 1749) and raised the quality of judicial personnel, but also curbed the invidious system of capricious judicial charges (and bribery) by fixing court fees and raising judges' salaries and brought a much improved jurisprudence to rural Prussia by mandating professional supervision of the patrimonial courts. After a lapse of some years, Cocceji's organizational and procedural innovations were improved, expanded and reissued as a new code in 1781; this was the contribution of J. H. von Carmer (1721–1801), who had been called from Silesia to Berlin as Minister of Justice and Grand Chancellor in 1779. But the crowning achievement of Prussian legal reform in this century was the compilation and codification of various royal decrees, cabinet orders, ordinances and other regulations undertaken by Carmer's younger contemporary Carl Gottlieb Svarez (1746–98); issued seriatim between 1785–94 and originally intended only as a supplement to provincial legislation, the final product (known as the Prussian General Legal Code [*Preußisches Allgemeines Landrecht*]) ended up giving the entire Prussian state a single body of legal norms for the first time in its history. Not a true constitution by today's standards, this impressive achievement nevertheless embodied much of the Frederician vision of a state defined by the observance of known and comprehensive laws designed to activate the enlightened principle that the essential purpose of government was the moral growth and improvement of the citizenry. The *Landrecht* was not socially progressive, in the sense that it established legally distinct classes (nobles, burghers and peasants); but it did attempt to explain the different rights and duties assigned to all in terms of the organic contributions of each to the welfare of the whole society. This code, by virtue of its universality, was as important in its own way to the unification of the Prussian state as was the ubiquity of the army and the bureaucracy and, beyond that, was a significant contribution to the whole concept of the political rule of law – the *Rechtsstaat* – that was to become so vital a part of the history of Germany in the next century.

In the end, widely praised and admired though he was, Frederick II was something of an enigma to his German contemporaries and especially to the intellectuals among them, whose preference for the title 'Frederick the Unique' over 'Frederick the Great' is indicative of genuine puzzlement over the apparent contradictions in the king's personality and reign. Here was a 'philosopher-king' who mixed war with welfare, contempt for all organized religion with a policy of complete religious toleration and the composition of sensitive poetry with the unfeeling personal behaviour of a robot – a man who with great discomfort to himself toured his provinces regularly to listen attentively to the woes and grievances of his subjects, but who also ran his state like an army barracks and often treated his subordinates with an icy scorn far more wounding than the raging tongue-lashings or blows administered by his father. He was, to be sure, a genuine friend of the enlightenment, who encouraged discussion of all public issues (except those he defined as political, to which censorship applied) and whose ministers – Zedlitz and Hertzberg for example – were leading contributors to the vital Berlin enlightenment; but he was no admirer of German letters, which he regarded as inferior to the French and most of the major works of the German literary revival, to the extent he knew them at all, he deprecated as contrived, weird or uncouth. Such opinions did not endear him to luminaries such as Wieland, Lessing and Herder, who indeed glimpsed greatness in him, but who were inclined to see more of Sparta than of Athens in both his style and his state. Frederick admired and emulated the cool, rational scepticism of the earlier French enlightenment, but not the extremes he found in the later materialism of a Helvétius or a Holbach, or in the unfettered naturalism and emotionalism of a Rousseau. Voltaire was essentially his model and in spite of the quarrelling which ended the Frenchman's lengthy visit to Potsdam in the early 1750s, Frederick later resumed an extensive and engaging correspondence with him.

Few rulers have left as deep an impress on their countries as Frederick did on Prussia. Yet while he was everywhere revered as a king, he was not beloved as a human being – partly because his iron self-control and extreme personal reserve formed a hard shell which made it difficult to penetrate to the inner self and partly because the combination of qualities which distinguished him (intellectual discernment, political vision, stoicism, restraint, self-denial and unremitting hard work) raised him so far above the shallowness, pettiness and self-gratification characteristic of many other princes of his time as to make him seem inhuman by being so much more than ordinarily human. But the greatest oddity of all, perhaps, was that a ruler as demanding of his subjects as was Frederick could be so much more demanding of himself.

How rare this quality was among princes was immediately demonstrated by Frederick's nephew and successor, Friedrich Wilhelm II (1786–97), an affable but also unintelligent and irresolute man of middle age, who was incapable of following the sound advice personally directed at him by his uncle in the latter's *Political Testament* of 1768. Indeed, he fell into the two chief errors Frederick warned against: becoming a creature of his ministers and allowing both individual decisions and a sense of the overall direction of the state to slip out of his grasp. In an attempt to court popularity within the higher civil service and among the people, he abolished a number of the separate ministries established by Frederick, including the justifiably unpopular Regie, and assigned most of their duties to the mediocre and overworked General Directory, whose attempt to function as it had half a century earlier was unsuccessful. The king himself, more given to the pleasures of his office than to its public duties, allowed quotidian decision-making to bleed off to advisers without real accountability and encouraged the growth of a certain comfortability and laxity within the bureaucracy. The Rosicrucianism of his ministers J. R. von Bischoffswerder and J. C. Wöllner, with its strong anti-rationalist tendencies, inevitably trickled down into the subordinate levels of administration; the public service ethic and indeed the whole enlightened character of Prussian society and government, especially in Berlin itself, weakened in the face of new attitudes and patterns of behaviour reflective of cynicism, indifference and self-indulgence. There was, to be sure, a strong residual element of the dedicated self-sacrifice of Frederick's day still in sections of a younger and intellectually more cultivated civil service and elsewhere in Prussia; and these were soon to reemerge, tested and strengthened by military defeat and political collapse, to take the state in their self-confident grip. Until then, however, the spirit of Frederick the Great would roam a kingdom which preferred its memories of the rigours of his rule to those of his enduring achievements.

While Frederick II's reign has probably received more historical attention, especially in the English-speaking world, than that of his contemporary and sometime foe Maria Theresia of Austria, this imbalance was less apparent in the Germany of their own time. The empress-queen, to be sure, suffered in some ways by comparison to her more intellectual and restlessly active Prussian counterpart, not least because he had cast her in the persistently defensive role of a loser in two long periods of war. But contemporaries also recognized honour in this, praising the unwavering resolve and durability with which she had successfully defended most of her dynastic inheritance against forces which at several points had seemed to doom it. A much more serene and less complicated person than Frederick, Maria Theresia did not overawe her world as he did; but neither did she threaten or frighten it as did he and her personal warmth and open-hearted generosity, reinforced by a faultless reputation as wife and mother, endeared her not just to the peoples of her own dominions but to Germans everywhere. At her death in 1780, she was deeply mourned throughout the Empire and Frederick himself spoke of her with the kind of genuine admiration that is perhaps only possible among honourable and mutually respected foes of long standing.

From 1760, when he had eased Count Haugwitz into semi-retirement, until the accession of Joseph II as sole ruler in 1780, Prince Kaunitz was the leading and directing figure of Maria Theresia's government. Operating always and only with her knowledge and informed consent, his position as State Chancellor was virtually that of an uncontested prime minister and it was he who twisted together the threads of earlier piecemeal reforms to point Austria firmly in the direction of a more unitary state. His first administrative innovation was the creation of the State Council (*Staatsrat*) in 1760, which functioned as both an advisory council for the monarch and a supreme watchdog on all court administrative agencies. Its small size (seven persons, including Kaunitz himself) and independence from all other court offices permitted an expeditious transaction of business – a real necessity, since it not only determined which matters would come before the ruler, but also formulated the edicts and ordinances resulting from her decisions, transmitted them to the proper executive agencies and supervised their subsequent implementation. This body introduced a new self-assurance to both policy-making and central administration and retained its importance until the early years of Joseph's highly autocratic sole rulership. Kaunitz also essentially segregated political from financial administration by placing the latter back into the Court Chamber and restricting the *Directorium in internis* (now known as the 'United Bohemian and Austrian Court Chancellery') to political affairs – a change whose benefits for finance were mostly offset by unforeseen bureaucratic complications.

Far more important than these changes was the assumption of an ever tighter control of local government by the central administration in Vienna. In the towns and cities, after 1760, the District Officers took on more and more functions of municipal administration, operating under edicts which regulated more strictly the management of urban wealth and property. Undergirding this effort were a host of new police ordinances regarding luxury expenditures, popular entertainment, church practices, schooling and, in Bohemia, the imposition of German as the official language and of new (German) weights and measures. Behind these ordinances was the deliberate intention to alter bourgeois consciousness itself – to erase hallowed local customs as the prerequisite to weakening traditional provincial loyalties in favour of reliance on and allegiance to the larger unitary state beyond; perhaps the clearest evidence of this was the disarmament of the citizenry at large and the full or partial dismantling of city fortifications, designed to emphasize assumption by the state of all the rights and duties of military defence. In rural areas, a similar intensification of state controls can be glimpsed in the subjection of landlords' officials to closer and more regular scrutiny in the fulfilment of their various duties towards peasant dependants.

This scrutiny, on the other hand, is only further evidence of the closer and more direct relationship between state and peasantry solicited in the important agrarian laws of Maria Theresia's later years. Beginning in 1768, special commissions began an investigation of peasant labour services which over the next few years resulted in widespread reductions of this hated 'robot' and in its outright abolition on the crown lands. At the same time, the government created the opportunity for peasants to buy proprietary rights under certain conditions and set up state commissions to determine fair prices in cases of disagreement. Certainly the state's interest in such reform was conditioned as much by economic factors as by humanitarianism or its desire to reduce the aristocratic privileges which stood between it and the lowest rural subjects of the crown: in the absence of a vigorous mercantile and industrial economy, the importance of the agricultural sector was paramount and these measures aimed directly at improving agrarian production by liberating peasants' labour for employment on their own farms. This reliance on self-interest also guided industrial policy through the loosening of various guild regulations, as well as the freeing of some whole industries from guild restrictions and a general prohibition of new guilds. Such measures, together with the creation of schools to impart expert artisan skills and the establishment of permanent provincial commercial commissions, led to observably improved production, while the correspondingly increased need to transport goods efficiently was addressed through the improvement of roads and rivers. By 1780, the economy of the Habsburg core lands, if still not booming by western European standards, was in sound and growing condition; just as important, the government's credit was solid.

The religious policies of the last half of Maria Theresia's reign were significant both in themselves and because they laid the groundwork for many of the better publicized reforms later undertaken by Joseph II. A devout Catholic herself, the empress-queen nevertheless continued the long family tradition of insisting on the right of the state to police the church in a wide range of matters and, in particular, to limit the extent of Rome's control and influence on it. Her personal faith, conditioned by Jansenist doctrines of a simpler and more austere Catholicism, rejected the extravagances of baroque piety and inclined her towards a religion defined more by practical charity than by worldly wealth and endowments. This view tallied nicely with the economic principles of Kaunitz, who had long believed that the economic superiority of Protestant states was mostly due to the absence of an organized clergy and who wanted to reduce the church's claim on Austria's resources. The two could therefore agree not only on policies of political supervision of the church which included state review of all papal and episcopal decrees, prohibition of nuncial visitations and censorship of all ecclesiastical publications, but also on a host of measures which lessened both the authority of the church and the economic drain attributable to its organization and practices. Ecclesiastical jurisdiction was henceforth restricted to clergymen, monastic prisons were abolished, the right of asylum was cut back and the church's management of its own funds and property was subjected to governmental supervision, with specific prohibition of the transfer of capital investments and coinage outside of the hereditary lands. Pure economic considerations also prompted laws which reduced expensive and time-consuming religious holidays, pilgrimages and processions, eliminated most clerical tax exemptions and placed severe limitations on future property acquisition by the church, especially in land.

The strong trend towards state assumption of responsibilities previously left to the church was nowhere more evident or of greater long-range significance than in education. As early as 1749, Maria Theresia's chief educational adviser, the Dutch Catholic and court physician Gerhard van Swieten, had begun a reform of the University of Vienna; starting with the medical faculty, van Swieten gradually replaced the older staff with new and more scientifically trained instructors and de-emphasized the religious content of the curriculum. Soon the law faculty was also reformed, with the specific intent of training a new generation of bureaucrats in the cameral sciences and administrative law; by as early as the mid-1770s, the programme had produced enough graduates to permit the government to require exposure to such formal training of all candidates for civil service positions, resulting in a sharp and rapid improvement in the quality of personnel. The state's intention to intervene at lower levels of the educational system was proclaimed in 1760 by the establishment of a new board, the *Studienhofkommission*, whose growing importance elevated it from subordinate departmental status to that of a separate court agency by 1774. Through it, supervisory educational commissions were set up in the provinces and educational experts were appointed to the *Gubernia*; at the local level, the District Officers assumed oversight functions over both gymnasia and elementary schools. The reform of the village school system, already discussed in Chapter Thirteen, was also part of the state effort; while slow and beset by many serious difficulties, it was carried out with the same tendency towards greater secularization of curricula and teaching personnel that characterized reform of urban schools at all levels – and, of course, it was funded largely by wealth seized from the Jesuit order after its dissolution in 1773.

The total effect of all the reforms discussed above can scarcely be overestimated; taken together, they meant that a significantly new conception of the state had already struck firm roots in Austria by the time Joseph II succeeded to rulership of the hereditary lands in

1780. Joseph, to be sure, had chafed under what he regarded as the inadequate extent and pace of this reform and had constantly harassed his mother for a 'reform of the reform', as it were; but during the co-regency she was more ruler than he and had resisted the pressures brought by her impatient son. Mother and son were, in truth, very different people. Maria Theresia, while certainly neither timid nor irresolute, needed and took time to ponder the advisability of reforms in terms of their ultimate purpose and consequences and of her own deepest convictions and had a shrewd and realistic sense of what her various peoples, given their historical and political individuality, could or would tolerate by way of change. Joseph, on the other hand, who as a youth had been drowned in the abstruse natural law philosophy pounded into him by his teacher C. A. Beck, was filled with the most admirable motives of enlightened humanitarianism, but was also possessed of a rational idealism often divorced from reality and of an impatient and impetuous personality which rushed to transform theoretical constructs into actuality as soon as he became convinced of their correctness in absolute philosophical terms. 'Right', in this sense, justified whatever 'might' he had to employ to implement the changes he saw as rationally correct, while a broad streak of self-righteousness led him to see whatever opposition he encountered as ascribable not just to fear of innovation, or even to crass self-interest, but to malevolent misanthropy or downright stupidity.

Joseph immediately revealed his total commitment to the ideal of the unitary, all-embracing state when he refused to engage in the usual ceremonies of homage in his various possessions out of unwillingness to make the accompanying promises to respect the traditional constitutions of those lands; indeed, he removed the Hungarian Crown of St. Stephen to Vienna and was never crowned either in Hungary or in Bohemia. While Maria Theresia had at least continued to pay lip service to the integrity of territorial diets and their committees, Joseph seldom convoked the diets and abolished the committees altogether, assigning their duties to the *Gubernia* (into which two noblemen were introduced as the forlorn and wholly uninfluential remnant of the estates' representation in government). The higher officials of the estates now became crown agents and by 1789 even the co-responsibility of the estates in voting taxes had all but disappeared through fiscal legislation which removed their discretionary powers by fixing the land tax; even the estates' own funds were placed under strict state supervision. This virtual extinction of the autonomy of the nobility was also carried into the towns and cities, where new magistracies, divided into three functionally differentiated senates and operating on instructions handed down from the central administration, replaced such organs of self-government as had earlier existed.

Within the central government, Joseph made relatively few structural changes. Influenced by the example of the Prussian General Directory (ironically so, in view of Frederick II's increasing dissatisfaction with it), the emperor recombined the administration of political and financial affairs Kaunitz had separated in 1760s. In 1781, he also further strengthened the Supreme Judicature in Vienna as a real ministry of justice by increasing its authority over various provincial courts which were now integrated into a single state system. The effect of this and other judicial reforms (new civil and criminal codes of 1786–7 and abolition of all torture and of the death penalty, for example) had the double effect of creating a judiciary far more independent of political administration than existed in any other major continental state and of establishing a more equal justice for all classes – another aspect of the destruction of barriers to the common state citizenship Joseph so earnestly sought. The same motive, along with an intention to simplify government and make it more efficient, underlay the division of Austria, Bohemia and Hungary into thirteen entirely new administrative districts, deliberately ignoring all historic provincial boundaries; a *Gubernium* was installed in each, with the usual District Offices beneath. It is questionable whether the new arrangement brought any real benefit; but it is certain that it created very hard feelings in a number of places and especially among the always sensitive Hungarians, who were much less accustomed to Vienna's meddling with cherished traditions than were Austrians or Bohemians.

If indeed the structure of the central government changed little under Joseph, its tone was radically different from that of his mother. Thus, for example, while the State Council set up by Kaunitz in 1760 continued to exist, its heretofore important advisory function was often ignored in the extremely autocratic reign of Joseph, who much preferred giving orders to taking advice. His was a very personal regime in which, like Frederick the Great, he tended to avoid contact with the administration as such and instead to surround himself with a few trusted advisers on whom he called as needed. On the other hand, he delighted in bureaucratic detail, regularly involving himself in petty administrative transactions he might better have left to subordinates. His frequent but also unpredictable intervention in the routine work of various state agencies did nothing to bolster their confidence or sense of responsibility, of course, but Joseph saw in it merely another of the many methods by which he kept surveillance on a bureaucracy in whose honesty and motives he had, if possible, even less confidence than Frederick II had in his.[3] Kaunitz was almost the only high official he believed to be both high-minded and thoroughly competent and as opposition to the veritable explosion of reform edicts of his reign increased, so did his own conviction that the obedience of his officials at all levels had to be monitored. In a sense he was correct, because, considerations of honesty aside, few of his bureaucrats shared his enthusiasm for a reform programme they regarded as ill-considered, overhasty, difficult to implement and needlessly destructive of customs and traditions (and in some cases privileges) they believed in; and while few were willing to expose themselves by active opposition to that programme, passive nonperformance could be a very effective means of resistance. With no reliable investigative body in the existing administration to count on, Joseph therefore organized a separate and independent agency to police the attitudes of important citizens and the performance of his own officials. Under the leadership of Count J. A. von Pergen, this new instrumentality – partly watchdog, partly security police – was founded in Vienna, but was quickly expanded to the major provincial cities and in 1789 was topped off with the establishment of a central police administration as a state ministry under Pergen's control.

In economic affairs, Joseph broke no really new ground, continuing the liberalized industrial policy of his mother's reign with respect to guild production and the encouragement of new industries where possible and the standard protectionism in the export-import trade. But the agrarian sector was profoundly affected by a number of measures which originated both in Joseph's humanitarian impulses and in his continuing concern for increasing agricultural productivity. The first of these, in 1781, abolished all forms of hereditary servitude in Austria and Bohemia (later also in Galicia and Hungary) and transformed all peasants into immediate subjects of the crown,

---

3. In spite of the suspicions he harboured about his bureaucrats, Joseph continued efforts begun under Maria Theresia to improve the quality of officials and to make bureaucratic employment more attractive. He not only standardized salaries and raised them somewhat, but also instituted a better promotion system and, in 1781, rationalized and extended the general system of pensions and survivors' benefits. These measures, while laudable in themselves, were nevertheless insufficient to create a well-paid and happy civil service.

thereby eliminating a host of seigneurial prerogatives and placing the peasantry under the protection of the state. Later Land Tax Patents of 1785 and 1789 also fixed both the state taxes and the land rents of what had now become essentially a class of hereditary tenant farmers: just over 12 per cent of the peasant's annual income (based on a ten-year average) was to go for tax and just under 18 per cent to satisfy all claims of the landlord, leaving some 70 per cent of the gross to cover his own needs. Labour services, already abolished on the crown domains, remained in force on private lands, but their commutation into cash was encouraged by the requirement that they be reckoned as part of the peasant's payments and regulated by written contracts supervised by the District Office. While parts of this package of agrarian legislation did not apply to all peasants and much of it was dismantled altogether after Joseph's death (due primarily to pressure from disgruntled landlords), the peasantry did retain the important net gain of personal freedom.

The same mixture of pragmatism and humanitarianism that motivated Joseph's agrarian reforms also fuelled his policies on education and social welfare. Only in his reign did the government's long-standing desire that every child have access to a primary school approach realization. This was accomplished not only by the enforced requirement that every parish have a school, but also by a considerable growth in the number of parishes (made possible by an increased production of priests encouraged by the government itself) and by empowering the District Offices to see that cities, landlords and village communities provided adequate school funding. New Protestant schools that arose after Joseph's Edict of Toleration, discussed below, helped to swell the total number of new schools. Joseph also encouraged the founding of industrial or vocational schools as one answer to the stubborn problem of poverty. Such schools, however, were but one example of the emperor's determination to provide the state with a rational and comprehensive welfare policy that would improve the currently very haphazard delivery of social services and alter its charitable or voluntary character by recognizing such services as a responsibility of the state. This did not mean converting all eleemosynary institutions into state-run organizations, of course – much as Joseph might ideally have wanted that; but it did mean increased governmental scrutiny of such agencies, as well as significantly increased state funding for old and new charitable enterprises, private or otherwise. One of the most important institutional buttresses of poor relief, for example, was the so-called *Armeninstitut* of the Bohemian Count J. N.

Buquoy, which originated on his own estates as a lay religious brotherhood devoted to the care of the poor, but which attracted a great deal of financial support from the state and, while retaining its private character, eventually spread over the entire monarchy. Other government funds were poured into new hospitals, homes for invalids, foundlings and orphans and the aged, as well as institutes for the mentally ill, the blind and the deaf. Joseph often became involved in the most minute details of such projects, expressing particular concern for medical care and clean and healthful buildings. How extensive the state's financial commitment to this welfare programme was under Joseph's rule can be inferred from the fact that most of it had to be abandoned because of the expenses of Austria's involvement in the wars of the French Revolution and Napoleon until 1815.

In view of the many original initiatives of Joseph's reign, it may be a bit puzzling that the term 'Josephinism' evokes remembrance primarily of his religious policies, since these, after all, were so closely and organically linked to the changes in church-state relations carried out during Maria Theresia's lifetime. In one sense, indeed, Joseph merely walked further down a path trodden not only by his mother, but by his more distant ancestors for many generations already – a path whose direction was determined by the monarchy's inveterate position that the Catholic church was subject to the sovereign rights of temporal authority in all such worldly dealings as were not indisputably necessary to the fulfilment of its spiritual mission. To the extent that Joseph merely further narrowed in favour of the state the definition of what was disputable in this sense, there was nothing new in his overall approach. But Joseph was perhaps the first Habsburg to define and widen the scope of the state's responsibilities in such a way as to include some of the functions regularly performed by the clergy and even to add to their duties new activities designed to serve the interests of the state. In Joseph's view, priests had important social functions beyond their purely spiritual ones; in their parishes they were fire wardens, sanitation engineers, agricultural advisers, primary care providers for the sick, the poor, the disabled and other disadvantaged elements of society, as well as schoolteachers and, *if properly educated*, porters of the moral and practical insights of the enlightenment generally. This explains why the government instituted strict educational require- ments for applicants to positions at all levels of the clergy and, after 1783, closed up the episcopal seminaries and the educational organizations of the regular clergy and transferred their functions to general seminaries administered by the state, whose curricula were monitored right down to the assigned books. It also explains why the emperor dissolved all monastic establishments that were not involved in useful educational or hospital work and confiscated their wealth in order to increase the number of parishes, finance new churches for them and assure a decent minimal income for a priesthood greatly augmented in numbers. In this way, Joseph went well beyond earlier policies which had essentially aimed at neutralizing an obstructionist clergy by creating a *new* clergy as active supporters and agents of an enlightened government; in doing so, he actually brought about a closeness of church and state which was without parallel elsewhere and which was destined to last for a long time.[4]

Joseph thus created a 'state church' in a somewhat novel sense of the term; because of that, he went even further than Maria Theresia in sealing this church off from outside interference: he not only expanded his own right to fill ecclesiastical offices, but also, after 1782, ordered that communications of bishops and heads of religious orders with Rome be monitored routinely by the *Gubernia* and, finally, brusquely terminated the ecclesiastical jurisdiction of non-Austrian bishops (those of Salzburg and Passau in particular) inside Austria itself. While political motives were certainly foremost in these and many other of Joseph's religious policies, it is incorrect to think of him as personally irreligious (much less impious) in the same vein as, for example, Frederick the Great – though he was also not as devout in the same way or degree as his mother. On the contrary, he saw his actions as elevating and cleansing the church and if there was more than a hint of the enlightenment's anti-clericalism in him, that was something he shared with many of his subjects, who knew from long personal experience that the clerics in their midst were not always selfless servants of the Word of God. His dissolution of over 400 monastic houses in his German lands alone caused little popular resentment, for example – though much less important ordinances further restricting holidays, processions and popular religious observances (including burial customs), all of them intended to spare his people needless expense, created a real storm of protest from one end of the monarchy to the other, requiring quick revocation of some.

Some of Joseph's edicts clearly proceeded from a strongly secularized view of the proper provinces of church and state. The

---

4. Jeserich, *et al.*, *Deutsche Verwaltungsgeschichte*, I, 539–41.

Marriage Patent of 1783 which permitted civil marriage, recognized divorce and largely eliminated ecclesiastical jurisdiction over married couples is a good example. But perhaps the most important single religious reform of his reign was less clearly due to secular or political motivation alone. This was the famous Edict of Toleration of 1781, which not only removed most discrimination against Jews, but also gave the right of private worship to all non-Catholics. The largest number of people affected by the edict were Lutherans and Calvinists – unusually well educated groups on the whole – who were now admitted to full citizenship, thus becoming immediately eligible for official employment in the army and civil service. This measure went far beyond anything Maria Theresia had been willing to do; she had balked at forcible conversions, to be sure and had permitted resettlement of Protestants in Transylvania, but she believed firmly in religious uniformity in the core lands of the monarchy. Joseph, on the other hand, was not unaware of the dangers of toleration, but, strangely, seems to have believed that it would result in many Protestant conversions to Catholicism, thus in the end producing a greater and voluntary religious uniformity. But that he might be wrong in this belief – and he was, since existing Protestants remained firmly in their faith and some 70,000 conversions *to* Protestantism occurred in the first year after the edict – would not have deterred him from taking this step, convinced as he was that the necessity of religion to a well-ordered society did not require imposition of a single 'official' religion to the exclusion of others.

Joseph proceeded with his whirlwind programme of reform from a base of enlightened public opinion that was exceedingly small by any standard of the day. He often complained, with much justification, that no one in his dominions really understood what he was trying to do. Clearly he hoped to change that by imbuing his bureaucracy and other elites with a new sense of public service and by creating a small army of enlightened priests to explain the rationale of his reforms to the common people. He even more or less single-handedly created an enlightened periodical press to advertise and justify his programmes. But while nearly all of his major initiatives violated the traditional interests of important social groups and penetrated enclaves of ancient privilege of many kinds, Joseph appears not to have appreciated how clearly those who were adversely affected by his measures understood their own self-interest, or how determined they were, individually and as groups, to resist or subvert his reforms even in the face of justifications he regarded as unassailable on either rational or humanitarian grounds. The farther one moved away from Vienna and from the small group of like-minded innovators in the emperor's immediate vicinity, the less enthusiasm there was for Joseph's reform – even among his own civil servants, who understood better than he the limited capacity of their society to absorb changes hurled at it so fast and in such dizzying quantity as to make comprehension or compliance impossible even where good will existed.

The last years of Joseph's fairly brief sole rulership closed with a series of scenarios more nightmarish than could have been crafted by his worst enemy. Unable to rely on his bankrupt and dissension-ridden French ally in his foreign policy, Joseph in 1787 felt compelled to enter a joint war with Russia against the Turks to shore up his relations with St. Petersburg. This war, a very costly one which went badly almost from the first, also helped to provoke a serious rebellion in Hungary. The Hungarians were already angry with Joseph for his refusal to be crowned king and for his disregard of the Hungarian constitution through administrative redistricting and in other ways; and they were furious with his language edict of 1784, which mandated a knowledge of German for anyone wishing to enter public service and appeared to be nothing less than an assault on Hungarian culture itself. On top of that, now they were expected to carry the main burden of the war against the Turks; so they resorted to the kind of revolt against Vienna that was hardly new in their history. In the Austrian Netherlands, Joseph's attempt to impose the same language edict and certain other political and religious reforms as well, sparked a similar rebellion there, led by the Belgian bishops (with Prussian encouragement) and ideologically reinforced by the early events of the French Revolution. Overwhelmed by these events, which added to the force of his opposition in the German core lands as well, Joseph recalled many (but not all) of the changes he had decreed for Hungary and died very soon thereafter, in February 1790.

While Joseph died embittered by the stubborn ingratitude of a people he thought should have known better and convinced that his reign was a failure, the final judgment had yet to be given. Even after his brother Leopold II (1790–92) (who disagreed less with Joseph's aims than with his methods) dismantled other aspects of his reform legislation in order to pacify and stabilize the overstressed monarchy, what was untouched included many of the most important achievements of Joseph's reign. Religious toleration (and the civic entitlements that went with it), the abolition of peasant servitude and most of the ecclesiastical regulatory legislation remained in force throughout the hereditary lands; together, these amounted to a significant further step along the difficult road towards the socially cohesive and politically unitary state envisioned in the successful reforms of Maria Theresia and Count Kaunitz. The Austria of 1790 was a far different monarchy from the one Joseph had first seen a half century before; it is a pity he could not know how much of his own work was responsible for helping his beloved House of Austria to master the unprecedented challenges it was to face in the quarter century following his death.

CHAPTER TWENTY-TWO

The German Powers, the Empire and the Territories at the End of an Era

While many of the reforms enacted or attempted in Prussia by Frederick II and in Austria by Maria Theresia and Joseph II can be explained in terms of more or less distinct and subordinate objectives with their own rationale, one supreme and overriding goal was intended to be served by all of them: the steady strengthening of the state to meet challenges – chiefly military ones – from existing or future enemies on the international scene. This is true even of those humanitarian reforms which appear to have embodied the noblest and most charitable of motivations, for these too served to build the health and numbers of the labour force and to bring greater order and discipline to populations whose productivity and reliability were of vital importance to the unity of the state; the welfare state, as one historian has noted, has often been closely related to the warfare state.[1] In particular, the results of the three Silesian wars had decreed that the Empire was henceforth to contain two European great powers; this situation, novel to German history, was to have a profound effect not only on the relationship of the two German powers to each other, but also on their policies towards the Empire and the rest of Europe as well.

If indeed freedom from clientage to a foreign power was the positive long-term result of the Seven Years War for Prussia, diplomatic isolation was its short-term negative counterpart – and something that greatly worried Frederick II. His relations with Britain, his only great-power ally in that war, after cooling steadily since 1760, had ruptured almost altogether by 1763; while, on the other hand, the alliance between his foes Austria and France not only

1. R. J. White, *Europe in the Eighteenth Century*, (N.Y., 1965), p. 203.

continued into the post-war period (if rather cheerlessly so, in view of the war's results) but was even strengthened by the engagement and later marriage of Maria Theresia's youngest daughter, Marie Antoinette, to the dauphin – the later Louis XVI. Aware of Prussia's continuing vulnerability and with no friendly power in western Europe to rely on for the immediate future, Frederick turned his eyes towards Russia, the emergent eastern power whose participation against him in the late war would almost certainly have destroyed Prussia without the incredible turnabout occasioned by the sudden death of Tsaritsa Elizabeth. An opportunity to propose an alliance with Catherine II (1762–95) arose out of the disagreement between Russia, on one side and Austria and France on the other, about the succession to the Polish throne, vacated by the death of Augustus III in late 1763: while both Vienna and Paris supported a continuation of the Saxon dynasty, Catherine was committed to installing her favourite, the Polish nobleman Stanislaus Poniatowski. Against various assurances of support from Frederick, Catherine entered into a defensive alliance with him in April 1764, after which the Russian empress was secure in employing measures which guaranteed Poniatowski's election.

But Frederick's satisfaction at having gained a great-power ally quickly turned to apprehension as the new Polish government soon in effect declared independence from its Russian 'protector', appealing to Austria for support; eventually, hostilities broke out between Polish forces and Russian troops sent by Catherine into southern Poland, ostensibly to protect the rights of Orthodox Christians against the Catholic majority. The situation was then further complicated by a Turkish declaration of war on Russia in late 1768. Determined as he was to maintain his only important alliance, Frederick reluctantly subsidized Catherine's war from his depleted treasury, but he also brought pressure to bear on the empress for a stronger commitment to Prussia by appearing to negotiate with Austria through goodwill meetings with the young Joseph II in 1769 and 1770. When unexpectedly large Russian gains against the Turks in the Balkans threatened to force an alarmed Austria into the war against Russia, Frederick, faced with the possibility of entering another war for Russian interests rather than his own, agreed to help mediate the rapidly escalating dispute between Vienna and St. Petersburg. Since all three powers were anxious to avoid a general eastern European war, they agreed on a solution which both obviated such a conflict and brought material benefit to all.

That solution, perhaps suggested by Austria's effortless seizure of some small Polish territories bordering Hungary in 1769, came at the expense of a feckless Poland, which had the misfortune of sharing borders with three expansion-minded great powers. In August, 1772, those powers agreed on annexations which stripped Poland of about a third of its population and territory.[2] While both Russia (which took Polish Livonia and much of Lithuania and Byelorussia) and Austria (which annexed Polish Galicia) received more territory than Prussia, their shares were of lesser geopolitical importance than that of Frederick, since the territories he appropriated – Ermland, the Netze district and the newly-named West Prussia – now linked East Prussia to Pomerania and Brandenburg by a deep land corridor. This so-called First Partition of Poland had therefore given Frederick, on the cheap, a strategic objective both he and his predecessors had long sought but had despaired of achieving without great cost. Russia, on the other hand, though gaining new territory and avoiding a war with Austria, had sacrificed Moldavia and Wallachia in the Balkans and a controlling voice in the affairs of a Greater Poland, while bringing closer that dangerous day when three restless great powers would have common borders. While no one in 1772 really foresaw that day, which finally arrived with the two subsequent partitions of 1793 and 1795 that dissolved Poland as a state altogether, the first partition did leave some unfinished business which the continued weakness of the Polish government, in spite of some energetic efforts at political regeneration, gave every reason to suppose could be concluded by future agreements of the great powers and at little expense to themselves.[3]

The cooperation between Austria and Prussia in the Polish partition did not bring any permanent warming of relations between the two governments: Vienna's feeling that it had to continue to shore up its position in Europe generally and in Germany in particular was as strong as ever and was matched in intensity by Frederick II's defensive watchfulness against the Habsburgs, which approached the level of permanent paranoia. Joseph, to whom Maria Theresia

2. Maria Theresia's strong moral scruples about this 'rape of Poland' were overcome only by the strenuous efforts of Joseph II and Kaunitz, leading to Frederick's famous witticism: 'She weeps, but she takes.'
3. Prussia, in particular, had reason to look towards some further gains at Poland's expense, since both the district of Thorn and the rich port of Danzig (through which the profitable trade of the Vistula passed on its way to the sea) had been denied it, chiefly at Russian insistence, in 1772. Since these objectives were unlikely to be gained without compensation for Austria or Russia, or both, further partitions of Poland were a logical prospect.

permitted a generally freer hand in foreign than in domestic affairs during the co-regency (1765–80), first attempted a reinvigoration of the German imperial office itself by a series of modest proposals which included the restoration of certain lapsed prerogative rights and the reform of the imperial courts; but when even these minor (and mostly well-intentioned) initiatives failed because of the habitual suspicion of Habsburg intentions among the German princes, Joseph abandoned his illusions of a revitalized emperorship and thereafter devoted his energies to more pragmatic projects designed to strengthen the dynastic lands themselves. The most important such project of Joseph's reign revolved around the idea of incorporating some or all of Bavaria into the German territorial nucleus of the House of Austria – an idea with a long history already, but which had gained a renewed and even urgent appeal after the final loss of Silesia to Prussia. By the mid-1770s, Elector Max III Joseph of Bavaria (1745–77) seemed likely to die without male heirs and Austrian diplomats had begun to negotiate with his presumed successor from a collateral Wittelsbach line, Karl Theodor of Sulzbach (1724–99), Elector Palatine and duke of Jülich and Berg, for an eventual exchange of Bavaria for the Austrian Netherlands. The Austrians, of course, had long since come to regard the Netherlands as fully expendable under the proper circumstances, while Karl Theodor cared nothing about Bavaria but was infatuated with the notion of consolidating his current possessions with the Austrian Netherlands into a single 'Kingdom of Burgundy' on the lower Rhine. While discussions envisioning some such outcome as this were proceeding in desultory fashion in Vienna, Max III Joseph died suddenly in late December 1777. Within days, Austrian diplomats presented Karl Theodor's startled representatives with a treaty authorizing immediate Austrian occupation of approximately a third of Bavaria's territory – the price, essentially, for continuing negotiations on any future exchange. Karl Theodor accepted the treaty with that understanding and Austrian troops crossed the Bavarian border in mid-January 1778.

These events, naturally enough, produced a convulsive reaction from Frederick II of Prussia, who not only prevailed upon Karl Theodor's presumptive heir, Duke Karl of Zweibrücken, to protest the partition of his future inheritance at the imperial diet, but also entered into a military alliance with Elector Friedrich August III of Saxony (1763–1827), who also had claims on parts of Max III Joseph's legacy. Frederick's further attempt to enlist military help from his ally Russia failed, but was balanced by the refusal of France to provide direct assistance to Austria. After briefly toying with the possibility of territorial compensation for himself as a solution to the Bavarian issue, Frederick instead decided to confront Vienna directly and in July 1778, he sent troops from Silesia and Saxony across the Bohemian frontier. The ensuing War of the Bavarian Succession (sometimes called the 'Potato War' because the troops spent most of their time digging potatoes from the cold and cheerless fields in which they camped) witnessed little military action. Maria Theresia's reservations about Joseph's judgment throughout this affair led her early on to appeal for a settlement to Frederick; but while this direct approach had no success, both rulers became increasingly nervous about Russia's obscure position and when Vienna finally proposed French mediation of the dispute, Frederick accepted, but on condition that Russia join the effort. This most dreary of wars was thus settled in the Peace of Teschen (May 1779): Frederick permitted Austria to absorb a small piece of Bavarian territory – the so-called Inn Quarter – in return for Austria's formal recognition of Prussia's expectancy to the margraviates of Ansbach and Bayreuth upon the death of their single Hohenzollern ruler.[4] Karl Theodor was awarded the rest of a Bavaria he despised and to which the succession rights of Karl of Zweibrücken were confirmed. The treaty, which also contained the whole text of the Peace of Westphalia, was formally guaranteed by both foreign mediators, thus allowing Russia to join France (and Sweden) as guarantors of the German political order.

The perception awakened in much of Germany that the Bavarian episode marked a distinctly aggressive reorientation of Austria's foreign policy and that this novel direction was due mostly to the restless ambitions of Joseph II, was soon reinforced by several actions ascribable to his influence. In 1780, only a few months before Maria Theresia's death in November conferred undivided sovereignty on Joseph, he had engineered the appointment of his youngest brother Max Franz as coadjutor bishop of Cologne and Münster, with presumptive right to succeed to the rulership of both upon the death of the reigning archbishop and elector (which occurred in 1783). This was a major coup, establishing not only a strong Habsburg presence on the lower Rhine, but also a penetration of the German Catholic church which took on an increasingly ominous character through

---

4. These principalities, containing some 400,000 people, lay just to the north and west of Bavaria. Their reversion to Prussia would create hostile outposts in what Austria regarded as its German sphere of influence, a prospect which contributed to Austria's overall discomfort after 1763. Both territories were finally absorbed by Prussia in 1791, during a period of Austro-Prussian reconciliation.

several other of Joseph's initiatives over the next few years: he restricted ancient ecclesiastical rights exercised in Austria by neighbouring prince-bishops, revived a long dormant imperial prerogative to appropriate certain monastic funds in the Empire for the support of his loyalists and actively manoeuvred to bring other sees under Habsburg control. What all of this suggested to a suspicious Empire was that Joseph wanted complete control of the Catholic *Reichskirche*, perhaps as a prelude to a massive secularization intended to increase Austria's territorial holdings – a possibility made suddenly more real in 1784 by the emperor's openly announced intention to annex both Salzburg and Berchtesgaden. These events, which began to take on the hues of an Austrian offensive within the Empire, also gave a far more menacing significance than it deserved to the paralysis which halted the operations of the imperial diet between 1780–85; this had resulted from nothing more than a petty procedural quarrel, but it was widely rumoured to be a deliberate Austrian plot to prevent concerted resistance from the diet to Austria's nefarious plans for Germany. The time-honoured response of territorial princes who felt threatened by the emperor's policies, of course, was that of alliance in some form of association of imperial estates; but while the above events gave rise to much discussion of this possibility, the actual formation of such a union resulted from an altogether different issue – Joseph II's resurrection of the Bavarian exchange project.

In spite of the disappointing outcome of the War of the Bavarian Succession, the prospect of acquiring all of Bavaria had lost none of its appeal for Joseph. No problem was to be expected from Elector Karl Theodor, who remained as eager as ever to exchange Bavaria for the Austrian Netherlands; but in the face of certain Prussian opposition, it was clear that without attracting the support of other great powers for the scheme Joseph had no real hope of realizing it. To obtain such support, the emperor first began a diplomatic courtship of Catherine II, gradually drawing her away from an alliance with Prussia that had been showing many signs of stress since the Bavarian war anyway; this policy culminated in Austrian mediation of a Russo-Turkish treaty in early 1784 which allowed a jubilant and grateful Catherine to annex the Crimea. By roundabout means, Joseph also worked to create a favourable disposition on the part of a France still formally allied with Vienna. This he did by making some harsh demands on Holland – also a French ally – and then, after receiving warnings from Versailles, moderating those demands with a show of sweet reasonableness which he expected the

French to reciprocate as his new plan for the Bavarian exchange ripened.[5] As subsequent events demonstrated, his efforts did him little good. It is true that Catherine's able diplomatic representatives did some circuit-riding to various German courts to create an atmosphere favourable to the project – with generally indifferent results – and, in particular, tried without success to coax agreement to the exchange from Karl of Zweibrücken; but France, always privately dubious about Austria's unilateral gain from the realization of the exchange, effectively stopped it by making French support dependent on some form of yet to be attained (and clearly impossible) Prussian agreement to it.

While in the final analysis, therefore, it was France's deliberate disassociation from the Bavarian project that forced Joseph to abandon it[6], Frederick II had also been busy encouraging German opposition to the exchange. Taking advantage of the general alarm Joseph's recent policies had aroused in the Empire and of the disposition towards the formation of defensive associations it had created, he was able to coax both Hanover and Saxony into a formal 'Association for the Preservation of the Imperial Constitution' (better known as the League of Princes) in July 1785 and, through them, eventually to attract fourteen more signatories, including not only several medium-sized states but also the imperial archchancellor, the archbishop-elector of Mainz.[7] From the standpoint of its most powerful member, Prussia, the real purpose of the league was not the protection of the constitutional order of the Empire that was expressed in the public articles of the treaty of alliance, but in the secret provisions which bound the three original signatories to oppose territorial exchanges or annexations within the Empire by armed force. In this sense, the league was simply insurance against

---

5. The pugnacious Joseph regarded the right of the Dutch to garrison the 'barrier fortresses' in the Austrian Netherlands, as well as the closure of the mouth of the Scheldt, as limitations on his sovereignty (even though both had been guaranteed by Karl VI at Rastatt in 1714). The Dutch were agreeable to withdrawal of their garrisons, but balked at opening the Scheldt, putting them for a time under the threat of Austrian military sanctions.

6. Karl Theodor himself remained eager for the exchange until 1788, when rebellions in the Netherlands against various of Joseph's policies there all but destroyed his enthusiasm.

7. The addition of Friedrich Karl von Erthal of Mainz (and his coadjutor, Karl von Dalberg) was a real coup, not only because of his high constitional position in the Empire but also because of his Catholicism, which allowed the league to escape confessional identification as a purely Protestant union and thus to attract sympathy from many ecclesiastical princes, including some who were tradition-ally friendly to the emperor. Hanover, of course, like Saxony, was an important electorate, with the added advantage of providing a loose connection to England.

any renewal of Joseph's acquisitive policies. Not all members were asked to subscribe to the secret articles and few did; indeed, several of them (Duke Carl August of Weimar in particular) ardently hoped that the new union might provide the impetus for a general reformation and strengthening of the imperial constitutional system. Frederick, however, had no interest whatsoever in the Empire except as a foil against Austria, a means whereby the German balance of power between Berlin and Vienna could be maintained.

After Frederick's death in 1786, the initial attitudes of his successor Friedrich Wilhelm II (1786–97) gave some hope to the reformist princes that the new king might support their plans for strengthening the imperial constitution. But by 1788, Prussia's earlier need for the league had diminished considerably: Austria, by virtue of disastrous performance in a joint war with Russia against the Turks, now seemed to present a much lesser threat in Germany, while an Anglo-Prussian treaty signed in August 1788 gave Prussia the much sought-after reassurance of a great-power alliance that had been absent since 1781, when the Russo-Prussian agreement of 1764 had lapsed. Prussia's declining interest in the league was by this time echoed in some other members; never very happy about the strong Prussian flavour of the union to begin with, these princes became steadily more uncomfortable as Austria's mounting misfortunes seemed to present an imbalance of power in Prussia's favour – a perception greatly strengthened by Prussia's unconcealed attempt in late 1789 and early 1790 to utilize for its own selfish purposes its contribution to an armed intervention against rebels in the bishopric of Liège that had been mandated by the Imperial Cameral Tribunal. While a last flicker of cooperative purpose can be glimpsed in the efforts of the four electoral members of the league to formulate a common policy in the imperial election of 1790, following Joseph's death, their failure to reach agreement revealed that the real reasons for their association had by now faded away entirely. Indeed, even before the election of Leopold II in September, Berlin and Vienna had achieved a partial reconciliation in the Convention of Reichenbach of July 1790.[8] Perceived now as essentially superfluous by Prussia, which also had no intention of letting it live on under the leadership of any other member, the League of Princes quickly suffocated in its own inactivity and purposelessness.

8. This agreement, though not ending the Austro-Prussian rivalry, did settle a number of immediately outstanding causes of friction between the two states and for a time eased the tensions which their continuous hostility since 1740 had brought to Germany.

Not all of those princes who had earnestly but vainly sought to use the league for a general reform of the Empire and who represented the smaller territories almost exclusively, received the news of the Convention of Reichenbach with the relief one might have supposed would greet any agreement that seemed to establish peace between the two German great powers. On the contrary, while many such princes rejected the suggestion that the Empire had degenerated into a balance of power system in which all territories not Austrian or Prussian – the 'third Germany', as it were – owed their continued existence chiefly to the mutual jealousy and watchfulness of Berlin and Vienna, preferring instead to think that the rights of all imperial estates were safeguarded by the imperial constitution itself, the fact is that many of them had come to rely on an effective balance of power between Habsburgs and Hohenzollerns as the condition for the preservation of the political and territorial *status quo* in Germany. This accounts for the widespread fear that Reichenbach, by establishing a basis for cooperation between Austria and Prussia, could ultimately lead to a partition of Germany between the two by a common agreement involving some mixture of secularization of ecclesiastical states, annexations of other territories on flimsy legal pretexts, or simple land-grabs. The interest in strengthening the constitutional order of the Empire stemmed mostly from the recognition of the lesser states that the negative centrifugal effects of the fragmentation of Germany, reinforced by other kinds of divisions – Protestant vs. Catholic, large states vs. smaller ones, ecclesiastical vs. secular states, emperor vs. Empire and so on – could be overcome, while preserving the rights of all imperial estates (that is, the territorial *status quo*), only by redefining the Empire as a juridical system and by reforms designed to strengthen the various components of that system in such a way as to justify commitment to the imperial nexus as a reliable, working legal order.

This is essentially what the two most famous students of imperial public law in the last century of the Empire's existence tried to do in their work. Both Johann Jakob Moser (1701–85) and Johann Stephan Pütter (1725–1807) abandoned the attempt to explain the Empire as a political body and instead tried to analyze and explicate the myriad relationships and obligations of imperial law which, if correctly understood and observed (and perhaps with some reforms to facilitate both comprehension and performance), adequately defined the imperial system. Both scholars believed that system to be a sound one, which could work to the advantage of all *if all wanted it to work*. That was a solution not much if at all different from the reforms in the operations of the diet, the Circles, the imperial courts and so on, solicited by the smaller princes such as Carl August of Saxe-Weimar and others, all of which, in the final analysis, were designed to preserve peace in an eternalized *status quo*. Yet even if these reforms had been adopted (and they were not), the predicate of their success was the existence of the good will to make them work – a 'common spirit' (*Gemeingeist*) or 'national spirit' (*Nationalgeist*) whose total and glaring absence was constantly lamented in the public press of the time.

But all of this begs the question of what was so admirable about the Empire as to justify efforts to preserve it, especially since almost no one thought it either possible *or* desirable that any reform aim at restoring such real power to any imperial institutions as might disturb the intricate balances which guaranteed the Empire's external and internal immobility. Prussian and Austrian statesmen (and many other Europeans, too) might well have answered that there was nothing particularly admirable about it, but that it had to be maintained, at least provisionally, simply to prevent its dissolution from upsetting either the German or the European balance of power – especially in ways which favoured one of the German powers at the expense of the other. Other territorial princes – the majority, certainly – would also doubtlessly have argued that the imperial structure had to be sustained because it was all that stood between their independence and their absorption by the more powerful states around them. But the raw self-interest that dictated such views as these was matched by a more elevated and fairly widespread approach which found in the territorial fragmentation of the Empire one immense advantage which more than compensated for the political paralysis it brought. That advantage was *diversity* – diversity in the forms and policies of governments, in social structures and attitudes, in cultural and educational milieus, in religions, in economic activities and levels of well-being and, in short, in virtually all of the conditions of human existence. That diversity, it was said, provided Germans with choices which the citizens of other countries did not have – especially those living in large states under the absolute rulership of centralized monarchies, single official religions and imposed uniform standards in everything from social behaviour to cultural and artistic taste. In the sense that freedom cannot exist without choice, furthermore, it therefore brought freedom itself. The generous but not uncritical receptivity to the contributions of other peoples in all areas of human endeavour which so many Germans saw as uniquely characteristic of their race was also inseparable from the variegated nature of the national community in which they lived. And finally, even the enervation of political will which made the Empire the diplomatic and military laughing-stock of Europe and which was of course traceable to its fractured sovereignty, could be seen as a boon to Europe: it lay as a dead mass in the heart of Europe, separating the quarrelsome great powers from each other, possessing too little power to be a threat to any of them but with just enough of it to protect its independence, thereby protecting the European balance of power. The Empire did have its admirers, therefore, who spoke for moral ideals that were becoming less and less comprehensible to a world in which continuous international competition had made the cultivation of power an all-consuming dictate. In this sense, the Empire conceived as a passive system designed merely to protect its members stood as the last grand institutional rebuke to – and victim of – the cynical maxims of *raison d'état*.

Even its staunchest defenders, however, could scarcely deny that the immobility of the Empire also served to protect the existence of several types of polities increasingly viewed as hopelessly anachronistic and impossible to reconcile with 'modern' concepts of competent (much less 'enlightened') government. The ecclesiastical principalities, for example, attracted growing criticism from a variety of sources. These states, products of a long forgotten struggle for power between medieval popes and emperors, appeared by now to have little purpose beyond guarding their political independence and defending themselves against undue interference from Rome. The German *Reichskirche* was fundamentally a bishops' church and conciliarist in outlook – tending, that is, to locate supreme ecclesiastical authority not in the papacy but in the collective will of the bishops expressed through councils. What this meant in practice, however, was a high degree of episcopal autonomy, with much touchiness among the bishops about taking orders not only from the Vatican but even from their metropolitan superiors. The most radical statement of episcopal supremacy within the German church was produced in 1763 by an auxiliary bishop of Trier, Nicolaus von Hontheim, writing pseudonymously as 'Febronius'; most German bishops, while refusing to identify with his extreme views, nevertheless accepted the general tendencies of his argument. The sensitivity of the suffragan bishops to the authority exercised by their metropolitans is well illustrated in the disagreements that arose over the Ems Punctation of 1786. This document, a vigorous protest against Rome's interference in the German church by the archbishops of Trier, Mainz, Cologne and Salzburg, was a response to the establishment of a special nunciatura in Munich, solicited from Rome by Elector Karl Theodor as part of an attempt to discipline his Bavarian bishops. The Punctation also called for the restoration of the ancient constitution of the *Reichskirche*; but since this was seen by nearly all subordinate bishops (including both territorial suffragans and prince-bishops) as an attempt of the metropolitans to increase their ecclesiastical authority over them, the archbishops' initiative failed to gain widespread support and soon vanished as an issue.

While self-interested squabbling over issues such as these hardly helped the public image of the ecclesiastical states, they faced much more serious criticism for other reasons. They were commonly accused not only of lax, corrupt and inefficient government, but of fostering a Catholic obscurantism inimical to most of the intellectual and practical ideals of the enlightenment. Critics pointed out that all the prelatic governments were in a sense nothing but ambitionless caretaker regimes, since their rulership was elective rather than hereditary, and that their chief purpose was to provide good livings for the otherwise unemployable fathers and sons of imperial nobility who filled the cathedral chapters and other official positions. Many of these principalities were, in fact, magnets for beggars and layabouts and most had economies and fiscal systems which were anything but progressive. There were indeed a few ecclesiastical princes who conducted reformist and enlightened regimes, or who were at least personally of high moral character[9]; but these were perceived as exceptions in a picture dominated by insouciance, malfeasance and incompetence. The chief defence offered up for the continued existence of the ecclesiastical states was that the lack of hereditary rulership removed all temptation to play dangerous and expensive power politics for dynastic reasons, resulting in governments which could devote their energies to improving the well-being of the citizenry instead of to war and diplomacy; bad government, in this argument, thus became mild government – the origin of the oft-cited phrase 'living is good under the crozier'. Such apologetics got

9. Perhaps the most notable reformer among them was Maria Theresia's youngest son, Max Franz, who was elected coadjutor of Cologne in 1780 and who succeeded to the electorship in 1784. Strongly influenced by the ideas and policies of his brother Joseph II, he pursued progressive economic and governmental policies and by elevating the Bonn academy to the status of a university sought to counteract the conservative influence of the nearby University of Cologne. Other examples would include Clement Wenzeslas, the last elector of Trier, Franz Ludwig von Erthal of Würzburg-Bamberg and the last prince-archbishop of Salzburg, Hieronymus Joseph.

little hearing outside the self-interested circles of the prince-prelates themselves and by the last two decades of the century the spectre of widespread secularization or annexation of these territories by the larger secular princes, made more substantial by Joseph II's well publicized intention to absorb Salzburg, had become a much discussed issue of German political life.

The Imperial Cities, as a group, had an even worse reputation than the ecclesiastical territories. The handful of larger and more prosperous of them – Hamburg, Bremen and Frankfurt, for example and even some of the old and venerable south German cities such as Nürnberg, Augsburg and Ulm – still possessed enough diversity and civic vigour to earn a measure of respect and even admiration in public opinion. But the majority of them, as victims of fundamental changes in the geography of trade and commerce since the sixteenth century, had lost much of their earlier population and economic vitality; more than a few, indeed, had sunk to the level of mere villages, in which the desperate attempt to maintain the traditions of a time long past now impressed outsiders as a ludicrous and unwarranted vanity. Subjected to periodic harassment by the annoyed rulers of the larger territories which surrounded or enclosed them and who coveted such little wealth and territory as they had, many cities, once at least semidemocratic in political structure, had degenerated into rigid patrician oligarchies whose grip on the government became even tighter as economic distress and popular discontent created increasingly serious challenges to their misrule. Unequal tax burdens, mismanagement of municipal property and funds and large and growing public debts were common features of far too many Imperial Cities and were widely known and reported. Like the ecclesiastical states, the Free Cities had some defenders; but their arguments tended to be based on the cities' historical contributions to German civilization in a much earlier age and except for the somewhat dubious proposition that as oases of political neutrality they tended to encourage greater freedom of thought and speech than other less inert territories, little justification for the continued independence of these small enclaves of imperial immediacy was offered. The critics' suggestion that the vast majority of these cities would benefit from the greater economic opportunities offered by absorption into the larger secular states was essentially correct and was proved to be so soon after the end of the century.

In addition to the ecclesiastical states and the Imperial Cities, there was another group of territories whose existence was called into

question in the later eighteenth century and whose final disappearance early in the nineteenth removed one of the last components
of the territorial mosaic that defined the old Empire. These were the
tiny lands of the hundreds of Imperial Knights who, though not
estates of the Empire, had provided a significant source of support
for the emperor, the ecclesiastical states (through their penetration of
the cathedral chapters and many prince-prelacies) and the whole
imperial constitutional order. They, more than any others, depended
on the protective shield of the imperial constitution to prevent
absorption by princes of whatever degree of power within whose
states their own lands lay as irritating pockets of independent
government and jurisdiction. Under more or less constant threat
from numerous princes' leagues formed against them after 1648, the
knights found enough support from the emperor, the Aulic Council
and their own employers among various ecclesiastical and even some
secular princes to preserve their precarious existence throughout the
eighteenth century. But in their capacity as territorial lords they had
very little support in the general public, which perceived their
minuscule lands as absolutely the most anachronistic, worst
governed and administered and most poverty-stricken in the Empire
and which not only rejected the historical and constitutional
arguments thrown up by the knights in their own defence, but also
hooted at their suggestion that their admittedly severe financial woes
actually protected the freedom of their subjects by making
impossible the establishment of absolutist military regimes. The
knights, who were particularly numerous in southern and southwestern Germany and along the Rhine, had long had a loose collective
organization which grouped them into fourteen cantons spanning
three imperial Circles; but while some liked to think that this
constituted them as a 'state' in the Empire in their own right and
advocated reforms to strengthen this organization as a means of self-
protection, the fact is that this state, like the Empire itself, could not
act like one and in the event failed to preserve the knights'
sovereignty and independence much past the end of the century.

While the existence of these three sorts of polity was clearly
fragile, depending as it did on the preservation of an almost absolute
status quo in the Empire, many of the secular territories could look to
the future with greater confidence. This was particularly true of the
larger states, whose interests were secured either by ties to a foreign
great power (as in the case of Hanover) or by their relative
importance as weights in the German political balance (Bavaria and
Saxony in particular, but including other middle-sized states such as

Württemberg and Hesse-Kassel). Hanover's history in the eighteenth century is interesting because it was the only German state without a resident prince – a circumstance which spared it considerable court expenses and enabled it to weather the financial exactions of the two mid-century wars without undue distress. The government lay in the hands of a privy council, consisting of high nobility, which communicated with the king-elector in England through a Hanoverian minister in London, though day-to-day administration was conducted by a sort of bureaucratic bourgeois patriciate. Few financial demands were made on the country from London and few troops were raised from it for service in the British empire (none of whom served in the American war). Its governance was generally mild and relaxed and its landowning nobility, sparse in numbers, supported laws which preserved and protected a moderately prosperous peasantry. With no ambitious ruler to stress its economy, Hanover was a generally well-off (if thinly populated) territory of some one and a half million souls, whose almost laissez-faire internal policies account for much of the excellent teaching and research carried on at its renowned university in Göttingen. That institution, in particular, served as an important conduit by which English culture and liberal political ideas were introduced into Germany. Unlike his two predecessors, King George III (1760–1820) never visited his German electorate, but his lively interest in agriculture produced several benefits for Hanover: the establishment of the Agricultural Society in Celle (1764), land reclamation on the moors around Bremen and the beginnings of peasant liberation on the electoral domains.

The equanimity of Hanoverian public life was much less in evidence in Bavaria, where serious financial problems plagued the entire reign of Max III Joseph (1745–77). These problems were the result not only of an unusually inefficient financial administration but also of woefully inadequate revenues of which, around 1760, nearly half were devoted to debt service and court expenditures alone. A conscientious application of new statistical techniques helped to correct some fiscal mismanagement and even to improve the overall economy to some extent; but even with forced loans and new taxes the problem of revenues remained intractable, due chiefly to the hugely excessive land holdings of tax-exempt churches and monasteries. New laws and ordinances of the 1760s were intended to address this issue by limiting new land acquisition by conventual establishments, controlling the growth of their membership and intensifying state supervision of church wealth. The fact that such measures were not very effective says much about the persistent strength of a Catholic church still riddled with superstitious and pagan practices and implacably hostile towards those currents of enlightened thinking which were becoming dominant elsewhere in Germany; indeed, even the dissolution of the Jesuit order in 1773 did not provide the window of opportunity for the desperately needed educational reform on which the elector and some of his advisers had counted. Apart from his establishment of the Bavarian Academy of Sciences in 1759, the only permanent successes of Max III Joseph's commitment to enlightenment were the rationalization and reform of criminal, procedural and civil law codes achieved by his able vice-chancellor W. von Kreittmayer between 1751–56.

The succession of Karl Theodor (1777–99) to the Bavarian throne brought an institutionalized electoral neglect of nearly all policies of public improvement, resulting in increased public indebtedness and an economic stagnation which filled the streets of Munich with beggars and raised highway robbery to the status of an honourable vocation. The new elector's distaste for Bavaria, made glaringly obvious by his repeated attempts to trade it to Joseph II for territories elsewhere, did not endear him to Bavarians, whose growing hostility only increased his intolerance towards them; eventually relying chiefly on his confessor Ignaz Frank, a former Jesuit with a fanatical hatred of the enlightenment, Karl Theodor instituted a severely custodial regime, replete with a censorship and police presence which became particularly intense after the discovery and suppression of the secret *Illuminatenorden* in 1784–5.[10] This harsh government stood in rather sharp contrast to the rather enlightened and easygoing policies which characterized Karl Theodor's rule in his other chief territory, the Palatinate, for which he had genuine affection. Though luxury-loving to a fault and a womanizer of heroic proportions, he maintained a refined and intellectually stimulating court in Mann-heim; he acquired splendid art collections, patronized excellent architects, kept one of the best operatic stages in Germany and, with an active interest in literature, founded the first court theatre for German drama – where, interestingly, Schiller's *The Robbers* was first presented in 1782.

Unlike Bavaria, where escape from the perils and expenses of high international politics after 1745 was insufficient to restore fiscal stability and economic prosperity for the remainder of the century, Saxony benefited immediately from its elector's virtually simul-taneous renunciation of all future royal ambitions in Poland and the

10. See below, Chapter Twenty-three.

treaty of peace with Prussia which restored him to his throne in Dresden after the Seven Years War. Since 1741, Friedrich August II's involvement in the Silesian wars had brought financial disaster and economic decline to the electorate – certainly contrary to the purposes of the generally well-intentioned but ultimately failed policies of his chief minister, Count Heinrich Brühl, who directed the government's foreign policy, economy and finances from 1738 until his death in 1763.[11] As early as 1762, however, as peace approached, a group of younger officials had begun planning for the reconstruction of the country through a special commission that worked closely with the crown prince, Friedrich Christian (who became elector, but reigned for only a few months in 1763) and, after his death, with Electress Maria Antonia. She, together with her administrator Prince Xaver, governed Saxony for Friedrich August III (1763–1827) during his minority and were able to restore respectability to both the fiscal system and the military establishment. After the new elector attained majority, he followed a cautious and unremarkable foreign policy based on friendship with Prussia and generally correct relations with Austria. In domestic affairs, a sober and conscientious administration reminiscent of the paternalistic governments of an earlier time contributed to a gradual but steady increase in economic productivity, both in textiles such as damask, velvet and silk which had good external and internal markets and in various mineral products from a superbly administered mining industry. Though Catholic himself, Friedrich August did not interfere in the affairs of the official Lutheran church, which by now had lost much of its stiff-necked and intolerant orthodoxy to the mildening and progressivist influences of the enlightenment. Dresden, meanwhile, remained one of the most pleasing cities in Europe, with its brilliant architecture, its collections of paintings and statuary and a modestly elegant court – for all of which the continuing musical and literary achievements of her sister city Leipzig provided an artistically perfecting counterpoint. While Saxony could never

---

11. Brühl, whose questionable financial management was probably as much a result of desperation as of incompetence or personal corruption, has received harsh treatment by many older historians, but has more recently been viewed with greater sympathy. Many of his economic initiatives were imaginative and productive and his fiscal policies were conducted without much help from a lazy and indifferent master and against an often ill-informed and self-interested opposition from the territorial estates. Brühl is frequently blamed for Saxony's misfortunes in the last Silesian war, but his treaty of alliance with France in 1756 was intended to secure peace in Germany, not to ignite a war with Prussia. French intentions, in fact, were essentially similar.

again hope to attempt a major role in German or European politics, it therefore continued to nourish a rich cultural tradition whose importance for Germany not even the now-rising lights of Weimar could diminish.

Among the larger territories of the Empire, probably the most notorious for arbitrary government was Württemberg, where Duke Karl Eugen (1737–93) fell into bitter and continuous quarrelling with the territorial estates immediately after his assumption of full control of the government in 1755. His extravagant spending on palaces, mistresses, court festivities, hunting and especially on the military, caused him to impose illegal taxes, collected by armed force, as well as to traffic in state offices and even to sell some of his soldiers into the colonial service of the maritime powers. His arbitrary imprisonment of such well-known figures as the legal scholar Johann Jakob Moser and the poet and journalist C. F. D. Schubart spread his notoriety well beyond the borders of his own duchy. The estates' desperation led finally not only to appeals to the imperial courts, but also to a diplomatic interposition of Prussia, England and Denmark which eventuated in a formal compromise (*Erbvergleich*) between the duke and his estates in 1770. Unfortunately, the strengthening of the small (standing) committee of the estates in which this agreement resulted did not much benefit the country, since the committee began to practise a form of corrupt absolutism in its own sphere, forfeiting much public confidence; the populace reacted to their increasingly dismal government by turning inward, submerging themselves even more deeply in the very strong Pietism which was the earmark of their territorial church. Karl Eugen himself experienced a spiritual and political 'conversion' of sorts in 1777 and reached a more or less cordial understanding with the estates which lasted for the rest of his reign, though his often aberrant and sometimes violent behaviour continued to make him and his court objects of a lively critical interest in the public press.

Princes were not the only possible source of despotic government, however, as was amply demonstrated in the example of the duchy of Mecklenburg-Schwerin. Here, the early attempts of Duke Karl Leopold (1713–47) to terrorize the estates and to erect a military absolutism led to an imperial execution by Hanover and Brunswick by which he was eventually deposed. After a long period as administrator of the duchy, Christian Ludwig II (1747–56) succeeded his brother and was forced into an extraordinary *Erbvergleich* with the territorial nobility; by its terms, the duke all but abdicated effective sovereignty over that three-fifths of the land area of the duchy composed of private estates, leaving their noble owners free to impose on their peasant dependants a harsh and unforgiving servitude unrestrained by any higher authority. The growing profitability of cattle-raising produced a movement towards enclosures which deepened the sufferings of the peasantry through widespread evictions which were legally prohibited elsewhere in Germany. Under Duke Friedrich the Pious (1756–85), the urban population was also made to suffer, if in a different way: a puritanical Pietist, Friedrich ran a blue-nosed regime in which popular amusements and entertainments, including the theatre, were forbidden; and he crippled higher education by quarrelling with the Lutheran faculty of the territory's only university at Rostock, eventually splitting that faculty by founding a second and much inferior 'anti-university' at Bützow which, happily, survived his own death by only four years.

Fortunately, the dark picture of misgovernment painted by the last two examples was alleviated by the existence of some genuinely enlightened rulers whose beneficent policies received as much attention in the public press as did the misdeeds of the malefactors among their fellow princes. Apart from the small but brilliant court of Carl August of Saxe-Weimar (1775–1828), which became virtually a literary and philosophical Camelot for many years, two larger territories deserve particular mention. Baden-Durlach (which also absorbed Baden-Baden in 1771) was gifted with two exceptional princes whose combined rule spanned more than a century. Margrave Karl Wilhelm (1709–38), who laid out his capital city of Karlsruhe around a new palace he built there, set the tone for a mild and benevolent government through an edict of toleration of 1722, whose practical implementation he further assisted by constructing separate churches or temples for Lutherans, Calvinists, Catholics and Jews. His son, Karl Friedrich (1738–1811), inherited his father's forward-looking disposition and with the help of his talented minister Wilhelm von Edelsheim, conducted a progressive government in the best traditions of humane princely paternalism. Personal enlightenment, combined with a strong pragmatic bent, attracted him to the economic doctrines of the French Physiocrats and he became the first ruler to attempt implementation of their theories. While many Physiocratic ideas proved unworkable and were abandoned, the overall attention they focused on agriculture produced some significant results in the form of improved soils, model farms, better transport facilities through new roads and canals, and, most impressive of all, the abolition of serfdom in 1783.

Karl Friedrich also had a genuine interest in education and not only ordered compulsory schooling at the primary level but also founded seminars for the training of teachers and ministers to make it possible.

Cut from much the same cloth was Duke Karl Wilhelm Ferdinand of Brunswick (1780–1806), whose merits as a sometime general in the Prussian army were matched by his achievements as an enlightened ruler; he carried out many economic improvements, practised complete religious toleration, granted more freedom to the press than it enjoyed anywhere else in Germany and punctuated his interest in education by appointing the progressive educator J. H. Campe superintendent of the duchy's school system. He also had a very active interest in the mature German enlightenment, including the literary revival, and was responsible for attracting G. E. Lessing to Wolfenbüttel as head of the ducal library there.

Among other rulers of medium-sized territories who lived up to at least some of the standards of enlightened government must be reckoned the two Hessian landgraves, Ludwig IX of Hesse-Darmstadt (1768–90) and Friedrich II of Hesse-Kassel (1760–85); the latter, in particular, tried to emulate his Prussian namesake of the same period and in spite of his dubious reputation as the chief German trafficker in soldiery for foreign states he ran a generally efficient administration and by his generous patronage of education, architecture and the arts turned the previously rather drab city of Kassel into a pleasing and tasteful capital. Most of the millions he made through his *Soldatenhandel* was eventually managed by the Jewish banker Meyer Rothschild, who founded the greatness of his family's banking business in Frankfurt and London chiefly on this Hessian capital. Friedrich's successor, Wilhelm IX (1785–1821), inherited a large fortune which he greatly increased by cutting back on the extravagances of his predecessor and by his own prudential financial management, eventually becoming one of the richest princes of his time.

It should be understood of course, that the many references in this and earlier chapters to 'enlightened' (or 'unenlightened') governments and rulers derive from the broader term 'enlightenment' not as an absolute theoretical norm, but as it was understood by contemporary commentators themselves. They employed all these terms freely in their descriptions of the public affairs of their times, though with a somewhat variable meaning which included some but not all of the connotations still carried by the adjective 'enlightened' today. For that reason, it is now necessary, in the following chapter, to examine the general (and unique) character of the later enlightenment in Germany.

CHAPTER TWENTY-THREE

The Later German Enlightenment

The later enlightenment in Germany – a period from roughly the end of the Seven Years War to the beginning of the French Revolution in 1789 – was characterized by two chief continuities with its earlier phases, discussed in Chapter Fifteen: it had no single geographical locus and was consequently a dispersed and diffuse movement; and it had no single one or even a few individuals whose views and reputations were so universally impressive as to set a single stamp on the entire movement, which therefore continued to be remarkably eclectic and syncretic with regard to both the sources and the applications of its ideas. But it is also different from its early years in two major respects: first, by reason of the extraordinarily rapid diffusion of new and progressive ideas from their original home in the universities, academies, learned journals and the studies of individual scholars to a wider and rapidly increasing public composed of all educated elites and to a limited extent of all the genuinely literate, including sections of the petty bourgeoisie; and second, by virtue of the growth of a more direct and specific criticism of existing society – a criticism largely absent in an earlier literature which was either so broadly theoretical as to be politically innocuous, or which tended to identify bad conditions and to propose remedies for them, but without penetrating to the root causes of those conditions. To a certain extent, the latter change may also be described as a shift from a criticism of moral attitudes alone to one which also included institutions and the practices unavoidably linked to them.

On the whole, even this new criticism cannot be termed radical, much less revolutionary; with few exceptions, both major and minor figures of the German enlightenment were remarkably tolerant of the basic features of their society. The moderation they showed in their approach to it was due primarily to two circumstances peculiar to Germany: first, almost all the figures who produced and disseminated enlightened ideas were active participants in and beneficiaries of the system they critiqued. This meant not only that there were both external and self-imposed constraints on what they could say or write, but also and just as important, that most of them had as much appreciation of the complexities and strengths of the system to which they belonged as of its weaknesses – which meant that their criticism was tempered by constructive intentions aimed at improving a system they accepted as both vital and their own, not at destroying or replacing it. The smaller scale of political life in the numerous German territorial states also nourished not only a familiarity and even fondness for a comfortably traditional society and its institutions, but also the realistic hope that socially meaningful reform could successfully be implemented in an environment small enough to be manageable.[1] These characteristics of the German enlightenment are fundamental to its nature and reveal its orientation as a basically conservative one, behind which lay the assumption that enlightenment itself could be made triumphant within the socio-political structure of the old regime as it then existed.[2]

Second, the purveyors of the enlightenment in Germany did not, for the most part, have to pursue their goals from outside of or without support from the two most important (and interconnected) institutional complexes of their time – church and state. In both, traditions existed which at least to a point reinforced the progressivist tendencies of the enlightenment, even when they diverged

---

1. In some important figures, this familiarity produced interesting ambiguities towards the theoretical foundations of the enlightenment and many of the attitudes and reforms associated with it. A particularly fascinating example is that of Justus Möser, the oracle of Osnabrück, whose many and important writings contained ideas ranging from the radically progressive to the stubbornly conservative and even reactionary. An illuminating recent study of this very unusual and ambiguous personality is Jonathan B. Knudsen, *Justus Möser and the German Enlightenment* (N.Y., 1986).
2. 'Enlightenment', by the 1780s, had come to be understood not just as the means by which the well-being and happiness of mankind was improved, but also as the process by which the theoretical capabilities of the human mind, operating through its independent power of reason, were developed and refined. That was the basic sense of the separate answers given by the philosophers Immanuel Kant and Moses Mendelssohn to the prize question 'What is Enlightenment?' posed in the periodical *Berlinische Monatsschrift* in 1783. Both men, though in different ways, also acknowledged a distinction between the value of intellectual cultivation as the theoretical education of man and its utilizations by him as a member of civil society.

from it in language and other ways, including final purpose. In Protestant areas, for example, which for the whole period remained the primary home of the German enlightenment, the influence of Pietism (even when no longer specifically identifiable as such) had pushed many Lutheran and Reformed clergy so far in the direction of 'practical' piety as to produce an insistence that the function of religion was to help man, not God, that the genuine worship of God implied assumption of a responsibility for the practical welfare of the entire Christian community and, therefore, that religious education also had to mean social education.[3] The utilitarianism of the enlightenment both benefited from and helped to strengthen these reformist tendencies, especially since a strong community of interest existed between a significant proportion of the clergy which thought of itself as 'enlightened' and the vast majority of the enlightened laity which remained firmly committed to religious tradition – even if, for both groups, this was by now a tradition amended by a progressive or rationalist theology. In the Protestant churches, in any case, the pulpit became almost as often the lectern of the enlightenment as of traditional piety.

Enlightened figures in Germany could also preach and work openly for various changes from within the governmental apparatus by virtue of the venerable traditions of Cameralism, which (especially as ethicized by Thomasius and rationalized by Wolff) had long since legitimized the advocacy of governmental social intervention and reform in the name of economic growth and fiscal efficiency. Cameralists were comprehensive in their utilitarian critique of traditional practices and procedures and it might be argued that they fell short of true 'enlightenment' only because of the lesser purity of their motives (which had more to do with the fiscal health of the state than with the happiness of mankind) and the relative shallowness of their reform proposals (which largely avoided fundamental institutional criticism). But even this characterization ignores the fact that most of the mid- to late eighteenth-century heirs of the early Cameralists were themselves eager participants in the enlightenment and that many of the more penetrating reforms they advocated in the name of that movement were present in the work of their predecessors, if only as briefly-mentioned and wistful desiderata known to be unrealizable under then-existing conditions. By the

3. Joachim Whaley, 'The Protestant Enlightenment in Germany', in Roy Porter and Mikulas Teich, eds., *The Enlightenment in National Context* (Cambridge, 1981), p. 113.

1760s and later, conditions had changed enough to permit and even to mandate the advocacy of reforms considered unrealistic only a single generation before, while the almost universal acceptance of the existence of a natural law accessible to reason had eliminated the earlier need to distinguish between justice and utility, since what was 'right' in the natural law was also by definition useful, just as what was 'wrong' (or 'unnatural') was useless or detrimental. This is why almost all debates about the changes advocated by the enlightened community were conducted largely in terms of relative social utility. It was of great importance, furthermore, that on this basis the principles of the enlightenment had penetrated many of the princely courts by and after the mid-century, including those of Frederick II of Prussia and Joseph II of Austria, thus lending high and impressive official sanction to enlightenment as the proper guide to the conduct of public affairs (even when in practice it operated that way only fitfully in some aspects of policy and not at all in others). This monarchical acceptance of enlightened ideals was vital because it not only permitted and indeed encouraged the diffusion of those ideals, but also because it seemed to prove that society, with all those inequalities which even the most enlightened believed to be both necessary and ineradicable, did not have to be insufferable; inequality, indeed, 'could be made palatable by rational and benign government in a spiritual and material welfare state'.[4]

The conservative nature of the German enlightenment is further exemplified in the distinction drawn or accepted by many of its champions between 'theoretical' and 'practical' enlightenment (see note 2 above), indicative of the view that attempts to draw reformist consequences from the intellectual results of the exercise of pure reason would in fact be revolutionary and therefore socially dangerous. This separation of the world of individual thought from that of practical social action demonstrates a lack of political self-confidence in an intellectual elite composed of official functionaries and professional men, not framers of policy and, in spite of the almost universal advocacy of a free press, shows some tolerance of censorship as long as it did not invade the world of private thought and conversation. The widely-held concept of 'relative' enlightenment also underlines both the good intentions and the limits of enlightenment as a social philosophy in Germany. In essence, this concept proposed different kinds and levels of enlightenment for different groups in society, distinguished primarily by vocation; it

4. Ibid., 117.

was enlightenment on a 'need-to-know' basis, in which both the uselessness and the dangers of overenlightenment were stressed as much as the urgent need for such elevation as was necessary to produce a reasonably happy and productive citizen – 'a good and, in his class, a sensible, useful and active man', as the Prussian Minister of Education Baron von Zedlitz put it in 1787. Zedlitz spoke for the great majority of the enlightened elites, who were genuinely concerned to improve not only the material well-being of the individual, but also his ability to cope successfully with the totality of his own environment; but as these environments were different, so was the degree and kind of enlightenment necessary to them.

Conservative though it may have been, however, there was an undeniable incrementalism in the German enlightenment's criticism of many of the institutions of traditional society. Religion is a case in point. Christian Wolff had already rejected some specific Christian beliefs and, in spite of his acceptance of revelation as supplementary to reason, had opened the door to the doctrines of 'natural religion' which had earlier made headway in much of western Europe, especially in England, and which tended to reduce all religions, including Christianity, to a core of common truths present in all major religions and compatible with reason and natural law, meanwhile rejecting special revelation, miracles and most or all liturgical and ritual trappings. The reductionism of this approach was to a degree reinforced by Pietism by virtue of its orientation towards individual rather than institutional devotion. The progress of such ideas had the gradual effect of dissolving certain previously accepted practices such as kneeling, confession and penance (in the Lutheran church, especially), while the traditional scripturally-based morality began to weaken in the face of a secularized utilitarian ethics which increasingly found justification before God in service to one's fellow man – another point of affinity with Pietism. Orthodox opposition to these trends – and there was much of it – soon persuaded moderate theologians (known as 'neologists') that they must attempt to find a middle ground between church tradition and rationalist innovation; but how little successful this attempt was is evident in the example of the Pietist Johann Semler (1725–91), a Bible scholar and professor of theology at Halle, whose well-intentioned efforts, like those of most other neologists, ended in reformulations much closer to natural religion than to orthodoxy. It was equally discomfiting to the guardians of the old faith to find such academics as J. L. Mosheim, first chancellor of the University of Göttingen and the historian L. T. Spittler (1752–1810) beginning to integrate the

Christian church into the general history of Europe as merely another man-made institution – one with specific and important social functions, to be sure, but also without sacred character.

Genuinely radical rejections of Christianity were rare, but aroused real sensation when they appeared – as in 1774–7, when the famous Gotthold Ephraim Lessing, seeking to stoke the fires of public debate, published fragments of the extreme *Apologia for Rational Worshippers of God* written by H. S. Reimarus of Hamburg before the latter's death in 1768. The checkered career of the free-spirited and half-crazy Karl Friedrich Bahrdt (1741–92), son of a theology professor at Leipzig, also sent shock waves through conventional Protestantism, reinforced by his unorthodox retranslation of the Bible and his many wild and scandalous interpretations of many biblical episodes. The steadily increasing alarm of the orthodox party that radical elements had taken charge of the Protestant churches led, in Prussia, to the promulgation of the infamous 'Wöllner Edict' of 1788, which attempted to restore traditional purity of doctrine to Lutheran and Reformed pulpits by a policy of combined censorship and purge; in doing so, it led to an explosion of vituperative debate in the public press, the angry nature of which is largely attributable to the shock the edict occasioned among enlightened groups which had become used to the steady progress of their point of view within the Protestant establishment.[5] What is important about this issue in the current context, however, is its demonstration that an immensely significant shift in religious thinking had taken place in much of Protestant Germany – a shift great enough to cause eventual official intervention, but one which had proceeded slowly, over many decades, pushed along gently by two or three generations of enlightened souls of whom the vast majority were anything but revolutionary.

In the churches of Catholic Germany, the response to similarly enlightened stimuli was played out somewhat differently, but no less self-consciously. It took the form of an increasing criticism of the

5. J. C. Wöllner, the author of this edict, was minister of education and religious affairs under Friedrich Wilhelm II (1786–97). Both men were members of the Rosicrucian Order, a society with a mystical-religious, anti-rationalist and romantic orientation. Politically conservative – even reactionary – its members opposed most of the tendencies of the enlightenment in the name of tradional morality and religion. The repressive provisions of Wöllner's edict should not, however, obscure the fact that it also institutionalized toleration for such religious minorities as Jews, Mennonites and Moravian Brethren, whose freedom of worship had previously rested only on the personal guarantee of Frederick II. Klaus Epstein, *The Genesis of German Conservatism* (Princeton, N.J., 1966), p. 143.

elaborate and deliberately dramatic observances of baroque piety and specifically of the teaching methods, curricula and other activities of the Jesuits, who had built so much of their earlier successes on the emotive approach to stimulating popular piety. A strong movement towards an enlightened form of Catholicism, involving a purification and return to the simpler practices of early Christianity, as well as rejection of 'superstitious' accruals of more recent origin, was begun in the early decades of the century in a number of Benedictine and Augustinian monasteries of southern Germany, whence it gradually spread to the lay clergy and into the ecclesiastical hierarchy. Parallel to and generally supportive of these reforms was a strong revival of episcopalism (vs. papalism) in a number of important Catholic universities, including Trier, Mainz and Salzburg. A noticeably stronger trend towards practical charity, reminiscent of the same emphasis in the Protestant churches, became obvious after the mid-century, especially, and was assisted from within the laity by the significant numbers of Catholics who had studied at such enlightened Protestant universities as Jena, Halle and Göttingen; now acquainted with the rationalist doctrines of Christian Wolff and his disciples and of other enlightened luminaries, these students returned to their Catholic homelands to become teachers, officials and professionals of other kinds, forming the active nucleus of a growing group of supporters of both social and religious reform.

In both Catholic and Protestant Germany, but especially in the latter, religious toleration was solicited by nearly all enlightened personalities, but the most impressive single plea for it was Lessing's famous drama *Nathan the Wise*, which appeared in 1779 as a response to the debate caused by his publication of Reimarus's fragments a few years earlier. Official toleration was observed in Prussia by Frederick II, of course and later in the Habsburg lands by virtue of Joseph II's edict of 1781; it was also adopted in at least limited form in a number of smaller territories as well – including even the Catholic electorate of Trier. But the record of success was a very spotty one; while many princes found toleration intellectually defensible (or fashionable) and believed that it might help to eliminate the many minor disturbances of public order still attributable to confessional quarrelling, it was generally very unpopular among the clergy and citizens of the majority faith whose vocal opposition was able to discourage its implementation in many places – especially, it would appear, in those with governments in which traditional social corporations (such as the estates) still played a large role. While Catholic areas were generally less favourably disposed towards toleration than Protestant ones, some of the least tolerant individuals could be found within the north German enlightenment; chief among them, perhaps, was the high priest of the Berlin enlightenment, Christoph Friedrich Nicolai (1733–1811), who constantly fulminated against the 'fanaticism' and 'obscurantism' of the Catholic church and who continued to detect Jesuit plots and conspiracies in all sorts of ordinary occurrences long after the order was dissolved in 1773. The evidence suggests, in any case, that of the entire population the friends of genuine toleration remained to the end of the period a distinct minority – even if a dedicated and intellectually influential one.

Both Protestant and Catholic populations, whether majorities or minorities in particular territories, were even less hospitable to the toleration of Jews than of each other, though the physical segregation of Jews in their own ghettos reduced the incidence of actual abrasion to some degree. Even toleration, however, was a far cry from emancipation – the granting of full civil equality – which was advocated in only a handful of relatively unimportant writings from the 1730s and 1740s and did not become a major public issue until the 1780s. Christian Wilhelm Dohm, a young Prussian official, published his widely-read *On the Civic Improvement of the Jews* in 1781, in which he proposed the social and economic assimilation of Jews over a period of several generations, without requiring religious conversion. The book created a storm of debate and criticism to which Dohm responded with a second volume, under the same title, in 1783. His point of view was vigorously defended by most (but not all) of the enlightened community in Berlin, of which the Jewish philosopher Moses Mendelssohn was an important and highly respected member. While this controversy brought no immediately favourable results for the Jews, it was significant for its demonstration that a secularized concept of citizenship in which confessional allegiance played no role was making inroads into even this most difficult area of long-standing prejudice.

Besides religion, politics and political life also received an abundant share of attention from the community of enlightened poets, publicists and commentators. Their most pointed and persistent critique was directed at princely 'tyranny', an omnibus term which included such sins as militarism, press censorship, profligate court expenditures (and the arbitrary and excessive taxation which supported them), inhumane treatment of critics and general insouciance towards the welfare of the citizenry. This sort of criticism was sustained partly by the existence of a number of 'enlightened' princely governments – including those of Frederick II and Joseph II, in particular – to which critics could point as successful examples of policies and personalities very different from the 'despotisms' they were attacking and partly by the rich body of evidence of princely misdeeds made available by the very widespread dissemination of news in the later decades of the century. As enlightened government increasingly became not only an accepted but also an expected standard, furthermore, criticism of 'tyrants' (and praise for their opposite numbers) became more frequent and more specific. It says much about the confined political experience of these critics, however, that the most frequently advanced proposals for eliminating despotism involved the moral conversion and regeneration of individual rulers – a solution with a long and honourable (if also generally ineffective) history already. Friedrich Karl von Moser's *The Master and the Servant* (1759) was of this venerable genre (in this case reinforced by the author's Pietist background), as was the play *Don Carlos* (1787) of the young poet and dramatist Friedrich Schiller, in which a trenchant indictment of a princely tyrant was accompanied by no prospective remedy other than the pious wish for an enlightened successor. Even Christoph Martin Wieland's *The Golden Mirror* (1782) fits the category, since while it contained a specific educational programme designed to produce enlightened princes (on the model of Joseph II, in this instance), it also assumed that good or bad government was determined by the ideas and attitudes of the ruler alone.

Essentially inefficacious as this approach may appear, it was probably more realistic than such institutional solutions as appeared here and there and which either harked back to German traditions that were themselves hardly models of good government – the old regimen of the estates (the *Ständestaat*), for example, or a republicanism modelled on the Imperial Free Cities – or were based on foreign examples, including contemporary Switzerland and England. The poet Friedrich Gottlieb Klopstock even conjured up an unhistorical ancient Germanic tribal democracy to support his vision of a return to a form of government natively and originally German. Most progressive spirits, however, found it impossible to entertain the prospect of reverting to aristocratic government or to find much that was admirable in the backward-looking and corrupt patrician governments of the Imperial Cities and adamantly refused to follow Klopstock into the swamps and forests of primeval Germania; the majority, though favourable to Swiss freedoms, also found the Swiss form of government (as well as most other republican or democratic constitutions) unsuitable to German conditions. England was indeed widely admired, but the quick turnabout in enlightened opinion occasioned by the War of American Independence shows that there was also much resentment towards Britain just below the surface, based on hostility to Britain's maritime and commercial supremacy after 1763 and on a widespread perception that English society was fast becoming a plutocracy – a tyranny of the wealthy as bad or worse than other tyrannies. Generally, but not universally, the German enlightenment applauded the course and results of the American Revolution (which was widely reported but also poorly understood and badly misinterpreted) and enthusiastically greeted the new government in North America as the exemplification of an ideal bourgeois republic.[6] But neither this reaction nor any other expressions of support for forms of government other than monarchy was accompanied by advocacy of any programme of practical political action for their implementation. It is therefore hardly surprising that princely governments tolerated such opinions, at least before 1789, recognizing them as the politically innocuous philosophical exercises they largely were. Thus, in spite of a sober awareness that the power to do great good was also the power to do great harm, most enlightened figures continued to cleave to one or another variation of enlightened absolutism as the best kind of government for their time and place, supporting this point of view by repeated reference to the words and actions of rulers who approached their ideal as well as to the steady and hope-inspiring progress of the 'enlightened spirit of the age'.[7]

Among the social issues which attracted the greatest public attention of the later German enlightenment, two were of particular significance: the existence of serfdom and the special social status of the nobility. Serfdom – legally sanctioned hereditary servitude – became the special *bête noire* of enlightened reformers on both philosophical (natural law) and humanitarian grounds because of its

6. See Horst Dippel, *Germany and the American Revolution, 1770–1800: A Sociohistorical Investigation of Late Eighteenth-Century Political Thinking*, trans. by Bernhard A. Uhlendorf (Chapel Hill, N.C., 1977), *passim*.
7. Admiration of such princes as Frederick II and Joseph II was not untempered by criticism from both major and minor figures, of course; both Lessing and Herder were especially soured by the excessive militarism of the Prussian state and of the blind obedience expected of its subjects. Such conditions could not be associated with truly enlightened government; but they were also not altogether incompatible with the distinction commonly drawn between 'theoretical' and 'practical' enlightenment referred to earlier. The inflexibility and harshness of Joseph's methods of enlightening his peoples also drew fire from some who otherwise approved of his intentions.

similarity to slavery and because of the sheer human debasement it entrained; and it had long been opposed by many Cameralists (and even some landlords) on the grounds that the compulsory labour required of serfs was less efficient and productive than free wage labour. By the later eighteenth century, reinforced first by the economic liberalism of the French Physiocrats and later by the teachings of Adam Smith, an economic literature which had earlier been characterized by a judgmentally neutral notation of the economic inefficiencies of serfdom had become more harshly critical of it, often to the point of recommending its abolition. Even when joined to the outraged humanitarianism spoken of above, this groundswell of criticism could not claim much success in accomplishing the outright elimination of peasant servitude, which in much of Germany was so vital to the overall social structure (and, as in Prussia, to the military system) as to make its abolition impossible in isolation from other and much more far-reaching changes; but the significant reforms of Karl Friedrich of Baden were certainly a response to both ethical and theoretical economic stimuli, as were the various partial measures taken in other territories to ease some of the burdens of serfdom in the absence of its actual elimination.

Serfdom was to a degree implicated in the second social issue which provoked much controversy in the last three decades of the century: the social position and privileges of the nobility. The censure of aristocratic abuses such as arrogance, cruelty to subordinates, licentiousness of life style and so on, was nothing new; it had a history as long and honourable as that of tyrant-thumping – with which it had often been linked, in fact. But by the mid-1770s, a distinctly new direction of criticism had emerged, in which the principle of aristocracy itself began for the first time to be questioned on a broad front by a growing legion of bourgeois writers and intellectuals. Pointing to the disjunction between the socially preferential status accorded the nobility and the virtual disappearance of the feudal military and governmental functions which had originally justified that status, critics argued that a host of aristocratic privileges were no longer defensible on rational grounds; these included the special legal protection given to aristocratic land holdings, seigneurial rights (including patrimonial legal and police powers, ecclesiastical patronage and the hunting rights which so damaged and outraged the peasantry) and privileged access to court, military and civil service positions. Why this criticism emerged in such force at this time is not altogether clear, though there is a certain logic to it as a corollary to the utilitarianism and economic liberalism involved in the attack on serfdom. A well-publicized debate that had been raging in France for some time already over the origins and justification of feudal land tenure may also have helped to draw attention to the general issue of noble privilege and at a time when an employment crisis in government service – one which favoured noble over bourgeois candidates – was beginning to be felt in various parts of Germany. The German nobility replied to its critics with a stout defence of its status and privileges, which of course remained fully in place. But as with other kinds of issues in the area of politics and religion, what was important at this point was not the amount of change wrought as the result of criticism, but the simple fact that a series of important traditional pieties had been recognized as legitimate objects of public discussion and reevaluation.

The vast scope of the social criticism and ameliorative proposals of literally hundreds of enlightened publicists and commentators on scores of issues of lesser import than those discussed above is impossible to comprehend in a short space. The journalists were alert to news of even the smallest evidences of notably bad (or good) government, of effective schemes of local improvement in everything from fire insurance to health, hygiene and legal and penal reform, of determined campaigns against superstitious beliefs and practices of all kinds and of both misanthropic and philanthropic activities of individuals and groups all over Germany and elsewhere in Europe; and they dutifully and efficiently reported such information and their judgments on it to the wider public, especially in the burgeoning periodical press. The explosion in the number of books and journals published in Germany, especially after the mid-1770s, is one of the most remarkable features of German history in the entire period and demonstrates a very rapid increase in both advanced literacy and interest in extensive reading, particularly among the emergent class of the *Bildungsbürgertum* – the well-educated bourgeoisie, regardless of specific vocation, but including officials and other state servants, the middle and upper strata of businessmen, scholars, artists, writers and professional men, especially lawyers and doctors.[8] The insatiable appetite for reading materials, as well as for a forum in which to discuss them, was partly satisfied by the establishment of various kinds of reading societies which by virtue of

8. By 1800, probably 20 per cent or more of the whole population was potentially involved in this readership, which was served by a small army of authors numbering over 10,000 – a four- or five-fold increase since only the mid-1760s.

collective buying power were able to acquire numerous publications whose expense was beyond the means of their members as individuals. By 1800, some 420 such societies had been founded, the vast majority after 1700; some lasted longer than others and they were of greatly differing size: a handful may have had 200 members and a few more as many as 100, but most were much smaller. Two interesting characteristics of such societies were the equality of rights and obligations of members, regardless of class, observed in nearly all and their democratic organization, which required election of the chairman and of new members and participation of the whole membership in the selection of new acquisitions. The nucleus of membership in most societies consisted of the university-educated bourgeoisie, but this could vary according to the principal employments of the place – more merchants in cities like Frankfurt, for example, or civil servants and official nobility in territorial capitals. The sociability afforded by the reading rooms (and by specially designated 'discussion rooms' in some) was an intentional feature of these societies and was a significant indicator of the desire of the members of these bourgeois self-help organizations to have an at least intellectual access to exciting developments in which they were still denied political participation.[9]

The journals which formed the bulk of the collections of the reading societies were so many and varied that it is impossible to mention more than a few; some had publishing histories as short as one or a few issues, or as long as several decades.[10] Friedrich Nicolai's *Allgemeine Deutsche Bibliothek* (1765–1806), published mostly in Berlin, was one of the longest-lived and most venerable periodicals, whose immense importance to the German enlightenment lay in its largely realized goal of reviewing every book of any importance published in Germany and which for that purpose employed critical reviewers drawn from the highest circles of the scholarly and literary worlds. The other chief organ of the Berlin enlightenment was the *Berlinische Monatsschrift* (1783–1811, under this or other titles), edited by J. E. Biester and Friedrich Gedike, but also published by Nicolai, which presented a great variety of articles on

9. Herbert G. Göpfert, 'Lesegesellschaften im 18. Jahrhundert', in Franklin Kopitzsch, ed., *Aufklärung, Absolutismus und Bürgertum in Deutschland. Zwölf Aufsätze* (Munich, 1976), pp. 403–11.
10. A convenient summary of the history of some of the most important journals and of their editors, is in Frederick Hertz, *The Development of the German Public Mind: A Social History of German Political Sentiments, Aspirations and Ideas.* Vol. II: The Age of Enlightenment (London, 1962), pp. 401–17.

enlightenment topics and public affairs generally, a majority of which were written by members of the official class or by the editors themselves, whose personal connections with such high Prussian officials as Baron Zedlitz and Count Hertzberg were useful in attracting both contributors and readers. More literary in emphasis, but not inattentive to social and political issues as well, was *Der teutsche Merkur* (1773–1810), published in Weimar by C. M. Wieland; it became one of the favourite publications of enlightened Germans and attracted some readership away from Nicolai's journal, which, like its editor, became somewhat too narrowly and mechanically rationalistic in its later years.

The first two real political journals were founded in 1774 by C. F. D. Schubart and August Ludwig Schlözer, respectively. Schubart's *Deutsche Chronik*, started in Augsburg and later moved to Ulm, was a satirical journal, full of condemnation of despots and of obsequiousness and servility to the mighty; its tone and contents so angered Karl Eugen of Württemberg that he lured Schubart (a former employee of the duke) back into his territory and clapped him into prison for ten years. By 1787, however, the two men had become reconciled and Schubart ended his life in 1791 as poet to the court and theatre of Württemberg; he was even permitted to edit a new journal, the *Vaterlandschronik*, which attracted twice the readership of the first one, but (predictably) was also much less controversial. Schlözer, professor of history, politics and statistics in Göttingen after 1769, published a journal from 1774–93 which under its final title of *Staats-Anzeigen* had an impressive circulation of 4400 copies and was perhaps at once the freest and most comprehensive of all periodicals of its type; benefiting from the more relaxed political climate of Hanover and from a steady stream of secret government documents sent to him for publication by high officials, diplomats and occasionally even by princes, Schlözer's journal was regularly and carefully read in all the major and most of the minor German courts.

It might almost seem, from the sheer number of new journals appearing with every passing year, that anyone with a viewpoint and a relatively small amount of money could (and did) found a periodical; certainly printers and publishers were becoming ubiquitous – Leipzig alone had eighteen presses employing nearly 1500 people by 1800 – and the reading mania showed no signs of weakening. The scandalously independent Württemberger Ludwig Weckherlin found an eager market for his *Der graue Ungeheuer* (1778–88), which was far too free-spirited to adopt the orthodoxies of the enlightenment on many issues (though it did on others) and preached such heresies as free love, polygamy, the positive values of war and of the aristocratic code of honour, and the evils of parliamentary government; the magazine had to be published under the special protection of the prince of tiny Öttingen-Wallerstein. German Physiocrats for a time had their own journal in Johann August Schlettwein's *Archiv für den Menschen und Bürger* (1780–84); and Catholic Germany – not nearly as prolific in periodicals production as Protestant territories – got its first major enlightened journal in the *Journal von und für Deutschland* (1784 and after), edited by Philipp Anton von Bibra, brother and chief minister of the prince-abbot of Fulda. It is worth noting that the personalities and opinions of the editors of these various publications did much to determine the nature of the publications themselves, because they not only chose what would be printed from both solicited and unsolicited contributions, but also usually wrote a substantial portion of the contents themselves.

While books, newspapers and journals, together with the members of the reading societies which bought them, were immensely significant disseminators of the ideas and spirit of the enlightenment, other kinds of societies made their contribution as well. Learned academies and societies, of which some ten new ones were founded after 1750, added an academic tone to enlightened discourse, especially by means of their published transactions and papers. There were also dozens of 'patriotic-utilitarian' societies, the vast majority established after 1770, whose purpose was to develop and disseminate information on improvements in everything from agriculture to mechanical arts and manufactures and whose members sought involvement in the practical implementation of the projects they discussed. Some of the literary and reading societies also evolved in this direction, or were reconstituted for the purpose of effecting practical improvements.

The Patriotic Society of Hamburg is a good example. Originally founded in 1724 as a literary society, it died out from lack of interest by the mid-century; when it was revived in the early 1760s it had the same name, but a different purpose corresponding to the practical and cosmopolitan humanitarianism conveyed by the term 'patriotic' as employed in this period. An unusually energetic association of civic-minded citizens, this society capped its many years of impressive good works with the creation of the famous *Allgemeine Armenanstalt* in 1788 – an institution for poor-relief which was widely acclaimed and imitated throughout Europe and which exemplified a gradual but general shift away from the harsh concept of merely policing the poor towards what would eventually become a more modern system of public welfare.

Freemasonry continued throughout the period to be the most important society – by this time an only semi-secret one by virtue of its large membership and geographical diffusion – dedicated to the cultivation and propagation of enlightened ideals; its lodges included princes, high officials, wealthy bourgeoises and much of the scholarly and literary elite, including Klopstock, Lessing, Wieland, Herder and Goethe. Tarnished here and there by puerile quarrelling over rituals, symbols and degrees and occasionally abused by swindlers and opportunists, the society eventually proved unappealing to some early members such as Frederick II of Prussia, who quit it in the early 1750s after a membership of some fifteen years and who forbade his ministers from attending meetings. Joseph II neither joined nor approved of Freemasonry, but tolerated it because of the many charitable initiatives which were a noteworthy public aspect of the lodges' activities. Though non-political in concept, the very nature of its elite membership meant that Freemasonry, as a forum for like-minded individuals with the power to shape both public opinion and public policy, was at least indirectly politically influential.

Far more deliberately political in orientation was the secret Order of the Illuminati (*Illuminatenorden*) founded at Ingolstadt in 1776 by the young Bavarian law professor Adam Weishaupt. Inspired by the vision of a Rousseauvian 'natural' world from which princes and sovereign states had been eliminated by the force of ideas alone and in which mankind had become one through the triumph of reason among all peoples, Weishaupt sought to work observable social change by means of a society whose membership would not only publicize its ideals to the broader public, but would also gradually attain leadership positions in the state from which to launch reform programmes. The movement spread to central and northern Germany chiefly through the energetic efforts of Baron Adolf Knigge, a Hanoverian by birth, who used his position as a Freemason to bring many fellow masons of high social rank into the order and to gain effective access to some of the smaller courts and princes.[11] His membership efforts were particularly successful

11. The total membership of the order at its height may have reached 4000, of whom it appears that over one-third were nobles and a majority were Freemasons.

among student youth, many of whom became major statesmen at a later time – Count Montgelas in Bavaria and Prince Hardenberg in Prussia are two examples; and the movement exercised some influence in a few of the progressive lower schools and in some universities, as well as on certain journals, especially those associated with the Berlin enlightenment. Divisive leadership quarrels among the Illuminati soon developed, however; Knigge himself quit the order in disgust and denunciations of the society (some of them from former members) eventually persuaded the elector of Bavaria to command its dissolution (and that of Freemasonry) in 1785, the same year it was officially condemned by Pope Pius VI. The outbreak of the French Revolution brought hysterical accusations that the order was in the business of assassinating princes; Leopold II forbade it in Austria in 1792 and most other German princes who had not already dissolved it followed his lead.

The *Illuminatenorden*, though the most extreme of the pre-Revolutionary secret societies, was actually much less threatening than the authorities who banned it believed it was: its founder, Weishaupt, was far more a dreamer than a danger and this characterization would apply to much of its youthful and idealistic membership as well, while no organization (and this would include Freemasonry as well) which numbered as many princes, noblemen and other social and political dignitaries among its adherents as this one did can be termed 'radical' in any very genuine sense of the word. The history and membership of both Illuminati and Freemasonry do demonstrate, however, how pervasive the progressive spirit of the enlightenment was among nearly all of the educated elites in Germany by the later decades of the century; the belief in both the desirability and the possibility of reform within the existing German political structure had become so general as to suggest that 'enlightenment' in some sense of the term was a force for nearly every educated person in Germany – including those who often opposed it by the distinction they drew between 'true' and 'false' enlightenment. In both the above organizations, individuals may have experienced a pleasurable shiver of wickedness by joining a secret society; but that it was a fashionable thing to do for so many who were deeply involved in the social, political and intellectual leadership of their country says much about the triumph of enlightenment as a cultural mindset, however different its programmatic implications may have been for different individuals or groups.

The doctrines of the enlightenment were also disseminated by the institutions of higher learning in Germany – the places where they had originated from. Universities such as Göttingen and Jena became examples of schools where new fields of study and new approaches to teaching led to a whole new concept of liberal education in the philosophical faculties; others, such as Halle, continued to honour the more dogmatic and slowly weakening traditions of Wolffian rationalism, but were by no means closed to the fresher intellectual currents of the later years of the century. Below university level, the picture was a mixed one. A slow seepage of enlightened ideas and attitudes into some of the Latin schools and academies resulted in piecemeal changes and improvements at that level, but on nothing approaching a national scale. Perhaps the most interesting experiment in lower education arose from the work of Johann Bernhard Basedow (1723–90), who had been impressed by the idea of 'natural education' preached by Rousseau in his *Émile* (1762) and who developed an educational theory stressing cultivation of philanthropic sentiments and attitudes in children by methods which quickened interest through observation of the real world, hands-on labour and sports, meanwhile abjuring reprimands and punishments in favour of encouragement – praise, small gifts and so on. Foreign languages were to be learned 'naturally' through conversation, while complex concepts were not to be taught whole but gradually formed from simpler facts and ideas. A superb publicist, Basedow awakened interest in his theories among the political and educational elite and in 1774 was given financial backing by Prince Leopold of Anhalt-Dessau to set up a model school in Dessau, which he called the *Philanthropinum*. Its good results, approvingly noted by such luminaries as Immanuel Kant and Baron Zedlitz in Prussia, led to imitations elsewhere; over sixty schools on Basedow's model were founded by 1790 – though most did not last long. Tuitions were expensive and the schools were therefore attended chiefly by nobles' and merchants' sons, with some scholarships available for the deserving poor. Basedow had quit his own *Philanthropinum* in 1778, mainly because of quarrels with his colleagues there and it survived his death in 1790 by only three years.

While Basedow was probably the most widely known educational reformer in Germany before 1790, he was certainly not the only one and was in fact less important than several others in one area particularly in need of improvement: peasant education. The Prussian nobleman Friedrich Eberhard von Rochow (1734–1805), who in 1772 had published an instructional manual for village schools, set his ideas for the enlightenment of peasant children to work in a model school on his estate at Reckan, near the city of

Brandenburg. Here, vocational training was combined with a loving emphasis on moral and religious instruction and on combating the multitude of false and superstitious beliefs which were not the least of the burdens borne by this oppressed class. His writings and his school were widely reported and were admired by the ever-alert Baron Zedlitz and later by Frederick II himself, who subsequently ordered his education minister to reorganize the Prussian village schools on Rochow's plan – a directive which, however good its intentions, remained largely without effect.

Rochow's theories hinted at the notion that even lower-class children ought to receive an education which not only provided information, but also stimulated their ability to think for themselves; this insight gained ground steadily thereafter, supported by the experience of other model schools for peasant youth established by reformers such as Christian Salzmann in Schnepfenthal or the Swiss P. E. von Fellenberg, who also utilized his estate for this purpose. By the mid-1790s, the ground already well prepared for his ideas, the Swiss Johann Heinrich Pestalozzi (1746–1827) had emerged as the most impressive theoretical mind in peasant education for many years. In addition to his writings (especially the famous three-volume *Lienhard und Gertrud* (1781–5), a loose compendium of didactic dialogues centred around a 'rational' peasant couple who raised their children to observe and reason about their environment of home, farm and village), Pestalozzi's several model peasant schools attracted enormous attention for placing sound and effective moral and vocational instruction squarely in the context of the children's familiar world of fields, meadows and barns.

These expanding efforts to bring practical enlightenment to peasant children was accompanied by a campaign of sorts to educate their parents, though by different means. A notable increase in peasant literacy and in the reading of books and periodicals by peasants in the last quarter of the century led a number of reformers (many of them members of one or another of the 'patriotic' scientific-agricultural societies of the time) to produce publications aimed directly at the peasantry, containing practical advice and information for daily life and work. Most of the periodicals established for this purpose were short-lived, partly because they quickly exhausted their basic message (and, in some cases, woefully under- or overestimated the taste and intellectual levels of their intended readership); their chief problem, however, was lack of steady funding and it is therefore no surprise that the most successful one of them was governmentally funded. This was the *Schlesische*

Volkszeitung, which grew out of an economic-patriotic society founded by the Prussian Grand Chancellor von Carmer; published from 1789 to 1803, it was eventually distributed free – a decisively important feature – by official order in every Silesian village and reached a yearly edition of 33,000 German and 10,000 Polish copies. Much more effective in this period than newspapers or magazines, however, were the peasant calendars and almanacs which became trusted household friends in many a rural dwelling; these compendia contained information and advice on everything from hailstorms to hygiene, cooking and lawsuits and were sometimes revised and reissued annually. The *Noth- und Hülfs-büchlein für Bauersleute* of Rudolph Z. Becker (1759–1822), a convert to Basedow's educational philosophy, was one of the most widely circulated works of this type, especially in northern Germany and appeared in several editions in the last two decades of the century.[12]

Nowhere, on the other hand, was the pervasive concept of 'relative enlightenment' more in evidence than in the public discussion of peasant education. For somewhat different reasons, personalities as different as Frederick the Great, the Osnabrück sage Justus Möser and the Swiss reformer Isaak Iselin had deep reservations about the amount and kind of education appropriate for peasants. Frederick was not altogether convinced that even basic literacy was such a good idea, since peasants thus enlightened might run off to the cities to become clerks and secretaries and Iselin believed that a peasantry educated to an awareness of the misery of its own circumstances might better be left in the lesser unhappiness of its ignorance; Möser, for his part, full of distrust for the mechanical rationalism he saw in much of the enlightenment and equally convinced of the cunning beneficence of tradition, was prepared (at the extreme) to protect the peasant's illiteracy to keep the socially and vocationally destructive influences of all 'philosophical' education as far away from the farm as possible. These dissents from the increasingly influential stream of 'progressive' pedagogical thinking in the later years of the century say much about the limits of the German enlightenment, because they point to the possibility of undesirable social change as an unintended result of otherwise praiseworthy humanitarian impulses. As in political and social criticism, so in peasant education there was a line which could not be crossed without touching something important to the very quiddity

---

12. Gagliardo, *From Pariah to Patriot*, pp. 105–8.

of the old regime. As a whole movement, the German enlightenment understood and accepted this; but while some years had yet to pass before that line could safely be crossed, the thinkers and writers of eighteenth-century Germany had nothing to be discouraged about in their work, which tapped about as much of the reform potential of the old regime as there was in it – and there was, in fact, more in it than has commonly been recognized; in doing so, they not only eased much human misery but also succeeded in creating a cultural climate in which 'enlightenment', by whatever definition, became as much the motto of the age in Germany as in any other country of Europe.

CHAPTER TWENTY-FOUR

The Revival of German Letters after 1740

While the assignment of fixed dates to the beginnings and ends of major movements in human history is always a somewhat artificial exercise, there is much to recommend the year 1740 as the beginning of a literary revival which by before the end of the century had elevated a long unappreciated German literature to a level of equality with the other major national literatures of Europe. In that year, in Zürich, appeared separate works by the two Swiss professors, J. J. Bodmer and J. J. Breitinger, which together launched the first salvos of a theoretical attack on the then dominant literary canons of Johann Christoph Gottsched. Influenced by the imaginative naturalism of early eighteenth-century English literature, as well as by the inspiring nature poetry of their countryman Albrecht von Haller and insights gleaned from translations from a simple but powerful medieval German literature, Bodmer and Breitinger turned away from the cool and abstract rationalism of Gottsched's literary prescriptions in favour of a more emotional style, one more naturally 'cluttered' with metaphors, exclamations, asides, interrupted speech and other similarly 'realistic' devices. To Gottsched's chagrin, the unfettering effects of this new approach, together with the continuing influence of English letters, soon showed up among his own younger disciples in Leipzig, some of whom founded a new and more 'liberal' journal, the Bremer Beyträge (1744–8), to satisfy needs not theretofore addressed in the existing 'official' magazine of the Gottschedian orthodoxy. The most popular writer in what now became a new literary circle in Leipzig was Christian Fürchtegott Gellert (1715–69), who not only helped to popularize and elevate the quality of the epistolary style (adopted from the English novelist Samuel Richardson), but also became the best-known German author of fables and tales in a period when this genre enjoyed immense popularity all over Europe. Not quite so directly responsive to the stimuli mentioned above, but still indicative of the fresher climate of literary creativity, were the Anacreontic poets of Halle, centred around a generation of young Prussians including J. P. Uz, J. N. Goetz, J. W. L. Gleim and Ewald von Kleist, whose many drinking songs and poems of love, friendship and the beauties of nature were superficial and often even fatuous, but represented another pan-European literary fad of the mid-century which provided appropriate accompaniment to the light-hearted rococo style in the arts.

A far more direct result of Swiss and English influences was the early work of Friedrich Gottlieb Klopstock (1724–1803), who more than any other single person was responsible for bursting the bonds of Gottsched's rationalistic restraints in actual practice. Greatly moved by Haller's naturalism and by Bodmer's translation of Milton's *Paradise Lost*, Klopstock early resolved to write a religious epic for the Germans as grand as Milton's for the English; the result was *The Messiah*, the first three cantos of which appeared in 1748. The sheer force of its religious fervour, expressed in a thunderously passionate language of emotion and sentiment, created an instant sensation and awakened unabashed admiration throughout a whole generation of the younger literary set. While the initial popularity of *The Messiah* diminished considerably over the quarter century required to bring forth all of its not very distinguished twenty cantos, Klopstock maintained a high visibility through publication of some fine lyric poetry (the *Odes* of 1771) and a number of dramas. Of the latter, the historically most noteworthy (for their subject matter rather than their quality) were the three devoted to the ancient world of the German tribal chieftain Arminius – an essentially imaginary world conjured out of a mixture of Teutonic and Celtic mythologies in order to postulate an original, simple, unspoiled and noble German national character as the basis for a new national literature which would abandon foreign models and concentrate on native German themes.[1] Klopstock's direct influence on German letters was perhaps most evident in the Göttingen Sylvan League (*Hainbund*), formed in 1772 by a group of close young friends including J. H. Voß, Ludwig Hölty and J. M. Miller, who then

---

1. In this way, Klopstock became the founder of what is sometimes called the 'German Movement' (*Deutsche Bewegung*) in literature, an often aggressively anti-foreign (and especially anti-French) current particularly noticeable among many of the lower- and middle-range poets and writers in Germany after 1770 or so.

attracted others into what became a loose circle of like-minded poets. Devoted to Klopstock, this group remained loyal to many of the themes raised by him – admiration for manliness and simplicity, love of virtue and piety and a fierce hatred for all forms of tyranny; in the *Göttinger Musenalmanac* which they controlled, as well as in other literary journals which began to arise in profusion, they frequently added their poetic voices to the chorus of enlightened criticism of various social injustices of the old regime.

Besides Klopstock, two other figures made an immense contribution to the rapid progress apparent in German letters in the two decades or so after 1750. The first was Gotthold Ephraim Lessing (1729–81), whose multifaceted additions to literary life did much to build up the confidence of a younger generation of German writers that their own language and talents were adequate to the highest standards of the literary arts. Born and educated in Saxony, Lessing became a leading figure in the Berlin enlightenment in his early twenties and, together with his close friends Nicolai and Mendelssohn, entered the struggle against religious fanaticism as a champion of toleration. Here, too, he first developed the skills of brilliant and impartial literary criticism upon which an important part of his reputation came to rest. In *Miss Sara Samson* (1755), he produced the first bourgeois drama of the German theatre – a prose tragedy modelled on Richardson's *Clarissa*; this successful play, exemplifying Lessing's conviction that a native German drama had to be based on the naturalism of English drama, also gave the *coup de grâce* to the Gottschedian dramatic school. Lessing went on to establish impressive credentials as an aesthetician in his *Laokoon* of 1766, a comparative treatise on the visual and poetic arts written as a response to the aesthetic theories of J. J. Winckelmann; and in 1767 he published his dramatic comedy *Minna von Barnhelm*, also a milestone of the German theatre.

Always convinced that the theatre was the most effective literary medium and perhaps even that it had possibilities for effecting social change, Lessing in 1767 accepted appointment as critic and adviser to a new 'German National Theatre' in Hamburg, a city with a long and diverse theatre tradition and a history of lively dramatic controversy. Though this new experiment failed in a few years, it left the positive residue of a renewed determination to efface the distinction between literature and drama – something Gottsched had worked for as well – and to replace the tired dramatic repertory of foreign translations with original German works, among which Lessing's quickly became standard. It also produced the *Hamburg*

Dramaturgy (1767–9), an attack on French dramatic theory and an important contribution to the art of dramatic composition. Lessing's continuing growth as a dramatist in his own right was demonstrated in 1772 with the completion and staging of *Emilia Galotti*, a tragedy of common life similar in some ways to *Miss Sara Samson*, but better organized and with a setting more evocative of the author's own world. While an undercurrent of critical social commentary had always been present in his bourgeois dramas, Lessing's last years (made materially secure by virtue of the permanent position as court librarian to the duke of Brunswick-Wolfenbüttel he had obtained in 1770) witnessed a more or less full-scale rededication of effort to his earlier concern for spiritual freedom and religious toleration; these were the years in which he published the sensational Reimarus fragments discussed earlier, his famous *Nathan the Wise* (1779) and, no less notably, the two prose expositions which contained the general principles of his enlightened philosophy: the *Conversations for Freemasons* (1778) and *The Education of Mankind* (1780).

Christoph Martin Wieland (1733–1813), though neither as scholarly nor as literarily talented as his slightly older contemporary Lessing, was nevertheless a figure of first-rate importance to the literary and intellectual movements of later eighteenth-century Germany. An early admirer of Klopstock and of the emotional naturalism preached by him and the popular English writers of his youth, Wieland soon abandoned this enthusiasm in favour of other sources of inspiration, including Greek antiquity and French literary models. He developed into a very self-conscious cosmopolitan, as supple and eclectic in his employment of literary themes and styles as in his personal philosophy, which was a curious but interesting mixture of Pietism, hedonism, rationality and sensuality, all of them tempered by a cool scepticism which occasionally approached cynicism. He was a magnificent stylist, with a light and affable touch (the source of much of his popularity and influence) who had few peers in his ability to manipulate the German language and to adapt it to different tastes – an undertaking he carried out as much in the many articles and reviews he wrote for his own journal *Der teutsche Merkur* as in his major literary works. Of the latter, the first of real note was *The Story of Agathon*, a moralistic novel set in ancient Greece, combining Wieland's own brand of hedonistic rationalism with an effort to explore the changing thoughts and moods of its hero Agathon – a literarily significant first attempt at the 'psychological novel'. After a three-year stay in Erfurt as professor of philosophy from 1769–72, he was called to Saxe-Weimar by the Duchess Amalie as tutor to her two sons – largely because she was impressed by his *Golden Mirror* (1772), a work of moral and political education for princes mentioned earlier. Wieland remained in Weimar for the rest of his life as the first member of a small but extraordinary circle of intellectuals and *littérateurs* that was destined to leave a huge and indelible stamp on the cultural history of the German people.

On the other hand, Wieland frustrated those of his contemporaries who might have liked to categorize his views as belonging to one or another of the identifiable literary movements of the time. Klopstock and the earnest young 'potato poets' of the emotive school disliked his open admiration for French literature and cannot have approved the satirization of German provincial life represented by his *The Abderites* (1774), a prose work set in the ancient land of Abdera, whose inhabitants were all stupid. But this work was equally displeasing to the unsentimental rank-and-file of enlightenment rationalists because of its scepticism about the ability of reason to alter reality; and the best of his many verse romances, *Oberon* (1780), a sympathetic exploration of the values-system of the nobility, was a source of annoyance to those anti-aristocratic writers who were just now busily condemning all such 'feudal' values as socially retrograde. Wieland's greatest contribution to German letters, in the end, may have had much to do with this sort of intellectual ambiguity, which was the result of an unwillingness to be overwhelmed (and thus narrowed) by excessive attachment to any single approach to life and letters, whether that of unfettered emotionalism or of an equally fanatical rationalism. The 'middle way' of that ambiguity may have helped to deny him some of the originality that identifies the greatest literary geniuses of the period; but it also helped him to become midwife to the majestic German classicism that eventually emerged from his own Weimar circle.

Before that mature classicism could appear, however – and that is a subject beyond the scope of this volume – it had to experience the turbulence of a remarkable period of adolescence. That period, sometimes called 'the period of genius', but more commonly known as the Storm and Stress (*Sturm und Drang*), was one of self-conscious rebellion against tradition on the part of a group of passionate young authors who were as disaffected with the social and literary conventions of their time as they were full of confidence in their own abilities to attack them successfully through prose, poetry and drama. While historical explanation of individual genius can be no more successful in this case than in any other, the conditions for its appearance at this time lie in everything written above about German literature since 1740 or so: the general movement towards greater emotionalism and naturalism associated with Swiss and English writers and critics; the admiration of simplicity and primitivity which appears in the work of Klopstock and his disciples (powerfully reinforced by the writings of Jean-Jacques Rousseau from the 1760s); and the steady growth in self-esteem of the German literary community as a whole arising from the identification of legitimate native German themes and increasing comfortability with a more standardized, flexible and sophisticated German literary language.

Against this background, in 1766–7, appeared the first *Fragments on Modern German Literature* of the young East Prussian Johann Gottfried Herder (1744–1803), a work which already contained most of the seminal ideas for which he later became famous (and which, though elaborated in other later works, were never set down in truly systematic fashion). Herder had studied with Immanuel Kant at Königsberg, but was more strongly influenced there by the writer Johann Georg Hamann (1730–88), whose Pietism had led him away from rationalism and back into the heart and the intuition of the individual as the key to the discovery of truth. Herder thus began to conceive of truth as the multiple and variegated expression of individual human beings regarded not as rational creatures alone, but as the totality of their personalities, which included the emotions and sentiments of awe and wonder, faith and fear, love and anger and so on. Since 'humanity' thus conceived consisted of multiple individual truths, diffused throughout time (history) and space (the whole world) and since each of these truths was coequally valid, Herder believed, it was impossible (as the enlightenment proposed) to set the 'rational truths' of contemporary Europe (or the later phases of any civilization) on a higher level than the truths of other times and places, or of earlier phases of civilizations – more especially so in the case of his own time, as Herder saw it, because rational reflection tends to repress and confine the expression of the wholeness of human personality. The key to the understanding of human truths lay in the empathetic study of language, poetry, song, myth and religion, said Herder and especially among primitive peoples whose spontaneity of expression had not yet been repressed and disciplined by reflective artifice and overrefinement.

Poetry in general therefore had to be regarded as the evolutionary product of particular peoples and could not be judged by abstract and universal criteria. With this principle, a historical as well as literary insight of first-rate importance, Herder at once denied the typical enlightened view that literary endeavours could be subjected to any single set of standards and also suggested that the peculiar genius of any people's literature lay in the unique genius of its language. Herder discussed these ideas in a number of works published between 1770 and the early 1790s – all of them, in a sense, fragments; but while the profound implications of his thinking for historiography and the philosophy of history did not become apparent until the nineteenth century, their impact on literature was immediate and dramatic, first appearing in the emotion-fired work of the young Johann Wolfgang (von) Goethe (1749–1832). Born in Frankfurt as the son of a well-to-do lawyer and jurist, Goethe was intended for a career in law; he studied at Leipzig from 1765–8, but illness forced him to return home until the spring of 1770, when it was decided that he should finish his university training at the University of Strassburg. It was there, in the autumn of the same year, that he met and fell under the influence of Herder.

The small body of Goethe's existing literary work at the time (some lyrical poems and short plays) was pleasant and modestly talented, though in no way distinguished; but Herder's message of the autonomy and genius of individual human personality and his conviction that great poetry arose more from spontaneous reaction to powerful inner feelings than from the laborious artifice of conscious artistry was eagerly absorbed by a young poet whose emotional engagements were already beginning to show much of the remarkable receptivity to life, love and nature that characterized the later works of his mature genius. The first major product of Goethe's new enthusiasm was the drama *Götz von Berlichingen* (1773), a passionately turbulent description of political rebellion, love and personal betrayals set amidst the upheavals of the German Reformation era, whose radically unconventional language and action made it an instant sensation (and scandal). This was followed in 1774 with *The Sorrows of Young Werther*, an epistolary narrative of the trials and tribulations of a sensitive young man trapped between the irresistible force of his own passions and the immovable walls of the social observances of the time; its popularity is attested not only by its immediate translation into other languages, but also by the flood of emulative sentimental literature it occasioned in Germany and elsewhere and even by the rash of suicides among tortured young romantics imitating the tragic fate of the unfortunate young Werther himself.[2] During this period, Goethe continued to write lyric poetry, as well as a number of lesser known domestic dramas and dramatic satires; but his ultimately most fruitful effort was the fragment known as the *Urfaust*, an unfinished piece which became the basis for his later and very famous two-part drama *Faust*. In 1775, Goethe accepted the first of several official appointments in the government of Saxe-Weimar which he would occupy with distinction from that time forward. In the same year, he began work on *Egmont*, a drama about the unjust and tragic fate of a leader of the Netherlands revolt against Spain, which was not finished and published until 1788. Its characteristics type it as belonging among his more youthful works, though its superb dramatic characterizations also point ahead to the quieter, more controlled and wiser classicism which first made its appearance in the splendid *Iphigenie on Tauris* (1787), a drama whose final form was deeply influenced by Goethe's journeys to Italy from 1786 to 1788 – journeys which immensely exalted and forever changed his vision of beauty, truth and art.

Important as he was to defining the characteristic features of the Storm and Stress period, Goethe was not the only individual who carried out this explosive break with literary convention. A number of his own friends from the early 1770s contributed a variety of plays couched in sometimes violent and extreme language and which had considerable dramatic appeal in spite of their often loose construction. Many of these dramas showed an interest in exploring individual personality that was common in the Storm and Stress and were typically coloured by the social concerns of the bourgeois enlightenment; such was the case, for example, with *The Soldiers* (1776) of J. M. R. Lenz, with its strong anti-militarist themes and with F. M. Klinger's *Chaos, or Storm and Stress* (1776), a love affair set in the midst of the American struggle for independence, which gave its name to the whole movement of which it was but a small part. Klinger also published *The Twins* (1776), a darkly murderous tale of fraternal jealousy and hatred. Of all of the minor dramatists of the movement, Johann Anton Leisewitz (1752–1806) was probably at once the most talented and most restrained; his *Julius von Tarent*, composed in 1774, was a well-constructed tragedy, whose excellent character depictions were accompanied by an artistic control not much in evidence among his fellows. One of the problems of these

---

2. The unabashed sentimentality of *Werther* was anathema to a significant part of the literary establishement, including especially Friedrich Nicolai, who hated it and tried very unsuccessfully to drive it off the market by his parody *The Joys of Young Werther* (1775).

lesser dramatic lights, in a sense, was that they all wanted to write the brilliantly successful *Götz von Berlichingen*; but that had already been done and their imitations (with the exception of Leisewitz's work) generally showed signs of the forced contrivances and artificiality that so often accompany deliberate emulation. Furthermore, just as their works were beginning to attract some public attention, they were blown off the stage and into permanent obscurity by the appearance and unheard-of popularity of the greatest revolutionary drama of the German theatre: Friedrich Schiller's *The Robbers*, published anonymously in 1781.

Schiller was the son of an army surgeon in Württemberg; originally intended for theological studies, he was forced against his and his family's will into the *Karlsschule*, the military cadet school of Duke Karl Eugen. He was able to transfer to a new military medical school when the academy was moved to Stuttgart in 1775 and began practice there as a regimental physician in late 1780. In the intervening years, he had read widely and enthusiastically in the *belles-lettres* of his time, moving from unabashed admiration of Klopstock's *Messiah* to an equally avid interest in most of the popular dramas mentioned above and certainly not excluding *Werther*, which made a deep and lasting impression. *The Robbers*, written throughout 1780, was privately published in 1781 and met with an instant acclaim that quickly led not only to a second edition but to its first stage performance in Mannheim in early 1782. The play's popularity stemmed not only from its theme of fraternal conflict with which other authors had had great success, but also from the social and political criticism it contained; by presenting the anti-social actions of his robber-hero in a favourable light, Schiller condemned the multiple and even more sociopathic tyrannies and injustices of church, state, law and social convention – and in a setting commonly understood to be that of contemporary Germany. Now convinced that literature was his true calling, Schiller fled his military medical employment in Stuttgart to a small village in Thuringia, where he finished his second major drama, *Love and Intrigue* (*Kabale und Liebe*) in 1784. The best 'bourgeois tragedy' of the century, this play, building on the huge popularity of the genre established by Lessing's *Emilia Galotti*, was at once love story, political commentary and a condemnation of the dehumanizing effects of the class-based social strictures of the age.

Schiller's reputation as a playwright was thus already fairly well established when he finished his next great drama, *Don Carlos*, in 1787. Composed in iambic blank verse in partial imitation of

Lessing's *Nathan the Wise*, this is perhaps the most potent and energetic work of political criticism he had written so far; set in the Spain of Philip II and the Spanish inquisition, it drives the double theme of hatred for tyranny and advocacy of free thought and expression which was so close to the heart of the later enlightenment and of the German literary world since Klopstock. *Don Carlos* was also the last major literary work of the Storm and Stress. Schiller's own interests were already turning more fully towards the writing of history, which had provided such a rich background for *Don Carlos*; as early as the fall of 1788 he published the first (and only) volume of a projected six-volume narrative history of the long Netherlands revolt against Spain and his famous *History of the Thirty Years War* followed not long thereafter (1791–3). What fascinated him about both periods was the restless conflict which filled them; and while it is certainly too strong to say that he fictionalized the events he wrote about, it is at least clear that his interest in them remained that of the playwright and the passionate 'freedom fighter' rather than of the historian: both works are very uneven as histories because of Schiller's unapologetic emphasis on dramatic episodes and colourful personalities and his highly subjective interpretations, which evaluated persons and events by their perceived relevance to the burning social, political and philosophical issues of his own time. Whatever their faults as history, however, both works are splendid contributions to literature and can still be read profitably for stylistic hints by historians today.

The Netherlands history had the additional benefit of bringing Schiller a faculty appointment at the University of Jena, in 1789, where he first established permanent connections with the Weimar talents to whom he had looked with admiration for some years already. Goethe, after a period of some coolness to the younger poet, eventually became a close friend to him; and with Schiller's admission to the Weimar group in the early 1790s, that circle of literary and intellectual giants was close to complete. Goethe and Schiller had done much for German letters and in particular for the rapid rise of a German national theatre – an endeavour in which Lessing had already pioneered. Schiller had a better sense for the visual impact of drama – its actual staging – than did Goethe, who tended to look at it as just another literary medium, if also one with special possibilities for certain themes in chosen scenarios. Together, though not without an appreciative nod to some of the lesser dramatists of the time, they provided much of the native German repertory which was so major a factor in the revival of a vital theatre all over the Germanic world in the later years of the century.

It should be obvious, in retrospect, that the enlightenment and the literary revival of the second half or so of the eighteenth century in Germany were closely related movements – always parallel and frequently intersecting. The themes of enlightened social criticism, in the broadest sense, pervaded every genre, medium and movement of German letters, from Klopstock's productive excesses through Lessing's calm but engaged rationalism and from the elegant and often lightly sardonic eclecticism and scepticism of Wieland to the youthful ragings of the authors of the Storm and Stress. The enlightenment also made a great contribution to the basic vehicle of all literary effort – the German language itself, which by the end of the century was employed in a considerably more standardized form with a pride and confidence that reflected its greater precision and subtlety. The enlightenment must also be credited with the steady progress of a new social attitude towards creative writing in general: in educated circles, at least, it began to be seen as a legitimate profession in itself, not as an amusing pastime or as something done by the very young until they 'grew up' to do something 'useful' with their lives.[3] That the professionalization of the literary vocation still had a long way to go, on the other hand, is demonstrated by the fact that almost literally none of the German authors of this century, major or minor, were able to make a living by sales of their works alone, since the profits from such sales, even in those rare instances where they were quantitatively large enough to provide a living income, were shared by the printer-booksellers who shamelessly pirated any works which seemed to promise any market at all. The result was that authors had no choice but to continue working careers in bureaucratic, professorial or other positions in the liberal professions, or else, like Friedrich Nicolai, to be publishers and booksellers themselves. The best that can be said is that many authors seem to have been able to rescue from their daily work a considerably greater amount of time for their literary endeavours than was true of their counterparts of the late seventeenth and early eighteenth centuries. That was progress, no doubt; but as was true of so many other aspects of life under the old regime, so in the literary profession full material independence had to await the advent of a new and more generous century.

---

3. Franklin Kopitzsch, 'Einleitung: Die Sozialgeschichte der deutschen Aufklärung als Forschungsaufgabe', in Kopitzsch, ed., *Aufklärung*, p. 71.

Bibliography

The following bibliography is intended as a basic guide for the general reader, not the specialist; it is also deliberately weighted in favour of the English-speaking student. This means both that some older (though still respectable) English titles which might not be included in an up-to-date bibliography that ignored language as a criterion will be found here and that some fairly specialized works will be cited partly *because* they are in English, while on the other hand most of the enormous body of equally or even more highly specialized studies of the period in German will be ignored. *Adequacy* of coverage of various topics in English has in some cases been used as a criterion for the exclusion of German works, even where the latter may be more recent or complete. Even so, the English-speaking reader may find a dismayingly large number of German titles here – evidence of the fact that in spite of the steady and encouraging growth of English-language works on early modern German history, including translations, the period is still not widely worked in English. Since virtually all of the works listed here have their own bibliographies, the reader is encouraged to use them as further aids; and it should be noted that titles listed in one or another of the following topical sections may be relevant to other sections as well.

I. Bibliographical, Biographical and Reference Aids

By far the most extensive bibliographical guide to German history, still in process of publication but now nearly complete through the eighteenth century, is Friedrich Dahlmann and Georg Waitz, eds.,

Quellenkunde der deutschen Geschichte, 10th ed. (Stuttgart, 1965/69 and continuing); this enormous compilation replaces the much shorter two-volume edition of the same work (Leipzig, 1931–2). Much more compact, but now somewhat dated, are the German and Austrian sections of the American Historical Association's *Guide to Historical Literature* (N.Y., 1961) and the numerous but scattered citations which appear in John Roach, ed., *A Bibliography of Modern History* (Cambridge, 1968), a guide designed to accompany the 12 volumes of the *New Cambridge Modern History* mentioned below. The most complete biographical dictionary remains the old but essential *Allgemeine deutsche Biographie*, 56 vols. (Leipzig, 1875–1912); it will remain useful for some entries even after completion of its worthy successor, the *Neue deutsche Biographie*, 15 vols. to date (Berlin, 1953 and continuing), published by the Historical Commission of the Bavarian Academy of Sciences. A shorter but convenient desktop biographical compilation is Hellmuth Rössler and Günther Franz, *Biographisches Wörterbuch zur deutschen Geschichte* (Munich, 1952); Rössler and Franz have also published an immensely useful short encyclopaedia of German history, the *Sachwörterbuch zur deutschen Geschichte*, 2 vols. (Munich, 1958; reprinted 1970).

II. General Histories

Among recent or relatively recent English-language works dealing with all or large parts of this period of German history, Hajo Holborn's *A History of Modern Germany*, 3 vols. (N.Y., 1959–69), is especially valuable for political, intellectual and cultural history, but is less satisfactory for economic and social developments and is not without organizational flaws. Rudolf Vierhaus, *Germany in the Age of Absolutism*, trans. Jonathan Knudsen (Cambridge, 1988), first published in German in 1978, is a fairly short but imaginatively structured survey of the period 1648–1763, though it is weakened by a not altogether felicitous translation. W. H. Bruford's *Germany in the Eighteenth Century: the Social Background of the Literary Revival* (Cambridge, 1935), though old, still has much detail on social, economic and cultural matters otherwise hard to locate in English. Volumes 4–8 of the *New Cambridge Modern History*, 12 vols. (Cambridge, 1957–71) contain many excellent and detailed but also scattered chapters on all aspects of German and central European history for the period 1609–1793.

In German, two older works, in particular, remain worthy of attention for their careful scholarship and wealth of information: Bernhard Erdmannsdörffer, *Deutsche Geschichte vom Westfälischen Frieden bis zum Regierungsantritt Friedrichs des Großen*, 2 vols. (Berlin, 1892–3) and Karl Biedermann's richly detailed *Deutschland im achtzehnten Jahrhundert*, 2 vols. in 3 (Leipzig, 1880). The trustworthy handbook of Bruno Gebhardt *et al.*, *Handbuch der deutschen Geschichte*, vol. 2: *Von der Reformation bis zum Ende des Absolutismus*, 9th ed. (Stuttgart, 1970) is a comprehensive narrative which contains good bibliographical notes and which can be expected to be continuously updated in future editions. Of the most recent German works, Heinrich Lutz, *Das Ringen um deutsche Einheit und kirchliche Erneuerung: von Maximilian I bis zum Westfälischen Frieden, 1490 bis 1648* (Berlin, 1983) and Rudolf Vierhaus, *Staaten und Stände. Vom Westfälischen Frieden bis zum Hubertusburger Frieden, 1648 bis 1763* (Berlin, 1984) (volumes 4 and 5, respectively, of the series 'Propyläen Geschichte Deutschlands') are masterful examples of the successful integration of narration and analysis. Heinz Schilling's two volumes in the series 'Das Reich und die Deutschen', *Aufbruch und Krise: Deutschland, 1517–1648* (Berlin, 1988) and *Vom alten Reich zum Fürstenstaat: Deutschland, 1648–1763* (Berlin, 1984), along with Horst Möller's *Fürstenstaat oder Bürgernation: Deutschland, 1763–1815* (Berlin, 1989) in the succeeding series 'Die Deutschen und ihre Nation', also deserve mention among newer general histories. The strongly structuralist approach of Hans-Ulrich Wehler, *Deutsche Gesellschaftsgeschichte*, vol. 1: *Vom Feudalismus des alten Reiches bis zum defensiven Moderisierung der Reformära* (Munich, 1987), while not without its problems, is both interesting and erudite and has copious notes and references.

III. The Thirty Years War

The best recent general history of this war is Geoffrey Parker, ed., *The Thirty Years' War* (London, 1984), whose chapters, though written by different specialists, are nicely integrated into a continuous narrative and analysis. Older, but still very worthwhile, is C. V. Wedgwood, *The Thirty Years War* (London, 1938 and later editions), a book which again proves that excellent history can also be exciting and colourful reading.

While neither of the above neglects the European international aspects of the war, the latter are more central to the themes of Georges Pagès, *The Thirty Years War, 1618–1648*, trans. David Maland and John Hooper (N.Y., 1970), S. H. Steinberg, *The Thirty Years' War and the Conflict for European Hegemony 1600–1660* (N.Y., 1966) and David Maland, *Europe at War, 1600–1650* (London, 1980). Josef Polisensky's *The Thirty Years War*, trans. Robert Evans (Berkeley, Cal., 1971) gives more attention to Bohemia and its centrality to the origins and course of the conflict than do others.

An excellent, topically organized survey of the economic, social and cultural effects of the war as it proceeded can be found in Herbert Langer, *Kulturgeschichte des 30jährigen Krieges* (Stuttgart, 1978). On more specialized topics, both Robert Bireley's *Religion and Politics in the Age of the Counterreformation: Emperor Ferdinand II, William Lamormaini, S.J. and the Formation of Imperial Policy* (Chapel Hill, N.C., 1981) and Thomas M. Barker's *The Military Intellectual and Battle: Raimondo Montecuccoli and the Thirty Years War* (Albany, N.Y., 1975) deliver more information of general interest than their titles might suggest. News, rumour and propaganda – important adjuncts to the war – are capably treated in E. A. Beller, *Propaganda in Germany during the Thirty Years War* (Princeton, 1940) and G. Rystad, *Kriegsnachrichten und Propaganda während des Dreißigjährigen Krieges* (Lund, 1960). Fritz Redlich has written two fine works which explore different but equally important social and financial aspects of the war in detail: *Die deutsche Inflation des frühen siebzehnten Jahrhunderts in der zeitgenössischen Literatur: die Kipper und Wipper* (Cologne and Vienna, 1972) and *The German Military Enterpriser and His Work Force: A Study in European Social and Economic History*, 2 vols. (Wiesbaden, 1964–5). Golo Mann's brilliant *Wallenstein*, trans. Charles Kessler (N.Y., 1976), is a detailed and subtle interpretation of this enigmatic figure and his times, but this translation does not contain the profuse notes and enormous bibliography of the original German edition (Frankfurt, 1971).

Finally, while the Peace of Westphalia and the effects of the war on Germany are discussed in a number of the books mentioned in this and the preceding section, Fritz Dickmann's *Der Westfälische Frieden*, 5th ed. (Münster, 1985) is by far the most extensive analysis of the peace, while Günther Franz in *Der dreißigjährige Krieg und das deutsche Volk*, 4th ed. (Stuttgart, 1979) and Robert R. Ergang, *The Myth of the All-Destructive Fury of the Thirty Years War* (Pocono Pines, Pa., 1956) reach very different conclusions about the severity of the war's impact.

IV. Constitutional and Political History

The two most comprehensive yet manageable constitutional histories which include the period 1600–1800 are Conrad Bornhak, *Deutsche Verfassungsgeschichte vom Westfälischen Frieden an* (Stuttgart, 1934; reprinted, Aalen, 1968) and Fritz Hartung, *Deutsche Verfassungsgeschichte vom 15. Jahrhundert bis zur Gegenwart*, 7th ed. (Stuttgart, 1959). Invaluable for its wealth of information on numerous aspects of constitutional, political and economic history, as well as for its detail on the development of administrative institutions and practices in the territories, is Kurt G. A. Jeserich, Hans Pohl and Georg-Christoph von Unruh, eds., *Deutsche Verwaltungsgeschichte*: vol. 1: *Vom Spätmittelalter bis zum Ende des Reiches* (Stuttgart, 1983). The first two chapters of Leonard Krieger's *The German Idea of Freedom: History of a Political Tradition* (Boston, 1957), though dealing more with the history of ideas than of institutions, reveal much about the background of constitutional development in the period.

The persistence of strong representative traditions in many German states even during the 'age of absolutism' is well argued (though also occasionally forced) in F. L. Carsten, *Princes and Parliaments in Germany from the Fifteenth to the Eighteenth Century* (Oxford, 1959).

A good summary and analysis of Cameralism and the 'police state' in the internal development of the territories is in Marc Raeff, *The Well-Ordered Police State: Social and Institutional Change through Law in the Germanies and Russia* (New Haven, 1983). The doctrines of various Cameralist thinkers themselves are most recently explored in Erhard Dittrich, *Die deutschen und österreichischen Kameralisten* (Darmstadt, 1974) and in still more detailed fashion in Louise Sommer, *Die österreichischen Kameralisten*, 2 vols. (Vienna, 1920–25) as well as in the even older and unimaginative (but still informative) Albion W. Small, *The Cameralists: the Pioneers of German Social Polity* (Chicago and London, 1909).

V. General Economic and Social History

With the exception of Eda Sagarra's not very satisfying *A Social History of Germany* (London, 1977), there are no social or economic histories in English which cover the early modern period in Germany. There are a number of excellent ones in German; all of them are good as general surveys, though each is different, containing insights and statistical and other details not available in the others.

Among economic histories, Heinrich Bechtel, *Wirtschaftsgeschichte Deutschlands vom 16. bis 18. Jahrhundert* (Munich, 1952) and Hermann Kellenbenz, *Deutsche Wirtschaftsgeschichte*, vol. 1: *Von den Anfängen bis zum Ende des 18. Jahrhunderts* (Munich, 1977), are good, while on social history alone, the long article by Eberhard Weis on 'Gesellschaftsstrukturen und Gesellschaftsentwicklung in der frühen Neuzeit' in Karl Bosl and Eberhard Weis, *Die Gesellschaft in Deutschland*, part 1: *Von der fränkischen Zeit bis 1848* (Munich, 1976), pp. 131–287, constitutes almost a small book in itself. Hans-Ulrich Wehler's *Deutsche Gesellschaftsgeschichte*, mentioned in section I, is also very strong on social structure.

A number of works successfully combine social and economic history, among them: Hermann Aubin and Wolfgang Zorn, eds., *Handbuch der deutschen Wirtschafts- und Sozialgeschichte*, vol. 1: (Stuttgart, 1971); Heinrich Bechtel, *Wirtschafts- und sozialgeschichte Deutschlands* (Munich, 1967); Rolf Engelsing, *Sozial- und Wirtschaftsgeschichte Deutschlands* (Göttingen, 1973); Friedrich Lütge, *Deutsche Sozial- und Wirtschaftsgeschichte*, 3rd ed. (Berlin, 1966); and George Droege, *Deutsche Wirtschafts- und Sozialgeschichte*, 3rd ed. (Frankfurt, 1979).

For the history of agriculture, the most important economic sector throughout the period, and of the peasantry, consult especially volumes 2, 3 and 4 of the series 'Deutsche Agrargeschichte', ed. Günther Franz, respectively as follows: Wilhelm Abel, *Geschichte der deutschen Landwirtschaft vom frühen Mittelalter bis zum 19. Jahrhundert* (Stuttgart, 1962); Friedrich Lütge, *Geschichte der deutschen Agrarverfassung* (Stuttgart, 1963); and Günther Franz, *Geschichte des Bauernstandes vom frühen Mittelalter bis zum 19. Jahrhundert* (Stuttgart, 1970). John G. Gagliardo, *From Pariah to Patriot: the Changing Image of the German Peasant, 1770–1840* (Lexington, Ky., 1969), analyzes the factors which led to a gradually enhanced social respectability for the peasantry in German public opinion.

Titles listed elsewhere in this bibliography and particularly in sections II and VII–IX, should also be reviewed for relevance to social and economic topics which concern individual territories rather than Germany as a whole.

VI. Cultural History: Religion, Education and the Arts

For the general history of religions and religious doctrines in Germany in the early modern period, consult titles listed in sections II and VII–X.

The powerful impact of Pietism on German and especially Prussian history has attracted a great deal of attention. The founder of the movement dominates the works of K. James Stein, *Philipp Jakob Spener: Pietist Patriarch* (Chicago, 1986) and Johannes Wallmann, *Philipp Jakob Spener und die Anfänge des Pietismus* (Tübingen, 1970), while the multiple influences of the movement as a whole on German society have been described in F. Ernest Stoeffler's *German Pietism during the Eighteenth Century* (Leiden, 1973). The involvement of Pietism in both political ideology and political practice are separately treated in Gerhard Kaiser, *Pietismus und Patriotismus im literarischen Deutschland: ein Beitrag zum Problem der Säkularisation*, 2nd ed. (Frankfurt, 1973) and in the German sections of Mary Fulbrook, *Piety and Politics: Religion and the Rise of Absolutism in England, Württemberg and Prussia* (Cambridge, 1983).

On education, no single history has yet replaced the now rather badly dated Friedrich Paulsen, *Geschichte des gelehrten Unterrichts auf den deutschen Schulen und Universitäten vom Ausgang des Mittelalters bis zur Gegenwart*, 3rd ed., 2 vols. (Leipzig, 1919–21), though various German works now in preparation will soon change that. Several recent English-language works have made significant contributions to social, political and economic aspects of the history of education in Germany at various levels and all are excellent bibliographical resources. James Van Horn Melton's *Absolutism and the Eighteenth-Century Origins of Compulsory Schooling in Prussia and Austria* (Cambridge, 1988) examines the increasing official concern for popular education in the context of social and economic imperatives of the regulative order of old regime society; the practical effect of such concern in Prussia was earlier elaborated in Wolfgang Neugebauer, *Absolutistischer Staat und Schulwirklichkeit in Brandenburg-Preußen* (Berlin and N. Y., 1985). Anthony J. LaVopa has looked at teachers, students and educational and clerical careers in *Prussian Schoolteachers: Profession and Office, 1763–1848* (Chapel Hill, N.C., 1980) and *Grace, Talent, and Merit: Poor Students, Clerical Careers, and Professional Ideology in Eighteenth-Century Germany* (Cambridge, 1988); and Charles McClelland's *State, Society and University in Germany, 1700–1914* (Cambridge and N.Y., 1980) has examined the unique place and changing functions of universities in German society. Karl Schleunes, *Schooling and Society: the Politics of Education in Prussia and Bavaria, 1750–1900* (N.Y., 1989) makes some shrewd observations about education in the eighteenth century, but is chiefly concerned with the nineteenth. A rare study of female education in the period is Peter Petschauer, *The Education of Women in Eighteenth-Century Germany* (Lewiston, N.Y., 1989).

Whether in German or in English, both general surveys and specific studies of German literature (*belles-lettres*) for the period abound. Perhaps the most venerable among a number of good English-language surveys is J. G. Robertson, *A History of German Literature*, 6th ed. by Dorothy Reich (Edinburgh and London, 1970), which also gives attention to the social background and personal histories of the many authors it discusses. More specific works for the seventeenth century include Roy Pascal, *German Literature in the Sixteenth and Seventeenth Centuries: Renaissance, Reformation, Baroque* (London, 1968) and, in German, Marian Szyrocki, *Die deutsche Literatur des Barock: ein Einführung* (Stuttgart, 1979). For the eighteenth century and the literary revival, see Friedhelm Radandt, *From Baroque to Storm and Stress, 1720–1775* (N.Y., 1977); Victor Lange, *The Classical Age of German Literature, 1740–1815* (N.Y., 1982); and Werner Kohlschmidt, *A History of German Literature, 1760–1805*, trans. Ian Hilton (N.Y., 1975). Eric Blackall, *The Emergence of German as a Literary Language, 1700–1775*, 2nd ed. (Ithaca, N.Y., 1978) emphasizes growing dexterity in the use of the German language itself as part of the literary revival; and for the later years of the eighteenth century, Ludwig Kahn's *Social Ideals in German Literature, 1770–1830* (N.Y., 1938) points to the importance of fictional literature as social commentary. A number of other works relevant to literary history, particularly of the eighteenth century, can be found in section X below.

For the history of the arts in general, the best survey remains that of Georg Dehio, *Geschichte der deutschen Kunst*, 4 vols. (Berlin and Leipzig, 1919–34), with an additional four volumes of plates, of which vol. 2 covers the early modern period. A good introduction to architecture for the English reader is Nicolas Powell, *From Baroque to Rococo: an Introduction to Austrian and German Architecture from 1580 to 1790* (N.Y., 1959); in German, Werner Hager, *Die Bauten des deutschen Barocks, 1690–1770* (Jena, 1942) is excellent for a shorter part of the period. For painting, see Max Goering, *Deutsche Malerei des siebzehnten und achtzehnten Jahrhunderts, von den Manieristen bis zum Klassizismus* (Berlin, 1940). The best history of German music of the period is Hans Joachim Moser, *Geschichte der deutschen Musik*, vol. 2: *Vom Beginn des Dreißigjährigen Krieges bis zum Tode Joseph Haydns*, 5th ed. (Stuttgart and Berlin, 1930; reprinted, Hildesheim, 1968). It is supplemented in some areas by Hans Mersmann, *Eine deutsche Musikgeschichte* (Potsdam and Berlin, 1934) and, for the serious musicologist, by Rolf Dammann, *Der Musikbegriff im deutschen Barock* (Cologne, 1967).

VII. Austria

As one of the great powers of Europe throughout the early modern period, Austria has commanded an immense interest among historians; even in English, the number of works devoted to its history is considerable, though coverage is much more spotty than in German. Robert A. Kann's *A History of the Habsburg Empire, 1526–1918* (Berkeley, Cal., 1974), though covering a very long period, is a readable and intelligent text. For the seventeenth century, R. J. W. Evans, *The Making of the Habsburg Monarchy, 1550–1700: an Interpretation* (Oxford, 1979) is an original work of first-rate importance, while for the eighteenth Ernst Wangermann's *The Austrian Achievement, 1700–1800* (London and N.Y., 1973), though of lesser weight, is both competent and interesting. More specific topics in the seventeenth century are not well represented in English, but John Spielman, *Leopold I of Austria* (New Brunswick, N.J., 1977) is a good look at both the man and his times; and in French, Jean Berenger has provided a splendid examination of the fiscal system of the monarchy in his *Finances et absolutisme autrichien dans le second moitié du XVIIe siècle* (Paris, 1975). The first two chapters of Robert A. Kann's *A Study in Austrian Intellectual History: from Late Baroque to Romanticism* (N.Y., 1960) provide insight into the cultural climate and 'crisis' of the late Austrian baroque. Important aspects of the monarchy's foreign policy and military history of the same period are illuminated in Thomas M. Barker, *Double Eagle and Crescent: Vienna's Second Turkish Siege and its Historical Setting* (Albany, N.Y., 1967) and Derek McKay, *Prince Eugene of Savoy* (N.Y., 1977). The brief reign of Joseph I has been well surveyed by Charles W. Ingrao, *In Quest and Crisis: Emperor Joseph I and the Habsburg Monarchy* (West Lafayette, Ind., 1979).

While no biography or other comprehensive study of Charles VI and his whole reign exists, greater attention has been given to Maria Theresia. Eugen Guglia, *Maria Theresia, ihr Leben und ihre Regierung*, 2 vols. (Munich 1917) remains the most reliable detailed biography; Robert Pick, *Empress Maria Theresa: the Earlier Years, 1717–1757* (N.Y., 1966) is sound and better overall (in spite of its only partial coverage of her reign) than Edward Crankshaw's more complete *Maria Theresa* (N.Y., 1970). G. P. Gooch, *Maria Theresa and Other Studies* (London and N.Y., 1951) contains two long and shrewd essays on the empress–queen; and much can be learned about her from Derek Beales's splendid biography of Joseph I, mentioned below. The economic policies of her reign have been well presented in Gustav Otruba, *Die Wirtschaftspolitik Maria Theresias* (Vienna, 1963); and the model work of P. G. M. Dickson, *Finance and Government under Maria Theresia, 1740–1780*, 2 vols. (Oxford, 1987) provides a wealth of information and insights on many more aspects of her reign than those suggested by the title alone. The military historian Christopher Duffy has filled an important gap with *The Army of Maria Theresa: the Armed Forces of Imperial Austria, 1740–1780* (N.Y., 1977).

Four books represent something of a transition from Maria Theresia's reign to that of Joseph II, since they deal with persons or policies important in both and even beyond. Georg Küntzel's *Fürst Kaunitz-Rittberg als Staatsmann* (Frankfurt, 1923) details the career of the most important minister in the Austrian government for over thirty years; the incremental progress of emancipatory and other agrarian legislation in Austria and Bohemia is sketched out by Edith Link, *The Emancipation of the Austrian Peasant, 1740–1798* (N.Y., 1949) and William E. Wright, *Serf, Seigneur and Sovereign: Agrarian Reform in Eighteenth-Century Bohemia* (Minneapolis, 1966); and the difficult but extremely important campaign to reform and unify legal codes as part of the process of modern state-building is the subject of Henry Strakosch, *State Absolutism and the Rule of Law: the Struggle for the Codification of Civil Law in Austria, 1753–1811* (Sydney, Australia, 1967).

The most recent and impressive biography of Joseph II in English is by Derek Beales, *Joseph II*, vol. 1: *In the Shadow of Maria Theresa, 1741–1780* (Cambridge, 1987), which when complete promises by a wide margin to overshadow the serviceable but not very profound biography by Saul K. Padover, *The Revolutionary Emperor: Joseph II, 1741–1790*, 2nd ed. (London, 1967) and the even shorter sketch by Paul P. Bernard, *Joseph II* (N.Y., 1968). Paul von Mitrofanov's *Josef II: Seine politische und kulturelle Tätigkeit*, 2 vols. (German translation of the 1907 Russian edition, Vienna, 1910) is no biography at all, but a close and still very useful analysis of Joseph's reform projects in the 1780s. The changed relationship between church, state and society, along with the longer-term results of it (which together have become known as 'Josephinism'), have so far been treated in systematic fashion only in German works, among them: Fritz Valjavec, *Der Josephinismus: zur geistigen Entwicklung Österreichs im achtzehnten und neunzehnten Jahrhundert*, 2nd ed. (Munich, 1945) and Eduard Winter, *Der Josefinismus: die Geschichte des österreichischen Reformkatholizismus, 1740–1848* (Berlin, 1962); but religious issues play a large part in Paul P. Bernard, *Jesuits and Jacobins: Enlightenment and Enlightened Despotism in Austria* (Urbana, Ill., 1971), as well as in Charles H. O'Brien, *Ideas of Religious Toleration at the Time of Joseph II* (Philadelphia, 1969). An important aspect of Joseph's foreign policy – his obsession with the Bavarian exchange project – has been studied in Paul P. Bernard, *Joseph II and Bavaria: Two Eighteenth-Century Attempts at German Unification* (The Hague, 1965).

Leopold II has received little attention in English, but an excellent German biography is Adam Wandruska, *Leopold II*, 2 vols. (Munich and Vienna, 1965); various aspects of Leopold's short reign have also been treated in general histories mentioned above, as well as in Henry J. Kerner, *Bohemia in the Eighteenth Century* (N.Y., 1932), which deals chiefly with the reigns of Joseph and Leopold. Section X should also be consulted for works touching on Austrian history.

VIII. Prussia

The history of Brandenburg-Prussia in the seventeenth and eighteenth centuries is better served in English than that of any other German state – which is natural enough, given Prussia's importance to the unification of Germany in the nineteenth century. Peculiarly, however, no comprehensive history of this state has emerged in English to challenge the short and sturdy, but somewhat dated Sidney B. Fay, *The Rise of Brandenburg-Prussia to 1786*, rev. ed. by Klaus Epstein (N.Y., 1964), or Otis C. Mitchell's abbreviated *A Concise History of Brandenburg-Prussia to 1786* (Lanham, Md., 1980). In German, a recent history of the period, written by a competent scholar for a general readership, is Ingrid Mittenzwei, *Brandenburg-Preußen 1648 bis 1789: das Zeitalter des Absolutismus in Text und Bild* (Cologne, 1987). For Prussia's early history to 1688, see F. L. Carsten's well-respected *The Origins of Prussia* (Oxford, 1954), which is helpful on the formation of basic social patterns which persisted throughout the old regime. For Elector Friedrich Wilhelm, Ferdinand Schevill's *The Great Elector* (Chicago, 1947) is a good introduction, but is considerably less substantial than the old, standard biography, M. Phillipson, *Der große Kurfürst Friedrich Wilhelm von Brandenburg*, 3 vols. (Berlin, 1897–1903). Linda and Marsha Frey's *Frederick I: the Man and His Times* (N.Y., 1984) is a generally unsuccessful and uneven effort to rehabilitate this ruler's reputation. Robert R. Ergang, *The Potsdam Fuehrer: Frederick William I, Father of Prussian Militarism* (N.Y., 1941) is solid and a good deal more objective than its title suggests; in German, see Gerhard Oestreich, *Friedrich Wilhelm I: Preußischer Absolutismus, Merkantilismus, Militarismus* (Göttingen, 1977). Two good studies by Reinhold Dorwart, *The Administrative Reforms of Frederick William I of Prussia* (Cambridge, Mass., 1953) and *The Prussian Welfare State before 1740* (Cambridge, Mass., 1971) have opened up important areas in this early period previously closed to English readers.

Some other works on various aspects of Prussian society of the pre-Frederician era, some of them ranging into the second half of the eighteenth century as well, should be mentioned: on the powerful influence of Pietism, Klaus Deppermann, *Der hallesche Pietismus und der preußische Staat unter Friedrich III.(I.)* (Göttingen, 1961) and Carl Hinrichs, *Preußentum und Pietismus. Der Pietismus in Brandenburg-Preußen als religiös-soziale Reformbewegung* (Göttingen, 1971); and on the special features of Prussian state and society attributable to its military system and its bureaucracy, Otto Büsch, *Militärsystem und Sozialleben im alten Preußen, 1713–1807: die Anfänge der sozialen Militarisierung der preußische-deutschen Gesellschaft* (Berlin, 1962) and the now classic work of Hans Rosenberg, *Bureaucracy, Aristocracy and Autocracy: the Prussian Experience, 1660–1815* (Cambridge, Mass., 1958).

Among the numerous biographies of Frederick II (the Great), one is truly monumental: Reinhold Koser, *Geschichte Friedrichs des Großen*, 4th and 5th eds., 4 vols. (Berlin, 1912–14), characterized by careful scholarship and a complete command of the sources; it will not soon be equalled. Of other German biographies, the most recent are Ingrid Mittenzwei, *Friedrich II. von Preußen: eine Biographie* (Berlin, 1979) and Theodor Schieder, *Friedrich der Große: ein Königtum der Widersprüche* (Frankfurt, 1983); the latter, more imaginatively organized than most biographies, will soon appear in an English edition. In English, the very recent biography of Frederick by Robert B. Asprey, *Frederick the Great: the Magnificent Enigma* (N.Y., 1986) is flawed by overemphasis on the king's diplomacy and wars and by inadequate attention to his peacetime achievements, especially after 1763. Two other studies provide good introductions for the English reader. Gerhard Ritter, *Frederick the Great: a Historical Profile* (Berkeley, Cal., 1968), first published in German in 1936, emphasizes Frederick's rational and restrained use of power; and G. P. Gooch, *Frederick the Great: the Ruler, the Writer, the Man* (London, 1947), is an admiring but not uncritical evaluation of the diverse talents and policies of this unusual monarch. Edith Simon's *The Making of Frederick the Great* (Boston, 1963) is a partly psychological explanation of the growth of the young Frederick into the mature king of the late 1740s.

Frederick's administration and bureaucracy have been the subject of many studies in German, fewer in English; of the former, a good overview is Walther Hubatsch, *Friedrich der Große und die preußische Verwaltung* (Cologne, 1973), while among the latter Hubert C. Johnson's valuable *Frederick the Great and His Officials* (New Haven, 1975) is as much about institutions as about personnel and conveys a good sense of the tenor of the king's administration. A relatively obscure work by Hermann Weill, *Frederick the Great and Samuel von Cocceji* (Madison, Wisc., 1961) examines the 'revolution' in the Prussian judicial administration brought about between 1740 and 1755 by one of the few royal servants who commanded the full trust and admiration of the king. The most accessible studies in English of Frederick's army and of his military career, both of superior quality, are by Christopher Duffy: *The Army of Frederick the Great* (N.Y., 1974) and *The Military Life of Frederick the Great* (N.Y., 1986).

Prussian mercantilism and economic policy in general are examined in W. O. Henderson's *Studies in the Economic Policy of Frederick the Great* (London, 1963) and to some extent in his *The State and the Industrial Revolution in Prussia, 1740–1870* (Liverpool, 1958). Two very different books which lead from Frederick's reign into the 1790s and beyond are Robert M. Berdahl, *The Politics of the Prussian Nobility: the Development of a Conservative Ideology, 1770–1848* (Princeton, 1988), which traces the growth of a coherent aristocratic political ideology as reaction to increasing challenges to the social assumptions of the old regime; and Henri Brunschwig's fascinating study *Enlightenment and Romanticism in Eighteenth-Century Prussia*, trans. Frank Jellinek (Chicago, 1974; 1st ed., Paris, 1947), an analysis of the decay of the melioristic rationalism on which the 'enlightened' government of Frederick II had rested and their partial replacement by a cultural pessimism, accompanied by currents of sentimentality, mysticism and irrationality. As in the case of Austria, the reader is referred to sections II, IV–VI and X for other references applicable to Prussia.

IX. Empire and Territories

The history of the last 150 years of the Holy Roman Empire is better represented in the many German monographic studies of it whose sheer number prevents their listing here than it is in either general studies in German or in English-language works in general. The best summary of the basic character and structure of the Empire in English is in chapters 1–3 of John G. Gagliardo, *Reich and Nation: the Holy Roman Empire as Idea and Reality, 1763–1806* (Bloomington, Ind., 1980), an analysis of German reaction to the decaying reality of the Empire under the pressures of political change in Germany and Europe in the later eighteenth century. Karl Otmar Freiherr von Aretin, *Heiliges Römisches Reich, 1776–1806: Reichsverfassung und Staatssouveränität*, 2 vols. (Wiesbaden, 1967) is a close political analysis of the last thirty years of the Empire's existence, with an immense bibliography useful for the last several centuries of imperial history; vol. 2 consists of important documents of the period.

The huge corpus of commentaries on imperial public law published after 1600 or so is summarized and analyzed in Hanns Gross, *Empire and Sovereignty: a History of the Public Law Literature in the Holy Roman Empire, 1599–1804* (Chicago, 1973).

Mack Walker, *Johann Jakob Moser and the Holy Roman Empire of the German Nation* (Chapel Hill, N.C., 1981), has described the multifaceted career of one of the most famous and prolific public lawyers of the eighteenth century, illuminating numerous other aspects of the history of the time in the process. James A. Vann has studied the possibilities and the limits of cooperation among some of the smaller territories of the Empire in *The Swabian Kreis: Institutional Growth in the Holy Roman Empire, 1648–1715* (Brussels, 1975); and various other imperial institutions and procedures receive attention in James A. Vann and Steven W. Rowan, eds., *The Old Reich: Essays on German Political Institutions, 1495–1806* (Brussels, 1975). Finally, Gerhard Benecke, *Society and Politics in Germany, 1500–1750* (London and Toronto, 1974), is a study of the continuing efficacy of the imperial nexus for the smaller territories, using the County of Lippe as his example.

Still 'national' in scope, but not dealing with the imperial structure as such, are Adrien Fauchier-Magnan, *The Small German Courts in the Eighteenth Century* (London, 1958), a perhaps excessively anecdotal survey of court life in a number of the lesser territories, especially Württemberg, but one which conveys some impression of both the positive and negative aspects of small-scale German politics; and

Mack Walker's very important *German Home Towns: Community, State and General Estate, 1648–1871* (Ithaca, N.Y. and London, 1971), which describes and analyzes the communal or 'home town' mentality that defined so much of the social, economic and political character of early modern Germany.

Descending to the territorial level, the only general historical survey covering this period is Georg Wilhelm Sante and A. G. Ploetz-Verlag, eds., *Geschichte der deutschen Länder: 'Territorien-Ploetz'*, vol. 1: *Die Territorien bis zum Ende des alten Reiches* (Würzburg, 1964), whose entries tend to be brief except for the largest territories. Territorial histories in English are few, but the ones that exist are good. Helen Liebel, *Enlightened Bureaucracy vs. Enlightened Despotism in Baden, 1750–1792* (Philadelphia, 1965), while mainly concerned with the origins of 'enlightened' policies in the regime of Margrave Karl Friedrich, also says much about the character of society and government there in general. James A. Vann, *The Making of a State: Württemberg, 1593–1793* (Ithaca, N.Y., 1984) paints this territory's history with a broader brush over a longer period of time than does Charles Ingrao that of Hesse-Kassel in his *The Hessian Mercenary State: Ideas, Institutions and Reform under Frederick II, 1760–1785* (Cambridge, 1987), but both authors provide a wealth of information on government and society in two different yet similar territories.

Of the larger states, Bavaria's history is particularly well documented in Michael Doeberl's old but sturdy *Entwicklungsgeschichte Bayerns*, 2 vols. (Munich, 1908–12), as well as in Michael Strich, *Das Kurhaus Bayern im Zeitalter Ludwigs XIV. und die europäischen Mächte*, 2 vols. (Munich, 1933), which is the classic account of Bavaria's failed bid to become a major international power; H. Rall, *Kurbayern in der letzten Epoche der alten Reichsverfassung, 1745–1801* (Munich, 1952) is a balanced history of Bavaria's domestic and foreign policies in its final half-century as an electorate.

The fascination long attached to the small but luminous court of Carl August of Weimar has resulted in several excellent studies: Fritz Hartung, *Das Großherzogtum Sachsen unter der Regierung Carl Augusts, 1775–1828* (Weimar, 1923) and W. H. Bruford's elegant *Culture and Society in Classical Weimar, 1775–1806* (Cambridge, 1962), as well as the fine biography by Willy Andreas, *Carl August von Weimar: ein Leben mit Goethe* (Stuttgart, 1953). Almost as much territorial history as biography is Max Braubach's *Maria Theresias jüngster Sohn Max Franz, letzter Kurfürst von Köln und Fürstbischof von Münster* (Vienna and Munich, 1961), an account of the life and achievements of the

421

Habsburg Maximilian Franz, one of the most enlightened of the ecclesiastical princes.

In urban history, the Free Imperial Cities have attracted the most attention among non-German historians, chiefly because of their self-governing character; among recent urban histories in English, only T. C. W. Blanning's *Reform and Revolution in Mainz, 1743–1806* (N.Y., 1974) deals with a 'territorial' city, but one which was also the seat of an archbishopric and electorate and interesting in its own right partly for that reason. Of three others, each has a different emphasis (as reflected in its title), but as a group they present a rich mosaic of the characteristics and problems of German cities of the old regime: Gerald L. Soliday, *A Community in Conflict: Frankfurt Society in the Seventeenth and Early Eighteenth Century* (Hanover, N.H., 1974); Christopher R. Friedrichs, *Urban Society in an Age of War: Nördlingen, 1580–1720* (Princeton, 1979); and Joachim Whaley, *Religious Toleration and Social Change in Hamburg, 1529–1819* (Cambridge, 1985). In German, Ingrid Batori's *Die Reichsstadt Augsburg im 18. Jahrhundert: Verfassung, Finanzen und Reformversuche* (Göttingen, 1969) is particularly informative.

X. The German Enlightenment

The enlightenment of the seventeenth and eighteenth centuries has been dealt with in general texts listed in section II as well as in a number of separate works in sections VI–IX; these may variously be regarded either as broad introductions or as commentaries on special topics. Probably the best one-volume surveys of the German enlightenment as a whole are Frederick Hertz, *The Development of the German Public Mind: a Social History of German Political Sentiments, Aspirations and Ideas*, vol. 2: *The Enlightenment* (London, 1962), which tends to concentrate on social and political attitudes and issues; and the more comprehensive but slightly shorter Horst Möller, *Vernunft und Kritik: deutsche Aufklärung im 17. und 18. Jahrhundert* (Frankfurt, 1986). Next to these, two volumes of essays present a variety of subjects important to an understanding of the peculiar features of the German enlightenment: the much larger of the two is Franklin Kopitzsch, ed., *Aufklärung, Absolutismus und Bürgertum in Deutschland. Zwölf Aufsätze* (Munich, 1976), while the collection in English of Roy Porter and Mikulas Teich, eds., *The Enlightenment in National Context* (Cambridge, 1981) presents brief but informative essays on Protestant and Catholic Germany by Joachim Whaley and T. C. W.

Blanning, respectively, and on Austria by Ernst Wangermann. The final and most 'political' phase of the enlightenment, from about 1770 onward, has been extensively and effectively examined in Fritz Valjavec, *Die Entstehung der politischen Strömungen in Deutschland, 1770–1815* (Munich, 1951) and Klaus Epstein, *The Genesis of German Conservatism* (Princeton, 1966).

On special topics, the vigorous public debate about the position and privileges of the nobility in German society (also discussed by Valjavec and Epstein) is well described in Johanna Schultze, *Die Auseinandersetzung zwischen Adel und Bürgertum in den deutschen Zeitschriften der letzten drei Jahrzehnte des 18. Jahrhunderts* (Berlin, 1925). Horst Dippel, *Germany and the American Revolution*, trans. Bernard Uhlendorf (Chapel Hill, N.C., 1977) examines the impact of the revolutionary war and the new American government on German public opinion; and the stimulative role of English political and social ideas and practices on the German enlightenment is addressed by Michael Maurer in *Aufklärung und Anglophilie in Deutschland* (Göttingen, 1985).

Since a notable increase in both literacy and extensive reading was an essential feature of the progress of the enlightenment in Germany, Rolf Engelsing's two books *Analphabetentum und Lektüre: zur Sozialgeschichte des Lesens in Deutschland zwischen feudaler und industrieller Gesellschaft* (Stuttgart, 1973) and *Der Bürger als Leser: Lesergeschichte in Deutschland, 1500–1800* (Stuttgart, 1974) are particularly significant. Reading and discussion, however, were but one aspect of an increasing sociability, especially among the literate bourgeoisie, which played a crucial role in defining the social scope of the German enlightenment; the growing institutionalization of that sociability is the subject of important works by Ulrich Im Hof, *Das gesellige Jahrhundert: Gesellschaft und Gesellschaften im Zeitalter der Aufklärung* (Munich, 1982) and by Richard van Dülmen, *Die Gesellschaft der Aufklärer: zur bürgerlicher Emanzipation und aufklärerischer Kultur in Deutschland* (Frankfurt, 1986).

On the whole subject of 'enlightened absolutism', about which much debate has raged on both sides of the Atlantic in recent years, C. B. A. Behrens provides some interesting insights in her comparative study *Society, Government and the Enlightenment: the Experiences of Eighteenth-Century France and Prussia* (London and N.Y., 1985); but the most convenient and current source of information on the current historiography of the issue for Germany will be found in H. M. Scott, ed., *Enlightened Absolutism: Reform and Reformers in Later Eighteenth-Century Europe* (Ann Arbor, Mich.,

1990), especially in chapters 5 (H. M. Scott, 'Reform in the Habsburg Monarchy'); 7 (R. J. W. Evans, 'Joseph II and Nationality in the Habsburg Lands'); 8 (Charles Ingrao, 'The Smaller German States'); and 10 (T. C. W. Blanning, 'Frederick the Great and Enlightened Absolutism').

A scattering of works in English on individual figures and their role in the German Enlightenment can be recommended. Leonard Krieger's *The Politics of Discretion: Pufendorf and the Acceptance of Natural Law* (Chicago, 1965) describes Pufendorf's reinterpretation and reformulation of natural law and its enthronement as a chief doctrine of the German Enlightenment. On G. E. Lessing, see Henry E. Allison, *Lessing and the Enlightenment: His Philosophy of Religion and its Relation to Eighteenth Century Thought* (Ann Arbor, Mich., 1966); and on C. M. Wieland, consult John A. McCarthy's *Christoph Martin Wieland* (Boston, 1979). Like Wieland and Lessing, J. G. Herder was a figure of major importance, but his work led in directions very different from theirs; his unique contributions to both literature and philosophy are examined in Frank McEachran, *The Life and Philosophy of Johann Gottfried Herder* (Oxford, 1939) and F. M. Bernard, *Herder's National and Social Thought* (Oxford and N.Y., 1965).

The bewitching and in many ways confusing Justus Möser, widely known and respected in his time as official, historian and commentator on public affairs, is the subject of two intellectual biographies: William F. Sheldon, *The Intellectual Development of Justus Möser: the Growth of a German Patriot* (Osnabrück, 1970); and, more recently, Jonathan B. Knudsen, *Justus Möser and the German Enlightenment* (Cambridge, 1986), which locates in Möser's often ambiguous views on many issues the kind of intellectual compromise that was not untypical of mainstream enlightenment thinking in Germany. In German, finally, Horst Möller has contributed a fine study of a pivotal figure in the Berlin enlightenment in his *Aufklärung in Preußen. Der Verleger, Publizist und Geschichtsschreiber Friedrich Nicolai* (Berlin, 1974).

Maps

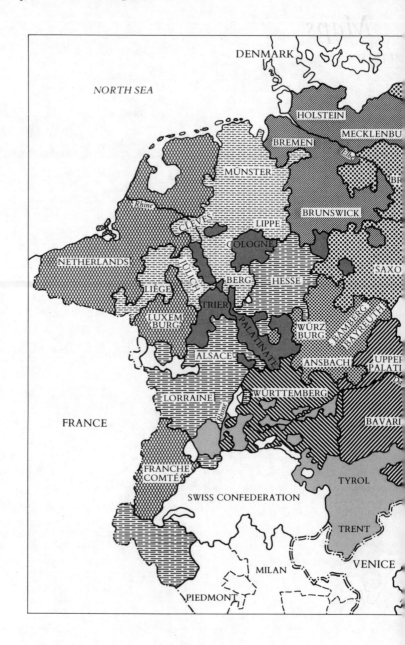

Map 1 The Imperial Circles of 1512

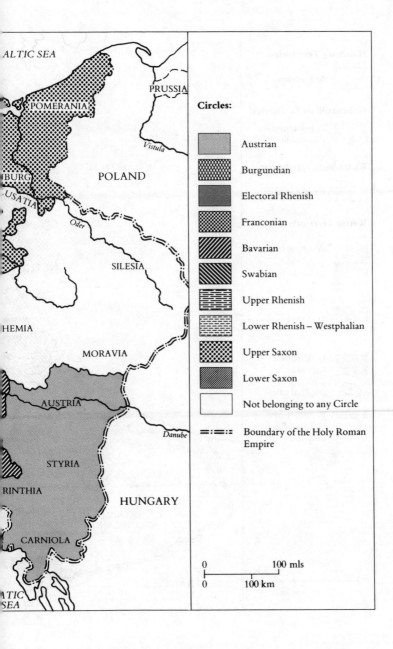

Map 2 North-western Germany after the Peace of Westphalia, 1648

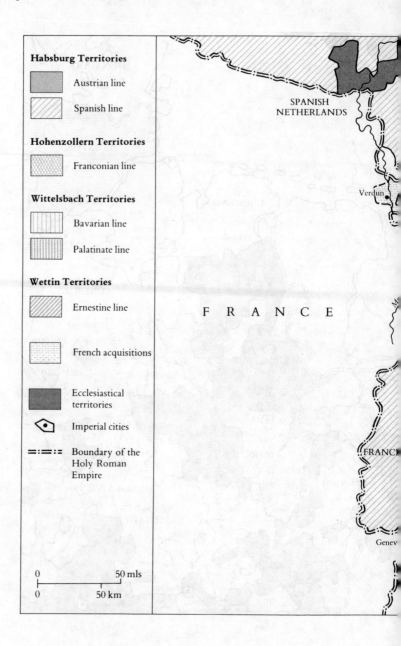

Habsburg Territories

Austrian line

Spanish line

Hohenzollern Territories

Franconian line

Wittelsbach Territories

Bavarian line

Palatinate line

Wettin Territories

Ernestine line

French acquisitions

Ecclesiastical territories

Imperial cities

Boundary of the Holy Roman Empire

0   50 mls
0   50 km

SPANISH NETHERLANDS

Verdun

F R A N C E

FRANCE

Genev

Map 3 South-western Germany after the Peace of Westphalia, 1648

Wetzlar

Fulda

Koblenz

ARCHB TRIER

BISH

Trier

Frankfurt

Luxemburg

Mainz

Darmstadt

Würzburg

Bamberg

ARCHB MAINZ

Worms

Metz

ELECTORAL

Heidelberg

PALATINATE

Rothenburg

ANSBACH

Speier

Hall

Heilbronn

LORRAINE

Rhine

BADEN

Stuttgart

Moselle

BISH
Strassburg

WÜRTTEMBERG

Ulm

Freiburg

BREISGAU

Ravensburg

*BISH
AUGSBURG*

SUNDGAU

Monbéliard

Basel

Konstanz

*BISH
BASEL*

Zürich

Besançon

OMTÉ

Bern

Vorarlberg

SWITZERLAND

Lausanne

GRISONS

Locarno

BISH
Trent

AVOY

Map 4 North-eastern Germany after the Peace of Westphalia, 1648

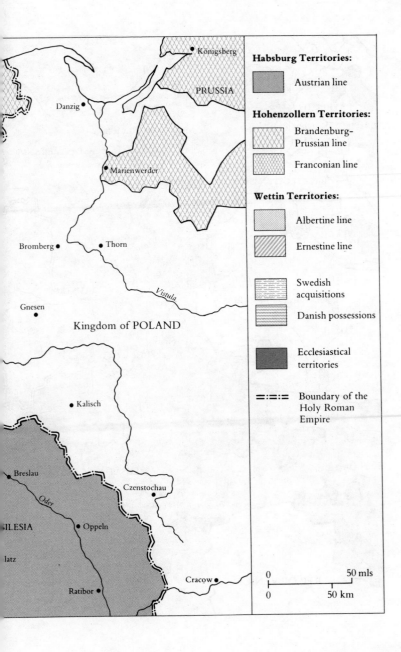

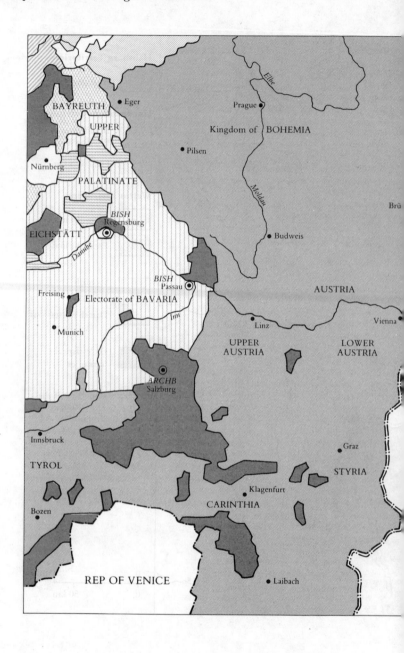

Map 5 South-eastern Germany after the Peace of Westphalia, 1648

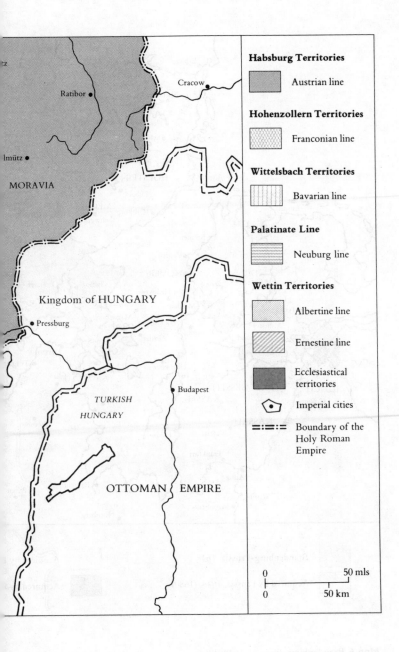

Habsburg Territories

Austrian line

Hohenzollern Territories

Franconian line

Wittelsbach Territories

Bavarian line

Palatinate Line

Neuburg line

Wettin Territories

Albertine line

Ernestine line

Ecclesiastical territories

Imperial cities

Boundary of the Holy Roman Empire

Ratibor

Cracow

lmütz

MORAVIA

Kingdom of HUNGARY

Pressburg

TURKISH HUNGARY

Budapest

OTTOMAN EMPIRE

0   50 mls

0   50 km

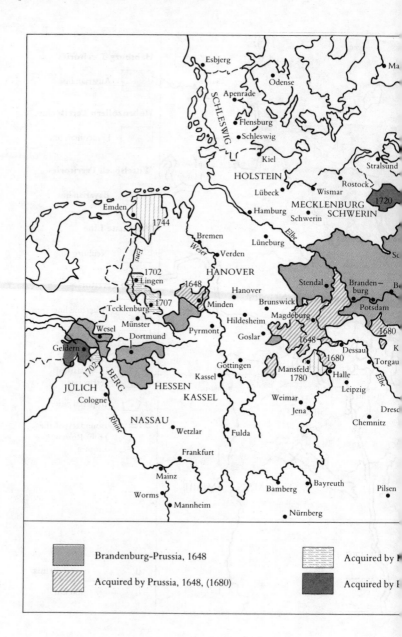

Map 6 Brandenburg-Prussia, 1640–1786

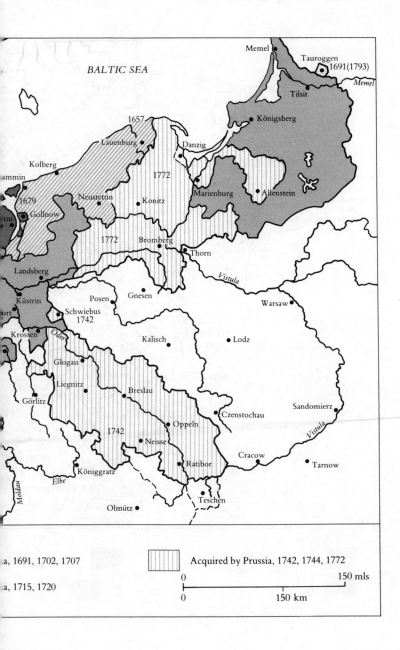

BALTIC SEA

Memel

Tauroggen
1691(1793)

Memel

Tilsit

Königsberg

1657

Lauenburg

Danzig

Kolberg

ammin

1772

1679

Neustettin

Konitz

Marienburg

Allenstein

Gollnow

1772

Bromberg

Thorn

Landsberg

Vistula

Küstrin

Posen

Gnesen

Warsaw

urt

Schwiebus
1742

Krossen

Oder

Kalisch

Lodz

Glogau

Liegnitz

Breslau

Görlitz

Sandomierz

1742

Oppeln

Czenstochau

Vistula

Neisse

Cracow

Königgratz

Ratibor

Tarnow

Moldau

Elbe

Teschen

Olmütz

a, 1691, 1702, 1707

Acquired by Prussia, 1742, 1744, 1772

a, 1715, 1720

0   150 mls

0   150 km

437

Map 7 Austria in the 18th century

Index

Index

Index

Index